IEG WORLD BANK IFC MIGA
INDEPENDENT EVALUATION GROUP



# Environmental Sustainability

## An Evaluation of World Bank Group Support

http://www.worldbank.org/ieg
http://www.ifc.org/ieg
http://www.miga.org/ieg

2008
The World Bank
Washington, D.C.

1818 H Street NW
Washington, DC 20433
Telephone: 202-473-1000
Internet: www.worldbank.org
E-mail: feedback@worldbank.org



1 2 3 4 5 11 10 09 08



Cover: Top left: Wastewater treatment plant in Honduras; photo courtesy of Jouni Martti Eerikainen. Top right: Planting coffee trees; photo courtesy of Jouni Martti Eerikainen. Bottom left: Logging road through deforested area of Bornea, in Sabah, Malaysia; photo ©Frans Lanting/CORBIS, reproduced by permission. Bottom right: Coal manufacturing plant along the Three Gorges of the Yangtze River in China; photo ©Keren Su/CORBIS, reproduced by permission.

ISBN-13: 978-0-8213-7670-6
e-ISBN-13: 978-0-8213-7671-3
DOI: 10.1596/978-0-8213-7670-6

**Library of Congress Cataloging-in-Publication Data**

Environmental sustainability : an evaluation of World Bank Group support.
p. cm.
Includes bibliographical references.
ISBN 978-0-8213-7670-6
1. Economic assistance—Developing countries—Environmental aspects. 2. Sustainable development—Developing countries.
3. World Bank—Developing countries—Evaluation. I. World Bank.
HC60.E53 2008
338.9'07091724—dc22

2008028078

World Bank InfoShop
E-mail: pic@worldbank.org
Telephone: 202-458-5454
Facsimile: 202-522-1500

Independent Evaluation Group
Knowledge Programs and Evaluation Capacity Development (IEGKE)
E-mail: ieg@worldbank.org
Telephone: 202-458-4497
Facsimile: 202-522-3125

Printed on Recycled Paper

# Contents

## Tables

Forestry operation in northwest Russia. Photo courtesy of Jouni Martti Eerikainen.

# Abbreviations

| | |
|---|---|
| AAA | Analytical and advisory activities (World Bank) |
| CAO | Compliance Advisor Ombudsman (IFC) |
| CAS | Country Assistance Strategy |
| CEA | Country Environmental Analysis (World Bank) |
| CES | Environment and Social Development Department (IFC) |
| CESP | Country Environmental Strategy Paper (World Bank) |
| CMU | Country management unit |
| CPS | Country Partnership Strategy |
| DFID | Department for International Development (U.K.) |
| DPL | Development Policy Loan/lending (World Bank) |
| EAP | Environmental Action Plan |
| EBRD | European Bank for Reconstruction and Development |
| EHS | Environmental health and safety |
| EMP | Environmental Management Plan |
| EMS | Environmental management system |
| ENRM | Environmental and natural resource management |
| EPFI | Equator Principle financial institution |
| ESE | Environmental and Social Effects (IFC) |
| ESMS | Environmental and Social Management System |
| ESW | Economic and sector work (World Bank) |
| FI | Financial intermediary |
| GDP | Gross domestic product |
| GEF | Global Environment Facility |
| IBRD | International Bank for Reconstruction and Development (World Bank) |
| IDA | International Development Association |
| IDF | Institutional Development Fund (World Bank) |
| IEG | Independent Evaluation Group |
| IFC | International Finance Corporation |
| ISO | International Standards Organization |
| IUCN | World Conservation Union |
| MDB | Multilateral development bank |
| MIGA | Multilateral Investment Guarantee Agency |
| NEAP | National Environmental Action Plan |
| NGO | Nongovernmental organization |
| OECD | Organisation for Economic Co-operation and Development |
| PPG7 | Pilot Program for the Conservation of Brazilian Rainforests |
| PRSC | Poverty Reduction Strategy Credit (World Bank) |
| PRSP | Poverty Reduction Strategy Paper |
| QAE | Quality at entry (MIGA) |

| | |
|---|---|
| UNDP | United Nations Development Program |
| UNEP | United Nations Environment Program |
| WDR | *World Development Report* |
| XPSR | Expanded Project Supervision Report (IFC) |

# Acknowledgments

The report was prepared by a team led jointly by John Redwood (Independent Evaluation Group [IEG]-World Bank), Jouni Eerikainen (IEG-International Finance Corporation [IFC]), and Ethel Tarazona (IEG-Multilateral Investment Guarantee Agency [MIGA]) under the supervision of Cheryl Gray (director, IEG-World Bank) and Marvin Taylor-Dormond (director, IEG-IFC, and acting director, IEG-MIGA). It draws on significant research and contributions provided by Dinara Akhmetova, Debora Brakarz, and Lauren Kelly (IEG-World Bank); Rex Bosson, Kenneth Green, and Clive Mason (IEG-IFC); and Roger Batstone and Stephan Wegner (IEG-MIGA).

World Bank country case studies were led by Anthony Hall (Brazil), Fernando Manibog (China), Sergio Margulis (Arab Republic of Egypt), George Keith Pitman (Ghana), John Redwood (India), Lauren Kelly (Madagascar and Senegal), Daniel Gross (Russian Federation), and Walter Arensberg (Uganda). Assistance was also provided by Ashwin Bhoursakar, Ramachandra Jammi, Antine Legrand, and Caitlin Sanford (IEG-World Bank) and Carlos Nuñez and SangHee Park (IEG-MIGA).

New project assessments were carried out as inputs to the study in Brazil (Tim Campbell and Jouni Eerikainen), China (Ashwin Bhoursakar, Jouni Eerikainen, Fernando Manibog, and George Keith Pitman), Ghana (Jouni Eerikainen and George Keith Pitman), India (Rex Bosson, Kenneth Green, Daniel Gross, John Redwood, and Colin Rees), Madagascar (Patrice Harou and Lauren Kelly), Russian Federation (Jouni Eerikainen and Colin Rees), Kenya (Kenneth Green), and Uganda (Walter Arensberg, Kenneth Green, and Patrice Harou).

Soon-Won Pak provided valuable administrative assistance. Bank Group local staff supported visiting IEG teams in field offices in Accra, Antananarivo, Beijing, Brasilia, Cairo, Dakar, Kampala, Moscow, Nairobi, and New Delhi. The team is grateful to peer reviewers Ken Chomitz, Amar Inamdar, John Shilling, and Claudio Volonte. Helen Chin, Heather Dittbrenner, William Hurlbut, and Caroline McEuen edited the report.

The team gratefully acknowledges the contributions of present and former World Bank Group managers and staff at Headquarters and in the field and representatives of governments, the private sector, academic and civil society organizations, and other development partners who provided information in the case study countries and elsewhere during the course of the study. The team also gratefully acknowledges the guidance and support provided by Shahrokh Fardoust and former IEG manager Alain Barbu and former IEG directors Ajay Chhibber and Aysegul Akin-Karasapan.

The report benefited from an external advisory panel composed of Christian Averous (head, Environmental Performance Division, Environment Directorate, Organisation for Economic Co-operation and Development), Yolanda Kakabadse (special advisor and former president, Fundacion Futuro Latinamericano, and former Minister of Environment of Ecuador), Olav Kjorven (director, Bureau for Development Policy, United Nations

Development Program), Julia Marton-Lefevre (director-general, World Conservation Union), and Bjorn Stigson (president, World Business Council for Sustainable Development). It also benefited from comments received from other World Conservation Union staff, especially Nancy MacPherson (special advisor, performance evaluation) and Erich Vogt (senior multilateral policy advisor).

This report is dedicated to the memories of Roger Batstone, Loretta Sprissler, and Ricardo Tarifa, environmentalists who devoted their lives to the mission of the World Bank Group.

Director-General: *Vinod Thomas*
Directors: *Cheryl W. Gray* (IEG-World Bank); *Marvin Taylor-Dormond* (IEG-IFC, IEG-MIGA)
Joint Task Managers: *John Redwood* (IEG-World Bank)
*Jouni Eerikainen* (IEG-IFC)
*Ethel Tarazona* (IEG-MIGA)

*Note:* John Redwood recused himself from work on Latin America, given his previous position as the director of the Environmentally and Socially Sustainable Development Department in that Region.

# Foreword

The environmental concerns on our planet have expanded dramatically in recent decades and are now among the most serious challenges affecting people's well-being around the globe. All nations are affected, but often the poorest countries and the least privileged populations bear the greatest burden. They are hit hardest by environmental destruction and climate change and have the fewest resources available to adapt to changing situations. Addressing environmental degradation and ensuring environmental sustainability are inextricably linked to the World Bank Group's mandate to reduce poverty and improve people's lives.

This evaluation looks at the effectiveness of World Bank Group support to the environment from 1990 to 2007. While there are difficulties in comparing the experience of the public and private sectors, a contribution of this evaluation is in bringing together findings on the World Bank, IFC (International Finance Corporation), and MIGA (Multilateral Investment Guarantee Agency), and assessing the effectiveness of the World Bank Group as a whole. In doing so, it also attempts to identify the external and internal constraints on Bank Group effectiveness, and suggest ways in which some of them, particularly the internal ones, can be reduced.

This period has seen an expansion in World Bank Group attention to environmental issues. The World Bank has provided analysis and financing to governments to help address priorities in biodiversity, land and water resource management, pollution control, and environmental policy. IFC has developed environmental standards for private investment, offered Advisory Services to companies for environmental and social performance, and promoted energy efficiency and clean technology. The World Bank, IFC, and MIGA have implemented safeguards or standards to minimize adverse environmental impacts from their financing.

The World Bank Group has been a leader in calling for environmental sustainability. But the institution has not been able to integrate environmental stewardship centrally or integrally into country programs, incorporate them as requirements for sustainable growth, and provide lending for environmental priorities—often because of lukewarm interest from the countries. Environmental sustainability must become a core part of the World Bank Group's strategic directions and receive fuller attention in regional and country assistance strategies. Operational teams need to collaborate more effectively across sectoral boundaries and build stronger skills in vital environmental areas, from pollution control to biodiversity conservation. The institution needs to work more effectively across the World Bank, IFC, and MIGA and with external partners to take advantage of synergies. And the three parts of the World Bank Group need—in somewhat different ways—to improve substantially their ability to assess the full environmental impacts of their interventions.

Environmental damages and the dangers of climate change worldwide are a central threat to economic growth and poverty reduction. With strategic shifts, the World Bank Group can play a critical part in the transformation for promoting environmental protection by governments and private agents as an essential aid to growth and well being.

*Vinod Thomas*
Director-General, Evaluation

Leaking oil drums outside a facility in Ghana. Photo courtesy of Jouni Martti Eerikainen.

# Preface

The purpose of this evaluation is threefold. First, it seeks to assess how—and how well— the World Bank Group has supported its public and private sector clients in their efforts to achieve greater environmental sustainability over the past 15 years. Second, it attempts to identify the principal external and internal constraints on Bank Group effectiveness. And third, it seeks to suggest how some of these constraints, particularly the internal ones, can be reduced.

Environmental issues are many and far-reaching, and this evaluation does not seek to address the entire scope of the subject. A central element of the approach followed, however, was to examine environment-related activities of the Bank Group as a whole, to provide an integrated corporate focus to the assessment of the recent experience of the IBRD/IDA (World Bank), IFC, and MIGA. This approach presented many challenges due to the differing, but complementary, development roles and instruments of the three parts of the institution, as well as their distinct information constraints. Within the Bank, the evaluation examined efforts to promote environmental improvement at the country level, not only through its strategic and analytical work, but also its lending and grant operations. For IFC and MIGA activities with the private sector, the main focus was on performance in meeting environmental requirements in projects and on the performance of IFC's environment-oriented Advisory Services and partnerships.

IEG has sought to bring together relevant evaluation findings and offer recommendations for all three parts of the Bank Group, but recognizes the limitations imposed by the differences and difficulties involved. The longer-term and cross-sectoral perspectives adopted here are also relevant and consistent with the nature and requirements of environmentally sustainable development itself. However, they, too, result in methodological and substantive challenges for both the public and private sector parts of the analysis.

It is also important to stress what the evaluation does not do. It does not attempt to evaluate the implementation of the Bank's 2001 Environment Strategy, though it does use the major themes of this strategy, together with the fourfold environment agenda put forward by the World Bank during the 1990s, as lenses to view Bank Group experience over the past 15 years.

Finally, this is just one of several IEG evaluations under way or about to begin that focus on Bank Group involvement with the environment. These include assessments of recent experience involving forests, climate change, and environmental due diligence and safeguards. Thus, the present exercise does not go into detail in these areas. It also builds on the findings and recommendations of other recent evaluations, including those of natural hazards, middle-income countries, financial intermediaries, renewable energy, and regional and global programs, and therefore should be seen as one of a number of IEG products that examine past performance and suggest possible courses of action that have a bearing on future Bank Group support for environmental sustainability.

Smoldering pastureland cleared for cattle in the Amazon rainforest. Photo reproduced by permission of Michael K. Nichols/National Geographic Image Collection.

# Executive Summary

Climate change is front page news. But other environmental problems are also becoming more serious, from local air and water pollution to soil erosion, water scarcity, deforestation, and loss of biodiversity. These problems are especially severe in developing and transition economies and have a particularly adverse impact on the poor.

Both the public and private sectors have critical roles to play and must act together to address domestic and transnational environmental issues. In an increasingly globalized world, moreover, what happens in one country, especially a large one, often has impacts well beyond its borders, and its environmental footprint expands in tandem with national economic growth. Solutions to these problems are among the most significant and overarching challenges faced by the World Bank Group, the countries in which it operates, and the development community as a whole. More effective action by all is needed.

This evaluation assesses the Bank Group's support for environmental sustainability—in both the public and private sectors—over the past 15 years. It identifies several crucial constraints that need to be addressed, perhaps most importantly insufficient government commitment to environmental goals and weak institutional capacity to deal with them. But constraints within the Bank Group, including insufficient attention to longer-term sustainable development, must be reduced as well. The Bank Group needs more adequate systems in place—in different respects, across the World Bank, IFC, and MIGA—to monitor environmental outcomes and to assess impacts. Better coordination among the three parts of the Bank Group is also among the key challenges.

Bank Group support for the environment has grown during the past 15 years. Performance has improved over time, though it has been weaker in Sub-Saharan Africa than elsewhere. Meanwhile, as documented in recent United Nations and World Bank/International Monetary Fund reports, environmental challenges, including those related to the Millennium Development Goal for environmental sustainability, have increased, and problems in the critical areas of pollution, congestion, loss of species, and climate change have worsened. In view of the public goods nature of these concerns, the Bank Group has a special role to play with respect to environmental issues—and has indeed been a leader in the analysis and advocacy that helps countries focus on them. But far greater progress is needed in giving these concerns operational priority, including in how the Bank, IFC, and MIGA work together, recognizing that long-term economic growth, poverty reduction, and environmental sustainability are interlinked.

## The Bank Group and the Environment

Bank Group support for the environment was largely limited to assessing the potential impacts of selected projects until the mid-1980s, when external pressures helped induce a broader approach. By the early 1990s, many countries were preparing National Environmental Action Plans with World Bank support, and International Bank for Reconstruction and Development (IBRD), International Development Association (IDA), and IFC environment-related financing had grown. Soon after the 1992 U.N. Earth Summit in Rio de Janeiro, the Bank adopted a fourfold agenda comprising safeguards, stewardship, integration of environmental concerns into macroeconomic and sectoral interventions (mainstreaming), and global sustainability.

The Bank Group's first formal environment strategy was approved in July 2001. It placed the environment within the institution's poverty reduction mission and highlighted three objectives: improving the quality of life, enhancing the quality of growth, and protecting the regional and global commons. The strategy also enunciated an institutional commitment to facilitate partnerships between the public and private sectors, as well as with civil society, to address environmentally sensitive issues and to promote better environmental management at both the country and global levels. Over the past 15 years, support for the environment has grown. The Bank Group is now the largest multilateral source of environment-related financing, including administration of Global Environment Facility (GEF) grants, and an important source of advice to many country and private sector clients.

## Evaluation Approach

Bank Group effectiveness ideally would be judged on the basis of observable improvements in the environment resulting from the interventions it supports. However, even when information on changes in environmental quality is available, which all too often is not the case, obtaining a precise measure of the impact of Bank Group support is difficult because of our inability to separate its influence on policy and environmental improvements from that of other forces.

In view of these constraints, which are common to many evaluations, this assessment relied significantly on country case studies, undertaken in 2006, to explore the influence of various instruments on the environment. The case studies included at least one country from each of the Bank Group's six operational Regions, with particular attention to Sub-Saharan Africa and the Bank's largest clients in lending volume and/or global environmental significance—China, India, Brazil, and Russia. The case study countries account for more than half of the population and nearly half of the land area and gross domestic product of all lower- and middle-income countries.

The evaluation considered the period since 1990, when the Bank Group stepped up its environmental support. Different evaluative approaches and methodologies were used for the various parts of the Bank Group, reflecting their different roles, instruments, and information constraints. The assessment of World Bank interventions considered lending and analytical work intended for environment-related issues together with the evolution of country strategies and policy dialogue. For IFC and MIGA, IEG focused on the performance of all projects (finance and guarantees) in meeting project-level environmental standards, using the Environmental and Social Effects Indicator and assessing IFC's environmental work quality at appraisal and supervision. Also examined were recent environment-oriented Advisory Services, complemented in the case of IFC by case studies in most of the same countries considered in the World Bank analysis.

The evaluation sought to answer five questions:

(1) How and how effectively has Bank Group support contributed to improving environmental quality and sustainability?
(2) How well have Bank Group interventions been aligned with national environmental priorities and private sector needs, and how well have environmental considerations been mainstreamed into Bank Group assistance?
(3) Have the design and implementation of the Bank's environment-related investment projects improved, and, if so, what factors have contributed to this? And have IFC and MIGA Investment and Advisory Services enhanced their private sector clients' management of environmental risks?
(4) To what extent—and how—have partnerships and World Bank Group coordination enhanced the effectiveness of its support for the environment?
(5) What internal and external constraints have limited effectiveness of Bank Group support, and how might they be reduced?

## Portfolio and Performance Overview

The Bank Group is involved with the environment in a number of ways, interacting with governments, other financial institutions, private sector clients, and civil society. The World Bank assists countries through analytical, advisory, and lending services to help them address environmental priorities and support policy reforms. Engagement of IFC and MIGA with the private sector has generally sought to ensure that investments adhere to environmental standards, but during this decade, IFC has launched several environment-oriented Advisory Service programs and developed partnerships with the Equator Principle financial institutions. Hence, while IFC and MIGA have fewer direct investment projects designed to improve the environment per se than does the World Bank, all of their financing operations, like World Bank investment projects, need to meet environmental due diligence requirements. Moreover, many IFC projects have built-in environmental benefits, such as improvements in energy efficiency.

Total World Bank commitments between fiscal 1990 and 2007 were $401.5 billion in 6,792 projects. The 2,401 projects specifically identified as involving the environment and natural resource management (ENRM) are officially estimated to include relevant commitments on the order of $59 billion. However, this figure is an approximation and appears to overstate the actual volume of resources going directly for environmental improvement. Apart from environment-related Development Policy Loans (general budget support in exchange for policy reforms), in which total lending had reached $3.5 billion by the end of fiscal 2007, ENRM commitments in investment projects considered to be at least 80 percent for environmental improvement were $18.2 billion (the remainder of the $59 billion was in projects with smaller shares devoted to the environment). The total includes Bank-administered GEF grants, Montreal Protocol projects, and carbon finance. An important part of this figure was for sanitation infrastructure (for example, wastewater treatment plants in China and elsewhere). Because of the way Bank commitments are identified, it is unclear how much lending has gone directly for environmental improvement. But the priority given to lending for ENRM appears to be modest.

World Bank environmental project performance, while slightly below the average for its portfolio as a whole, has improved, with a better record from the second half of the 1990s to the present decade than in the early and mid-1990s. This reflects learning and discontinuation of some less successful project approaches. Performance of environmental projects has been weakest in Sub-Saharan Africa, but there has been a range of successful and unsuccessful operations in all Regions.

IFC's engagement with the private sector overall (that is, not dealing specifically with the environment) has grown rapidly in recent years, with annual commitments more than doubling from $3.9 billion to $8.2 billion between 2003 and 2007. From fiscal 1990 through 2007, IFC committed about $56 billion. IFC's environmental support includes GEF projects for about $1 billion, including $320 million from IFC and $185 million in Dutch-funded carbon facilities. It also includes Advisory Services for environment and social sustainability business line projects totaling $208 million by end-2007, which represents a quarter of IFC Advisory Services funding.

MIGA issued guarantees between fiscal 1990 and 2007 for a total exposure of $16.7 billion in 510 projects (again, an overall figure, not referring to the environment per se). The largest share of MIGA operations in the nonfinancial sectors has been in infrastructure, manufacturing, and the extractive industries. As with IFC, there seem to be few MIGA operations specifically intended to avoid damage to the environment. But financing modern technologies in the private sector, while intended primarily to improve productivity and product quality, also generally reduces harmful environmental impacts, given the older technologies they replace.

IFC and MIGA have increased their efforts to engage their clients on environmental issues in recent years. In April 2006 IFC established its

Policy and Performance Standards on Social and Environmental Sustainability, which were adopted (and adapted) by MIGA, effective October 1, 2007. The impact of these new standards cannot yet be assessed. However, environmental compliance and performance gaps in IFC projects over the past 15 years have been most notable in Africa, in part because of weaker sponsor capacity, and (sometimes) wavering sponsor commitment to the sustainability agenda, and in some industry sectors. MIGA has also given increasing attention to environmental issues in its underwriting and has used its contracts to identify applicable safeguard policies, guidelines, and requirements for remedial action. But improvements are needed, particularly in less environmentally sensitive (Category B; see glossary for category descriptions) projects, whose potential impacts typically receive less attention.

## Principal Evaluation Findings

The World Bank Group has been a leader in calling attention to the global importance of environmental sustainability. It has made progress in including environmental concerns in its strategies and analytical and lending products since 1990, and increasingly since 2001, and has provided support for the environment through a range of financial and nonfinancial services, private sector investments and guarantees, and regional and global programs and partnerships. When requested, the Bank Group usually has been able to help countries set environmental priorities (although this is ultimately the responsibility of the countries themselves) and private sector clients to identify and address potential direct environmental impacts. It has been far less able to integrate these efforts centrally into country programs, incorporate them as requirements for sustainable growth and poverty reduction, and provide lending to help countries address environmental priorities—often because of lukewarm interest in such support from the countries themselves.

### *Country strategies*

The Bank's country strategies generally take account of national environmental priorities, although insufficient attention has often been given to longer-run sustainability concerns. Treatment of ENRM issues in country strategies has improved over the past 20 years in Brazil, China, and Madagascar, for instance. But there have also been important cases where treatment has not improved. For example, Bank strategies for Russia have reduced the priority given to the environment, which reflects declining central government interest in borrowing and in policy advice for environmental problems. Attention to the environment has been uneven over time in Arab Republic of Egypt, Ghana, India, Senegal, and Uganda.

Most Bank country strategies have not integrated IFC and MIGA environment-related activities. However, environment has been a strategic priority for IFC and MIGA in recent years. IFC *Strategic Directions* documents approved by the Board over the past decade have emphasized environmental and social sustainability. The importance of integrating depends on the extent of IFC and MIGA engagement in the countries, the nature and scale of the environmental impacts of their operations, and the degree of coordination needed between policy efforts and private sector investments. In many areas—such as avoiding deforestation, protecting biodiversity, and emerging efforts to address climate change in many parts of the world—it is essential that Bank, IFC, and MIGA approaches that affect the environment be better coordinated to improve overall corporate effectiveness.

### *Analytic, financing, and guarantee activities*

The results of World Bank nonlending activities have often been as significant as those of lending operations in terms of environmental improvement, as in the case of industrial pollution control in Indonesia and river basin management in China. However, even where environmental problems are particularly serious, they have been treated unevenly in Bank analytical and/or lending activities. Performance in this regard has been relatively positive in countries such as Brazil and China, but less comprehensive or well integrated (particularly in lending) in Egypt, India, Russia, and the case study countries in Sub-Saharan Africa. Among the reasons for these differences are the size of resources available for country programs, the lack of client demand, and the capabilities of national and local institutions.

Based on assessments of completed operations in the case study countries and a review of the Bank's ENRM portfolio as a whole, the effectiveness of project types has varied. Land and watershed management operations, community-based forest management projects, and grants to reduce ozone-depleting substances, for example, have generally been satisfactory, as have most biodiversity conservation projects (although there were performance problems in the initial years of such operations). Water resource management projects at the river basin level and urban environmental operations, despite shortcomings, have also been largely satisfactory based on overall project outcome ratings.

In contrast, Bank-supported operations to combat industrial pollution through credit lines have been only partially satisfactory from the perspective of environmental quality. However, the Bank learned from this experience and discontinued the credit line approach in most countries in favor of alternative approaches, such as public disclosure programs, which have been more successful. Environmental capacity-building projects have often shown weak results as well, but such projects have generally been more successful when they have sought to achieve concrete environmental improvements, rather than focusing mainly or exclusively on institutional development. Environment-related Development Policy Loans, in turn, hold potential to influence relevant policies and institutions. However, given that these are recent projects and that programmatic approaches have typically been applied, only changes in policies and institutions can be measured at this stage. It will be important to measure environmental outcomes over the longer term to determine the success of these projects in achieving environmental sustainability objectives.

In Sub-Saharan Africa and elsewhere, integration of ENRM concerns into Poverty Reduction Strategy Credits, and the country-prepared Poverty Reduction Strategy Papers on which they are based, has not been given sufficient priority. Climate change is another critical area in which Bank Group interventions have been limited. The gap is especially serious with regard to the rising adaptation needs in Sub-Saharan Africa and South Asia. But this is beginning to change. Both the Bank and IFC envisage giving much greater attention to climate-related challenges in the years ahead.

Finally, even though the World Bank applies environmental due diligence to all of its investment projects, it lacks an aggregate monitoring and reporting system (such as in IFC) that would allow it to more systematically assess the environmental aspects and results of the projects it supports. This is a task that both self- and independent evaluation need to undertake.

Turning to IFC, about two-thirds of investment projects met their environmental and social requirements and standards. Significant gaps were found in investment projects in Sub-Saharan Africa, in part for the reasons mentioned above, and in the textile, food and beverage, tourism, and agriculture and forestry sectors. IFC has had a positive influence in helping its clients develop management systems to better address environmental and social aspects companywide. This is important, considering IFC's increasing focus on corporate loans and equity investments that cover all of its clients' activities, compared with narrower project finance. The overall effectiveness of IFC/GEF initiatives was found by an external evaluation to be satisfactory, with mixed project outcomes. A partial review of environment-oriented Advisory Service projects found some positive outcomes, but often there was not enough information to assess them against expected impacts.

IFC's environmental work quality at appraisal has generally been adequate, but supervision of financial intermediary projects has been insufficient. Project appraisal has been adequate in identifying direct environmental, social, and health and safety risks in real sector projects and in diligent translation of IFC generic requirements for financial intermediary projects to legal documents. But greater attention is needed to the assessment of indirect and induced environmental and social impacts, which can be significant—for example, in agribusiness projects. IFC's 2006 Performance Standards provide new tools to help define projects' areas of influence, supply chain management, and cumulative impacts, and the new environmental and social review procedure in implementation since May 2006 includes risk-based appraisal and supervision of FIs. However, it is too soon to assess implementation of these standards and the impact they are having on environmental performance.

IFC's measure of project environmental and social effects is confined generally to environmental impacts and performance in meeting standards and requirements at the company level. However, as part of the Bank Group, IFC's impact also includes the sectorwide or Regionwide effects of the operations it supports. Therefore, both self- and independent evaluation should be given broader focus to assess these effects.

Turning to MIGA, performance in meeting environmental requirements and standards in MIGA guarantee operations differed between projects with more (Category A) and less (Category B) serious potential environmental and social impacts. For Category B projects, measures agreed to in the early stages are not always being fully carried out, suggesting the need for additional support and monitoring. As in the case of IFC, MIGA needs to give greater consideration to the broader environmental effects of the investments it supports.

More generally, differences in project-level environmental requirements between the World Bank, on the one side, and IFC and MIGA, on the other, deserve assessment. The Bank follows environmental and social safeguards (operational policies, procedures, and guidelines, last partially revised in August 2004), while in 2006 IFC adopted new Policy and Performance Standards on Social and Environmental Sustainability. A similar approach was adopted by MIGA in 2007. Another key difference is the recourse to an independent Inspection Panel for external complaints in the case of the Bank, while IFC and MIGA rely on the Office of the Compliance Advisor Ombudsman (CAO), reporting to the president of the World Bank Group. The crucial question is the environmental impacts of these differing approaches. They need to be evaluated and the findings incorporated into policies. The forthcoming IEG evaluation of environmental and social due diligence across the Bank Group could be helpful in this regard, but greater self-evaluation is also needed.

### Need for more strategic and coordinated approaches

Government ownership of environmental objectives is of particular importance. In addition to enforcing its own legislation, the public sector needs to create an investment climate that will encourage and support environmentally sustainable private sector investment and growth. This is especially important for the energy, water, wastewater, and waste management and recycling sectors, which have significant impacts on both the environment and public health. Furthermore, mainstreaming environmental concerns needs to go farther. Because most environmental problems are spatial externalities and involve more than one sector, they are often best addressed in a cross-sectoral and location-specific way. Many Bank-supported interventions do not go far enough in this respect. More coordinated action is frequently needed among public and private stakeholders, as well as across investment sectors, areas where the Bank Group could be of greater assistance to interested clients.

In supporting sustainable development and poverty reduction, the Bank Group also needs to give more attention to the increasing transnational environmental impacts of rapidly growing developing—as well as Organisation for Economic Co-operation and Development—countries, including the effects of rising trade in raw materials and agricultural and forest products from Sub-Saharan Africa and South America to Asia, as well as within Asia. Given associated global environmental problems, including the impacts of climate change and biodiversity loss, such pressures are being noted by various analysts as important and growing concerns.

### Partnerships

The Bank Group has worked with and through a number of regional and global environmental programs and networks, including the Global Environment Facility, the Montreal Protocol, and the Poverty-Environment Partnership with other U.N. and bilateral assistance agencies. Such partnerships have often enhanced the effectiveness of Bank Group support for environmental sustainability at both the country and global levels. However, IEG visits to Egypt, Ghana, Senegal, and Uganda revealed that other donors sometimes view the Bank as an insufficiently responsive partner. At the same time, Bank collaboration with environmental nongovernmental organizations and other donors in Brazil, China, India, Madagascar, and Russia appears to have enhanced mutual effectiveness. One factor associated with these positive outcomes is the presence of Bank environmental specialists in the field, which varies according to the size and complexity of its portfolios in the countries involved.

IFC has sought to extend use of its Performance Standards for private sector investments in developing countries by working with commercial and other multilateral development banks. The Equator Principles, initiated by IFC in 2003, had been adopted by 60 of the world's leading banks by March 2008. These now cover the majority of large-scale project financing in the developing world. To assess their impact, however, financial institutions will need to demonstrate greater transparency and improved reporting with respect to implementation.

### External constraints

Several significant constraints at the country and firm levels limit greater effectiveness of Bank Group and other donor support for the environment. A principal obstacle in many settings is insufficient commitment to environmental objectives, policies, and interventions at the national, subnational, and/or firm levels. Rapid population growth, economic expansion, and persisting poverty, together with market, governance, and institutional failures, continue to play an important role, as do political instability and civil unrest, especially in fragile states. Notable too are the frequent inadequacy of information about and understanding of the nature and causes of environmental problems; unclear definition of the domestic environmental agenda and its links to economic growth and poverty reduction; and weak legal, regulatory, financial, technical, human, and institutional capacity.

### Internal constraints

Among the constraints within the World Bank Group are competing priorities for the attention of senior managers, insufficient staff technical and operational skills, and suboptimal use of limited administrative budgets. Organization of the World Bank into country and sector departments, while helpful in many ways, nonetheless means that geographic and sectoral boundaries between management units represent potential barriers to more effective assistance, especially for regional and global challenges. Resolution of environmental problems often requires interventions across national or regional boundaries (as in the Mediterranean and Nile Basins). This means that certain internal inertias often need to be overcome.

Given the demand-driven nature of Bank programs at the country level, global public goods, including environmental quality and sustainability, tend to receive insufficient priority. Similarly, not enough attention is given to sustainable development obstacles and opportunities in Bank country and Regional strategies. Addressing these constraints requires strong leadership at the corporate, Regional, and country levels, supported by high-quality analytical work and other tools.

An additional impediment stems from insufficient coordination of action within the Bank Group. For IFC and MIGA to operate effectively, adequate legal and regulatory frameworks need to be in place and enforced at the country level. This depends on government policies and practices, including transparency, areas in which the Bank often has greater leverage, although Bank influence varies significantly across countries and over time. IFC is also increasingly working with governments—for example, in providing advice on private sector sustainability, corporate governance, and public-private partnership reforms. The feasibility of private investments may also depend on adequate physical and economic infrastructure, such as facilities for treatment of industrial waste and wastewater, which are often undeveloped or nonexistent and provided by public utilities that are World Bank clients. In turn, regulatory reforms supported by the Bank can be made more effective with parallel IFC/MIGA efforts to induce its clients—and the private sector more generally—to comply with these regulations. Such opportunities for coordinated action in support of greater environmental sustainability need to be better identified and exploited.

Achievement of the objectives of Bank Group strategies—including the 2001 Environment Strategy, in which IFC and MIGA were not significant participants—depends partially on private sector actions to stem environmental damage and improve environmental quality, areas where IFC and MIGA can play a vital role. Good collaboration between the Bank and IFC is increasingly seen in several urban and rural programs. However, absent a common framework that allows the Bank Group to understand the full range of environmental effects of its interventions, there is a risk that the public and private sector arms of the Bank Group may be working with different criteria in relation to the environment. This could happen, for example, in the energy, transport, and agribusiness sectors and other future investments that are particularly critical to climate change. Thus, it is important that new investments in both the private and public sectors (for instance, new power investments in Asia and agribusiness investments involving tropical forests in Africa, Asia, or Latin America) meet the same environmental performance standards and consistently seek to reduce environmental damage, including deforestation and greenhouse gas emissions. Better intra–Bank Group coordination of strategies, approaches, and interventions at both the corporate and country levels is essential.

## Recommendations

In view of the increasing importance of environmental sustainability for economic growth, poverty reduction, and human well-being, as documented in recent U.N. and World Bank/International Monetary Fund (IMF) reports and the findings of this evaluation, the World Bank Group should seek to enhance the effectiveness of its activities in support of environmental sustainability. IEG recommends the following (details are provided in chapter 6):

1. **Increase the attention to environmental sustainability in the World Bank Group by ensuring that environmental issues enter fully into discussions of its strategic directions and in Regional and country assistance programs.**

Promotion of environmental sustainability (including, but not limited to, addressing climate change) should be a central pillar of the Bank Group's strategic directions in its efforts to support inclusive and sustainable globalization. The World Bank Group should jointly reformulate and update the 2001 Environment Strategy in light of the increasingly important role of the private sector, global public goods, and transnational environmental footprints. The World Bank Group should jointly consider both medium-term (5–10 year) and longer-term (10–20 year) approaches to strengthening environmental sustainability at the Regional and national levels and should incorporate short-term (3–5 year) environmental programs into country assistance and partnership strategies where feasible, especially for countries with large investment portfolios, great environmental challenges, and carbon footprints of global significance. IFC should continue supporting market transformation toward sustainability with its Advisory Services and direct and financial intermediary investments, emphasizing technology transfer and development in clean production, energy efficiency, and sustainable supply chain management.

**2. Move to more cross-sectoral and spatially oriented approaches to environmental support and strengthen staff skills.**

The Bank Group should help its clients adopt more cross-sectoral and spatially focused approaches to addressing environmental challenges. Staff technical and operational skills for the delivery of environmental support also need to be strengthened. While the World Bank Group must be responsive to client demand in its policy advice and lending, it can still be proactive in analyzing environmental issues and seeking to identify strategic entry points in countries with significant environmental concerns.

**3. Improve the Bank Group's ability to assess its support for the environment and to monitor and evaluate the impacts of its environment-related interventions.**

The Bank Group needs to do a better job of measuring the environmental performance and impacts of its activities. The Bank needs to improve monitoring, evaluation, and reporting of environmental aspects and results of lending operations at both the project and portfolio levels. While IFC has evaluated its environmental and social effects since 1996, and recently developed new tools to track and analyze environmental performance indicators at the project level, and MIGA has scaled up its assessment and monitoring of project environmental and social performance, both institutions could improve their attention to baseline and performance indicators for later monitoring and evaluation. IFC and MIGA should also be concerned with and measure more fully the aggregate and supply chain impact—beyond individual project performance—of projects with large environmental dimensions—for example, in oil, gas, mining, energy, or agribusiness projects in high-biodiversity regions.

The Bank Group needs to develop and apply methods to assess its environmental impact. Together with agencies such as United Nations Development Program and United Nations Environment Program, it needs to help quantify progress toward achievement of the crucial Millennium Development Goal 7 for environmental sustainability, a goal that is not now being tracked adequately.

**4. Improve coordination among the Bank, IFC, and MIGA and between the World Bank Group and external partners (both public and private) in relation to the Bank Group's environmental mission and ensure consistent and effective implementation at the corporate and country levels.**

Senior management across the World Bank, IFC, and MIGA needs to give greater attention to ensuring Bank Group consistency and effectiveness in this area. Mechanisms should be established at the top management, Regional, and (where pertinent) country levels to promote, monitor, and report on intra-institutional coordination and collaboration with respect to environment-related strategies (including but not restricted to those concerned with climate change), policies, and interventions. Specific actions are recommended with regard to: (1) corporate strategies for the environment; (2) environmental aspects of country assistance and partnership strategies; (3) monitoring, evaluation, and reporting on environment-related interventions and outcomes; and (4) assessing experience with differing approaches to environmental due diligence for lending, equity, and guarantee operations. Furthermore, strengthening external partnerships with both the public and private sectors should be a central theme in an updated World Bank Group environmental strategy. Effective partnerships will be essential to success in addressing the world's urgent environmental concerns.

Polluted water in the Philippines. Photo by Curt Carnemark, courtesy of the World Bank Photo Library.

# Advisory Panel Statement

## Introduction

The external Advisory Panel, consisting of Julia Marton-Lefevre;[1] Bjorn Stigson;[2] Christian Avérous;[3] Yolanda Kakabadse;[4] and Olav Kjorven,[5] met on May 2, 2008, at World Bank Headquarters to consider the draft IEG report, "Supporting Environmental Sustainability: An Evaluation of World Bank Group Experience, 1990–2007," and prepared this statement afterward.

## Terms of Reference

The Advisory Panel was asked to consider whether the evaluation succeeded in answering the questions it set out to examine, whether there were gaps in conclusions and recommendations, and whether the key messages were effectively communicated.

## Overall Conclusions

Overall, the Advisory Panel found that the evaluation report was of high quality and contained sound findings. The panel supports the findings in relation to the following issues:

- ***Mainstreaming of environment.***
  The World Bank Group has yet to internalize sufficiently the environmental challenge in its operations and business. Despite many excellent achievements around the world, despite major intellectual accomplishments and many policy innovations, and despite state-of-the-art environmental safeguards, the Bank Group continues to give low de facto priority to the goal of enhancing the environmental sustainability of development. This is documented convincingly by the evaluation report, particularly in terms of the levels of financing dedicated to this purpose, and the lack of integration of a systematic environmental sustainability perspective across policy and financial instruments. For example, the Bank (International Bank for Reconstruction and Development/International Development Association) has too often failed to translate its environment agenda effectively from upstream analytical work, via Poverty Reduction Strategy Papers and Country Assistance Strategies, through to its downstream lending operations.

- ***Integrate energy and climate strategies and deploy low-carbon technologies.***
  To support broad-based economic growth, developing countries will need substantial investments in infrastructure, particularly energy. The Bank Group is uniquely positioned to help countries integrate energy and climate strategies into their national development plans, and it should play a stronger role in this, in partnership with other agencies. On the financing side, the Bank Group could be more active in identifying and setting up financial mechanisms as well as further developing the carbon markets to deploy low-carbon technologies for energy access projects in developing countries.

- ***Focus on environmental management through investments.***
  While Bank lending is by-and-large subject to environmental safeguards to minimize negative impact, only a small fraction of lending goes directly to strengthen environmental management, advance environmentally sound growth and investment through and with the private sector, and promote transitions toward environmental sustainability in key sectors such as transport, agriculture, and energy.

- ***Coordination of actions in-house and building momentum with partners.***
  The Bank Group has not sufficiently acted "as one" in addressing strategic environmental challenges. In most cases, International Bank for Reconstruction and Development/International

Development Association, IFC, and MIGA have pursued, separately, what they considered to be their particular niche "in the market." While we agree that mandates should remain distinct and clear for each of the three, greater efforts to jointly identify and pursue opportunities for synergy is expected.

The Bank Group should look beyond itself and its relations with client countries, not least in the context of developing new strategies in the environment and climate areas. The imperative of broader partnerships is recognized in the evaluation, but more reflection is needed. The reality of the environmental sustainability challenge is such that the Bank Group cannot realistically take it on in isolation from others. It must approach partnership with the United Nations, with the private sector, and with civil society in a qualitatively new and strategic way.

***The Advisory Panel considers these findings to be central to the ability of the World Bank Group to influence environmental sustainability and development and recommends that these findings concerning policy and operations be addressed as a matter of urgency.***

The Advisory Panel also found that the evaluation did not adequately address some strategic evaluative issues. These shall not be listed here in their entirety; however, the following areas are of particular concern to the Advisory Panel.

- More evenly represent the balance between project and strategic-level questions. While it has produced interesting findings and data related to some strategic-level issues, these are overshadowed by the heavy emphasis on project and portfolio analysis and performance.
- Provide more data on whether the Bank Group addresses the drivers for sustainability, and make recommendations on how to strengthen the Bank Group's strategy and approach.
- Produce a comprehensive analysis of the effectiveness of the Bank Group's performance as it relates to gender equity dimensions of environmental sustainability.
- Address the criteria with which the Bank Group makes its investment decisions, in the first place, to meet broader environmental objectives.
- Examine how the Bank Group establishes its comparative advantage in environmental programming in relation to other players/partners in the field of environment and development, including the regional development banks, which have a distinct relationship with country governments in their regions, as well as the United Nations and international nongovernmental organizations.
- Provide sufficient qualitative analysis of the breadth and depth of stakeholder/partner consultation and their views.

***The Advisory Panel recommends that IEG sharpen the focus and methodology of future evaluations to include these key performance factors.***

## Specific Recommendations

The Advisory Panel understands and appreciates that, following its review meeting with IEG, a number of its observations have been considered and some have been adapted and incorporated into the evaluation report. The Advisory Panel would like to draw attention to some of these issues:

- The Bank Group must step up its efforts—together with other partners—to make the economic case for strong environmental action, such as by systematically showing the health benefits of environmental improvements. A Stern-like report on the economics of environmental action versus inaction should be considered.
- Given the global, watershed developments in the larger environmental field over the last 10 years, the Bank Group needs a new, transformational environmental policy that addresses today's (known) needs and tomorrow's (still evolving) challenges. This policy must look beyond a useful 10- to 20-year time horizon, to a 40- to 50-year time horizon as well. This time horizon is, at the very minimum, necessary to take into consideration the lifecycle impacts of investments made today, such as in the power and transport sectors.
- Recent efforts to strengthen IFC's environmentally oriented operations and IFC's im-

plementation of its environmental safeguards system, to ensure their effectiveness and impact, must be redoubled. IFC's record to date is mixed.

- MIGA needs to strengthen the implementation of its environmental safeguards as well as embrace a stronger commitment to proactively "do good" as an important area of its business.
- The Bank Group should more broadly support the transfer and effective application of low-carbon technologies and promote more systematically enhanced technology collaboration among developed and developing countries.
- Small and medium enterprises are critical for pursuing sustainable economic growth and halting environmental degradation. The Bank Group needs to pay more attention to this sector and provide more support, particularly in building much needed capacity.
- Declaring that the Bank Group is a unique and special institution of knowledge and learning, a "brain trust" of applied knowledge, is not sufficient. The role of the Bank (and the entire Bank Group) as a knowledge bank must go beyond this to delivering, expanding, and testing this learning—in tandem with partners. The report has little to say about the impact of knowledge and learning in the area of environment.

***The Advisory Panel recommends that the areas listed above be urgently given priority in further strategic thinking, action, and evaluation by the World Bank Group.***

## Conclusion: A Forward-Looking Perspective

The Advisory Panel feels strongly that the Bank Group needs to interpret the findings and recommendations of this evaluation against the backdrop of environmental, economic, and political realities. A number of environmental and natural resource challenges are now attracting the attention of heads of states and governments, as well as macroeconomists and development economists. The forthcoming climate change framework and a host of evolving climate-related funds and facilities, as well as efforts to pull the Bank's various forestry initiatives together, provide the ideal backdrop for setting clear conceptual and strategic priorities on environmental sustainability for the Bank Group. President Zoellick has stressed that the time has come for a transformation in the way the Bank Group approaches development. We support this view.

In this context, the Advisory Panel wishes to flag four areas of strategic importance with real consequences for policy and operational priority-setting, in the context of promoting sustainable development and poverty reduction:

- Transitioning toward low-carbon economy, coupled with expanding clean and affordable energy access for the poor
- Preserving biodiversity while improving rural livelihoods
- Improving resource productivity
- Protecting water resources, coupled with expanding access to water and sanitation.

The global environmental challenge is unprecedented and it requires collaboration among a large number of development partners, including the United Nations system, the Global Environment Facility, regional development banks, bilateral donors, the private sector, research institutions, and civil society. To succeed in implementing a transformative vision of environmentally sustainable development, partnerships are a *conditio sine qua non*. The Advisory Panel believes the most central partnership must continue to be with the client countries, but the challenge of environmental sustainability reaches beyond the "confines" of that relationship alone. Much more systematic and stronger partnerships must be built and harnessed across the entire spectrum of shareholders and stakeholders. We specifically mention a few, as follows:

- ***The United Nations.*** Over the past several decades, there has been no real concerted attempt at defining and implementing a complementary and mutually supportive approach about the roles and responsibilities of the Bank

Group and United Nations agencies in the area of environment. It is time for this to change. Beginning with climate change, but broadening the scope gradually to other areas, the Bank Group and key United Nations agencies should work out a practical and pragmatic way forward, aimed at being able to offer partner countries stronger and more strategic support. The emerging environmental crisis requires a forceful and concerted multilateral response. Countries and people deserve nothing less.

- ***Development banks.*** The Bank Group should develop more strategic relationships with the multilateral and bilateral development banks by building on their distinct relationships with local shareholders and stakeholders in delivering coordinated support to key environmental initiatives. The new partnership approach adopted in the design and implementation of the new climate investment funds could serve as a model for pursuing other, Bank Group/multilateral development bank–supported environmental sustainability efforts.
- ***The private sector.*** The importance of the private sector can hardly be exaggerated. The Bank Group must take a hard look at how it works with the private sector, and the signals it sends to the private sector about its commitment to environmental sustainability, and the opportunities and challenges involved in promoting it. The opportunities for partnership with firms and business groups at all levels are vast. Taking a truly strategic and "picky" approach is essential, as is working more seamlessly across the Bank Group. The Advisory Panel agrees strongly with the evaluation on the need to design a much more strategic approach to market transformation for environmental sustainability (including transition to low-carbon economy), something which requires coordinated work in relation to both public and private sectors.
- ***Civil society organizations.*** Strategic partnership with civil society organizations and networks can greatly expand the reach, effectiveness, and legitimacy of Bank Group efforts. Many civil society organizations have a stronger technical capacity than government institutions, and can promptly react to immediate needs. While working at local or national levels, many are active networkers with similar organizations worldwide, generating and sharing information, experiences, and lessons.
- ***The scientific community.*** The evaluation does not state much about how the Bank Group has worked with or tapped the knowledge of the scientific community. While recognizing the progress that has been made in instituting modern knowledge management and networks in the organization, it is not clear if the Bank Group has effectively harnessed scientific knowledge to develop "cutting-edge" approaches. The Bank Group should consider options for ensuring how best to do this for the future, including the option of reestablishing a senior environmental science position.

As the international community focuses on the need to urgently address global and local environmental challenges, large amounts of resources will hopefully be made available to find solutions to these challenges. However, new resources are not sufficient. The Bank Group needs to complement them with transformational changes of its corporate culture, making environmental sustainability fully part of its development role.

The report's evaluation provides the Bank Group with an excellent basis and opportunity for setting a new course, commensurate with the most pressing challenges of our time.

The Advisory Panel looks forward to the decisions of the governing bodies with great anticipation.

# Management Response

## Introduction

Management welcomes the opportunity to comment on the evaluation of the World Bank Group experience with the environment agenda, covering the period from 1990 through 2007 prepared jointly by the three units of the World Bank Group's Independent Evaluation Group (IEG): IEG-World Bank, IEG-International Finance Corporation (IFC), and IEG-Multilateral Investment Guarantee Agency (MIGA).

It is useful to take stock of progress on this important element of World Bank Group's vision to contribute to inclusive and sustainable globalization—to help reduce poverty, enhance growth with care for the environment, and create individual opportunity. Management concurs with several aspects of IEG's main findings. Many of these findings reinforce important messages already captured in the Bank's Environment Strategy and recent update (World Bank 2001b, 2003a, 2008c), or in the findings from Bank economic and sector work, internal reviews and self-evaluation, and emerging lessons from operational experience across the World Bank Group.

At the same time, management expresses concern over the evaluation methodology employed by IEG, the gaps in evaluated areas, and the resulting use of findings to draw broad conclusions. The metrics and evaluation scope are inconsistent across the institutions; as a result, some findings, conclusions, and recommendations are not drawn from the entire set of environmental sustainability-related activities across the World Bank Group. Therefore, on several aspects, management differs, sometimes markedly, with IEG's findings and recommendations.

***Lack of adequate coverage of IFC's Sustainability Strategic Pillar.*** In particular, the report falls short in achieving the necessary depth of coverage of activities and programs under IFC's Sustainability Strategic Pillar. Sustainability is a core element of IFC's strategy, encompassing a range of initiatives that include standard setting in social and environmental performance, sustainability advisory services, promoting sustainable investing, scaling up renewable energy and energy efficiency project financing, and reducing IFC's environmental footprint. The report's shortcomings in this respect are partly a function of an evaluation that centers on different sets of activities for the Bank and IFC and MIGA.

***Limited Group-wide relevance.*** Given the aforementioned fundamental evaluation limitations and the report's objective of presenting group-level findings on the World Bank Group's full range of environmental sustainability activities, the report in some key areas has "over-synthesized" issues as Bank Group-wide and/or as sustainability-wide, while in fact they are relevant to only certain parts of the Bank Group or to certain parts of the World Bank Group's sustainability initiatives. Management, therefore, differs with IEG's recommendations on several aspects, as outlined below in some detail.

## Key Issues of Agreement and Divergence

This management response first outlines the areas in which management broadly agrees with the analysis in the review. It then discusses areas in which management believes that IEG has drawn generalized conclusions from incomplete analysis or conclusions that may go beyond the findings or do not fully take into account the underlying context. It also notes areas where IEG could have given a fuller account of efforts the World Bank Group is already making.

### A. Areas of agreement

There are several areas of agreement that management would highlight. These include the centrality of environmental sustainability in the Bank's work, the importance of country ownership, the key role for analytical support to countries, and the need for strong collaboration across sectors and across World Bank Group institutions on environmental sustainability issues.

***Centrality of environmental sustainability.*** Management concurs that environmental sustainability is an important part of the World Bank Group work. The 2001 Environment Strategy highlighted how environment was crucial from the perspective of both growth and poverty reduction; it also underscored that it was a theme applied across the World Bank Group (World Bank 2001b). More recently, this theme has been reflected in the priority and management attention across the World Bank Group devoted to climate change, an important environmental sustainability issue, Bank-wide and across Regions. Significant efforts on the nexus of environment and growth/poverty reduction front have been made and more are under way at the Regional level. Each of the Regions has prepared a Regional environment strategy to customize the overall strategy to specific Regional conditions. The approach to climate change is similar, with Regional strategies or business plans being prepared. Also, as noted earlier, IFC has made climate change and environmental and social sustainability one of its five strategic pillars, and it has included sustainability as a core business driver in its fiscal 2009–11 Road Map, recently presented to the Board of Directors (IFC 2008).

***Centrality of country ownership and the difficulty of attribution.*** The report highlights the importance of country ownership and the priority that countries place on environmental sustainability as the main determinants of country outcomes. It also correctly highlights the difficulties associated with measuring and attributing environmental outcomes to specific support from the World Bank Group. Although these difficulties apply across all sectors and themes, in part because countries' own policies and actions are the key determinant, they are especially acute around environmental issues, because support is provided by a wider set of donors than in many other sectors normally working together; and separating out the World Bank Group contribution would not be possible. Similar challenges are encountered when considering the contributions made by the private sector on macrolevel sustainability indicators; however, project-level impacts are easier to delineate.

***Centrality of good analytic support to countries.*** Given that each country's policies and actions determine environmental outcomes, management concurs with IEG on the importance of supporting countries on a demand-driven basis with good analysis. The IEG evaluation highlights the role of Country Environmental Assessments (CEAs) and Strategic Environmental Assessments (SEAs). Management sees these as important but by no means unique analytical tools to help countries mainstream environment into their policies and programs, and, therefore, into the Bank's Country Assistance Strategies, which reflect country-determined priorities.

The Bank has devoted considerable attention in the last three years to improving the effectiveness of SEAs with regard to helping inform policy choices. A pilot program is under way on institution-centered SEAs, which focus specifically on strengthening institutions and governance. This pilot program is being carried out in close coordination with bilateral and United Nations partners on the Organisation of Economic Co-operation and Development–Development Assistance Committee Task Team on SEA. The Bank has also played an important role in this task team as a contributor to the preparation of good practice guidance on SEA in development cooperation.

CEAs are an important tool to initiate and conduct a dialogue with countries on key environmental priorities linked with both poverty reduction and economic growth. The Bank continues to apply this tool strategically to respond to different needs in different country circumstances, with good results. A recently completed review of five years of experience with CEA, which draws on good practice examples, emphasizes many elements that are consistent with this IEG evaluation. These include: (1) building on analytic work of other agencies (including CEAs, SEAs, and Environment Performance Reviews); (2) highlighting the poverty dimension through more distributional analysis; (3) applying institutional analysis at a sectoral and key environmental topic level to better derive recommendations that strive to tackle key environmental issues (that is, treating institutional analysis as a means rather than as an end); (4) presenting both short- and longer-term recommendations in the report, recognizing that some interventions take longer to implement; and (5) emphasizing ways the CEA can be used as a tool to better coordinate with donors. The Bank also continues to coordinate on a regular basis with the regional development banks, as well as bilateral donors, on country-level analytical work to share experiences and lessons learned.

***Need for strong collaboration across sectors.*** Management concurs with IEG's observations on the need for strong collaboration among those responsible for country support on health, water supply and sanitation, urban development, energy, and transport, both in urban and rural settings. The recent Health Strategy (World Bank 2007c) exemplifies the multisectoral collaboration that is essential to achieving outcomes that address the basic health challenges so prevalent in developing countries. This strategy was developed through close collaboration between the Sustainable Development Network and the Human Development Network.

A recent piece of economic and sector work, "Environmental Health and Child Survival" (from the Environment Department), highlights this same point and discusses the close synergies between health, infrastructure, and environmental programs and how these could be enhanced further to achieve better outcomes (World Bank 2008a). The recent work on the transport strategy (World Bank 2008d) also benefited from this kind of collaboration. As highlighted in the recent *Global Monitoring Report* (World Bank 2008b), this commitment to collaboration is evident not only within the Bank but across all development partners. Indeed, collaboration with other partners is being strengthened. For example, a forthcoming (June 2008) poverty-environment partnership joint-agency paper—endorsed by 19 agencies, including the United Nations Development Programme, United Nations Environment Programme, and the World Health Organization, and a group of bilaterals, as well as several nongovernmental organizations—focuses on poverty, health, and environment and how, from the perspective of meeting the Millennium Development Goals, these issues can be included in poverty-reduction strategies and development plans.

***Potential for significant leveraging effect through standard setting.*** Management agrees with IEG's finding that IFC has a role to play in continuing to promote Equator Principles as a global environmental standard for private sector investments in the developing world. This is an example of the leveraging effect the World Bank Group can have through a process of consultative standard setting and dissemination. The recent update of Part III of the *Pollution Prevention and Abatement Handbook* (that is, the industry-specific guidelines) (World Bank Group with UNEP and UNIDO 1999) led by IFC, in close collaboration with the Bank, is another example of both standard setting with global significance and of close collaboration between the two institutions.

***Strong coordination across MIGA, IFC, and the Bank.*** Management agrees that continually improved coordination across the Bank, IFC, and MIGA can yield even better results. Close collaboration among all three in the context of the preparation of the Clean Energy Investment Framework (World Bank 2007a) and a climate change strategic framework for development (World Bank 2007j) are good examples of the commitment to such coordination. The aforementioned update of Part III of the *Pollution Prevention and Abatement Handbook* is another example of such collaboration. A further example is provided by the work undertaken by MIGA, with the close cooperation and assistance of the IFC, leading up to the adoption in October 2007 of MIGA's new Social and Environmental Policies, Performance Standards and Policy on Disclosure. These policies were closely modeled on the new IFC policies and standards of 2006.

### B. Areas of divergence

Although noting several areas of agreement, management would also like to note several areas in which it diverges from the analysis and findings in the IEG evaluation.

***Different and incomplete scope of analysis leads to conclusions not drawn from the full range of World Bank Group sustainability activities.*** As noted earlier, the metrics and evaluation scope are inconsistent across the institutions and as a result, findings, conclusions, and recommendations are not drawn from the entire set of sustainability-related activities across the World Bank Group.[1] IEG's evaluation combines two noncomparable impact indicators of two different categories of projects: (1) the development outcome of the Bank's "do good" (notably environment and natural resources management) projects, representing a small portion of the Bank's portfolio; and (2) the environmental outcomes and performance of IFC's and MIGA's mainstream investment activities (therefore, their entire portfolios). Activities that IFC undertakes in the sustainability domain—notably other advisory activities and the groundbreaking innovative work over the last 10 years (including renewable energy/energy efficiency projects, among others)—are also missing from the analysis. The evaluation of IFC's non-due diligence activities (or "do good" activities, per the report terminology) is cursory and incomplete. The report states that "... IFC and MIGA have fewer investment projects designed to improve the environment per se ..." and then goes on to indicate that "IFC's environmental nonlending support includes Global Environment Facility projects for about $1 billion and $185 million in Dutch-funded carbon facilities. It also includes active Environmental and Social Sustainability business line projects which totaled $208 million by end 2007, or a quarter of current total advisory funding." The $1 billion actually includes some $320 million from IFC, $200 million from the Global Environment Facility, and $485 million from donors. If the study's objective was to identify observable improvements in the environment through "do good" actions/projects, then IEG should have included the Bank's environmental interventions along with the corresponding IFC activities and programs focused on the environmental sustainability agenda. IEG's review therefore does not fully capture the extent to which the mainstreaming of the sustainability agenda has occurred within IFC and the entire scope of operations that has resulted from the adoption of sustainability as a strategic pillar. This is a missed opportunity for IEG to provide a meaningful evaluation of IFC's full range of sustainability activities.

***Drawbacks of the country case study-based methodology.*** The IEG evaluation notes why it took a case study approach.[2] However, it is unclear why applying that methodology to the largest countries can lead to conclusions that can be applied across the board. In South Asia, for example, the Bank's environmental program in India is not representative of programs in much smaller countries. In general, the experiences of the BRIC countries (Brazil, Russia, India, and China) constitute an exception, given their large geographic mass and populations. Moreover, the evaluation is not clear with respect to whether a standard methodology was used across case studies. In addition, with these kinds of studies, local context needs to be taken into account. For all these reasons, it is difficult to generalize across the universe of countries based on the case study results.

***Difficulties with the analysis of portfolio trends.*** In its investment lending, the Bank supports countries in their investments in specific sectors—for example, agriculture, forestry, mining, sanitation, or transportation—that can have positive environmental and/or natural resource management benefits. Like social development or public sector governance, environment and natural resources management is a theme—corresponding to the goals of sectoral support. The IEG evaluation argues that the Bank's thematic coding system tends to overstate the amount of lending commitments supporting environmental improvements in investment projects.

Management would argue that the sector and thematic classification and coding system may well understate the Bank's environmental support to countries, particularly given (1) the limit on the number of thematic codes that task teams can assign to a country's operation that they are supporting (the system accepts a maximum of five subthemes per project) and (2) the practice adopted in the coding system that a single dollar of lending can only support one subtheme, although in reality the same investment dollar may support, for example, water resources management, biodiversity, and rural development. As it does periodically, management is reviewing its sector and thematic coding but notes that, even with the limitations noted above, the system provides a good degree of clarity on the goals of activities supported by the Bank.

***Development Policy Operations (DPOs), budget support, and the timeframe for environmental outcome improvements.*** The IEG evaluation recognizes the potential of environment-related DPOs to support policy and institutional reform. It considers DPOs separately because it observes that the environmental results of DPOs may not be directly related to amounts disbursed, as with investment operations. The evaluation states that moving to Poverty Reduction Support Credits and other forms of budget support in Africa may indicate uneven support for the environment. Many of the DPOs in support of the environment have been programmatic in nature (for example, Mexico). Environmental outcomes are best measured at the end of the program.

The report notes that stand-alone technical assistance and capacity-building projects have been less effective than others in the portfolio. This is an important finding and deserves greater scrutiny. Perhaps the reason (acknowledged in the conclusions of the report) is that capacity problems cannot be addressed in a single operation and require a long-term engagement. Management notes that programmatic DPOs, including Poverty Reduction Support Credits, exemplify such long-term engagement. They represent strong—not weak or uneven—Bank commitment, and their extended duration may permit continual opportunities to address environmental issues in dialogue with the country.

Management would also note that the Bank and other donors are moving to increase the share of external assistance flowing through country budgets (one of the Paris Declaration goals). Budget support recognizes the centrality of government ownership and also the importance of funds flowing through country budgets for fiscal discipline. A related point is pertinent: Bank support for a certain sector does not necessarily mean additional investment in that sector. Countries, as they should, set their own budget priorities and seek funding to meet overall budget financing needs. Often, seeking Bank support in a given sector is more related to the international experience and knowledge the Bank can bring to that sector. Specifically with regard to DPOs: as pointed out in the IEG evaluation, DPOs can help countries strengthen policies and institutions. Stronger policies and institutions can strengthen environmental outcomes across the whole spectrum of investments in a country, not just those supported by the World Bank Group, with much greater impact.

***Broader look at World Bank Group performance.*** Although the evaluation is focused on the environment portfolio, management would suggest a more substantial acknowledgement that often improvements in the environment can be brought about by macroeconomic or sectoral policies (for example, more open trade can facilitate the adoption of more clean technologies, and removal of energy subsidies can help reduce greenhouse emissions) and that Bank support to the environment needs to be even more systematically channeled through some of these economic policy support mechanisms that are usually managed by Bank units outside the environment family, notably the Bank's Poverty Reduction and Economic Management Network.

***The role of IFC in supporting environmental and social due diligence and the consideration of aggregate effects.*** The nature of some IEG recommendations suggests that there is confusion concerning IFC's role with regard to the mitigation of environmental and social impacts associated with projects IFC finances and the consideration of aggregate effects for large projects. Although IFC can provide advice on mitigating project-related impacts, it does not design nor does it implement mitigation plans for project-related impacts; ownership of mitigation plans and implementation responsibility remain with the project sponsor. IFC supports the process of developing the necessary mitigation and corrective action plans on the basis of environmental and social assessments commensurate with the potential impacts of a project under consideration and oversees the implementation of the mitigation actions through a program of risk-based supervision. Furthermore, potential aggregate effects of large projects are captured through numerous provisions in IFC's Performance Standards, including those relating to area of influence, cumulative impacts, associated facilities, and supply chain management.[3]

***Cross-sectoral integration.*** The IEG report also focuses on environmental portfolio and related operations rather than taking a broader look at cross-sectoral integration. For example, although Uganda is one of the case studies, there is no acknowledgment or review of the increased efforts in Africa in promoting regional, river-basin approaches. These efforts (Nile, Senegal, Niger, and Zambezi, for example) represent an important trend toward a more integrated, ecosystems-based approach that also aims at increased government commitment to an integration of sectors and to an examination of power, transport, agriculture, flood management, natural resource management, and environmental management as an integrated package in the context of basin development and poverty alleviation. The IEG report also fails to acknowledge the Africa Action Plan emphasis on these activities or the Regional Integration Assistance Strategy (World Bank 2007i), now endorsed by the Board, or the actions in other Regions on Regional priorities in response to the IEG review of Regional operations.

***Time dimension and learning from experience.*** As with all evaluations, IEG's product is necessarily backward looking. IEG's case studies are now two years old, and some of the lessons of experience cite operations from the 1990s.[4] As a consequence, for instance, the portfolio of carbon finance projects in Uganda is not mentioned, nor is the shift in support under current projects to urban environmental problems and decentralization and natural resource management. Another example is Ghana, where, after extensive preparatory work, the government recently finalized an environmental and natural resources governance program and has signed a Letter of Development Policy in that regard.

***Trust-funded activities.*** The Bank's various trust-funded instruments—including the Bank-Netherlands Partnership Program, Forest Law Enforcement and Governance, Program on Forests, and Trust Fund for Environmentally and Socially Sustainable Development—are mainly dedicated to the support of analytic work, and the IEG report would have benefited from their inclusion in the discussion on nonlending services. Similarly, the Development Grant Facility might also have been included in the evaluation as an instrument. In a similar vein, World Bank Group environment activities occur increasingly in a multidonor context where the World Bank Group (although often holding the fiduciary responsibility) is only one of several actors who determine and oversee the substantive aspects of project implementation. Accordingly, the evaluation would have benefited from a discussion that examined whether there is a qualitative difference in results and impact between World Bank Group-only environmental initiatives and multidonor efforts.

***The Bank's country-based demand-driven operational support.*** The IEG evaluation could be read as suggesting a supply-driven approach, which sits at odds with the evaluative evidence coming out of IEG showing that ownership and demand create successful results. The World Bank Group has a role to play in highlighting environmental issues to governments, and there is an important role for advocacy at the global, Regional, and country levels. However, in the end, countries set their own strategies. As a development cooperative, the Bank needs to respond to country demand, while, of course, maintaining its environmental standards in operations. Some of the IEG suggestions on long-term country plans or measuring the environmental impact of the activities that it supports in a given country would seem to take on roles that lie squarely with national governments.

## Conclusions

Management welcomes the opportunity to comment on this evaluation, notably because it covers a subject that is central to the overall vision of the World Bank Group. Management is in agreement with many aspects of IEG's findings and conclusions. However, because of the methodology employed in the evaluation, including the different methodologies applied across World Bank Group institutions, management does not concur with some of the conclusions and recommendations. Management's specific responses to IEG recommendations are outlined in the attached Management Action Record.

## Management Action Record

| Recommendation | Management Response |
|---|---|
| **1. Increase the attention to environmental sustainability in the World Bank Group by ensuring that environmental issues enter fully into discussions of its strategic directions and Regional and country assistance programs.** | ***Mostly agreed; divergence on some recommendations.*** Management broadly agrees with most of the recommendations, and the actions to which it commits are outlined below.<br><br>*Already the practice in IFC.* Environmental sustainability is at the core of IFC's corporate strategy as it is one of its five strategic pillars. The sustainability agenda is therefore an integral component of IFC's strategy development process across both investment and advisory work. This very general recommendation, and the very narrow focus of the report on IFC's environmental and social due diligence process, suggest that the IEG review has not captured the full extent of sustainability agenda as a public good and its substantial contribution to the private sector. IFC external client surveys since 2001 have consistently revealed two major trends: clients increasingly perceive "sustainability" as primarily helpful rather than a requirement, and IFC's work in sustainability has been a key factor in bringing the business case for sustainability into the private sector domain. |
| Jointly reformulate and update the 2001 Environment Strategy to reflect new realities—including the increasingly important role of the private sector, technology transfer to developing countries, global public goods, and transnational environmental footprints—and emerging Bank Group corporate priorities. | Management plans to update the environment strategy in fiscal 2010, building on the Strategic Framework for Climate Change and Development.<br><br>IFC's contribution to an update of the World Bank Group Environment Strategy would be anchored in the ongoing implementation of a sustainability agenda that is evolving rapidly in the private sector and in financial markets. Because sustainability issues are evolving so rapidly, they must be captured on an ongoing basis in policy and operational dimensions, not just through formal strategic exercises such as the update of the 2001 Environment Strategy. Examples of recent developments in the sustainability agenda include the rapid rise of supply chain management and labor issues in the private sector domain. The formal strategic framework must therefore be supported by a dynamic operational context that can respond to emerging issues or lead the way in identifying the next frontier in the sustainability agenda. |
| Consider both medium-term (5–10 year) and longer-term (10–20 year) approaches to strengthening environmental sustainability at the Regional and national levels and incorporate short-term (3–5 year) environmental programs into country assistance and partnership strategies. | Management accepts that there is value in taking longer-term trends into consideration in the development of short-term Regional and country strategies, when possible. However, management does not intend to formally establish new medium-term (5- to 10-year) and long-term (10- to 20-year) approaches. Man- |

## Management Action Record

| Recommendation | Management Response |
|---|---|
| | agement argues for much greater flexibility in pursuing the environmental agenda at the country and operational level. That is especially the case given the need for country ownership and customization, set out in the text. The preparation of 10- to 20-year Regional and country-based plans is essentially already being tackled through the preparation of Regional environmental strategies and CEAs. Note that within CEAs, it is already considered good practice to present recommendations with a short-, medium-, and long-term timeframe.<br><br>IFC's sustainability agenda is first set at the corporate strategy level, with sustainability being one of IFC's five strategic pillars. Furthermore, the detailed Regional and sector approaches are set in the Regional and industry department strategies. These are investment strategies with a near-term (3-year) horizon, in view of the rapidly evolving sustainability agenda globally and IFC's need to meet changing client mix and demand. As a result, it is rather unrealistic for IFC to set medium- (5- to 10-years) and long-term strategies (10- to 20-years). Enhanced coordination with the Country Assistance Strategy team for country strategies and integrated sector and thematic strategies (for example, the Strategic Framework on Climate Change and Development) of a shorter time horizon would nonetheless be more useful for IFC. |
| Identify opportunities for intra-Bank Group cooperation in helping clients address key national and global environmental challenges, including pollution reduction and long-term goals (up to 50 years) for greenhouse gas abatement and adaptation to climate change. | Agree with addressing global environmental challenges, but disagree with long-term goals of up to 50 years. With respect to global environmental challenges, this is already occurring currently in the context of the preparation of the Climate Change Strategic Framework for Development and in the context of designing the Climate Investment Funds. Both are key tools in addressing greenhouse gas abatement and adaptation to climate change. Further, management is also working with the regional development banks on the Climate Investment Funds, recognizing that the Bank is just one partner assisting clients to meet long-term goals.<br><br>As described above, such mechanisms already exist for the climate change agenda (including adaptation). Another example of collaboration is the process of developing and vetting IFC's Environment, Health, and Safety Guidelines for more than 60 different commercial and industrial sectors. These guidelines provide an important reference point for the World Bank Group and for other international financiers who look on them as a recognized |

## Management Action Record

| Recommendation | Management Response |
|---|---|
| | reference point, which is particularly important when building up long-lived infrastructure assets.<br><br>With respect to key national environmental challenges, management feels that this violates the sovereignty principle and undermines the Bank's country-based demand-driven model, described above. Rather than preparing World Bank Group-led long-term plans at a country-level to tackle local environmental issues, management's approach is to support countries in strengthening their own learning frameworks (both monitoring frameworks and supporting a culture of scrutiny and greater social accountability within the country and the strengthening of environmental constituencies) so countries can better manage new environmental issues as they arise in an informed way. |
| Work with development partners to help countries address environmental problems. Use Country Environmental Analyses (CEAs) and Strategic Environmental Assessments (SEAs) for this purpose at the national, policy, sectoral, and subnational levels. Treat institutional capacity building as a means rather than an end and link it to attainment of observable environmental outcomes. Give greater attention to improving the performance of projects that focus primarily on environmental policy and institutions. | The World Bank is already working closely with development partners, and management commits to further enhance this effort through continued coordination with development partners on CEAs and with the Organisation for Economic Co-operation and Development–Development Assistance Committee Task Team on SEA on the preparation of advisory notes (for example, on climate change and SEA) as well as implementation of the Organisation for Economic Co-operation and Development–Development Assistance Committee Good Practice Guidance on SEA through the institution-centered SEA pilot program. |
| Encourage the adoption and use of the Equator Principles as global environmental standards in private sector investments in the developing world and IFC Policy and Performance Standards on Environmental and Social Sustainability by multilateral development banks. | Encourage the adoption and use of the Equator Principles as global environmental standards in private sector investments in the developing world and IFC Policy and Performance Standards on Environmental and Social Sustainability by multilateral development banks. Encouraging the adoption and use of the Equator Principles as global environmental standards in private sector investments in developing countries is consistent with IFC's sustainability agenda. This is an ongoing activity that has been remarkably successful, given that 60 banks have adopted the Equator Principles, from 10 in 2003, and that these banks provided more than 70 percent of cross-border project financing in emerging markets in calendar 2007. IFC is actively supporting and promoting the adoption of the Equator Principles through various means and efforts, largely coordinated through the policy unit housed in IFC's Environment and Social Development Department. Also, through a Community of Learning practice group, man- |

## Management Action Record

| Recommendation | Management Response |
|---|---|
| | aged and convened by IFC, IFC continues to engage with Equator Principle financial institutions and other stakeholders globally, in sharing implementation experience, raising awareness, and building capacity.<br><br>In addition and more specifically, through direct and indirect interactions with financial institutions and, more broadly, through the sustainable investing practice area of IFC's Sustainable Business Innovator, IFC is pursuing strategic market interventions aimed at increasing the sustainability of emerging market portfolios and private equity investment. In 2005, IFC, in collaboration with local partners, was instrumental in the launch of the Sustainability Index in the Saõ Paolo stock exchange. This was the second Sustainability Index in emerging markets. In 2008, and again with a number of partners, IFC replicated this work in India, leading to the launch of the S&P Environmental, Social and Governance India Index. Both indices were the first in their respective Regions to promote adoption and disclosure of sustainable business practices and performance, thereby meeting investor demand to encourage good environmental and social risk management and corporate governance. |
| Continue to develop IFC's systems to improve accountability and transparency among Equator Principles signatories. Focus IFC Advisory Services and capacity building on Regions and sectors with low environmental performance, especially on Sub-Saharan Africa and the textile, food and beverage, tourism, and agriculture sectors, and continue supporting market transformation toward sustainability, emphasizing technology transfer and development in clean production, energy efficiency, and sustainable supply chain management. | *Already the practice.* IFC believes in a continuous process of development, implementation, evaluation, and learning across the entire scope of its operations, whether investments or advisory services. This operational philosophy therefore supports an ongoing process of improvement of internal systems and tools to support more effective implementation of the Performance Standards and garner the lessons of implementation, which are critical to improving overall learning by IFC and Equator Principle institutions. Processes such as the review and update of the Environmental and Social Review Procedures and Environment and Health and Safety Guidance Notes are two examples. Notwithstanding the above, addressing issues relating to accountability and transparency of Equator Principle signatories must be in accordance with each institution's governance framework and cannot be subject to any IFC authority or oversight.<br><br>As regards environmental and social sustainability, IFC Advisory Services and capacity-building efforts focus on Regions and sectors with the highest potential for development impact and continue to support market transformation toward more sustainable practices by emphasizing initiatives that address climate change, |

**Management Action Record**

| Recommendation | Management Response |
|---|---|
| | specifically sustainable energy and water issues, clean production and technologies, social responsibility and gender entrepreneurship, and biodiversity conservation and natural resource management. For example, since 2003, IFC has helped establish lending targeted to energy efficiency in six Central European countries. Until recently, the program supported close to $240 million in sustainable energy investments across the six countries, generating energy savings equivalent to more than $80 million per year and achieving carbon emission reductions of more than 160,000 tons a year. |
| Expand MIGA's environment-related technical assistance to clients. | *Agreed.* MIGA launched in 2007 a new trust fund-supported effort (with financial support from the government of Japan) to provide such technical assistance to clients in Africa. This is the first such effort by a provider of political risk insurance, and if it proves successful, MIGA would be interested in expanding such support to investors in all Regions. However, this will depend on the ability to mobilize donor funding. |
| **2. Move to more cross-sectoral and spatially oriented approaches to environmental support and strengthen staff skills.** | ***Mostly agreed; work is already ongoing.*** |
| Be more proactive on environmental concerns, including adaptation to, as well as mitigation of, climate change, but not neglecting other local and global environmental priorities. Better integrate environmental, health, and labor issues under the Bank Group's sustainability agenda in the short and longer terms. | *Already the practice.* Greater proactivity on the climate change agenda is already under way with the preparation of a Climate Change Strategic Framework for Development and the design, with other partners, of Climate Investment Funds, to support this agenda. The framework will address both adaptation and mitigation issues. That said, Bank management is mindful of the need for balance across climate change and other local and global environmental priorities. These issues will be addressed in the updated environment strategy, following the completion of the climate change framework.<br><br>IFC is continually seeking opportunities to innovate by capturing sustainability-related business opportunities. It does so through its Environment and Social Sustainability Business Line, across six themes: sustainable investing, sustainable energy and water, cleaner technologies, social responsibility, gender entrepreneurship, and biodiversity. The Sustainable Business Innovator in IFC's Environment and Social Development Department develops advisory products and service concepts for IFC teams in Regional advisory facilities and investment departments. |

## Management Action Record

| Recommendation | Management Response |
|---|---|
| | Climate change has been included as one key priority in IFC's sustainability pillar. Although still evolving, key features of the IFC's approach to climate change include near-term actions on (1) enhanced support for renewable energy/energy efficiency investment, (2) partnerships to address climate change mitigation and adaptation, and (3) extending carbon finance activities. IFC will further review (1) its role in adaptation to climate change, (2) measuring the greenhouse gas emissions in IFC's portfolio, and (3) the use of carbon shadow costs in project appraisal.<br><br>The rapid growth of climate-related work has not slowed innovation and operations in the other important environment and social areas across both the investment and advisory services dimensions. Also the environmental and social advisory services business of IFC is growing strong with solid portfolio and pipeline numbers and is managing to attract a healthy volume of donor support.<br><br>Finally, development and implementation of the Performance Standards have facilitated the improved integration of environment, social, health, and labor considerations in IFC clients' environmental and social assessment and management processes. |
| Give greater analytical and operational attention to addressing problems that cross national and regional boundaries as well as to increasingly serious environmental and carbon footprint concerns. In analytic work, increase emphasis on linkages between poverty and the environment. Strengthen collaboration on environmental health issues among those responsible for health, water supply and sanitation, energy, transport, urban development, and environment. | Regional environmental work has traditionally been funded through the Global Environment Facility and is now supplemented with Regional International Development Association (IDA) funds, continuing under IDA15, and, for example in Africa, the establishment of a Regional Integration Department. It is important to note, however, that the Bank primarily works on a demand-driven country model basis. Poverty and environment analytics have matured, and distributional analysis is being emphasized already in SEAs and CEAs. Program on Forests- and Bank-Netherlands Partnership Program-supported work on the Forests-Poverty Toolkit is another step in this direction. Cross-sectoral issues are an important part of the climate change framework being developed and will be central to the follow-on updated environment strategy.<br><br>Furthermore, under the World Bank Group strategy on climate change, IFC is looking into practical ways to measure its carbon footprint in its portfolio amid the challenges associated with developing a methodology that can be applied to a diverse portfolio of projects such as IFC's. This is being done in consultation |

## Management Action Record

| Recommendation | Management Response |
|---|---|
| | with the World Bank, other multilateral development banks, Equator banks, and other international financial institutions. Many of these financial institutions have expressed interest in using such a tool for their own portfolio analysis. IFC's focal areas in climate change work were mentioned above. |
| Strengthen staff skills in such areas as adaptation to climate change, carbon finance, and the ability to deliver environment-related investment and policy reform projects. | Management is continuing to strengthen staff skills in these areas, primarily through training and on-the-job learning. A new course, Climate Change for Development Professionals, for staff has been initiated, and a new course focused on sustainable development for managers and senior managers is under preparation.<br><br>Over the years, IFC has established various sustainability trainings for staff customized to specific skills and needs. Training has included: Sustainability Policy and Performance Standards training, offered throughout the year to World Bank Group staff through the Learning Catalogue; IFC Carbon Finance training offered on demand to industry and Regions; Sustainability Advisory Services training, including areas relevant to Climate Change (energy efficiency, renewable energy, cleaner production, biodiversity), offered to IFC Regions and industries on demand; and a combined environmental and social Advisory and Policy and Performance Standards training offered to IFC Regions on demand. At the corporate level, sustainability training is offered in both the induction and credit courses. Footprint training is also offered to new staff. To accommodate increased demand and staff growth under decentralization, an e-learning course on the Sustainability Policy and Performance Standards is also offered. IFC's Environment and Social Development Department has a team dedicated to development of such training content and the organization of its delivery. Finally, with the creation of IFC's Sustainability Knowledge Network, training and on-boarding has become a key strategic area of attention. |
| Improve IFC-Bank coordination on policy dialogue with governments to enhance structural reforms aimed at public-private partnerships in water, wastewater, and waste management, reuse, and recycling sectors, and ensure that industry views are present in the national and sectoral policy dialogues. | This recommendation would have been more solidly grounded and of greater clarity if it were substantiated with findings drawn from a systematic evaluation of IFC-World Bank coordination. Regardless of this shortcoming, increased World Bank Group collaboration is a strategic IFC goal, and IFC departments have laid out specific plans to enhance Bank Group synergy. The Bank and IFC are increasingly collaborating, as appropriate, in Country Assistance Strategies and in specific sustainability themes, such as climate change and gender, among others. |

## Management Action Record

| Recommendation | Management Response |
|---|---|
| | Although recognizing the importance of this coordination (and highlighting the example of India, where it has already been well advanced), it is important to recognize that the Bank works on a country demand-driven basis, and such collaboration is dependent on specific country demand. |
| Stress the need for IFC and MIGA clients, especially financial intermediaries, to develop and implement solid environmental and social management systems, ensure that engineering and pollution control system design and community engagement is integrated in the early project stage, and use more independent environmental audits as part of project completion tests. In IFC's project selection and marketing, emphasize the potential for environmental benefits. In MIGA's engagement with projects, provide advice on environmental (and social) issues to help bring clients closer to industry best practices. | *Already the practice.* Implementation of environmental and social management systems is a core provision under Performance Standard 1 (Social and Environmental Assessment and Management Systems). The need for IFC clients to develop and implement environmental and social management system is assessed during appraisal and is related to the size and scale of the environmental and social risks that they need to manage. Regarding financial institutions, IFC has established and is implementing a structured risk-based approach that emphasizes coverage of all high-risk and (at the supervision stage) poorly performing financial institution projects. The risk-based approach entails an analysis of the financial institution's portfolio and is carried out during appraisal to establish the risk level of the financial institution. The portfolio analysis and the performance of the financial institution's environmental and social management system are captured in an Environmental and Social Risk Rating measure that is established at appraisal and is calculated by IFC during project supervision. This risk-based approach allows IFC to be cost-effective by allocating resources to higher-risk projects and by not overburdening clients with few or no environmental and social risks that do not need an elaborate management system rather than taking a one-size-fits-all approach.<br><br>IFC enters projects at various points in a project's lifecycle, ranging from prefeasibility (preconstruction) to renovation/retrofit of existing facilities and operations. The ability to influence design of pollution-control systems is an opportunity that IFC takes advantage of if it enters a project at the design stage. In green field operations, IFC increasingly plays an important role in technology selection. Likewise, with community engagement, for projects that directly affect a community, IFC requires client engagement through Performance Standard 1; however, IFC can only require engagement after it has entered the project, which may be well past early project stage.<br><br>With regard to the last sentence, MIGA agrees (see the response to the recommendation concerning MIGA above). |

## Management Action Record

| Recommendation | Management Response |
| --- | --- |
| **3. Improve the Bank Group's ability to assess its support for the environment and to monitor and evaluate the results of its environment-related interventions.** | ***Partially agreed.*** |
| Improve World Bank monitoring, evaluation, and reporting of environmental performance and results of lending operations. Give greater attention to improving baseline environmental assessments in IFC and MIGA—and measure more fully the aggregate effects of projects with large environmental impacts—for example, in energy and agribusiness. Work with partners such as UNDP and UNEP to help quantify progress toward the achievement of Millennium Development Goal 7 for environmental sustainability. | See below with regard to World Bank lending operations. The Bank has worked with multiple partners, and continues to do so, with respect to agreeing on appropriate environmental indicators and disseminating them (for example, through the *Little Green Data Book,* an annual publication). However, it is unclear how the recommendation to quantify progress toward the Millennium Development Goals arises out of this IEG evaluation. Executive Directors and the Bank's Governors have been very explicit in setting out a clear division of labor—United Nations monitoring of the achievement of the Millennium Development Goals and the International Monetary Fund and Bank monitoring policies and actions needed to meet the Millennium Development Goals.<br><br>As noted in the IEG report, IFC already undertakes extensive monitoring and development outcome reporting of its investment operations.<br><br>Provisions relating to "area of influence" and "cumulative impacts" in IFC's Performance Standard 1 (Social and Environmental Assessment and Management Systems; also adopted by MIGA in October 2007) provide the reference framework for IFC and MIGA to capture potential environmental and social impacts more effectively through comprehensive baseline assessment, where and when warranted. There are, nevertheless, limitations associated with the roles and responsibilities of project sponsors, which make it challenging to extend accountabilities to regional levels or on a sectorwide basis. |
| Improve the way the World Bank determines how much of its total financing has supported environmental improvement and revise preparation guidelines for Implementation Completion Reports (ICRs) to require a more systematic review of environmental dimensions and results. A mechanism to track the influence of Bank nonlending services on environment-related policies and institutions in client countries would also be desirable. | Bank management agrees to strive for better measurement, monitoring, and evaluation of its environmental support. Management is in the process of updating and streamlining investment lending policy, is reviewing its sector and thematic codes, and is undertaking a review of economic and sector work, building on IEG's forthcoming economic and sector work evaluation. In connection with work on the Climate Change Strategic Framework for Development, and in the context of designing the Climate Investment Funds, management is exploring options for project analysis. Management commits to incorporate the goal |

## Management Action Record

| Recommendation | Management Response |
|---|---|
| | of better measurement, monitoring, and evaluation of its environment support into this work and reports to Executive Directors on progress, notably in connection with climate change updates and investment lending reform discussions. |
| For environmentally sensitive IFC agriculture and forestry projects, especially in areas of high biodiversity, undertake carefully designed baseline studies to identify indirect, induced, and cumulative (as well as direct) environmental and social impacts. Design, implement, and monitor adequate plans to mitigate any negative effects. Enhance sustainability of supply chains with certification schemes and third-party monitoring. Measure specific emissions and mass flows in advance of relevant projects and assess them afterward to gauge project impact on the abatement of effluent discharges and dust and greenhouse gas emissions. | IFC clients are required to conduct a process of social and environmental assessment in accordance with the requirements of the Performance Standards. For environmentally sensitive projects, clients will establish and maintain a social and environmental management system appropriate to the nature and scale of the project and the level of social and environmental risks and impacts. Such a system will typically incorporate social and environmental assessment, including indirect, induced, and cumulative impacts; an environmental and social management program; organizational capacity; training; community engagement; and monitoring and reporting.<br><br>IFC does not design or implement mitigation plans; its additionality in this regard is through advice at entry and during supervision to the project sponsor responsible for designing and implementing mitigation plans. The project sponsors also regularly report to IFC on their progress through the *Annual Monitoring Report*. IFC, through its supervision activities, oversees the client's implementation of the mitigation plans agreed with IFC. Supply chain management is the latest challenge in project assessment and management. IFC applies Performance Standard 6, through which application of certification for natural resources (for example, forest/marine resources) is required. In addition, IFC has begun enhanced due diligence for supply chain issues in high-risk sectors. Finally, IFC promotes new certification systems through participation in various commodity round tables (for example, palm oil, soy, cotton, sugar). |
| Improve the performance of projects on MIGA's environmental and social policies on a timely basis, as appropriate in a project cycle. Require investor-clients to establish environmental and social project management systems at a sufficiently early stage to effectively monitor impacts. Consistently incorporate provisions for regular reporting of safeguard performance during project implementation in MIGA's Contracts of Guarantee. | *Agreed.* Performance Standard 1, Social and Environmental Assessment and Management Systems, requires that such systems be in place on a timely basis, and compliance with this performance standard is required in MIGA's Contract of Guarantee. |

## Management Action Record

| Recommendation | Management Response |
|---|---|
| **4. Improve coordination among the Bank, IFC, and MIGA and between the World Bank Group and external partners (public and private) in relation to the Bank Group's environmental mission and ensure consistent and effective implementation at the corporate and country levels.** | ***Mostly agreed; some divergence.*** |
| • Establish mechanisms to promote and monitor coordination across the Bank, IFC, and MIGA with respect to environment-related policies, strategies, and instruments. In particular: | Collaboration already takes place across a number of relevant operational areas, as described above. Improving coordination among the Bank, IFC, and MIGA is a useful and desirable objective where it makes operational sense, given the different clients we service. |
| – Actively involve IFC and MIGA in updating the 2001 Environment Strategy and in monitoring and evaluating its implementation. | *Agreed.* |
| – Jointly identify environmental aspects of World Bank Group country assistance and partnership strategies and jointly plan, monitor, evaluate, and report on mitigation of adverse impacts. | This depends on the country. Country Assistance Strategies and Country Partnership Strategies already take this approach by planning in a coordinated way on World Bank Group activities in a country. Monitoring and evaluation, however, can only take place within the project context, rather than at a broader level, so that the sovereignty principle is respected. |
| – Increase efforts to share experience with assessment, monitoring, evaluation, and reporting on environmental aspects, results, and impacts of activities. | *Agreed.* Again, one needs to bear in mind that private and public sector projects face very different contexts and challenges and efforts to share experiences need to take this into account. Progress will be reported in the context of the fiscal 2010 Strategy. |
| – Systematically monitor and evaluate the application and results of environmental due diligence policies and procedures (safeguards and performance standards). | These are reported in Bank Quality at Entry and Quality of Supervision reports, including environmental annexes, as well as Environmental Sector Board Portfolio (Bank-wide and Region-specific) Updates, which include similar portfolio quality indicators specific to environment.<br><br>For IFC, as noted above, this is a standing operational practice and requirement. |
| • Make strengthening external partnerships a central theme in an updated World Bank Group environmental strategy. | *Agreed.* The Environmental Sector Board has hired a lead partnership coordinator in the past year, which has greatly enhanced Bank management's ability to strengthen and coordinate external partnerships. This will be formally reflected in the updated strategy. |

| Management Action Record | |
|---|---|
| **Recommendation** | **Management Response** |
| • Improve MIGA's coordination with global programs, such as the Global Environment Facility and the Bank's Carbon Financing Group, and identify potential partners whose clients might benefit from MIGA guarantee support. | *Agreed.* MIGA coordinates and works closely with such global programs, making available political risk insurance to cover governmental obligations to potential partners. Special workshops have been held to ensure that the staff of both MIGA and such global programs are aware of the instruments available. |

A farmer plants cassava on ground cleared by fire. Photo reproduced by permission of Michael S.Yamashita/National Geographic Image Collection.

# Chairperson's Summary: Committee on Development Effectiveness (CODE)

## Background

In September 2007, CODE considered the *Sector Strategy Implementation Update (SSIU): Third Review*. Part II of the report presented the implementation progress of four Bank sector strategies, including the 2001 Environment Strategy. Environmental and social sustainability has been one of IFC's strategic pillars since 2000. In April 2006, IFC updated its approach with the launch of its Policy and Performance Standards on Social and Environmental Sustainability. MIGA adopted its own Policy and Performance Standards on Social and Environmental Sustainability, modeled on the IFC policies, effective October 2007.

## IEG Evaluation

The evaluation assessed the effectiveness of World Bank Group (WBG) support for environmental sustainability—in both the public and private sectors—from 1990 to 2007. It identified constraints within the WBG, including insufficient attention to longer-term sustainable development. IEG recommended the following: (1) Increase the attention to environmental sustainability in the WBG; (2) Move to a more cross-sectoral and spatially oriented approach and strengthen staff skills; (3) Improve the Bank Group's ability to assess its support for the environment; and (4) Improve coordination and consistency among the Bank, IFC, and MIGA and between the WBG and external partners.

## Draft Management Response

Management concurred with several aspects of IEG's main findings, and noted that many of them reinforce important messages already captured in the Bank's Environment Strategy and recent update, or in the findings from Bank economic and sector work (ESW), internal reviews and self-evaluation, and emerging lessons from operational experience across the WBG. Management expressed concerns over the evaluation methodology employed by IEG, the gaps in evaluated areas, and the resulting use of findings to draw broad conclusions. The metrics and evaluation scope were considered inconsistent across the institutions and, as a result, some findings, conclusions, and recommendations were not drawn from the entire set of environmental sustainability–related activities across the WBG. Therefore, on several aspects, management differed, sometimes markedly, with IEG's findings and recommendations.

## General Conclusions

CODE welcomed the opportunity to deliberate on a topic of immense strategic importance for the WBG. It thanked IEG for a comprehensive, informative, and detailed paper that provided some comfort, especially regarding the increase in attention accorded to environmental sustainability in all three institutions and improvements in performance over the 15-year evaluation period. The IEG review also identified a number of areas where the performance could be improved and crucial constraints to be addressed, particularly those related to government commitment and weak institutional capacity. The committee also appreciated management's substantive response, which detailed areas of broad agreement with the findings and recommendations, as well as several points where its perspectives diverge from those of IEG. The lack of adequate coverage in the evaluation of IFC's strategic pillar on sustainability and the limitations of the attempt to synthesize Bank Group–level findings elicited some sympathy from speakers. Yet, the committee was gratified to note that management was committed to following up on all aspects covered in the evaluation. The rich discussion covered a wide range of topics and issues, including its strategic alignment and those related to translating objectives into effective development impact, and issues related to organization and staffing.

## Next Steps

The Strategic Framework on Climate Change and Development will be considered by CODE in early August. The new WBG Environment Sector Strategy will be prepared in fiscal 2010, with a concept note by spring 2009. Findings from various relevant IEG reviews over the next 12 months would be among the inputs for the new strategy. There was also a request for IEG to prepare a synthesis paper based on this report and related forthcoming evaluations that CODE felt would better serve as a basis for discussion than this evaluation.

The following main issues were raised at the meeting:

***Evaluation Methodology and Scope of the Review.*** Several speakers raised questions about IEG's evaluation methodology and the scope of the review, and a few noted that the evaluation could have been more focused or presented as a series of evaluations. Several speakers observed that the evaluation could have usefully included a more forward-looking approach; an analysis of aid architecture; more country-specific lessons from Country Assistance Evaluations; more preeminence to IFC's strategic pillar on sustainability, including efforts to promote energy efficiencies through financial intermediaries; and integration of IEG's review on global programs. A speaker felt that the differences between the views of IEG and management should have been addressed up front, before initiating the evaluation. *IEG noted that the methodologies applied to examine each member of the WBG are known and well accepted, and that the available data reflect reasonably the current and historical situations prevailing in each institution. Management replied that a more in-depth discussion on evaluation methodology may be undertaken when IEG presents the Approach Paper of future evaluations, and it suggested that perhaps there should be a CODE discussion of Approach Papers for WBG evaluations.*

A member underlined the difficulties in drawing general conclusions that apply to the entire WBG, given the different approaches and businesses of IFC/MIGA and the Bank. Another member felt that since the evaluation was not intended to make comparisons given the different group of clients and environmental standards, an artificial comparability between methodologies should not be imposed. This member found that the weakness was in drawing conclusions from the generalization of individual case studies, and the differences between evaluation and a general policy-advocacy role. In this vein, she added that any conclusion should be drawn from findings of these cases, and some policy advocacy may not be directly relevant to the cases.

***New Environment Strategy.*** Speakers felt that management should take into account some of IEG's key findings in preparing the new strategy, including cross-sectoral integration (such as climate change, water management, energy, and transport) across the Regions. Some speakers raised questions and comments about timing and articulation between the preparation of the Strategic Framework on Climate Change and Development, and the new environment strategy; alignment with the WBG strategy; high expectations about the WBG's role in environmental management; and use of knowledge of the scientific community. It was highlighted that environment is an integral part of the economic growth and development agenda. In this regard, the need to consider updates of other environment-related strategies, such as forestry or urban development, and due diligence and safeguard mechanisms was mentioned.

Some members noted that the formulation of the new strategy should involve extensive consultations with external stakeholders—governments, the private sector, and development partners. Given IEG findings that the WBG impact and efforts varied over time and across themes and countries, it was suggested that the new strategy should put more emphasis on operational changes and business modalities, establish internal control mechanisms, and include indicators to monitor its effective implementation. Questions were raised about the Bank's role in relation to other players in the international arena and the existence of two sets of social and environmental standards in the WBG.

***Country Focus.*** Members agreed with IEG's recommendation on the need for a fully integrated WBG approach to environmental issues in country programs. In this regard, the WBG should strengthen dialogue with its clients to mainstream environmental sustainability in Country Assistance Strategies (CASs) and focus on the regional context, like the case of the European Union. One member sought further clarification on implementation of this recommendation. She stressed the importance of the Bank's advisory role in encouraging the consideration of environmental programs in CASs and of avoiding additional conditionalities to clients. Several speakers remarked that the WBG approach should be demand-driven and based on the countries' ownership and institutional capacity. In addition, the WBG's role in raising awareness on the importance of environmental sustainability in client countries was highlighted.

Following the proposed Chairperson's Issues Note, some members commented on the need for a dynamic, flexible, and differentiated approach to meet the needs of different categories of clients—low/middle-income countries or fragile states. The various challenges of addressing the environmental agenda were noted, including those related to policy support lending, particularly Development Policy Lending, strengthening countries' institutional capacity, and the Bank's leadership in setting and promoting environmental best practices. Further clarification was sought on IEG's analysis of the Bank's role in assisting clients to anticipate and mitigate the effects of natural disasters (floods or droughts, for example).

***WBG Coordination.*** Speakers underscored the need to improve collaboration within the WBG to strengthen the effectiveness of its assistance at the country, regional, and global levels. They emphasized that organizational structure, staffing and incentives, and internal constraints should be considered in addressing the lack of an integrated WBG approach. One member felt that important emerging lessons from across the WBG's support to the public and private sectors should be incorporated to achieve greater environmental sustainability. One speaker stressed the importance of having more joint Bank-IFC-MIGA CASs.

***Global Public Goods.*** Some members felt that global issues cannot be addressed purely at the national level. In this vein, the question was whether the Bank Group is the most appropriate institution to address this matter, given that other development partners, such as the UN, should play the leading role.

***Monitoring.*** Speakers agreed with IEG's recommendation on the need to improve monitoring of impact of WBG's interventions, shifting from an input to an output indicators approach and setting clear benchmarks to measure progress in areas such as climate change and development. One speaker raised the related question of how to balance the impact of emissions compared to the overall developmental benefits of a project. He cautioned against embracing a certain methodology for measuring carbon footprints. One member, however, felt that carbon footprint measurement was not the key to address environmental sustainability, because it was not a question of lack of awareness, but of limited alternative viable ways of modern human life and production.

Jiayi Zou, Chairperson

Girls collecting clean water from well in Sri Lanka. Photo by Dominic Sansoni, courtesy of the World Bank Photo Library.

# Glossary

| | |
|---|---|
| **Adaptation** | Measures taken by societies and individuals to adapt to actual or expected adverse impacts on the environment, especially as the result of climate change. |
| **Biodiversity** | Short for biological diversity. Refers to the wealth of ecosystems in the biosphere, of species within ecosystems, and of genetic information within populations. |
| **Carbon offset** | A financial instrument representing a reduction in greenhouse gas emissions. Although there are six primary categories of greenhouse gases, carbon offsets are measured in metric tons of carbon dioxide-equivalent ($CO_2e$). One carbon offset represents the reduction of one metric ton of carbon dioxide, or its equivalent in other greenhouse gases. |
| **Category A (projects)** | Projects with potential significant adverse social or environmental impacts that are diverse, irreversible, or unprecedented. |
| **Category B (projects)** | Projects with potential limited adverse social or environmental impacts that are few in number, site-specific, largely reversible, and readily addressed through mitigation measures. |
| **Chlorofluorocarbons (CFCs)** | A family of inert, nontoxic, and easily liquefied chemicals used in refrigeration, air conditioning, packaging, and insulation or as solvents and aerosol propellants. Because CFCs are not destroyed in the lower atmosphere, they drift into the upper atmosphere, where their chlorine components destroy ozone. |
| **Civil society** | The totality of voluntary civic and social organizations and institutions that form the basis of a functioning society, as opposed to the force-backed structures of a state (regardless of that state's political system) and commercial institutions. |
| **Climate change** | Change of climate that is attributed directly or indirectly to human activity that alters the composition of the global atmosphere and that is in addition to natural climate variability observed over comparable time periods. |
| **Ecology** | The relationship of living things to one another and their environment, or the study of such relationships. |
| **Ecosystem** | The interacting system of a biological community and its nonliving environmental surroundings. |
| **Effectiveness** | The extent to which the development intervention's objectives were achieved, or are expected to be achieved, taking into account their relative importance. |

| | |
|---|---|
| **Emission** | Pollution discharged into the atmosphere from smokestacks, other vents, and surface areas of commercial or industrial facilities; from residential chimneys; and from motor vehicle, locomotive, or aircraft exhausts. |
| **Environment** | The sum of all external conditions affecting the life, development, and survival of an organism. |
| **Environmental and social effects** | IEG's indicator as a part of development outcome evaluation, covering: (1) the project's environmental performance in meeting IFC's requirements and (2) the project's actual environmental impacts, including pollution loads; conservation of biodiversity and natural resources; and, in a broader context, social, cultural, and community health aspects, as well as labor and working conditions and workers' health and safety. |
| **Environmental aspect** | Element of an organizations activities, products, and services that can interact with the environment. |
| **Environmental assessment** | A process whose breadth, depth, and type of analysis depend on the proposed project. Environmental assessment evaluates a project's potential environmental risks and impacts in its area of influence and identifies ways of improving project design and implementation by preventing, minimizing, mitigating, or compensating for adverse environmental impacts and by enhancing positive impacts. |
| **Environmental footprint** | A measure of human demand on the ecosystems and natural resources. |
| **Environmental impact** | Any change to the environment, whether adverse or beneficial, wholly or partially resulting from an organization's environmental aspects (as defined in ISO 14001). |
| **Environmental mainstreaming** | The integration of environmental concerns into macroeconomic and sectoral interventions. |
| **Environmental Management Plan (EMP)** | The synthesis of all proposed mitigative and monitoring actions, set to a timeline with specific responsibility assigned and follow-up actions defined. The EMP is one of the most important outputs of the environmental assessment process. |
| **Environmental management system** | Part of an organization's management system used to develop and implement its environmental policy and manage its environmental aspects. |
| **Environmental objective** | Overall environmental goal, consistent with the environmental policy that an organization sets itself to achieve. |
| **Environmental performance** | Measurable results of an organization's management of its environmental aspects. |
| **Environmental performance criterion** | Environmental objective, target, or other intended level of environmental performance set by the management of the organization and used for the purpose of environmental performance evaluation. |

| | |
|---|---|
| **Environmental Performance Evaluation** | Process to facilitate management decisions about an organization's environmental performance by selecting indicators, collecting and analyzing data, assessing information against environmental performance criteria, reporting and communicating, and periodically reviewing and improving the process (ISO 14031). |
| **Environmental Risk Assessment** | An evaluation of the environmental risks associated with a specific intervention. |
| **Environmental sanitation infrastructure** | Infrastructure such as a wastewater treatment plant or sanitary landfill designed, in part, to improve environmental quality, although its ultimate purpose is to protect human health and welfare. |
| **Environmental sustainability** | Ensuring that the overall productivity of accumulated human and physical capital resulting from development actions more than compensates for the direct or indirect loss or degradation of the environment. Goal 7 of the U.N. Millennium Development Goals specifically refers to this as integrating the principles of sustainable development into country policies and programs and reversing loss of environmental resources. |
| **Equator Principles** | A financial industry benchmark for determining, assessing, and managing social and environmental risk in project financing. |
| **Externalities** | Uninternalized costs or benefits resulting from one economic agent's actions that affect the well-being of others. They may be either positive or negative. Pollution and other forms of environmental degradation are frequently cited as an example of the latter. |
| **Financial intermediary** | An institution that performs financial intermediation between two or more parties. |
| **Greenhouse gas** | Gases in the atmosphere that reduce the loss of heat into space, and therefore contribute to global temperatures through the greenhouse effect. Greenhouse gases—water vapor, carbon dioxide, methane, nitrous oxide, ozone, and chlorofluorocarbons—affect the temperature of the Earth. |
| **Hazardous wastes** | Byproducts of society that can pose a substantial or potential hazard to human health or the environment when improperly managed. Substances classified as hazardous wastes possess at least one of four characteristics—ignitability, corrosivity, reactivity, or toxicity—or appear on special lists. |
| **Indigenous peoples** | Collectively, the members of cultures with historic, ancestral, spiritual, and functional connections to the land on which, and from which, they live. In popular usage, indigenous peoples are distinguished from members of cultures whose connection to the land on which they live is limited to the historical period. |

| | |
|---|---|
| **ISO (International Organization for Standardization) 14001** | The ISO 14000-series of standards specify the requirements for an environmental management system, which can be integrated with other management requirements to assist organizations in achieving environmental and economic goals. |
| **ISO 14031** | ISO standard "Environmental Performance Evaluation—Guidelines." |
| **Mitigation** | Measures taken to reduce adverse impacts on the environment. |
| **Natural resource management** | Human intervention to guide the use of renewable natural resources such as water, soils, and forests. |
| **Ozone-depleting substances** | Manufactured chemical compounds that reduce the protective layer of ozone in the Earth's atmosphere. The Montreal Protocol, administered by the U.N., maintains the list of ozone-depleting substances that are targeted for control, reduction, or phase-out. |
| **Performance standards** | The eight Performance Standards establish requirements that the client is to meet in IFC-financed projects. |
| **Prevention** | Measures taken to minimize the release of wastes to the environment. |
| **Safeguard policies** | Policies designed specifically to ensure that the environmental (and social) impacts of projects supported by the Bank Group are considered during appraisal and preparation. The Bank's safeguard policies cover environmental assessment, natural habitats, pest management, indigenous peoples, cultural resources, involuntary resettlement, forests, dam safety, international waterways, and disputed areas. |
| **Stewardship** | Responsible management of the environment and renewable natural resources, with an eye toward assuring their sustainability. |
| **Sustainable development** | Development that meets the needs of the present without compromising the ability of future generations to meet their own needs. |
| **Wastewater** | Spent or used water from individual homes, communities, farms, or industries that contains dissolved or suspended matter. |
| **Watershed** | The area drained by a particular watercourse, including the watercourse itself. |

# Chapter 1

## Evaluation Highlights

- Environment has a complex and important relationship with growth and poverty.
- The World Bank Group has engaged with environmental issues since the early 1970s, but most activity, including that of IFC and MIGA, has taken place since 1990.
- The first Bank-wide environment strategy was approved in July 2001, but it mostly reflected the World Bank's agenda and priorities.

Pristine Chinese countryside. Photo by Curt Carnemark, courtesy of the World Bank Photo Library.

# The Context

Global climate change is front page news. It is also the topic of the United Nations Development Program's (UNDP) *Human Development Report 2007/2008* (UNDP 2007) and the most recent *Global Monitoring Report* (World Bank and IMF 2008), which is concerned with progress toward achievement of the Millennium Development Goals (MDGs) and inclusive and sustainable development. But other environmental problems are also becoming more serious, from urban air and water pollution to soil erosion; desertification; water scarcity; and the loss of endangered species, vital natural habitats, coral reefs, and other biodiversity.

These growing environmental challenges have been well documented by the United Nations Environmental Program (UNEP) in its most recent *Global Environmental Outlook* (UNEP 2007), which concludes the following:

- The world has changed radically—socially, economically, and environmentally—since the report of the World Commission on Environment and Development (WCED 1987).
- The World Commission on Environment and Development recognized 20 years ago that the environment and economic and social issues are interlinked.
- Population growth, increasing economic activity, and changes in consumption patterns have increased pressure on the environment. Serious and persistent barriers to sustainable development remain.
- Environmental degradation is therefore undermining development and threatens future development progress.[1]

Environmental problems, including climate change, affect middle- and low-income countries (including fragile states) alike, but have a particularly severe impact on the poor. Addressing environmental degradation, therefore, is essential to achieving sustainable development and long-term poverty reduction, and is among the most important challenges faced by the World Bank Group and other development assistance providers, as well as by the countries themselves.

***Environmental degradation and the predicted effects of climate change are serious challenges for developing countries.***

## Growth, Poverty, and Environment

As the World Commission on Environment and Development first demonstrated, and the recent UNEP and World Bank/International Monetary Fund (IMF) reports reaffirm, economic growth, poverty, and environment are strongly interrelated (figure 1.1).[2] Investments to increase economic growth are important for poverty reduction, but in the absence of adequate mitiga-

**Figure 1.1: Relationships among Growth, Poverty, and Environment**

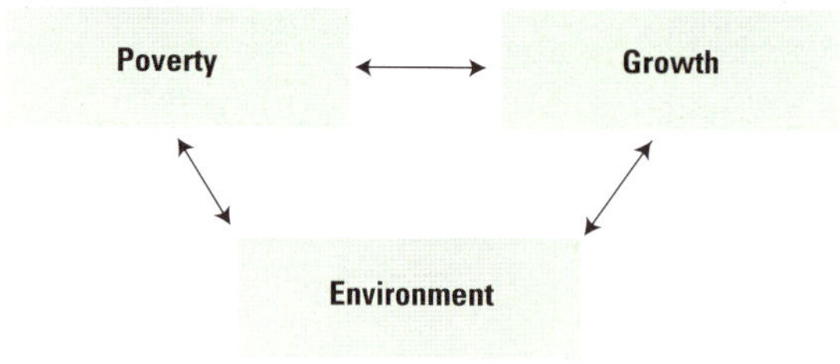


tion measures, certain types of investment, especially for new, large-scale infrastructure, may make some people poorer or harm the environment, as with forced resettlement or the flooding of natural habitats by major hydropower projects.

Links among growth, poverty, and environment are complex and run in both directions. Many (but not all) environmental problems improve as output levels rise, but, as with income disparities, they may get worse before they get better.[3] In addition, the costs associated with environmental degradation—such as the public health costs of pollution or soil nutrient loss from uncontrolled erosion—often reduce productivity, resulting in lower rates of economic growth than would otherwise be the case (World Bank 1992a, 2003d).[4]

*The complex interrelationship of poverty, growth, and environment may cause environmental problems to get worse before they get better.*

Beyond this, people are frequently impoverished by a declining natural resource base and forced by their circumstances to further degrade the environment (WCED 1987; World Bank 1992a, 2003d). In short, the natural environment often limits the economic opportunities of people in rural areas, and they, in turn, affect the quality of the resource base. Similarly, the health impacts of pollution most adversely affect the poor and may further restrict their chances to rise out of poverty, while poverty often forces low-income urban dwellers to reside in areas with poor or nonexistent sanitation and greater vulnerability to the negative effects of natural and man-made hazards.

*The public and private sectors must both address environmental problems.*

Strong growth over the past decade in both developed and developing countries has increased pressures on world agricultural, mineral, energy, and other resources. In an increasingly globalized world, moreover, expanding economic activity in one country, especially one of the largest,[5] may have a significant environmental impact or footprint outside its borders.

In this context, governments and the private sector must both act to prevent and mitigate the environmental risks associated with growth and persisting poverty. Governments promulgate laws and regulations to protect the environment, but often lack resources for proper enforcement. They are also charged with implementing international environmental conventions within their national boundaries. Private and public productive activities consume natural resources, including water and energy, often inefficiently, and can damage the environment through pollution and excessive and nonsustainable resource exploitation.

## Bank Group Involvement in the Environment

The World Bank Group engages with environmental issues in a variety of ways, interacting with governments, other financial institutions, private sector clients, and civil society. Bank Group lending, investment, and guarantee programs also have direct and indirect impacts on the environment (figure 1.2). World Bank environment-related support for the public sector is given mainly through advisory, analytical, and lending services to countries to help them better understand environmental issues and set priorities, support policy reforms, build capacity, and address specific environmental problems. Increasingly, it has also included engagement through regional and global environmental programs and partnerships. The International Finance Corporation (IFC) and the Multilateral Investment Guarantee Agency (MIGA) support to the private sector has generally sought to ensure that the investments they finance or guarantee adhere to environmental policies and standards and minimize or mitigate harmful environmental impacts. IFC has also launched a number of environmental (and social) Advisory Service programs.

**Figure 1.2: World Bank Group Environment-Related Activities**

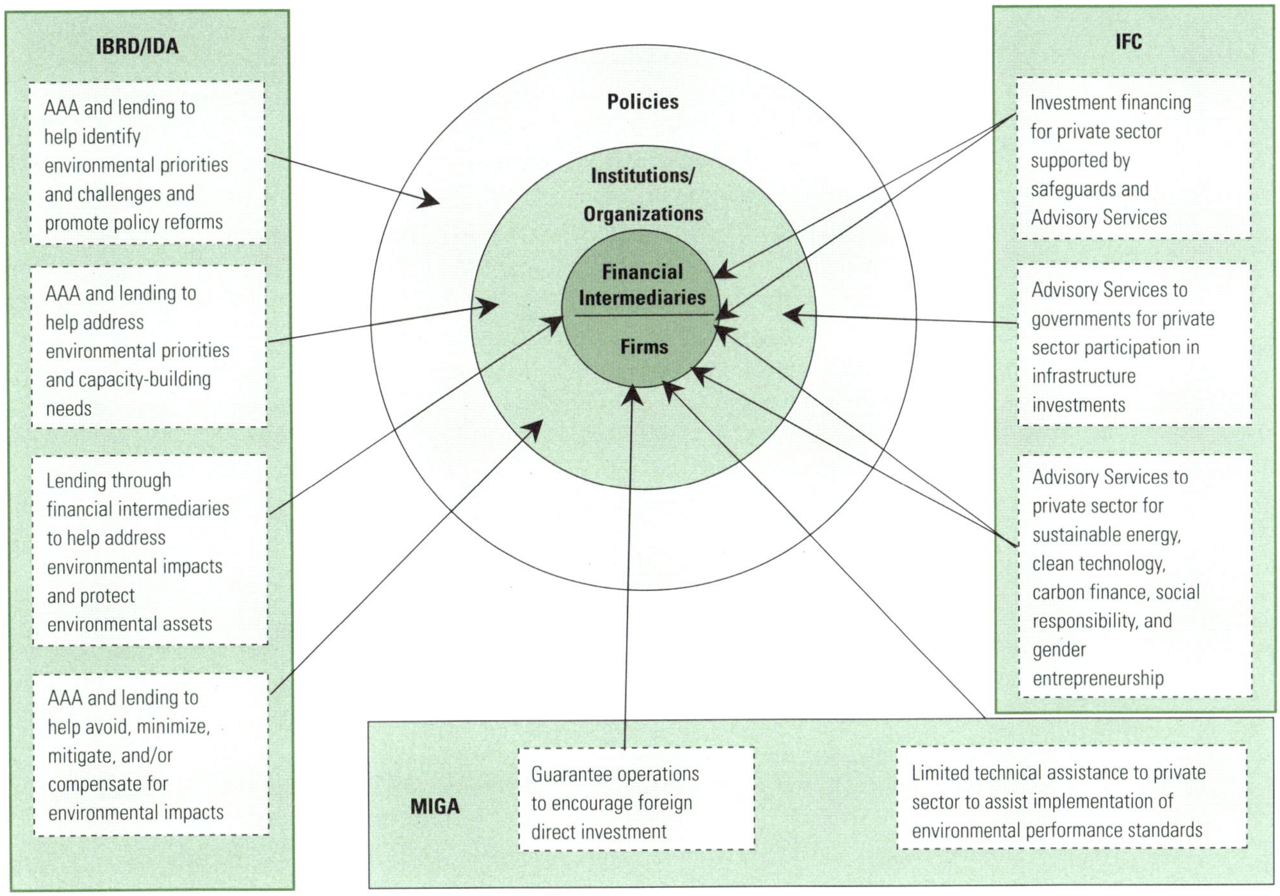


*Note:* AAA = analytical and advisory activities.

Environmental considerations became an explicit part of World Bank Group support starting in 1970, when an advisor was appointed to help assess potential environmental effects of World Bank investment projects. The Bank was the first international development agency to do so (Wade 1997). These activities gained further impetus—as new guidelines were developed and environment-related lending was stepped up—after the United Nations Conference on the Human Environment in Stockholm in 1972. In the mid-1980s, the Bank came under sharp external criticism for the environmental and social impacts of several large lending operations, including Polonoroeste in Brazil, the Narmada Dam in India, and the Transmigration Program in Indonesia.[6] Partly as a result of this experience, a central Environment Department and Regional environment divisions were established in 1987, new specialists were hired, environmental safeguards were strengthened, and lending for the environment expanded.

*World Bank Group environment-related support to the public sector is often direct; in the private sector, it is more indirect.*

The World Bank's first policy on the environmental aspects of its work was issued in May 1984.[7] But it was not until October 1989 that an Operational Directive formally required that all proposed investment operations be subject to environmental assessment, including use of public consultations and the disclosure of draft and final environmental assessment reports.[8] An Operational Directive on Environmen-

*The World Bank Group has been involved with environmental issues since the early 1970s.*

*World Bank Group environmental activities accelerated in the late 1980s and policies on environmental assessment and action plans were issued.*

tal Action Plans (EAPs) was issued in July 1992.[9] The Bank contributed to the United Nations Conference on Environment and Development in Rio de Janeiro in June 1992, mainly in the form of a *World Development Report* (WDR) affirming that environmental protection was an essential part of development.[10] A Vice Presidency for Environmentally Sustainable Development was also created.[11] Other key initiatives in which the Bank became engaged were the Multilateral Fund for the Implementation of the Montreal Protocol on Substances that Deplete the Ozone Layer in June 1990[12] and the Global Environment Facility (GEF), whose pilot phase began in October 1991, to help finance global conventions for biodiversity conservation and to address climate change.[13]

*IFC began to engage with the environmental agenda in the late 1980s.*

IFC hired its first environmental specialist in 1988, created an Environment Unit in its Engineering Department in 1991, a Technical and Environmental Department in 1992, and an Environmental Projects Unit in 1997. Its first procedure for project environmental analysis and review, issued in 1990, was revised in 1993. A set of Environmental and Social Safeguard Policies, based largely on those of the Bank, together with revised procedures and a manual on public consultation, were approved by the Board in 1998. The Environment and Social Development Department was established in 2000. The safeguard policies were reviewed in 2005 and replaced with a new Policy and Environmental and Social Performance Standards in 2006. In 2003, the Equator Principles were launched, based on IFC requirements and establishing standards for environmental and social due diligence by international commercial banks in emerging markets. A revised version of the principles, covering IFC's new Policy and Performance Standards on Social and Environmental Sustainability, was adopted in 2006 by 41 commercial banks that were investing in developing countries. IFC's Environmental and Social Advisory Service programs[14] were reorganized in 2006 under the Sustainable Business Innovator team. Sixty major banks had adopted the Equator Principles by March 2008.

*MIGA followed Bank policies from its inception in 1988.*

Since its establishment in 1988, MIGA's mandate has been to encourage the flow of private investment to World Bank Group clients by offering political risk guarantees. MIGA policy requires all the projects it supports to comply with applicable MIGA environmental policies and guidelines. Its work with clients focuses on environmental assessment and monitoring of project compliance with environmental and social guidelines and safeguards. MIGA followed applicable World Bank policies and used IFC staff for the environmental and social review of its operations during much of the 1990s, but established its own environmental office in 1998. MIGA's Environmental Assessment and Disclosure Policies were approved by the Board in 1999, and its issue-specific safeguard policies were approved on an interim basis in 2002. Following IFC, a new Policy on Environmental and Social Sustainability and associated Performance Standards became effective in October 2007.

## Bank Group Environment Strategies and Financial Support

During the 1990s, the World Bank Group stressed several aspects of its environment work, including project-level safeguards to "do no harm," national environmental strategies, financial and technical support to both the public and private sectors to "do good," and support to countries to address global sustainability issues. Nonlending outputs included many publications (such as Schramm and Warford 1989 and Munasinghe 1994), technical assistance, and a variety of environmental capacity-building initiatives aimed at both the public and private sectors. Starting in 1990, relevant activities (including those of IFC and MIGA as of 1993–94) were summarized annually in reports entitled *The World Bank and the Environment*. The fiscal year 1993 report presented a fourfold agenda, consisting of stewardship, safeguards, mainstreaming, and global sustainability, that would characterize the Bank Group's approach for the rest of the decade.[15]

The only explicit World Bank Group strategy for the environment, *Making Sustainable Commitments* (World Bank 2001b), was endorsed by the Board of Directors in July 2001. However, the participation of IFC and MIGA in its elaboration was limited, so that it primarily reflected the World Bank's agenda and priorities.[16] Regional strategies, prepared in parallel and as inputs for the Bank-wide strategy, were issued around this time (see, for example, World Bank 2002a, 2002b, 2005a). Placed clearly in the context of the World Bank Group's mission to combat poverty, the strategy affirmed that promotion of environmental improvement was a "fundamental element of development and poverty reduction strategies and actions." This would be achieved by helping countries "set and address their environmental priorities and challenges, including those of a regional and global nature, and by supporting the sustainability of its operations" (p. xx).

Three interrelated objectives were highlighted in relation to this central goal: (1) improving the quality of life, focusing on areas where environment, quality of life, and poverty reduction are strongly interlinked—that is, enhancing livelihoods, preventing and reducing environmental health risks, and reducing vulnerability to natural hazards and the adverse impacts of climate change; (2) improving the quality of growth (both how growth is generated and its pace; see Thomas and others 2000) by supporting policy, regulatory, and institutional frameworks for sustainable environmental management and sustainable private sector development; and (3) protecting the quality of the regional and global commons with an increased emphasis on local benefits of global environmental interventions (World Bank 2001b).

In reinforcing Bank efforts in the 1990s to integrate environmental concerns in its activities, the 2001 Strategy sought to clearly position environmental and natural resource management as development issues, rather than primarily as matters of conservation and doing no harm. This evolution of thinking also influenced approaches taken by other development institutions, as manifested in the series of *World Resources Reports* jointly sponsored by the World Resources Institute, UNDP, UNEP, and the Bank.[17] It also influenced the activities of several important international environmental nongovernmental organizations (NGOs), in part through new collaborations such as the Critical Ecosystems Partnership Fund with Conservation International and the World Bank–World Wildlife Fund Forest Alliance. And it was reflected in a second environment-related WDR (World Bank 2003d), launched 10 years after the Rio conference at the September 2002 World Summit on Sustainable Development in Johannesburg. This report reaffirmed that environmental improvement, institutional development, and empowerment of the poor are all essential for sustainable development.[18]

***A fourfold agenda for environment was put forward by the Bank in the early 1990s.***

Together with other inputs,[19] the 2001 Strategy drew on findings and recommendations of an IEG (then known as the Operations Evaluation Department, or OED) evaluation of World Bank environmental activity in the 1990s. That assessment, which used the above-cited fourfold agenda as its evaluation framework, concluded that Bank performance had been partially successful and recommended a number of changes that were incorporated in the strategy (IEG-World Bank 2002).[20] The present evaluation seeks to update—and expand to IFC and MIGA—that exercise, using both the earlier fourfold agenda and the main thematic thrusts of the 2001 Strategy as its principal lenses.

***The World Bank Group's first explicit environmental strategy was issued in 2001, but it mainly reflected the Bank's agenda and priorities.***

Even though the 2001 Strategy only briefly addressed IFC and MIGA, the environment has been a strategic priority for both institutions in recent years. IFC's Strategic Directions documents approved by the Board over the past decade have emphasized environmental and social sustainability. More recently, one of five strategic priorities in *IFC Strategic Directions FY08–10* is differentiation through sustainability, and one of four business drivers in IFC's recent Global/Local Strategy is strengthening development, including positive environmental impact. Similar examples can be provided for MIGA.

Even though the World Bank Group is only one among many donors that have provided significant support to developing countries, it has become the largest single source of multilateral development finance for the environment over the past 15 years.[21] World Bank funding for the environment and natural resource management (ENRM) has increased substantially since 1990; China, India, and Brazil have been the largest borrowers. It has also helped to leverage financing from other sources, including the GEF and bilateral donors, to support implementation of national environmental strategies and action plans and to address global environmental challenges, among other objectives. But the volume and nature of this support varies considerably from one country to the next, in accordance with their interest in borrowing and receiving policy advice from the Bank for environmental purposes and the extent to which they turn to other donors in this regard.[22] The Bank's influence is constrained accordingly. IFC[23] and MIGA have also stepped up their financing of private sector investments in recent years—both in general terms and relative to that provided to governments by the Bank—including their support for better internal environmental management systems (EMSs) at the individual project level, but they, too, are ultimately constrained by client demand.

# Chapter 2

## Evaluation Highlights

- IEG has evaluated the effectiveness of World Bank Group support for the environment through both the public and private sectors over the past 15 years, as well as the constraints on that effectiveness.
- Environmental and natural resources management are cross-cutting themes, and therefore multisectoral.
- The information base regarding environmental aspects, results, and impacts of World Bank Group projects is within its control. But the evaluation found some shortcomings in this regard.

Deforestation in Brazil's rain forest. Photo ©Douglas Engle/Corbis, reproduced by permission.

# The Evaluation

## Objectives and Framework

This evaluation has three objectives. First, it attempts to assess the extent to which World Bank Group support since 1990 has been effective in helping countries set and address environmental priorities and in helping private sector clients enhance their environmental management and mitigate adverse impacts. Second, it identifies the principal external and internal constraints on greater World Bank Group effectiveness in this area. Third, it suggests ways in which the World Bank Group can improve its effectiveness.

The analytical framework for the evaluation recognizes three generic requirements for public policy effectiveness: a clear definition of what is to be achieved (the mission), adequate institutional and political support for this mission (the authorizing environment), and the organizational capability to carry it out (capacity). These three elements can be visualized as intersecting circles (figure 2.1), where the challenge is to align them as closely as possible. For Bank Group managers and staff to achieve the objectives they seek, both internal and external support and resources must be mobilized (Moore 1995).

Relevant actors outside the World Bank Group include governments, private firms, civil society organizations, and other development agencies. In addition, two sets of intersecting circles matter, one within the World Bank Group (internal constraints), and the other within the Bank's country government and IFC and MIGA private sector clients (external constraints). Because the World Bank Group's role in helping to bring about desired improvements in environmental sustainability is ultimately of interest, its support

**Figure 2.1: Keys to Effectiveness**

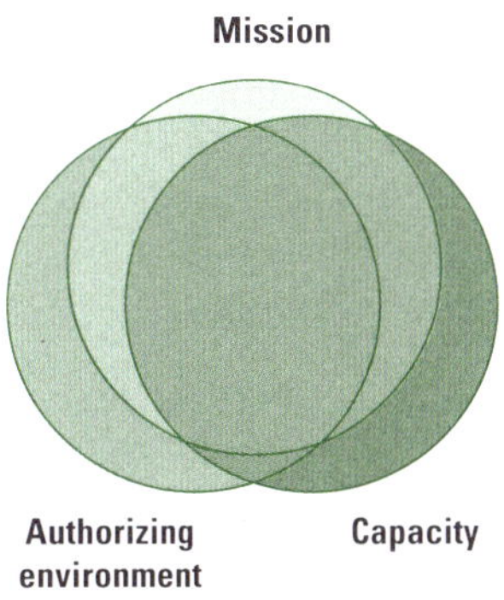

*The evaluation framework considers generic requirements for public policy effectiveness.*

can be considered effective to the extent that it has had a measurable positive and durable impact on environmental quality.

However, determining this with any precision is very difficult. An accurate assessment of World Bank Group effectiveness requires an ability to trace the key links on multiple causality chains between specific actions and specific environmental outcomes and impacts. A recent Bank paper on aid effectiveness identifies three types of links between donors and country outcomes, from external donors to policy makers, policy makers to policies, and policies to outcomes.[1] According to this source, "aid agencies, foreign NGOs, and international financial institutions influence local policy makers" by affecting policy formulation and providing financial and technical assistance. In addition, donors "try to impose policies through aid conditionality, but operate with imperfect knowledge of the local environment and, more importantly, imperfect control of the implementation of these policies" (Bourguignon and Sundberg 2006, pp. 3–4).

*But it is very difficult to trace multiple causal chains from specific World Bank Group actions to specific environmental results.*

All of these points are relevant to the present assessment. Moreover, particularly in the case of environment, it is important to state from the outset that the Bank, IFC, and MIGA are only three among a great number of actors (and normally are far from being the most significant among them) that influence relevant policies and institutions, as well as environmental outcomes, quality, and sustainability more generally in the countries where they operate. Thus, in considering Bank Group effectiveness in relation to the environment, it is critical to recognize both that:

- The Bank Group cannot—and should not be expected to—solve environmental problems that are ultimately the responsibility of the client countries and private firms themselves, although it should try to be as effective as possible in supporting its clients' efforts to do so.
- Any assessment of the performance of Bank Group environment-related interventions should ideally take into account the role and performance of all of the other major actors involved, not just the Bank, IFC, or MIGA.

*Environment and natural resource management is a cross-cutting theme, and a spatial focus is often needed.*

In attempting to carry out an evaluation of this sort, several methodological limitations, including those attached to the specific approaches taken in the present exercise, should be kept in mind.

## Methodological Approaches and Constraints

Despite the frequent absence of needed information on the actual environmental results of World Bank Group interventions, and in view of other methodological problems briefly described below, it is nonetheless possible to: (1) examine experience at the project, firm, country, and global levels to determine what has been attempted over time and through what means; (2) obtain a general sense as to how effective these interventions have been in helping clients achieve their environmental objectives; and (3) where such interventions have not been effective, to identify the principal external and internal constraints involved. Several considerations are important here, including differences in what it is possible to determine for the World Bank versus IFC and MIGA, given the differences in their roles and instruments, together with their varying information constraints.

Since November 2001 the Bank has considered ENRM as a cross-cutting theme[2] like economic management, public sector governance, gender, and social development, as opposed to sectors such as education, health, and transport.[3] Second, as is also the case for rural and urban development, a spatial focus is important both because environmental problems occur at different spatial scales, from local (watershed or urban area) to global, as the 2003 WDR points out, and because environmental problems are spatial externalities. In short, they are the negative (although often unintended) spillovers or by-products of productive and other human activities—for example, air or water pollution, greenhouse gases, or biodiversity loss due to land use changes, and so on—in a particular locality. The cross-sectoral and spatial nature of the environmental challenges faced by the Bank Group and its clients adds complexity to any evaluation of this sort.

As indicated above also, ideally the effectiveness of World Bank Group support would be evaluated on the basis of tangible improvements in environmental quality. However, this is often impossible, for at least four reasons. First, the needed environmental quality and project outcome data are either not available or of insufficient quality (the information problem). Second, such improvements often take considerable time to become evident, and thus may not yet be observable (the time horizon problem). Third, even when specific actions have positive environmental impacts, they may be offset or overcome by other factors that result in negligible overall improvement or actual worsening of environmental quality (the countervailing factors problem). Fourth, even where positive trends in environmental quality can be more readily observed, it may not be possible to identify their precise causes or the extent to which they were brought about by World Bank Group influence (the attribution problem) because of the involvement of other actors.

Effectiveness can also be assessed by attempting to gauge the influence of Bank support on country environmental priority setting; policy changes; and legal, regulatory, and institutional capacity development; and IFC and MIGA support for overall market transformation toward sustainability and individual firms' EMSs, clean production technologies, pollution abatement, and efficient and sustainable energy and resource use. Here again, however, there are often considerable information, time horizon, and attribution problems. In addition, having clear national environmental priorities; better policies; and stronger legal, regulatory, and institutional frameworks in place is not in itself sufficient to ensure improved environmental outcomes in the absence of adequate political will and institutional capacity to use these instruments appropriately. And, as suggested above, rapid growth and persistent poverty, among other factors, may impede resolution of environmental problems or exacerbate their severity in the short and medium term, with the former being especially important in middle-income countries, and the latter in lower-income countries. Civil unrest and political conflict, in turn, often represent another important set of factors that contribute directly to environmental degradation, particularly in fragile states.[4]

Many of these constraints are beyond the control of the World Bank Group. However, one of the most important—the information base regarding environmental aspects, results, and impacts of the investments it supports—is within its control. This evaluation has found shortcomings in this regard. For example, there is no requirement that World Bank Implementation Completion Reports assess the environmental results of operations.[5] As a consequence, even though these reports are not the only instruments needed for this purpose—strong individual project monitoring and evaluation systems are essential, and robust ex-post impact evaluations would also help—the Bank does not have a consistent idea of even the short-run environmental effects of its lending, although the 2001 Environment Strategy promised to introduce a monitoring and reporting framework that would track Bank performance. IFC's performance monitoring in relation to the environment (see below) is presently more systematic.

***It is not possible to assess effectiveness on observable environmental outcomes.***

***The impact of World Bank Group activities on country environmental policies and institutions is also difficult to gauge.***

### *Assessing World Bank effectiveness*

In part because of the methodological problems mentioned above, the World Bank portion of this evaluation is largely based on experience in the nine study countries, together with a portfolio review and survey of the relevant Bank and non-Bank literature. Four of the case study countries—India, China, Brazil, and Russia—are among the Bank's largest clients in total commitments over the 1990–2007 period. They rank first, second, third, and tenth,[6] respectively, and are also of great global environmental significance.

Most of the others (Ghana, Madagascar, Senegal, and Uganda) are in Sub-Saharan Africa, and, with Arab Republic of Egypt, on the African continent. Considered together, these nine countries represent close to 44 percent of the total land area, 56 percent of the overall population, and 46 percent of the combined gross domestic product of all lower- and middle-income countries. All of them also currently face serious environmental challenges, ranging from water scarcity, land degradation, and deforestation to severe air and water pollution, rising greenhouse gas emissions, and increasingly threatened biodiversity (see appendix C). And they house a broad range of geographic, ecological, and cultural diversity, as well as many of the world's most polluted megacities.[7]

*Country cases for the Bank evaluation were selected to ensure Regional coverage and inclusion of countries with the largest environmental footprints.*

The assessment of World Bank effectiveness considers both lending and nonlending instruments, together with the treatment of environment in country assistance/partnership strategies and borrower-prepared National Environmental Action Plans (NEAPs) and Poverty Reduction Strategy Papers (PRSPs).

On the lending side, a general portfolio review of all Bank ENRM loan, credit, and grant operations approved between fiscal 1990 and 2007 was carried out (see chapter 3 and appendix F), although more in-depth analysis of these projects was limited to the case study countries. The decision to follow a country case study approach for the Bank portion of the study was also prompted by the absence of a project environmental performance monitoring system similar to those of IFC and MIGA.

The case study approach has the advantage of permitting a deeper examination of experience with a range of strategic, analytical, and lending/grant instruments in a particular set of countries over time. However, it also has limitations, especially when the countries involved are not fully representative of the larger universe of clients, either in a specific Region or the full set of Bank Group client countries, which affected the ability of the evaluators to draw conclusions that would be fully applicable to that larger universe. This disadvantage can be partially offset, as in the present exercise, by selecting countries that include a substantial share of the overall population served by the Bank Group and have representative development and environmental management challenges, as well as by the more comprehensive portfolio review. But trade-offs are inevitable, so it is important to keep in mind that Bank findings, conclusions, and recommendations in this evaluation are based primarily on the experience in the case study countries, supported to the extent possible by findings from the broader portfolio analysis and information from other sources.

### Assessing IFC and MIGA effectiveness

The assessment of IFC effectiveness considers both lending and nonlending instruments, drawing on previous evaluations and nine country studies. In 1996, IFC developed a project-level Environmental and Social Effects (ESE) Indicator that is part of a specialized evaluation and rating system for analyzing the development outcomes of its investment projects. The ESE rating reflects a project's environmental and social performance in following the policies, guidelines, and project-specific requirements in place at the time of appraisal, as well as project environmental and social impacts. Starting in 2006, IFC also initiated a system to monitor and (self-) evaluate its Advisory Services, using an objective-based evaluation framework that comprises strategic relevance, outputs, outcomes, impacts, and efficiency. IEG started to validate these results in 2007. Thus, this evaluation is largely based on recent IEG validations and previous external program evaluations.

MIGA's evaluation is similar to that of IFC and assesses the extent to which the evaluated projects' performance adhered to MIGA policies and environmental, health, and safety criteria derived from its environmental assessment and disclosure policies and guidelines, applied both at approval and during implementation.

The different approaches reflect, in part, that World Bank clients are countries and governments and the Bank's assistance to the public sector takes place at the policy as well as at the institutional/organizational and financial intermediary (FI) levels, while IFC's support to the private sector occurs principally at the FI and individual firm levels, and MIGA's mainly at the firm level. It also reflects different information constraints regarding project environmental performance within the various parts of the World Bank Group (see appendix A for further detail concerning methodological differences between the World Bank and IFC and MIGA portions of this evaluation).

The portfolio approach also has advantages and disadvantages. The former include the possibility of more readily comparing performance across a broad range of sectors and drawing conclusions that apply to the entire universe of activities supported. At the same time, it is not possible by this method alone to bring out qualitative aspects of the experience under review, which must rely more on an individual case-by-case analysis. For this reason, the IFC part of the evaluation also included visits to selected client operations in most of the same case study countries selected for the Bank evaluation.

### Other evaluation and field inputs

In both the World Bank and IFC/MIGA assessments, maximum use was made of IEG evaluation materials, including project and country-level evaluations and previous sector or thematic assessments. Project-level evaluation materials were also used for IFC and MIGA. New assessments were carried out for completed environment-related World Bank operations in Brazil, China, Ghana, India, Madagascar, Russia, and Uganda (see appendix E) and first-hand inspection of relevant IFC projects in the same countries, except Madagascar and Senegal (where IFC's activities are limited), as well as in Kenya and (more selectively) South Africa. Many of IEG's IFC-related findings were based on project evaluations conducted between 1996 and 2006 (a random sample of projects with at least five years' maturity after approval and 18 months' revenue generation). The MIGA evaluation used results of past ex-post evaluations of mature guarantee projects (including field visits), an assessment of quality-at-entry of recent MIGA guarantees (involving a desk review and interviews with staff), and a country case study (desk review) of MIGA's entire portfolio in the Russian Federation.

*The IFC and MIGA evaluations focus on project impacts and performance in meeting environmental and social requirements.*

IEG-World Bank and IEG-IFC fielded missions to all of the case study countries during 2006 and selected development partner organizations to obtain the views of government officials, other multilateral and bilateral agencies, international environmental organizations, and a broad range of national stakeholders, including representatives of the private sector, academic institutions, trade associations, the media, and local NGOs concerning the nature, quality, and effectiveness of World Bank Group environmental support. World Bank and IFC field and headquarters professional staff were interviewed, as were current and former World Bank Group managers familiar with the case study countries, and World Bank Group environmental activities more generally.

*Reviews of evaluation materials were supplemented with field visits, stakeholder interviews, and new project assessments.*

In summary, evaluating effectiveness of World Bank Group support for the environment is a complicated task. First, as a cross-cutting theme, the environment itself is complex. Second, the World Bank Group is a small actor in this area relative to many others, most notably the governments and private sector in the countries themselves. This is particularly the case in the largest countries. Third, there are multiple constraints—information, time horizon, countervailing factors, and attribution among them—that limit the evaluator's ability to determine causal relationships between interventions supported by the World Bank Group and tangible changes in environmental quality or even environment-related policy and investment decisions by client governments, financial intermediaries, and firms.

This report divides Bank Group support for the environment into complementary "do no harm" (mainly safeguards) and more proactive "do good" approaches. Because of significant differences in the nature of their business models, project cycles, activities, and clients, the Bank, on the one hand, and IFC and MIGA, on the other, have addressed environmental aspects differently over the past 17 years. Because of these differences, as well as the aforementioned information constraints, the relative emphasis on the "do good" versus "do no harm" aspects of Bank Group environment-related activities in this evaluation varies, depending on the part of the institution involved.

Despite these limitations, a general sense of the effectiveness of World Bank Group support for environmental sustainability since the early 1990s can be obtained, especially in the nine case study countries. In undertaking this assessment, however, it has become evident to IEG that the World Bank Group, especially the Bank, needs to improve the coverage and quality of its own information base regarding the environmental aspects, results, and impacts of the investments it supports and other environment-related services it provides. This is itself one of the central findings of the evaluation.

# Chapter 3

## Evaluation Highlights

- Country strategies have increased their attention to environment, but analytic work on poverty and pro-poor growth has lagged.
- Projects mapped to the Environment Sector Board have performed slightly below the Bank average.
- Performance on safeguards, stewardship, mainstreaming, and global sustainability has improved, but further advances are needed.
- The Bank has done better at helping countries identify priorities than at helping to address them.
- The Bank has not been sufficiently strategic in addressing environmental linkages with health and vulnerability.
- The Bank's record on helping countries improve environmental governance has been mixed.

Motorcycles, which produce large amounts of $CO_2$, are a main form of transportation in cities in Vietnam. Photo by Tran Thi Hoa, courtesy of the World Bank Photo Library.

# The World Bank and the Environment

World Bank support for the environment has evolved over the past four decades from an initially preventive "do no harm" or safeguards approach to—especially after 1990—a proactive "do good" approach. The latter includes direct interventions to improve the local/national (stewardship) and global environments and increased integration of environmental concerns in a broad range of sectors and policies (mainstreaming), using a variety of instruments.

Both approaches were integrated with the World Bank Group's poverty-reduction mission by the 2001 Environment Strategy, which emphasized linkages among environment and poverty, health, and vulnerability. The approaches were also linked to environmental governance, global sustainability and local benefits, and the private sector, the last mainly through the activities of IFC and MIGA (see chapter 4).

## World Bank Instruments

### *Strategies and action plans*

IEG reviewed four types of strategies and plans: Country Assistance Strategies (CASs) and Country Partnership Strategies, NEAPs, Country Environmental Strategy Papers (CESPs), and PRSPs. CASs, Country Partnership Strategies, and CESPs are Bank products, the former two increasingly prepared jointly with IFC and in consultation with the countries involved. NEAPs and PRSPs are country products with varying degrees of Bank technical support.

IEG case study analysis found, and the Bank literature confirms, that environmental concerns have received growing attention in country strategies since 1990 (Kishore and Shyamsundar 2005; Bell, Shyamsundar, and Hamilton 2002; Bell and Shyamsundar no date; Shyamsundar and others 2001; Shyamsundar and Hamilton 2000). Their integration into national development priorities has likewise increased, although there is considerable variation across countries and over time.[1] The differing attention given to environmental concerns in such documents reflects the relative importance given to them by specific Regional vice presidents and country directors and their teams and, above all, by the government authorities with whom they primarily engage.

*Environmental concerns have received growing attention in country strategies since 1990.*

#### *National Environmental Action Plans and Country Environmental Strategy Papers*

Madagascar was the first country to produce a NEAP with World Bank support (1988).[2] Many others followed, including China, Egypt, Ghana, India, Russia, Senegal, and Uganda. Some countries (for example, Egypt) have produced second-generation plans, and others (such as India) have subsequently adopted National Environment Policies, but in many others NEAPs have not been updated. The Bank and/or other donors (including the GEF) have financed one or more projects in many countries (three each in Ghana and Madagascar and two in Uganda, for example) to help governments implement NEAPs or equivalent strategies. The Bank has used CESPs to help countries set priorities and identify ways of addressing them, including use of market-based instruments together with more traditional command-and-control approaches. CESPs also helped orient Bank support for the environment in China (1992) and Senegal (1994) prior to their NEAPs, and Bank economic and sector work (ESW) assessed the India NEAP (1996).

*NEAPs were elaborated for many countries, and in some cases CESPs were done in advance of them.*

NEAPs and CESPs made relevant contributions to identifying priority environmental problems; analyzing their causes; and specifying a range of policy, institutional, and investment measures to address them. However, earlier studies show that insufficient definition of priorities, poor country ownership, and weak internal capacity often constrained their effectiveness (World Bank 1995c; IEG-World Bank 1996).[3] Inconsistent donor support was also a factor in the incomplete implementation of some NEAP measures.

*Weak country ownership and capacity and inconsistent donor support have resulted in incomplete implementation of recommendations.*

### Poverty Reduction Strategy Papers

One goal of the 2001 Environment Strategy was to promote environmental improvements in PRSPs (first required of International Development Association [IDA] recipients in October 1999) and associated investments. The need to introduce ENRM considerations into PRSPs was stressed in a sourcebook and a general guidance document for such exercises (Bucknall, Hamilton, and Kishor 2000). But subsequent reviews by the Bank's Environment Department (Bojo and Reddy 2002, 2003a, 2003b; Bojo and others 2004) and experience in the four Sub-Saharan African case study countries for this evaluation suggest that ENRM concerns have been insufficiently incorporated in many PRSPs[4] and associated Poverty Reduction Strategy Credits (PRSCs), especially in view of the importance of natural resources for growth and poverty reduction in rural areas and of environment-health links, particularly in cities.

*Though IDA recipients are required to consider ENRM issues, they have not featured prominently in PRSPs.*

### Nonlending services

Attention to environmental problems in Bank nonlending services[5] has increased since 2001.[6] Among case study countries, examples include costs of environmental degradation estimates for China, Egypt,[7] and India, and Country Environmental Analyses (CEAs) for Egypt, Ghana, India, and Senegal. Strategic Environmental Assessments (SEAs) are also being used increasingly. Notable Bank environment-related research has focused on pollution management (World Bank 2000a), agricultural expansion, poverty reduction, environment in tropical forests (Chomitz and others 2007), and the "wealth of nations" (World Bank 2006f). The 1992 and 2003 WDRs are also examples (World Bank 1992c, 2003d), as are studies at the Regional (for example, Cleaver and Schreiber 1994) and country levels (World Bank 1997a, 2001a).

Nonlending services, including programs financed by the Development Grant Facility, such as the Consultative Group on International Agricultural Research system and the Critical Ecosystems Partnership Fund,[8] have been as important as lending operations in creating positive environmental results (see box 3.1). CEAs, one of which was recently published (Sanchez-Triana, Ahmed, and Awe 2007), are also a potentially valuable tool. Experience at the Asian and Inter-American Development Banks[9] shows that CEAs have been especially useful when prepared prior to country strategies. In the absence of Bank CEAs or other analytical work, the Bank should continue to draw on CEAs by other agencies, as well as Organisation for Economic Co-operation and Development (OECD) Environmental Performance Reviews[10] and other relevant reports, to provide input into country strategies.

Experience in India shows that the process of elaborating a CEA can be at least as important as its conclusions and recommendations, because they have strong potential for both raising awareness and helping build consensus.[11] Although CEAs should continue to provide the environmental background information required for Bank Development Policy Loans (DPLs),[12] as in both Egypt and India, these loans should be used primarily to analyze environmental priorities more generally.[13] The Environment Department has recently assessed the first five years of Bank experience with CEAs (World Bank 2007g); based on that assessment, further guidance[14] will be provided to country partners and Bank staff.

### *Lending services*

Since 1990 the Bank has provided financial support for ENRM through International Bank for Reconstruction and Development (IBRD) loans, IDA credits, GEF and Montreal Protocol grants, and, increasingly, carbon finance. This has included funding for five main thematic areas, or agendas, each having several subareas: (1) brown—industrial pollution and urban environmental management; (2) green—land, watershed, forest, and other renewable natural resource management; (3) blue—integrated water basin (including rivers, lakes, and seas), fisheries, and marine and coastal zone management; (4) institutional and policy—financial and technical assistance to build national and subnational environmental management capacity and induce policy and institutional reforms; and (5) global—(terrestrial and aquatic) biodiversity conservation, climate change, reduction of ozone-depleting substances, integrated ecosystem management, and management of international waters.[15]

*Attention to the environment in the Bank's AAA has increased since 2001.*

*The Bank's nonlending services have been at least as important as its lending operations because of their broader reach.*

Experience in the case study countries under each of these agendas is summarized in appendix D, which contains a set of matrices that indicate how the Bank responded to a range of key environmental issues in its country strategies, ESW, and lending and grant operations both before and after 2001, together with the relative severity of each issue in each country. An overview of the Bank's ENRM portfolio, including that part mapped to the Environment Sector Board,[16] is also provided. A more detailed review of the ENRM and Environment Sector Board portfolios is contained in appendix F.

*The CEA process is at least as important as its content and should be highly participatory.*

**Box 3.1: Positive Impacts of Nonlending Support: Three Examples**

1. In the course of their work on pollution management, researchers in the Development Economics department provided support to both their Regional operational colleagues and country partners in Brazil, China, India, Indonesia, Mexico, and elsewhere. This work was summarized in the book *Greening Industry* (World Bank 2000a). Among other impacts, this support helped the Indonesian government substantially increase the effectiveness of its actions to combat industrial pollution by publicly disclosing good and bad private sector performers through the national media. There was a similar experience in China.[a]
2. A World Bank Institute seminar on multipurpose river basin management in China in early 1990 led to a major Bank study for the strategic and holistic management of the Yellow River Basin. This was followed by major Bank investment projects in a variety of sectors in the Yellow and other major river basins (such as for the Yangtze and Tarim Rivers), as well as for the surrounding Loess Plateau (Sun 1994).
3. A Bank research paper was reportedly influential in persuading the Russian government to ratify to Kyoto Protocol on climate change (Lecoq and Shalizi 2004).

*Source:* IEG country case studies.

a. A recent external assessment of World Bank research activities found that *Greening Industry* was a "truly first-rate product" that revealed "many mechanisms that work to control pollution even in the absence of pollution control legislation, or in such situations where such legislation exists but is not implemented." See Deaton and others (2006, p. 18).

*The Bank has provided support for many environmental agendas.*

Between fiscal 1990 and 2007, 2,401 projects involving ENRM objectives or components ("the ENRM portfolio") were funded by IBRD loans and/or IDA credits, including fast-disbursing adjustment and development policy operations (DPLs) and GEF and other grants involving commitments officially estimated at $59 billion (table 3.1). This compares with nearly 6,800 Bank operations and more than $401 billion in total commitments. Thus, roughly 15 percent of all commitments approved between fiscal 1990 and fiscal 2007 reportedly involved ENRM objectives or components.

The $59 billion includes roughly $3.5 billion in DPLs with environment-related conditions.[17] These operations support policy and institutional reforms while providing clients with general budget resources. Thus, they are not used to directly finance investments for ENRM. However, given the importance of strengthening policies and institutions, such operations hold a great deal of potential. Clearly, it will also be important to measure environmental outcomes over the longer term to determine the success of these projects in achieving their environmental sustainability objectives.[18]

*The amount of Bank lending for ENRM purposes could not be determined, but official lending figures appear to be overstated.*

The Bank's thematic coding process, moreover, appears to overestimate actual commitments for ENRM; the Bank tends to overstate the amount dedicated to environmental improvement in many of the largest investment projects.[19] There may also be significant differences between commitments and actual disbursements during implementation as the result of loan/credit reallocations and cancellations.

Although it is not easy to determine precisely how much of the estimated ENRM commitments have been used to finance specific environmental improvements, the amount in projects primarily concerned with ENRM can be identified. Commitments in non-DPL operations with 50 percent or more of the total reportedly for ENRM-related purposes were $34.5 billion, much of which was for environmental sanitation infrastructure (such as wastewater treatment plants). The figures also include several large natural resource management projects. Even though any cut-off percentage is arbitrary, commitments in which at least 80 percent was estimated to be for ENRM purposes totaled $18.2 billion, or about 4.5 percent of the overall total.

**Table 3.1: Portfolio by Region, Fiscal 1990–2007 (official figures based on thematic coding)**

| Region | Total number of projects[a] | Total commitment amount ($ million) | Projects with ENRM content | ENRM (% of total projects) | Total commitment amount in ENRM projects ($ million) | ENRM commitment (% of total commitment) | Environment commitment amount ($ million) |
|---|---|---|---|---|---|---|---|
| Sub-Saharan Africa | 1,907 | 61,742.30 | 555 | 29.1 | 20,950 | 33.9 | 6,737.30 |
| East Asia and Pacific | 1,064 | 85,472 | 449 | 42.2 | 39,676.50 | 46.4 | 19,687.98 |
| Europe and Central Asia | 1,266 | 70,539.30 | 419 | 33.1 | 18,658.30 | 26.5 | 8,356.83 |
| Latin America and the Caribbean | 1,373 | 98,445.10 | 559 | 40.7 | 27,703.50 | 28.1 | 11,482.04 |
| Middle East and North Africa | 540 | 23,359.00 | 193 | 35.7 | 9,451.20 | 40.5 | 4,059.00 |
| South Asia | 636 | 61,923.80 | 223 | 35.1 | 23,635.40 | 38.2 | 8,757.63 |
| World | 6 | 29.50 | 3 | 50.0 | 29.00 | 97.3 | 20.75 |
| **Total (all World Bank)** | **6,792** | **401,511.30** | **2,401** | **35.4** | **140,103.40** | **34.9** | **59,101.52** |

*Sources:* World Bank databases.

a. The numbers cited here are based on the exact numbers for all individual commitments.

In Regional terms, Africa has the largest share of projects in the ENRM portfolio, followed by Latin America and the Caribbean and Europe and Central Asia. The Middle East and North Africa and South Asia have the smallest shares (figure 3.1). In terms of commitments, however, the largest share is in East Asia and the Pacific, followed by Latin America and the Caribbean and Europe and Central Asia, and the smallest is in the Middle East and North Africa, followed by Sub-Saharan Africa (figure 3.2).

The East Asia portfolio is dominated by China, which accounts for 36 percent of all ENRM projects and 57 percent of all ENRM commitments in the Region.[20] India (with 11 percent) and Brazil (6 percent) also have significant weights in ENRM commitment terms, with India's share alone exceeding that for all of Sub-Saharan Africa and Brazil's nearing that of the Middle East and North Africa. In short, three of the case study countries account for nearly one-third of ENRM commitments since fiscal 1990, while the nine together account for more than 40 percent.

The number of ENRM projects and commitments for environment-related purposes increased in the early 1990s, leveled off or fell between fiscal 1995 and 2003, and rose again subsequently (figure 3.3). The spike in commitments in fiscal 2005 occurred largely in Latin America, mainly reflecting large environmental DPLs in Brazil, Colombia, and Mexico. However, as noted above, the fast-disbursing resources transferred through these operations were not used to fund public investments for the environment, but to support policy/institutional reform.

***Though Africa has had a large number of projects, most were small.***

***China has borrowed a particularly large amount for environment-related projects.***

Bank-administered GEF operations increased fairly steadily between fiscal 1999 and 2005 but fell off in fiscal 2006–07. According to the Environment Department, total cumulative Bank financing through the GEF as of the end of fiscal 2007 was just over $4 billion, with IBRD/IDA cofinancing $7 billion and an additional $12.3 billion coming from other sources. This indicates that such grants have successfully leveraged significant amounts of funding, including,

**Figure 3.1: Share of Bank Projects in ENRM Portfolio, by Region, Fiscal 1990–2007**

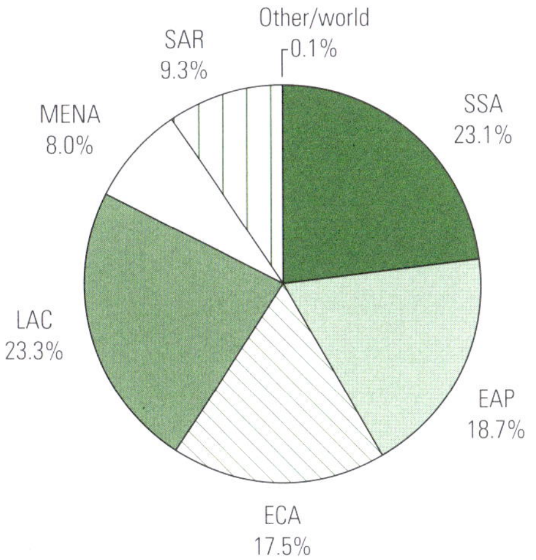


*Source:* World Bank data.
*Note:* SSA = Sub-Saharan Africa; EAP = East Asia and Pacific; ECA = Europe and Central Asia; LAC = Latin America and the Caribbean; MENA = Middle East and North Africa; SAR = South Asia.

**Figure 3.2: Share of Bank Environment Commitments in ENRM Portfolio, by Region, Fiscal 1990–2007**

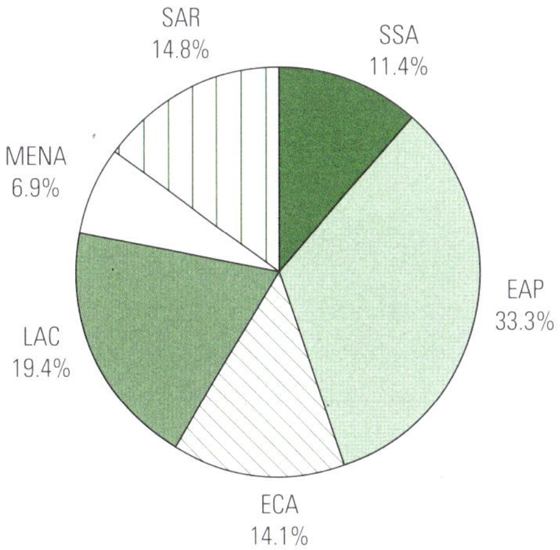


*Source:* World Bank data.
*Note:* SSA = Sub-Saharan Africa; EAP = East Asia and Pacific; ECA = Europe and Central Asia; LAC = Latin America and the Caribbean; MENA = Middle East and North Africa; SAR = South Asia. Percentages total 99.9 because of rounding.

**Figure 3.3: ENRM Portfolio Commitment Amounts (official figures) and Number of Projects, by Fiscal Year**

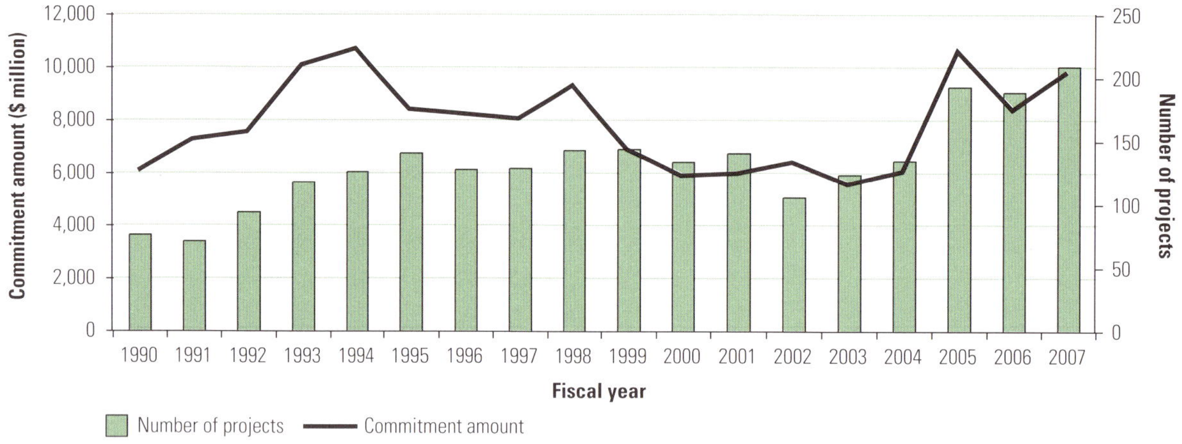


*Source:* World Bank database.

through blended operations, from the World Bank itself.

*Bank-administered GEF operations increased steadily between fiscal 1999 and 2005.*

Because the environment is a cross-cutting theme, ENRM projects are mapped to a large number of Sector Boards. Even though the Environment Sector Board has had the largest number of projects—almost one-quarter of the total—it is far from the most important in commitment terms—accounting for only about 8 percent. The Rural Development, Energy and Mining, Water Supply and Sanitation, Urban Development, and Transport Boards all had higher shares (see appendix F for details).[21]

*Many sector boards share responsibility for Bank environment-related projects.*

## Doing No Harm: Environmental Safeguards

Safeguards are designed so that potential adverse impacts of development projects are adequately identified, assessed, and addressed through application of the environmental assessment policy (Operational Policy 4.01) and associated policies on natural habitats, involuntary resettlement, indigenous peoples, and so on. Thus, safeguards continue to be an important instrument to address environmental impacts within the Bank. This section does not analyze Bank safeguards experience in depth, because that will be the subject of a future IEG evaluation.

*"Do no harm" remains an essential principle of Bank environment-related activities.*

Since 1990, the Bank has applied its environmental assessment policy to all investment and some adjustment operations. Between fiscal 1990 and 2007, the Bank processed 6,790 projects. Nearly one-fifth of these—and one-third of the total commitments in such operations—were in the nine case study countries. These countries, moreover, have a disproportionate share (45 percent) of the most environmentally sensitive Category A projects, which is even more striking in commitment terms (63 percent of the total). China alone accounts for 25 percent of all Category A projects and 34 percent of commitments in such operations because of the significant presence of large infrastructure projects in its portfolio. In contrast, all of Sub-Saharan Africa accounts for just 5 percent of such projects (and only 3 percent of total commitments in them).

Past reviews of Bank experience with environmental safeguards, including for China, India, and Sub-Saharan Africa, record increasing environmental assessment effectiveness over time.[22] But they also find persisting weaknesses in upstream analysis of alternatives; consideration of indirect, induced, and cumulative impacts, public consultation, and disclosure; and borrower implementation and Bank supervision of environmental management plans.

IEG previously assessed Bank performance regarding environmental safeguards as partially satisfactory (IEG-World Bank 2002). Although progress has been made since 2001, in part through establishment of a Quality Assurance and Compliance Unit, many of IEG's earlier findings and conclusions—such as in relation to the timeliness, scope, and quality of environmental assessments (see appendix B)—remain relevant. Consistent with this, the most recent Bank Sector Strategy Implementation Update affirmed that the goal of improving the safeguard system over the past five years has been only moderately achieved (World Bank 2007f).

Continuing difficulties associated with application of environmental safeguards are reflected in some requests to the Bank's Inspection Panel for projects where environmental safeguards have allegedly been violated, most recently in the Democratic Republic of Congo.[23] Such requests have also included operations in Brazil, China, India, and Uganda, several of which were found by the Panel not to have fully complied with Bank environmental requirements.[24] More generally, of all 49 requests for Inspection Panel investigation through October 2007, 65 percent have involved concerns about compliance with the Bank's environmental assessment policy.[25]

On the more positive side, growing use is now being made of SEAs, as recommended by the 2001 Strategy.[26] Although experience to date has been mainly in OECD countries, SEAs are now increasingly being used in the developing world[27] and, like CEAs, are a potentially valuable tool.

Quality at entry of Bank operations with respect to environmental aspects has improved over the past several years. A recent review of Bank projects under implementation in fiscal 2005–06 found that around 90 percent were marginally satisfactory or better in the supervision of environmental aspects, especially in relation to safeguards (QAG 2007). However, there were also still some concerns in this regard.[28]

*Since 1990, nearly 6,800 Bank projects have been screened for potential environmental impacts.*

Furthermore, while recent Bank efforts to rely more on country systems for safeguards may be realizable in the medium term in some sectors and places—among case study countries, there are ongoing or proposed future pilots in Brazil, Egypt, Ghana, India, and Uganda, for example. Yet experience to date suggests that, because of persistent institutional, political, and other constraints, this is less likely to occur soon in many countries, especially poorer ones.[29]

*Environmental concerns have received more attention since 2001, but earlier IEG findings regarding safeguard performance remain relevant.*

Although effectiveness with respect to application of environmental safeguards has improved since 1990, in light of recent Inspection Panel, Quality Assurance Group, and Environment Sector Board findings, it is still less than fully satisfactory. Progress has been made and a new approach to environmental due diligence in policy-based lending is also now being followed (see Mani and Sears 2006), but performance to date has been mixed, shortcomings persist, and a more systematic evaluation (including of IFC and MIGA experience) is needed.[30]

*Some recent Inspection Panel findings indicate persisting problems.*

## Doing Good: Stewardship, Mainstreaming, Global Sustainability, Partnerships, and the 2001 Strategy

Much of the Bank's support for environmental sustainability since 1990 has focused on "doing good." From the fourfold agenda, this can be considered under three subheadings—stewardship, mainstreaming, and protecting the Regional and global commons. This section assesses effectiveness of World Bank support in these areas and briefly discusses experience with partnerships and progress regarding the main thematic thrusts of the 2001 Environment Strategy.

*Internal reviews of Bank safeguard experience found improvement, but with persisting weaknesses in supervision.*

### *Improving environmental quality: Stewardship*

Supporting stewardship involves helping countries set environmental priorities, build institutions, and implement programs and projects for environmental improvement and sustainability. In addition to loans and grants, this is done by helping countries prepare action plans and integrate short- and long-term environmental concerns into country strategies, capacity building, and policy dialogue, as well as through ESW and research.

Updating earlier IEG assessments (see appendix B), the case studies suggest that the Bank has generally succeeded in helping countries set environmental priorities, but it has done less well in helping them address these same priorities through its lending. The Bank has provided support for NEAPs in all case study countries except Brazil, where there has nonetheless been much relevant ESW over the past 15 years.

*The Bank has helped countries set environmental priorities but has done less well in helping them address these priorities.*

In terms of nonlending instruments, a trend of declining environmental ESW in the 1990s has been reversed, although environment-related research may now be declining (except for climate change) because of staffing changes.

As with safeguards, experience with respect to environmental stewardship over the past five years has been uneven. This is reflected in the most recent Sector Strategy Implementation Update assessment, which analyzed how well environmental priorities have been addressed through project and program design since the 2001 Strategy was approved. This was considered to have been just moderately achieved (World Bank 2007f). Experience in case study countries supports this assessment (box 3.2).

Performance of completed ENRM and Environment Sector Board projects approved from fiscal 1990 to 2005 (see figure 3.4) can be compared with that of Bank operations as a whole. Projects mapped to the Environment Sector Board performed slightly less well than ENRM and Bank projects as a whole (figure 3.5). Over this period, about 76 percent of all ENRM projects were rated satisfactory or better on completion,[31] the same as for all Bank operations.[32] However, GEF, Montreal Protocol, and Rainforest Pilot Program projects performed better than IBRD/IDA projects.[33]

Performance also differed significantly across Regions and over time for both the ENRM and Environment Sector Board portfolios. Among Regions (figure 3.6), performance was best in Europe and Central Asia and worst in Africa for

**Box 3.2: Uneven Stewardship in Case Study Countries**

Bank support to India since 1990 has exhibited an imbalance. There has been a greater concentration of lending for natural resource management than for basic sanitation, pollution abatement, and urban environmental management—even though Bank ESW determined that surface water pollution and urban and indoor air pollution account for roughly 75 percent of the total costs of environmental degradation. The Bank cannot be expected to engage in every priority issue, but it could have done more to ensure greater consistency between its analytical and advisory activities (AAA) and lending in this particular case.

In Brazil, China, India, and elsewhere, land and watershed management projects have resulted in substantial socioeconomic and environmental benefits. The Bank has had a positive influence on policies and institutions for water resource management at the central and state government levels. Except in China, however, less has been done on urban environmental issues.

The Bank has perhaps been most proactive in promoting environmental stewardship in China, including in major river basins. Its support to land management, as in the Loess Plateau and elsewhere (through the Red Soils projects, for example), has resulted in significant environmental improvement and contributed to rural poverty reduction. Despite the importance of its natural resource base, however, the same has not occurred in Sub-Saharan Africa. In that Region, Bank environmental support since 1990 has focused mainly on capacity building and biodiversity conservation (Ghana, Madagascar, and Uganda). In Egypt and Russia, the Bank has also been involved in a number of environmental areas, but government ownership has often been weak and results sometimes less than fully satisfactory.

*Source:* IEG country case studies.

**Figure 3.4: Shares of Environment, ENRM, and All Completed Bank Projects Rated Satisfactory, by Fiscal Year of Approval, 1990–2005**

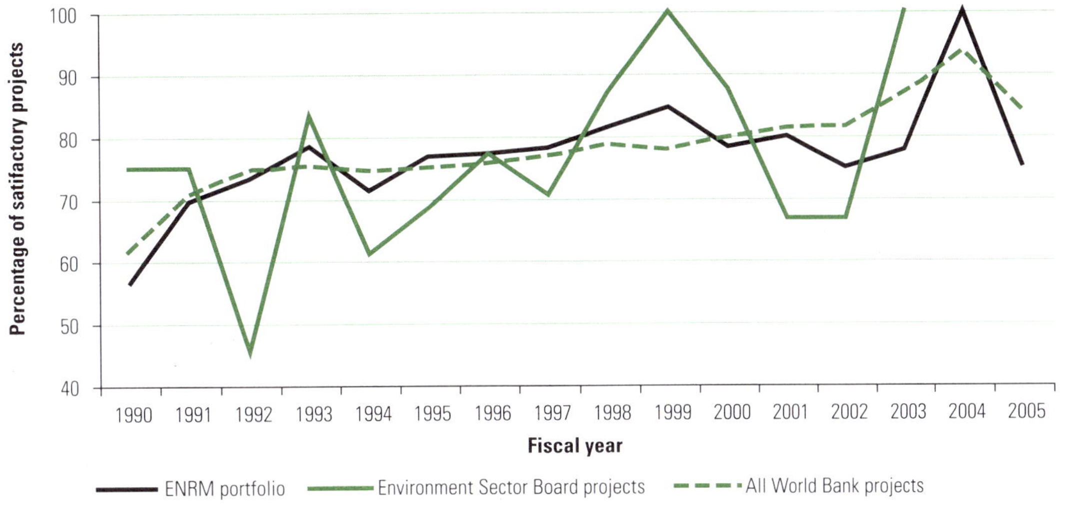


*Source:* World Bank database.
*Note:* Satisfactory projects are all those that received an IEG project outcome rating of highly satisfactory, satisfactory, or moderately/marginally satisfactory. ENRM = environmental and natural resource management.

both portfolios. However, although performance in Latin America and the Caribbean and East Asia and the Pacific was above average for the ENRM portfolio, in both cases it was below average for the much smaller Environment Sector Board portfolio; the reverse was true for projects in South Asia and the Middle East and North Africa.[34] In part, this reflects the way different Regions map their projects to the various sector boards (see appendix F).

**Figure 3.5: Share of Completed ENRM Projects Rated Satisfactory, by Sector Board Mapping, Fiscal 1990–2005**

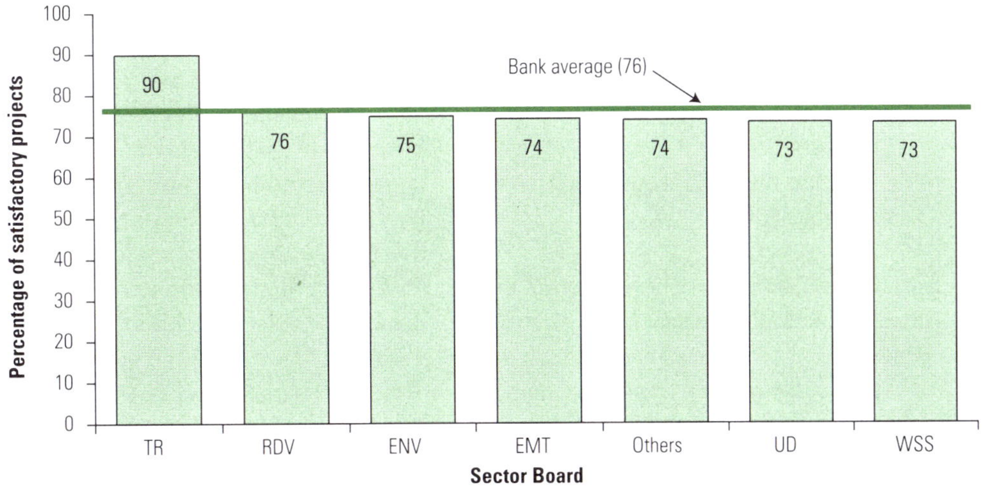


*Source:* World Bank database.
*Note:* Satisfactory projects are all those that received an IEG project outcome rating of highly satisfactory, satisfactory, or moderately/marginally satisfactory. EMT = Energy, Mining, and Telecommunications; ENV = Environment; RDV = Agriculture and Rural Development; TR = Transport, UD = Urban Development; WSS = Water Supply and Sanitation.

**Figure 3.6: ENRM and Environment Portfolio Performance, by Region, Fiscal 1990–2007**

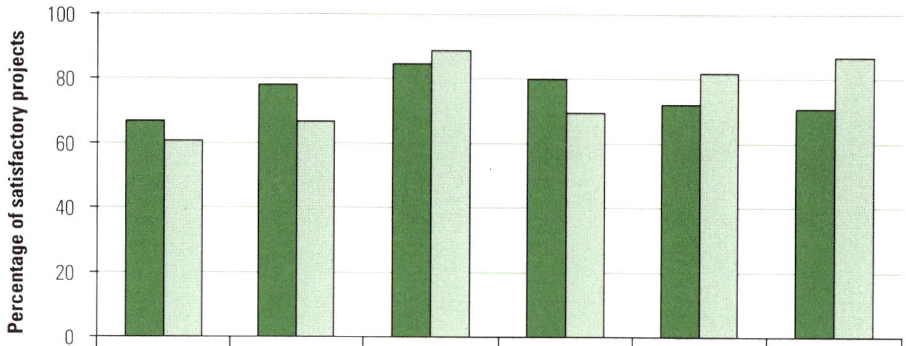


| | SSA | EAP | ECA | LAC | MENA | SAR |
|---|---|---|---|---|---|---|
| ENRM (%) | 66.8 | 78.1 | 84.6 | 79.8 | 72.0 | 70.8 |
| ENV (%) | 60.7 | 66.7 | 88.9 | 69.4 | 81.8 | 86.7 |

**Region**

*Source:* World Bank database.

*Note:* Regions: SSA = Sub-Saharan Africa; EAP = East Asia and Pacific; ECA = Europe and Central Asia; LAC = Latin America and the Caribbean; MENA = Middle East and North Africa; SAR = South Asia. ENRM = environmental and natural resource management; ENV = Environment Sector Board.

Over time, outcomes of the Bank-wide, ENRM, and Environment Sector Board portfolios have improved (figure 3.6); satisfactory percentage shares have increased for projects approved in the latter half of the 1990s and thus far in the present decade, compared with those in the first half of the 1990s. In the Environment Sector Board portfolio, for example, although just 66 percent of all projects approved between fiscal 1990 and 1994 were rated moderately satisfactory or better on completion, this share rose to about 78 percent for those approved between fiscal 1995 and 1999 and 80 percent for those approved between fiscal 2000 and 2003. These results suggest that the Bank has learned from its project experience.

That learning has occurred is borne out by a more in-depth examination of unsatisfactory Environment Sector Board projects, many of which were either for natural resource management—including some for biodiversity conservation—and institutional capacity building for environmental management or use of directed credit lines for industrial pollution abatement. This does not mean that all such projects have failed, as there have been clear exceptions, including satisfactory institution-building projects in Chile, China, and Poland.[35] However, since the late 1990s, the Bank has largely discontinued approaches that have proven less effective.

*Performance of both ENRM and Environment Sector Board projects has improved, and there are clear signs that learning has occurred.*

Project performance can also be assessed by environmental theme within the ENRM portfolio, as indicated in table 3.2. Although there are also some complications here,[36] the data in this table refer to projects for which one of the seven ENRM themes was indicated as the most important. The most significant themes based on numbers of projects are pollution management/environmental health and environment policy/institutions. Based on total commitments for ENRM purposes, the significant themes are pollution management/environmental health and water resource management (see appendix F).

The figures in table 3.2 reveal that the project subsets that have performed best are for pollution management/environmental health, land administration/management, and water resource management; those that have performed poorly are environmental policy/institutions and biodiversity. It must be cautioned, however, that some of these

**Table 3.2: ENRM Projects, by Theme, Fiscal 1990–2007**

| Theme | Number of times coded | Number of times primary | Total ENRM commitment ($ million) | Percent satisfactory completed projects |
|---|---|---|---|---|
| Biodiversity | 369 | 220 | 1,823.9 | 71.2 |
| Climate change | 310 | 144 | 3,594.7 | 75.0 |
| Environmental policy/institutions | 663 | 125 | 4,175.5 | 64.8 |
| Land administration/management | 370 | 101 | 2,135.8 | 80.0 |
| Pollution management/environmental health | 675 | 179 | 5,865.8 | 80.2 |
| Water resource management | 459 | 122 | 5,036.1 | 79.7 |
| Other ENRM | 205 | 59 | 1,024.1 | 75.0 |
| Total | 3,051 | 950 | 23,655.8 | 75.5 |

*Source:* World Bank database.

categories comprise very diverse projects whose performance has been quite different. The pollution management subset, for example, contains 13 completed Montreal Protocol and GEF projects for the phase-out of ozone-depleting substances, which were 100 percent satisfactory. But it also contains 6 projects consisting mainly of directed credit lines for industrial pollution abatement, which were just 50 percent satisfactory. This reflects an approach that has proven to be comparatively ineffective.[37] Performance of projects in the biodiversity subset has improved significantly over time, again suggesting institutional learning. However, performance remains lower than the Bank-wide average.

It should likewise be cautioned that the overall outcome ratings do not necessarily reveal how projects have performed in environmental terms, even for those mapped to the Environment Sector Board. Many ENRM and other operations, including infrastructure projects requiring more extensive up-front environmental assessment (Category A), are considerably relevant, but their environmental effects are not systematically reported at closing. Despite this, several findings about stewardship can be highlighted:

- The Bank has engaged in a wide variety of ENRM-related concerns, used a diversity of instruments, and provided significant levels of relevant lending and nonlending support to the case study countries, especially Brazil, China, and India, but also elsewhere (such as Madagascar), even before 1990.
- Land and watershed management operations have been particularly successful, as have projects to reduce ozone-depleting substances. Efforts to strengthen environmental management capacity through technical assistance operations have been less successful than those combining technical assistance with investments for environmental improvement.
- There have been differences across countries in the way certain instruments are used. Although there were numerous GEF biodiversity projects in Brazil, Ghana, and Madagascar, for example, GEF funding for biodiversity was used far less in China, India, and Russia.
- There also have been changes over time in Bank approaches to the environment in some countries. India is one example, but there were also significant shifts in Russia and parts of Sub-Saharan Africa, such as Ghana.[38]
- The most extensive Bank ENRM-related activity has been in China. With the exception of biodiversity conservation, there have been numerous Bank lending operations in all areas of environmental relevance.
- In some cases, the Bank did not adequately apply what had been learned from its own analytical and

*Projects involving reduction of ozone depletion, land management, and water resources have performed better than others.*

*China predominated in the Bank portfolio in nearly all ENRM areas.*

evaluation work in preparing follow-on ENRM operations; these also subsequently failed (for example, in the Brazilian Amazon in the early 1990s and with industrial pollution control projects in India). To avoid this, the Bank needs to fully understand the context, including the local ecology and political economy, in which it is intervening; truly learn from its mistakes; and systematically address them in the design of future operations.

- There were clear exceptions, but Bank lending for the blue and, to a lesser extent, green agendas (especially for land and watershed management) has often been more effective than that for the brown and institutional ones (see page 21 for "color" definitions). Outcomes with respect to different parts of the institutional and global agendas were likewise uneven (for example, ozone-related projects have been very successful, but those for biodiversity conservation have had mixed results).[39]
- Although Bank ENRM projects achieved much, there have also been shortfalls, especially when priorities reflected in NEAPs, CESPs, and other ESW products are compared with the substantive focus of Bank lending in some countries.[40]

In short, the results of Bank-supported interventions with respect to environmental stewardship over the past 15 years have been mixed. A broad range of activities was supported, and there were real accomplishments: helping to place 600,000 square kilometers of Amazon rainforest under legal protection; significantly influencing by means of public disclosure the way China, Indonesia, and other countries sought to curb industrial pollution; and helping both Brazil and China approach river basin management in a more integrated way. But there were also shortcomings.

### *Mainstreaming the environment in development*

Mainstreaming involves helping build positive linkages between poverty reduction, economic efficiency, and environmental protection. A concern since the 1992 WDR (World Bank 1992c), when the focus was on incorporating environmental considerations into sectoral and macroeconomic policies, mainstreaming was to be implemented, according to the 2001 Strategy, by making environmental sustainability a core objective of Bank ESW, using lending to address environmental issues, and integrating environmental objectives into a broad range of activities and sectoral projects. In the 1990s, however, there were limited incentives for mainstreaming and few independent Bank resources to integrate environmental components into other projects. Thus, in 2001 IEG concluded that Bank performance with regard to mainstreaming had been just partially satisfactory (see appendix B).

*Experience with mainstreaming has also been uneven.*

Mainstreaming has advanced since 2001, as indicated by the growing number of ENRM projects mapped to different sector boards. However, it is still incomplete for some of the same reasons previously identified and, as with other dimensions of recent Bank ENRM performance, effectiveness has varied both across countries and over time (box 3.3).

Equally significant as the need to further mainstream environmental concerns at the macroeconomic and individual sectoral levels—in both polices and investments—is the need to treat them in a comprehensive and holistic way. In short, how environmental considerations are integrated into development interventions is also important. Integrating appropriately generally means starting from the nature of the environmental problem and working backward to the solutions, and it normally means involving multiple sectors. In short, effectively addressing environmental problems often requires coordinated actions across several sectors in a given locality—such as energy, industry, transport, and land use planning in the case of urban air pollution. As the 2003 WDR emphasizes, it also requires a spatial focus.

These considerations have often been absent in Bank support for the environment. There are some notable exceptions—such as the multipurpose management of the Yellow River and Loess Plateau in China; efforts to improve water quality in Chinese and Brazilian metropolitan areas; and rural watershed management in Brazil, China,

**Box 3.3: Experience with Mainstreaming in Case Study Countries**

In India, Bank performance has been reasonably good regarding mainstreaming in country strategies, sector policy dialogue, and lending operations that do not have primarily environmental objectives. In many ways, efforts to promote stewardship and mainstreaming appear to have converged, although, as in other countries (China being an exception), this is more evident in the green and blue projects than in the brown and institutional ones.

In Brazil, the situation is similar, but two successive national environment projects have been better at strengthening environmental management capacity at the state level, so progress on the institutional front appears to have been greater than in India and China, not to mention Sub-Saharan Africa. The Bank has also attempted to promote improved environmental mainstreaming and associated policy and institutional reforms through programmatic DPLs in Brazil and elsewhere.

Bank lending and AAA have likewise played a significant mainstreaming role in China. Nearly 60 percent of all Bank projects approved between fiscal 1990 and 2007 have had environmental components, with the most significant results in the energy, agriculture and rural development, and forestry sectors. In Russia, Egypt, Senegal, and Uganda, mainstreaming initiatives have been more piecemeal and have been more the result of the efforts of individual champions among Bank staff than of fully institutionalized approaches.

*Source:* IEG country case studies.

and India—but many approaches have been insufficiently strategic or too fragmented, limiting their potential to improve environmental quality. Yet as IEG's *2006 Annual Review of Development Effectiveness* pointed out more generally (that is, not just in relation to the environment), "strong results demand attention to cross-sectoral synergies" (IEG-World Bank 2006a, p. xiv).[41]

### Managing risks to the Regional and global commons: Global and local benefits

Achieving global environmental sustainability[42] is also a major challenge, especially in large countries such as Brazil, China, India, and Russia. Bank support for global sustainability has become more important since the Montreal Protocol, GEF, and Kyoto Protocol were established. Growing international concern over climate change means it will be even more important in the future. Bank effectiveness has been mixed in this regard in the case study countries, both before (appendix B) and after 2001 (see box 3.4).

Bank use of global environmental financing mechanisms such as GEF has been uneven across Regions. Although Latin America, Sub-Saharan Africa, and East Asia have made significant use of such resources, this has been far less the case in South Asia, especially India. Reasons for these differences appear to be a combination of weak country interest and a preference by some past Bank Regional managers to avoid GEF-funded projects because of their perceived higher transaction costs. Competition among GEF implementing agencies has also played a role in some countries.

*Global commons issues and natural resource degradation at the global scale are both important—Bank performance on these has been mixed.*

One aspect that received particular attention both in IEG's earlier assessment of Bank performance (IEG-World Bank 1996) and in the 2001 Strategy concerns the local benefits of global environmental projects (World Bank 2001b).[43] Since 2001, the Bank has given increased attention in its global environmental operations to local benefits, including through a rising number of hybrid projects involving funding from IBRD, IDA, or both.[44] But, as in other areas, some of the shortcomings highlighted in the previous IEG evaluation seem to persist. These include comparatively weak performance of some environmental programs, such as the Lake Victoria Environment Program and the Guarani Aquifer, as another recent evaluation has shown (IEG-World Bank 2007a).

*Since 2001 the Bank has increased attention to local benefits of its global environmental operations.*

### Partnerships[45]

The 2001 Strategy stressed the importance of collaboration with other development institutions, civil society, and the private sector to help achieve Bank environmental objectives and leverage resources.[46] Particularly at the Regional

**Box 3.4: Global Sustainability and Local Benefits in Case Study Countries**

Considerable attention has been given to biodiversity conservation through the establishment and management of protected areas and through support to buffer zone communities in Brazil, India, Madagascar, and Uganda, among other countries. Attention has also been given to the reduction of ozone-depleting substances, especially in China, India, and Russia. In Brazil, however, although legal protection has recently been strengthened in ecological and indigenous reserves in the Amazon with Bank and other donor support, deforestation continues largely unabated.

The situation in Madagascar is similar but on a smaller scale. With the significant exception of China, less attention has been given to greenhouse gas mitigation. And until very recently, outside the Caribbean, almost no attention has gone to helping countries adapt to the likely future impacts of climate change.

Experience in the case study countries has had both positive and negative aspects. The India Ecodevelopment Project was able to reduce adverse impacts on biodiversity and increase locals' collaboration in conservation, while at the same time providing benefits to them. A recent global program review for the Bank-supported Critical Ecosystems Partnership Fund reached a similar conclusion but also pointed to areas where improvements are needed.

Examples can be drawn from other countries as well, including support to local communities around Lake Baikal under the Biodiversity Conservation Project in Russia and through the Rainforest Pilot Program and various completed and ongoing GEF projects in Brazil. Recent IEG assessments of biodiversity-related projects in Madagascar and Uganda provide similar findings. However, the new GEF Resource Allocation Framework establishes priorities to maximize global environmental benefits, which, as a result, may have an adverse effect on smaller countries such as those in the Caribbean, Mesoamerica, and Sub-Saharan Africa that will have less opportunity for GEF support in the future.

*Source:* IEG country case studies.

and global levels, the strategy affirmed that the Bank would engage in partnerships, especially in areas where (1) there was strong international consensus for action with the aim of contributing to global public goods, (2) close links could be established with country assistance programs, and (3) significant resources could be catalyzed.

Partnerships can enhance Bank development effectiveness, leverage resources, and reduce transaction costs, and they may exist at the subnational, national, Regional, and global levels.[47] One strong example can be drawn from the rich experience in Brazil (box 3.5). In general, the Bank appears to have been fairly successful at establishing productive partnerships with other donors and development agencies to help countries strengthen their environmental management. Given the often complex and cross-sectoral nature of work on the environment, multi-institutional partnerships seem increasingly to be the norm and are likely to be even more important in the future.

*Partnerships can increase Bank development effectiveness related to the environment.*

During this evaluation, IEG sought the views of various organizations that were collaborating with the Bank on environmental initiatives, including other multilateral and bilateral donors and environmental NGOs. IEG asked representatives of these institutions to comment on the Bank as a partner. In some cases, the Bank was seen as a helpful collaborator, as in the Poverty-Environment Partnership, initiated by the Department for International Development (DFID), UNDP, the European Commission, and the Bank in 2001. The Critical Ecosystems Partnership Fund and the World Bank–World Wildlife Fund Forest Alliance are also examples of mutually beneficial partnerships with major environmental NGOs.

However, some of those interviewed considered the Bank less collaborative. For example, in the case of TerrAfrica, which seeks to improve land management in Sub-Saharan Africa, a perceived tendency for the Bank to monopolize resources and other aspects of the multi-institutional initiative was seen during its early years; it is now reportedly resolved.[48] In general, all those interviewed thought there was scope for more and better environment-related collaboration in the future.

**Box 3.5: Successful Bank Partnerships for the Environment in Brazil**

In Brazil, environment-related collaboration has existed for some time among multilateral bodies, bilateral organizations, and civil society. The Bank was able to reestablish its environmental credibility, following the experience with Polonoroeste in the 1980s, after the G-7 heads of state asked it to help advance a new conservation and development agenda for the Amazon and Atlantic forests. The Bank undertook the effort together with the European Commission and various bilateral donors, led by Germany. This arrangement also allowed policy dialogue to move forward based on several analyses of the challenges posed by deforestation and sustainable development in Amazonia.

The Pilot Program for the Conservation of Brazilian Rainforests (PPG7) has proven to be an innovative experiment in international cooperation for tropical forest protection. It paved the way for the Amazon Regional Protected Areas Project. This project was the product of a pioneering financial partnership among the Brazilian and German governments, GEF, and the World Wildlife Fund, among others, with Bank oversight and technical support. Through these initiatives, the Bank has collaborated with a wide variety of organizations, including federal, state, and municipal governments, international and local NGOs, bilateral donors, and the private sector.[a] Although its complex institutional arrangements have generated high transaction costs, a long project cycle, and complex funding procedures,[b] PPG7 has strengthened local community and civil society participation, a legacy on which future initiatives can be built. It has also contributed to the establishment of extensive new indigenous, ecological, and extractive reserves, among other concrete results.

*Source:* IEG country case study.

a. In the Brazilian Amazon case, the government collaborators include bilateral representatives from Germany, France, Japan, the Netherlands, the United Kingdom, and the United States, as well as the European Union and UNDP.

b. This same criticism regarding the GEF was made by Bank clients, including Brazil, India, and Russia during IEG missions for this evaluation.

At the country level, the strength and effectiveness of Bank partnerships also varied. One factor appears to be the presence of Bank environmental specialists in country offices. Where there is a significant field presence—as in Brazil, China, India,[49] and Madagascar—donor and other interinstitutional collaboration appears to be strong. However, where Bank environmental staff are either few or absent from the local office—as in Egypt, Ghana, Russia, Senegal, and Uganda—the picture tends to be the reverse.[50] Experienced local Bank specialists and consultants appear to have been especially effective (particularly where English is not the primary language), reflecting their ability to better comprehend the local institutional and political economy considerations on which success of environmental policy and associated reforms often depend.

## Thematic priorities of the 2001 Environment Strategy

Building off the approaches of the 1990s, the 2001 Strategy explicitly linked the Bank's work on the environment to its poverty-reduction mission. In doing so, it gave special emphasis to three thematic objectives: (1) "quality of life," focusing on linkages between environment and poverty, health, and vulnerability; (2) "quality of growth," referring to how growth occurs, as well as its pace and including concerns with environmental governance and sustainability in the private sector; and (3) protecting the Regional and global commons.

*The Bank is seen as a good collaborator in the Poverty-Environment Partnership, the Critical Ecosystems Partnership Fund, and the Forest Alliance, but not in some others.*

### Poverty, livelihoods, and the environment

The 2001 Strategy recognized that "because poor people depend heavily on the productivity and environmental services of ecosystems and natural resources," the Bank would assist them in improving management and protection of these resources. This would include helping communities to manage land, water, and forest resources more sustainably as well as to clarify and establish property rights; strengthening or reforming incentive systems that influence how resources are used; and building the analytical base and institutional capacity to improve natural resource management (World Bank 2001b).

As noted in chapter 1, the relationship between rural livelihoods and the environment is complex and reciprocal (World Bank 2001b).[51] The World

Commission on Environment and Development observed in the late 1980s that people are often impoverished by a declining natural resource base and then are forced by their circumstances to degrade the environment further (WCED 1987; World Bank 1992a).

*Linkages between the natural resource base and rural livelihoods are especially important.*

Together with the role of population pressures, this has been documented in Bank ESW for Sub-Saharan Africa since the early 1990s (Cleaver and Schreiber 1994). However, it is equally the case elsewhere. Because of this reciprocal relationship, these impacts can be positive or negative, and both the Bank's Environment and Rural Poverty Reduction Strategies take such linkages into account.[52]

This evaluation finds that, although there has been increasing analytical work (including Development Economics research) on this topic since 2001, much mainstream Bank ESW and policy-based lending for poverty reduction still gives insufficient attention to linkages between rural livelihoods and the natural resource base. This is especially serious in South Asia and Sub-Saharan Africa, but has been the case in Northeast Brazil and China as well—that is, in precisely those areas where the bulk of the rural poor live (box 3.6).

In general, even though some data and methodological difficulties may be involved and there are some relevant exceptions (as in Malawi and Nepal), poverty assessments often give insufficient attention to the role of natural resources, an oversight that also characterizes some Bank analytical approaches to pro-poor growth, as in a recent publication entitled *Delivering on the Promise of Pro-Poor Growth,* which fails to consider links between natural resource access, use, and management on the one hand and rural economic growth and poverty on the other (Besley and Cord 2007).[53]

*Much poverty-focused analytical and strategic work gives insufficient attention to linkages between rural livelihoods and the natural resource base.*

Bank studies of rural poverty in Sub-Saharan Africa have also often given insufficient emphasis to the importance of natural resources. A recent Bank publication, *Down to Earth: Agriculture and Poverty Reduction in Africa,* for example, barely mentions natural resources (Christiaensen and Demery 2007). The need for better water, soil, and forest management at the microcatchment and river basin levels is not discussed. And although some attention is given to weather-related shocks, the need to help countries adapt to the potentially severe agricultural and associated socioeconomic impacts of climate change, whose importance has been highlighted in a recent IEG paper (IEG-World Bank 2007c) as well as in the Stern Report on the economics of climate change (Stern 2006),[54] is overlooked. Experience in Senegal and Uganda suggests that natural resource management-poverty links have also been largely neglected in Bank lending there.

Bank poverty assessments may be more effective if they systematically consider critical links between natural resources and rural livelihoods. This also applies at the subnational level, as there is clearly a spatial dimension here as well.

The importance of the spatial dimension can best be illustrated by the approach presented in the 2003 WDR[55] and subsequent ESW on the spatial incidence of poverty in Brazil, Indonesia, Madagascar, and elsewhere (Chomitz and others 2007). Another recent Bank publication on poverty mapping moves in the right direction but could go even further (Bedi, Courdouel, and Simier 2007). Another relevant example is analytical work that applies spatially differentiated, asset-based approaches for sustainable rural growth and poverty reduction in Central America.[56]

#### Health and environment

The relationship between health and the environment was the second major thematic focus in the 2001 Strategy under the heading "quality of life." The strategy affirms that "environmental factors, such as unsafe water and air pollution, are major contributors to the total burden of disease and impose significant economic costs, particularly for poor people. These risks are substantially greater in developing countries than developed ones." In response, Bank interventions were

### Box 3.6: Environment-Poverty Linkages in Brazil, China, India, and Madagascar

Linkages between environment, especially renewable natural resources, and poverty in rural areas have received significant attention in Bank lending activity over the past several decades. In India, there is a clear awareness of the complex two-way relationship between rural poverty and environment, as indicated in the National Environment Policy (India, MoEF 2006). These linkages have also been a principal concern of the Bank's natural resource management operations there, predating the 2001 Environment Strategy by more than a decade.[a] These links have been a prime focus of Bank rural development lending in all four countries, as reflected in the evolving approach to irrigation and drainage and water resource management more generally, land and watershed management, and forest resource management in numerous projects during the 1990s and early 2000s.

The Bank's record of supporting improved land management for environmental sustainability and poverty reduction in its lending in southern and southeastern Brazil and central and southern China provides similar examples. These projects have generated major economic and environmental benefits by raising soil productivity, resulting both in sustained increases in agricultural output and incomes and sharply reduced soil erosion, run-off, and sedimentation of watercourses, with associated improvements in water quality and reduction in water treatment costs.[b]

In view of this recognition of the importance of livelihood-natural resource linkages in the Bank's lending, it is surprising that much less attention has been given to this in the Bank's poverty-related analytical work there.[c] This shortcoming also characterizes the Bank's analytical work at the subnational level, as in recent assessments of poverty in the state of Uttar Pradesh in India.[d] This was also the case in Brazil, where a study of rural poverty that focused mainly on the northeast (which contains the largest concentration of rural poor in Latin America) failed to integrate this dimension either into its analysis or the resulting proposed strategy (World Bank 2003c).

There are indications in the most recent Development Policy Review for India that this neglect of environment-poverty linkages in Bank ESW may be beginning to change (World Bank 2006b). These links were also given considerable attention in pioneering ESW on rural development and environment in Madagascar in the early 2000s, as well as through several more recent lending operations.

*Source:* IEG country case studies.

a. The 1988 strategy for India observed that poverty-reduction strategies could only succeed over time within the framework of programs to sustain the natural resource base, as environmental degradation was "closely linked with poverty and population pressure" (World Bank 1988, p. 22).

b. Success of these operations can be attributed in part to such common factors as use of microwatersheds as planning and intervention units, which facilitated farmer cooperation and the adoption of an integrated, multisectoral approach (including road improvements by municipal governments, together with on-farm improvements such as terracing, use of "green" fertilizers, and zero or low-till cultivation techniques); strong political support from state governments and local economic political elites; adequate knowledge of land management problems, potential, and practices; and favorably uniform soil and other physical conditions.

c. A major Bank ESW report, although in many ways quite comprehensive, only touches on this relationship but does not explore it or develop the policy implications and operational relevance of the poverty-environment relationship (World Bank 2000b).

d. See World Bank 2002c. The links between poverty and environment are ignored despite the fact that 80 percent of the poor reside in rural areas and their livelihoods depend largely on access to and the quality, management, and sustainability of the natural resource base.

expected to focus on "cost-effective measures to prevent and reduce environmental health risks through reducing people's exposure to indoor and urban air pollution, waterborne diseases, and toxic chemicals." Measures would also include improved access to cleaner commercial fuels and improved design of safe water and sanitation services to increase health benefits (World Bank 2001b).[57]

The strategy identified China, India, and Sub-Saharan Africa as the places where the burden of disease from environmental risks was highest. There are significant differences among these three areas, however, with waterborne diseases being the most significant health risk in India, followed by indoor air pollution and urban air pollution, agro-industrial waste, and malaria. In Sub-Saharan Africa, in contrast, waterborne diseases and malaria are of nearly equal importance, followed by indoor air pollution. In China, indoor air pollution and urban air pollution account for nearly three-fourths of the total disease burden from environmental risks, followed by waterborne diseases (World Bank 2001b).

*Environmental factors are major contributors to total disease burden.*

As in the case of poverty and environment, there have been imbalances in the analysis of health-environment linkages across countries as well as between ESW and Bank lending. There has been relevant ESW on health-environment linkages in certain countries, such as on the relation between indoor and urban air pollution and respiratory diseases in India and between both air and water pollution and health problems in China (see box 3.7). Recent CEAs have also focused on environmental health issues.[58] But there has been little lending in India to help address such concerns in urban areas, although in China there has been considerably more, perhaps reflecting differing country interest in borrowing from the Bank for this purpose.

Less attention has been given to environmental health issues in Sub-Saharan Africa, where HIV/AIDS has dominated Bank health-related support. A review by the Environment Department found that treatment of environmental health in recent PRSPs (for the most part in Sub-Saharan Africa), for instance, has been inadequate and, where it was addressed, water and sanitation received greater attention than air quality and

### Box 3.7: Health and Environment in Selected Case Study Countries

Bank analytical work on health and environment in India is an example of good practice, especially in its treatment of the relationship between indoor and outdoor air pollution and respiratory problems. It also shows good practice in the relationship between water pollution and gastrointestinal diseases that have harmful effects on the very young and the elderly. Influenced by Bank ESW,[a] the Indian government recognized the critical links between health and environment in the new National Environment Policy (India, MoEF 2006, pp. 5–6).[b]

Environment-health links have also been stressed in recent CASs. However, the Bank has provided little financial support to help India address environment-related health problems (for indoor air pollution, for example). Even with respect to metropolitan water quality management, where the Bank was very active before the 1990s—with the exception of Mumbai—its support has virtually disappeared over the past 15 years. Water pollution meanwhile remains very serious in India, as just 58 percent of the urban population had access to improved sanitation in 2005, compared with 69 percent in China, 83 percent in Brazil, 84 percent in Egypt, and 93 percent in Russia (World Bank 2006d).

The situation in China is similar in that health impacts of urban pollution have received considerable attention in Bank ESW (World Bank 2007b). In contrast to the experience in India, the Bank has provided significant lending support to help deal with these issues, particularly water pollution, in many Chinese metropolitan areas. At the same time, curbing local and global emissions has also been a strong focus of Bank financial and analytical support.

Less analytical attention has been given to environment-health linkages in Brazil, even in ESW on pollution management that used cost-effectiveness criteria to rank priorities for health-related pollution abatement (World Bank 1998a).[c] Unlike India and elsewhere in Latin America (see, for example, Ahmed, Awe, and others 2005),[d] there has been no analysis of indoor air pollution, which is a concern in poor rural areas, especially in the northeast. Although urban-industrial pollution control in São Paulo pioneered Bank environmental lending, the comparatively low profile of this support relative to that for the green agenda has contributed to a reduced Bank impact on environmental health. Several metropolitan pollution control projects in southern and southeastern states recently audited by IEG, however, have positively affected local water quality and generated other health-related benefits through improved flood control.

*Source:* IEG country case studies and Project Performance Assessment Reports.

a. Even though it was removed from the final version of the document approved in May 2006, the draft of the National Environment Policy prepared in 2004 contained a specific reference to the Bank's study of environmental health in Andhra Pradesh, carried out in 2001.

b. The policy affirms: "It is increasingly evident that poor environmental quality has adversely affected human health. Environmental factors are estimated as being responsible in some cases for nearly 20 percent of the burden of disease in India, and a number of environment-related factors are closely linked with dimensions of poverty. It has been shown that interventions such as reducing indoor air pollution, protecting soil from contamination, improved sanitation measures, and better public health governance offer tremendous opportunities for reducing the incidence of a number of critical health problems."

c. The main priority for Brazil was extension of urban water networks; those for the south and southeast were control of industrial particulate sources in heavily polluted, densely inhabited large cities, extension of urban sewerage networks, and control of particulate emissions from diesel vehicles. Those for the north and northeast were the extension of urban sewerage networks and control of industrial and vehicular particulate emissions.

d. The CEA for Colombia also found indoor air pollution a serious problem.

energy-related concerns. Sanitation was also found to be secondary to water supply, leading the authors to conclude that such strategies needed to give greater attention to environmental health concerns (Kishore and Shyamsundar 2005).

Addressing vector-borne diseases such as malaria that are especially serious in rural areas is particularly important in Sub-Saharan Africa.[59] Diseases also include schistosomiasis, which remains a significant public health concern in five of the case study countries—Brazil, China, Egypt, Senegal, and Uganda—among other countries. High rates of schistosomiasis occur near bodies of fresh water and in areas of poor-quality housing, as in many poor rural areas. As experience in Sub-Saharan Africa suggests, Bank involvement has been uneven. In addition to varying degrees of country interest in borrowing for this purpose, limitations on the use of instruments, such as GEF grants, have constrained the Bank's ability to provide funding to help respond to these problems.

Finally, there are no examples of integrated health-environment projects in the Bank's portfolio. Such approaches have been supported by other donors with encouraging results.[60] A pilot health-environment project in Madagascar, for example, financed in part by the United States Agency for International Development, was associated with implementation of the NEAP (Mogelgaard and Patterson 2006).[61] An evaluation of this and similar projects in the Philippines and Tanzania concluded they were cost-effective (Pielemeier 2007) and may be an approach the Bank might also want to consider.

***Vulnerability and environment***

Vulnerability and its links to poverty and the environment was a third focal area in the 2001 Strategy, which observed more specifically that millions of poor people were "vulnerable to natural disasters and environmental hazards, a threat that is expected to increase as the result of climate change." Bank interventions would seek to reduce vulnerability and the cost of natural disasters by supporting upland resource management and payments for environmental services; assessing impacts of natural disasters; improving weather forecasting and dissemination of weather-related information; providing information to communities about the risks they face; and stabilizing hillsides and coastal areas (World Bank 2001b).

*PRSPs are weak on analysis of environmental health impacts, and insufficient attention has been given to environmental health in Africa.*

However, both this evaluation (box 3.8) and a specific IEG assessment of Bank support in response to natural disasters (IEG-World Bank 2006c) found that, although the record has been positive in some respects, the Bank has not been sufficiently strategic or effective in helping client countries anticipate and prevent the often disastrous consequences of severe weather and climate-related natural events such as droughts, floods, tropical storms, and other natural catastrophes. Because climate change impacts are likely to increase, helping countries address these concerns becomes even more important, especially in those parts of the world that are already impoverished and thus highly vulnerable to the effects of weather and climate-related phenomena. These areas include substantial portions of South Asia and Sub-Saharan Africa (see IEG-World Bank 2007c).

Although Bank management is taking steps to respond to the earlier IEG evaluation on natural hazards (IEG-World Bank 2006c), if the Bank is to achieve the objectives set forth in the 2001 Strategy, greater progress is needed with respect to the identification and implementation of effective measures to address environment-vulnerability linkages. This includes both predisaster vulnerability assessments and planning and improved environmental management to make rural and urban landscapes less susceptible to natural risks. It also includes increasing preparedness for the potential environmental and socioeconomic impacts of climate change. The challenges associated with adaptation to climate change will vary considerably across and within countries,[62] and the Bank is beginning to step up its support in this regard. Awareness within the Bank of the importance of doing so has risen significantly over the past few years, but concrete

*The Bank needs to be more strategic and effective in helping countries reduce their vulnerability to natural hazards and climate change.*

**Box 3.8: Environment and Vulnerability in India and China**

India has received the largest amount of Bank natural disaster-related support over the past two decades (IEG-World Bank 2007c).[a] Attention is given to the relationship between environment and vulnerability in the recent National Environment Policy, especially in relation to the management of coastal resources (India, MoEF 2006).[b] Despite India's considerable vulnerability to natural hazards—which was mentioned in several recent CASs—and the country's status as the Bank's largest client for natural disaster–related reconstruction support, the Bank's attention to the relationship between vulnerability and environment has been neither sufficient nor systematic.

This contrasts with recent experience in the Caribbean, Mexico, Central America (particularly Honduras and Nicaragua), and parts of South America. In these areas, the Bank has financed numerous projects, with varying degrees of success, to address vulnerability both to *El Niño* and to hurricane-related flooding, mudslides, and other natural disasters. The Bank has sought to help Caribbean islands adapt to the likely impacts of expected sea level rise associated with global warming; it has also financed an innovative project involving catastrophic risk insurance.

Bank lending for natural disaster–related projects in China has also been significant over the past two decades. Particular attention has been given to flooding problems in the Yellow, Yangtze, and other major river basins.[c]

*Source:* IEG country case studies.

a. Not including reallocation of resources from existing projects, which was also significant, India had 42 disaster-related Bank projects between 1984 and 2005, involving total commitments of nearly $8.3 billion. China, second overall, had 32 such projects, with total commitments of $4.9 billion; Bangladesh, third, has 28 projects and close to $2.9 billion in commitments.

b. The policy observes, for example, that "in the future, sea level rise due to climate change may have major adverse effects on the coastal environment," further aggravating the "significant degradation of coastal resources for which the proximate causes include poorly planned human settlements, improper location of industries and infrastructure, pollution from industries and settlements, and overexploitation of living natural resources" (p. 35).

c. This experience differs from that in countries such as Argentina because the associated Bank projects had broader objectives, including to reduce and manage water flows at the river basin level through multipurpose investments, rather than focusing largely, if not exclusively, on flood control.

efforts to respond to this challenge are still in an early stage.

#### *Environmental governance*

Promoting improved environmental governance in client countries is also an explicit goal of the 2001 Strategy.[63] This has both public and private sector dimensions that fall under the strategy's second major thematic objective—to improve the quality of growth. Regarding the public sector, the strategy affirmed that, in cooperation with its development partners, the Bank would help client countries (1) strengthen their environmental policy, legal, regulatory, and institutional frameworks with a special focus on local environmental institutions; (2) strengthen environmental assessment systems and practices; (3) reinforce the positive role of markets and the environmental benefits of sectoral and macroeconomic reforms; and (4) support good governance, institutions for collective action, increased transparency, access to environmental information, and public participation in decision making (World Bank 2001b).

*Experience with improved governance has been mixed.*

Experience in the case study countries suggests uneven effectiveness to date. In India, for example, many of the elements mentioned above have been concerns of Bank assistance, including an early focus on helping build an adequate policy, legal, regulatory, and institutional framework; improving environmental assessment practices; and strengthening decentralized environmental management, where much has been accomplished. Far less progress has been made with respect to the adoption of market-based instruments for environmental management or generation of environmental benefits through macroeconomic and sectoral reforms, despite Bank efforts to convince the Indian government of their importance (box 3.9).

Regarding land, watershed, and community forest management, experience has been generally positive in India and China. Forest cover has actually increased in both of these countries since the 1990s. This is due in part to the afforestation efforts supported by Bank-financed projects, but mainly in response to strong government policies.

This contrasts with experience elsewhere, including Brazil, Ghana, Madagascar, and Uganda, where deforestation has increased over the same period. Containing illegal logging remains a serious governance issue in most of these countries, as well as in Indonesia, Malaysia, and Russia, where deforestation has likewise increased. Together with corruption, these are among the factors associated with poor compliance with and weak or uneven enforcement of national forestry legislation. The Bank has attempted to help address these issues in part through its support to the Forest Law Enforcement and Governance Initiative (World Bank 2006e), but curbing deforestation and illegal logging remains a daunting challenge and is an area where Bank Group influence is clearly limited.[64]

Despite Bank-supported efforts to bolster national efforts to manage the environment and strengthen capacity for decentralized management in Brazil, China, Egypt, India, Russia, Sub-Saharan Africa, and elsewhere, important challenges also remain in addressing issues of water scarcity (especially in Egypt, India, and northern China) and enforcement of and private sector compliance with pollution legislation. Although it now appears that air and water pollution from larger industrial establishments in countries such as Brazil, China, Egypt, and India is under better control than in the early 1990s, in part because of Bank-funded projects, pollution from small and medium-sized enterprises and inadequate disposal of hazardous wastes are persisting problems. The same is true for municipal solid waste and sewage in many urban centers, including in Sub-Saharan Africa. Another area of environmental governance where Bank financial support has been limited is urban air quality management, although increasing proactivity of local civil society and the judiciary is beginning to make a difference (box 3.10).

***Important challenges persist, especially with respect to water scarcity and urban water and air quality management.***

The Bank cannot—and should not be expected to—address every environmental priority, and client countries may not seek its support in this regard. However, the record to date in relation to

**Box 3.9: Environmental Management Capacity—India**

The technical and institutional capacity of environmental agencies in India, as in many other countries, varies considerably across states and over time, reflecting differing levels of development and commitment to environmental goals. India nonetheless has strong policy, legal, and regulatory frameworks and good environmental institutions, compared with many other developing countries. Similar statements can be made about Brazil, China, and Russia, although in Russia commitment at the central government level has declined in recent years.[a] The Bank has played a significant institution-building role in these countries as well as in many Sub-Saharan African countries, including Ghana, Madagascar, and Uganda, where capacity is generally weaker.

In India, institution building was attempted through the Environment Management Capacity Building Technical Assistance and Industrial Pollution Control and Prevention Projects. Approved in the early and mid-1990s, these projects focused on federal and selected state agencies. There has been a gap in Bank financial support for environmental governance following closure of these projects, although several new operations are being prepared following up on recent ESW, including the CEA.

In contrast, state water resource, watershed, and forest management/ecodevelopment projects have had policy and institution-building components that have positively affected participating state water resource and forest departments. These projects have helped induce state agencies to take more holistic and strategic approaches to natural resource management, in most cases through participatory processes involving affected communities. Continuing Bank support over several decades and joint learning with client agencies contributed to project success.

*Source:* IEG country case studies.

a. This was clearly the view of those inside both the Bank and Russian civil society, including the former Minister of the Environment, who was interviewed by IEG during its mission to Russia in September 2006.

environmental governance has been mixed (box 3.11). Bank lending for the brown agenda has been less significant in Africa, Brazil, and India than in China, but recent IEG evaluations show that Bank support has made relevant contributions at the metropolitan, microwatershed, and river basin levels in both China and Brazil. This includes management, institutional, and governance aspects. However, the Bank could have done more in relation to natural resource management in Africa, biodiversity in China, and river basin management in India. It also needs to fully incorporate lessons of its experience in the Brazilian Amazon over the past two decades.[65]

More generally, Bank support for environmental governance has grown since 1990. The Bank has provided useful support with respect to national environmental policy and institutional development. In Brazil, China, and India, for example, the support has helped strengthen environmental institutions at both the national and subnational levels—and thus has helped decentralize environmental management capacity—although the nature, quality, and results of this support have varied over space and time.

The record with respect to industrial pollution control and urban environmental management, however, has been less impressive, except in China and to a lesser extent Brazil. In these two countries—and India in particular, but also Egypt, Russia, and elsewhere—environmental governance at the metropolitan and urban levels deserves greater attention. This is especially true as cities will continue to grow and the scale and complexity of this challenge will continue to increase.

**Box 3.10: Managing Air Quality in Metropolitan Areas**

Despite the relative absence of Bank lending,[a] notable progress has occurred over the past decade in several major Indian metropolitan areas, especially Delhi and Mumbai. This improvement is due to the intervention of environmental NGOs (mainly through the use of public interest lawsuits), the media, and the judicial system. Supreme Court actions have resulted in improved enforcement of pollution-related legislation and greater private sector compliance in the industrial, energy, and transport sectors, as documented in recent Bank ESW and elsewhere (World Bank 2005b; CSE 2006). Citizen awareness and intervention regarding pollution is reportedly also increasing in China, and even in Egypt, NGOs are now bringing lawsuits to force better government enforcement of legal requirements.[b]

The focus of NGO and court pressures has been mainly on air pollution, even though Bank ESW in India at least demonstrates that water pollution is responsible for a much larger share of the costs of environmental degradation. The experience in other developing countries with megacities, including Brazil and Mexico, has been similar. One possible explanation is that it is more costly to resolve urban water quality issues, which normally require large investments for sewage collection, treatment, and disposal. Another possibility is that, although water quality problems mainly affect the poor, everyone is exposed to polluted air. It is thus perhaps not surprising that recent actions have been more concerned with air quality than water pollution or indoor air pollution, which mainly affects the poor.[c]

*Source:* IEG country case studies.

a. Bank assistance has mainly taken the form of several capacity-building activities (URAIR associated with the former Metropolitan Environment Improvement Program in Asia; the Clean Coal Initiative; and, more recently, the Clean Air Initiative).

b. Personal communication with a former attorney general, who now heads an Egyptian environmental NGO, during an interview with the IEG evaluation team in Alexandria, Egypt, in June 2006.

c. In addition, the rural population—the poor in particular—generally have less political influence than their urban counterparts, so they are relatively less empowered when it comes to influencing government environmental and other priorities, a phenomenon that is by no means unique to India.

## Box 3.11: The Bank and Environmental Governance in Brazil, China, and Africa

**Brazil**

The Bank has helped strengthen regulatory and institutional frameworks through its management of international funds for the Amazon, Atlantic forests, and other biomes. It has provided support for the federal forest regulatory framework through GEF and, through technical assistance, for the Law on Management of Public Forests. The law aims to strengthen the role of decentralized management and markets in promoting sustainable forest resource use. Complementary GEF projects helped set up the institutional structure for biodiversity management in the Ministry of the Environment, and the Secretariat for Amazonia has been partly financed through the Rainforest Pilot Program. Other parts of the ministry have also been supported by Bank-funded projects.

Projects in Brazil have encouraged greater decentralization in environmental policy making and strengthened subnational institutions.[a] Some, such as PPTAL/PPG7, have had a significant impact (placing 40 million hectares of indigenous lands under stronger legal protection). PPG7 has also been instrumental in enhancing the influence of civil society by creating and supporting NGO networks that have been highly active in the policy arena. But their sustainability once the program ends remains to be seen.

Environmental governance has been addressed mainly at the sector, state, municipal, and project levels. Two national environment projects, however, have focused on such challenges for the country with positive results for both institutional capacity and protection of local environmental assets. These operations have combined institutional strengthening measures with investments to protect environmental assets, including federal protected areas. The Bank has also used development policy lending for the environment. But it is not yet possible to evaluate the environmental results of this approach.

**China**

The main environmental governance issues in China include inadequacy of the State Environmental Protection Agency's resources to fully address environmental challenges; institutional weaknesses among the subnational environmental pollution bureaus that represent a major constraint on effective enforcement and monitoring of compliance with environmental regulations; insufficient technical capacity and resources in the bureaus; and limitations on the long-standing pollution levies, which are often too low to induce polluters to reduce emissions or treat effluents. The Bank has made significant contributions in governance-related AAA and research, particularly on industrial pollution management, energy efficiency, greenhouse gas emissions reduction, environmental institution building, regulations, and public participation.[b]

In environmental management, the Bank has emphasized both economic incentives and the tightening of command-and-control measures. Much has been learned from ESW about local responses to regulatory measures and the value of public disclosure of polluters. But the uneven success of China's pollution levy system is a missed opportunity, as this system is complex to administer, and the marginal cost of abatement may be twice the current effective charge rate. Poorly designed incentive frameworks have resulted in weak compliance and contributed to continuing deterioration in environmental quality. China also needs to make greater progress in the use of environmental taxes on polluting inputs to complement the economic incentives from effluent fees and fines already in place.

As in India and Brazil, air pollution control in China's largest cities has benefited from increasing public awareness and government response. Bank lending support, however, has had mixed results in promoting environmental governance relative to the strong contributions of AAA. Bank lending to address brown issues has nonetheless been much more extensive in China than in any other case study country. Effectiveness on the blue agenda in China has also been impressive, as has that for watershed and forest management, if not biodiversity conservation. In that agenda, efforts have been far more limited than in Brazil or many countries in Sub-Saharan Africa, for example.

**Africa**

In Sub-Saharan Africa, the Bank has supported the creation and development of environmental institutions through lending operations for well over a decade in Ghana, Madagascar, and Uganda. But results have been mixed. A range of institutional coordination issues regarding environmental management also remains in Senegal. Continued Bank and donor assistance, including investment support, is essential, but government commitment to environmental objectives remains unclear in Senegal and Uganda, where relevant environmental governance problems persist.

In Uganda, the Bank has supported increased awareness and understanding of environmental issues, a strengthened policy and institutional framework for ENRM, and actions to address issues

*(Box continues on the following page.)*

**Box 3.11: The Bank and Environmental Governance in Brazil, China, and Africa (continued)**

such as management of Lake Victoria and protection of threatened biodiversity. However, its successes have mainly involved operations funded by GEF that respond to particular domestic and international constituencies and capacity-building projects that may also have been mostly donor driven. At the same time, efforts to mainstream environmental concerns across sectors and to decentralize environmental management capacity have been only partly successful, and the long-term financial sustainability of the National Environmental Management Agency remains uncertain. Despite this, Ghana and Uganda are generally regarded by the Bank as countries with comparatively strong institutions for environmental and natural resource management.

*Source:* IEG country case studies.

a. During the 1990s, for example, the Natural Resource Policy Project under PPG7 strengthened the technical capacity of state environmental agencies in the Amazon region. Joint resource management strategies involving local populations and government authorities, as in India, also formed a basic part of several subprojects, including those for extractive reserves and demonstration projects, PROVARZEA (which sought to improve environmental management of watersheds), and the participatory demarcation of indigenous reserves.

b. An important future role for the Bank could be to help the government strengthen subnational environmental pollution boards and improve the incentive framework for pollution management.

# Chapter 4

## Evaluation Highlights

- IFC's environmental assistance has achieved at least satisfactory environmental and social effects in about two-thirds of evaluated investment projects, which leaves room for improvement.
- Performance of projects in Sub-Saharan Africa and in some industry sectors fell short of expectations.
- IFC has taken actions to improve supervision of FI projects; previously, supervision had been insufficient.
- IFC has had a positive impact on its clients' environmental management, but MIGA has tended to give the issue too little attention.
- IFC has potential major indirect impact on the Equator Principles.
- MIGA Category B projects generally have adequate EAPs, but many of those plans are not fully implemented.
- Performance of the MIGA projects in Russia demonstrates the potential for a stewardship approach.

Ceramic tile manufacturing plant in Brazil. Photo courtesy of Jouni  Martti Eerikainen.

# IFC, MIGA, and the Environment

The 2001 Environment Strategy stated, "As parts of the World Bank Group, IFC and MIGA will promote through their investments and guarantees environmental and social responsibility and good environmental management in the private sector." In implementing this mandate, country strategies developed by the Bank are gradually including IFC and MIGA, as has been the case for the recent Brazil and China strategies.[1]

The approaches of IFC and MIGA are similar and based on meeting environmental and social standards applicable to individual projects and enterprises. The aim of IFC and MIGA is to ensure that the investments avoid or mitigate environmental damage and improve the environmental performance of the companies. More recently the institutions have also started initiatives (mostly Advisory Services) to promote a greater private sector role in improving the environment.

This chapter describes the financing and nonfinancing instruments of IFC and MIGA and evaluates the performance and impacts of their projects based on meeting project-specific environmental requirements and Performance Standards ("do no harm").[2] In addition, it assesses their more recent Advisory Services and other interventions to improve environmental performance of the private sector more broadly ("do good").[3] The evaluation draws on nine country studies and an examination of the specific environmental and social effects of a random sample of all projects implemented by IFC and MIGA during fiscal 1990–2006.

## Assessing IFC Performance

### *Description of IFC instruments*

IFC increased its attention to the environment during the 1990s by applying environmental strategies, policies, and standards in the provision of its financial and nonfinancial services. In addition, it has sought out environmental business opportunities and engaged in global environmental activities. These activities, which have expanded in recent years, include environmental management capacity building in investment projects, environment-oriented IFC Advisory Services, support for the GEF, and carbon finance. IFC has also established a partnership—known as the Equator Principles (discussed later in this chapter)—with commercial financial institutions that have agreed to use environmental and social standards similar to those followed by IFC in their developing-country investments.

*IFC increased its attention to environmental issues in the 1990s.*

Until 2006, IFC used the guidelines in the World Bank Group's *Pollution Prevention and Abatement Handbook* (World Bank Group with UNEP and UNIDO 1999) and 10 World Bank Group safeguard policies and directives,[4] together with its own guidelines and policies, as the foundation for its environmental due diligence and supervision work. In recent years, IFC has sought to amplify this approach with one that addresses the client's role in achieving outcome-based environmental and social performance, including new areas such as labor and community engagement.[5] The shift was based in part on a 2003 review of IFC safeguard policies by the Compliance Advisor Ombudsman (CAO), which proposed ways to enhance performance.[6]

In line with the CAO recommendations, in 2006 IFC adopted a new policy on social and environmental sustainability, designed "to promote sustainable private sector development in developing countries, helping to reduce poverty and improve people's lives." Under this new regime, clients are required to meet all applicable IFC Performance Standards and project-specific requirements (see box 4.1).

*After a 2003 review, IFC adopted a new approach that aims to mainstream sustainability and take up a stewardship agenda.*

The new approach recognizes sustainable development as a strategic priority and key business driver. With its 2006 Policy and Performance Standards on Social and Environmental Sustainability, IFC affirmed the importance of mainstreaming environmental and social aspects by integrating them into the private sector development and economic sustainability objectives in its investment projects. However, it is too soon to evaluate the results relating to environmental outcomes of this new initiative.

### Volume and nature of IFC investments

IFC's total investments (not referring specifically to the environment) have grown rapidly over the past four years, from $3.9 billion in fiscal 2003 to $6.7 billion in fiscal 2006. Investments reached $8.2 billion in fiscal 2007, reflecting similarly increasing private capital flows to the developing world. Commitments (again, not for the environment) in the nine case study countries were $13.4 billion during fiscal 1990–2006, representing 28 percent of IFC investments during the period, with the largest shares in Brazil, India, Russia, and China. In fiscal 2006, China ranked number one ($638 million), followed by Russia ($502 million) and Brazil ($412 million).

From fiscal 1990 to 2006, IFC's commitments were $47.9 billion in 3,419 projects (table 4.1). Most of the projects were in the financial market sector (39 percent by number of projects), comprising finance and insurance and collective investment vehicles, mainly funds, and in the process and manufacturing industry (29 percent).[7] Most of the 124 projects with high potential environmental risk (Category A; see box 4.2) were in the oil, gas, and mining (57 projects); electric power (28); processing and manufacturing industry (20); and transportation (11) sectors.

Although IFC is a relatively minor investor, with about a 4 percent share (including cofinanciers) of total private capital flows to the developing world, it is the largest multilateral development bank (MDB) investor in the private sector with $56 billion in disbursements. This sum represents 29 percent of total private sector investments by the MDBs from 1991 to 2007. Furthermore, according to IFC's annual client survey in 2006, IFC's assistance in managing environmental and social aspects was cited as the third most important factor in choosing IFC as an investment partner. Clients reported that IFC was regarded as having a sustainability "stamp of approval." Thus, measured by its investment volume, environmental capacity building, Performance Standards, partnerships, and efforts to stimulate sound environmental and social practices beyond its investments, IFC can be considered the leading private sector MDB investor in emerging markets.

### Volume and nature of IFC nonfinancial services

#### Advisory Services

IFC Advisory Services (previously technical assistance and Advisory Services) have grown since 1986 and accelerated over the past few years. Thirty-six percent of IFC's staff work full

**Box 4.1: Policy, Performance Standards, and Strategy to Promote Sustainability**

The new IFC approach, approved by the Board in April 2006, is a pyramid structure with a policy statement at the top, eight performance standards[a] in the middle, and detailed guidance notes supporting each standard at the base. The Policy on Social and Environmental Sustainability combines the "do no harm" approach with the postulate that client engagement is essential to achieving sustainable results.

The 2006 IFC Environment and Social Review Procedure (ESRP), approved by IFC management and revised in July 2007, likewise extends the 1998 ESRP, especially in providing more specific IFC requirements for financial intermediaries (FIs)[b] and giving guidance on how to mobilize additional resources and IFC Advisory Services to improve project performance.[c]

In late 2006, IFC's Environment and Social Development Department created a system to benchmark and rate investment project performance with the 2006 Performance Standards at both appraisal and supervision. These projects will mature in 2011 and will be evaluated as a part of IEG's review of project team self-evaluations (Expanded Project Supervision Reports, or XPSRs), which include environmental specialists when appropriate. IFC now has enhanced tools to assess performance, track indicators during supervision, and eventually evaluate projects' environmental and social impacts based on follow-up information.[d]

IFC strategies in this decade have addressed environmental sustainability as one of its corporate priorities. As IFC's business model, in accordance with its Global/Local Strategy,[e] shifts away from project finance toward corporate finance and frontier countries,[f] especially in Sub-Saharan Africa, IFC's business and environmental and social risks are also sharply increasing. Those risks will include not only the project's area of influence but also the client's business and environmental management as a whole. As part of the strategy, IFC's Environment and Social Development Department will move a significant part of its investment support staff to field offices by 2010. Bringing environmental specialists closer to clients is expected to improve client management and enable better project supervision, but maintaining the department's coherence and knowledge management with increasing duties and project volume will be a challenge.

*Source:* IFC Policy and Performance Standards on Social and Environmental Sustainability (April 2006); IFC data.

a. The Board approved IFC's Sustainability Policy, Disclosure Policy, and eight Performance Standards in April 2006: (1) Social and Environmental Assessment and Management System; (2) Labor and Working Conditions; (3) Pollution Prevention and Abatement; (4) Community Health, Safety, and Security; (5) Land Acquisition and Involuntary Resettlement; (6) Biodiversity Conservation and Sustainable Natural Resource Management; (7) Indigenous Peoples; and (8) Cultural Heritage.

b. The 1998 requirements vary depending on whether IFC finances the FI (FI type 1), directly finances the subprojects (FI type 2), or is "the lender of record" for the subprojects (FI type 3). The Environmental and Social Review conducted by IFC specialists first determines the significance of any business activities that have the potential to produce an environmental and social impact based on a review of the portfolio and industry sector information. IFC will thereafter tailor its requirements according to the portfolio environmental, safety, health, and social risks. Where the portfolio review indicates that the FI's investments could have potentially significant environmental and social impacts, the FI is required to ensure that its subprojects meet the relevant elements of the IFC Performance Standards in addition to applicable national laws and regulations.

c. The 2007 ESRP includes procedures for IFC's Advisory Services Department to self-determine when to seek assistance from the Environment and Social Development Department to identify environmental and social objectives and performance indicators and to monitor progress toward objectives.

d. Rating environmental condition and performance indicators at appraisal and project maturity will provide a better basis for evaluating their environmental impacts, assuming that the larger the difference between environmental performance at appraisal and at the time of evaluation, the greater the environmental impact will have been.

e. IFC's Global/Local Strategy identified four business drivers: (1) provide better services to clients; (2) strengthen development impact, including positive environmental impact; (3) move the business model to respond to the shift from project finance to corporate finance; and (4) hold IFC accountable.

f. IFC defines the frontier countries as IDA countries and frontier regions in non-IDA countries.

time on such services, the majority in 64 field offices. From 1986 to 2007, IFC received $1,271 million in donor commitments and contributed $657 million from its own resources to support Advisory Services. Spending on IFC Advisory Services in fiscal 2007 was $197 million—excluding investments—up 30 percent from the previous year. Data as of December 31, 2007, indicate that, among 1,011 active IFC Advisory Services projects, 190 were under the environment and social sustainability business line, involving total funding of $208 million, 24 percent of current total IFC Advisory Services funding.

### *Equator Principles*

IFC advised and guided 10 leading banks from 7 countries in adopting the Equator Principles in June 2003. A revised set of principles was launched in July 2006, reflecting

*IFC has established a clear position in sustainable finance with the Equator Principles.*

**Table 4.1: Commitments and Environmental Categories, by Sector, Fiscal 1990–2006**

| | IFC commitments | | | Environmental screening category | | | |
|---|---|---|---|---|---|---|---|
| **Sector group name** | **$ million** | **% ($)** | **Number** | **A** | **B** | **FI** | **C** |
| Financial markets | 16,975 | 35.5 | 1,326 | | 10 | 692 | 463 |
| Process and manufacturing industry | 14,397 | 30.1 | 983 | 20 | 749 | 4 | 91 |
| Oil, gas, and mining | 3,931 | 8.2 | 197 | 57 | 99 | 1 | 19 |
| Electric power | 2,829 | 5.9 | 102 | 28 | 59 | 1 | 13 |
| Transportation and warehousing | 2,559 | 5.3 | 163 | 11 | 125 | 2 | 12 |
| Information technology and publishing | 2,553 | 5.3 | 140 | | 75 | 2 | 58 |
| Tourism | 1,061 | 2.2 | 167 | 6 | 133 | | 7 |
| Agriculture and forestry | 930 | 1.9 | 129 | 1 | 104 | | 4 |
| Retail | 894 | 1.9 | 47 | | 44 | | 2 |
| Health and education | 599 | 1.3 | 89 | | 74 | 1 | 13 |
| Water and waste management | 520 | 1.1 | 22 | | 19 | 2 | 1 |
| Construction and real estate | 267 | 0.6 | 20 | 1 | 17 | | 1 |
| Gas distribution | 203 | 0.4 | 9 | | 9 | | |
| Professional and technical services | 150 | 0.3 | 25 | | 7 | | 13 |
| Total | 47,867 | 100 | 3,419 | 124 | 1,524 | 705 | 697 |

*Source:* IEG-IFC database.

*Note:* Process and manufacturing industry includes sectors from global manufacturing (713 projects); agribusiness (163 projects); and oil, gas, mining, and chemicals (102 projects) departments. A total of 369 currency swaps and early projects in 1990 had no categorization.

IFC's 2006 Performance Standards on Social and Environmental Sustainability. As of March 2008, 60 banks had declared adherence to the principles to manage social and environmental issues related to the financing of development projects. IFC's strategy also encourages other MDBs to adopt the Performance Standards in emerging markets. Implementation of the principles is still recent and cannot yet be evaluated.

**Box 4.2: Risk Categorization of IFC Projects**

As part of its review of a project's expected social and environmental impacts, IFC uses a system of social and environmental categorization to reflect the magnitude of impacts understood as a result of the client's SEA and to specify IFC's institutional requirements to disclose to the public project-specific information prior to presenting projects to its Board of Directors for approval, in accordance with the disclosure policy. These categories are the following:

- *Category A Projects:* Projects with potential significant adverse social or environmental impacts that are diverse, irreversible, or unprecedented
- *Category B Projects:* Projects with potential limited adverse social or environmental impacts that are few in number, generally site-specific, largely reversible, and readily addressed through mitigation measures
- *Category C Projects:* Projects with minimal or no adverse social or environmental impacts, including certain FI projects with minimal or no adverse risks
- *Category FI Projects:* All FI projects, excluding those that are Category C projects.

*Source:* IFC 2006 Policy on Social and Environmental Sustainability.

### GEF and carbon finance projects

By December 31, 2007, IFC had completed 30 GEF-funded projects totaling just over $1 billion, including $320 million from IFC, $203 million from GEF, and $485 million from other cofinanciers. IFC has managed $185 million in two Dutch-funded carbon facilities since January 2002.[8] In this role, IFC takes no financial risk but acts as a trustee. It has used this arrangement to engage in the carbon market and to gain understanding about the needs of the market. The results include the development of new commercial products and the creation of an internal carbon finance unit.

*IFC has engaged with GEF and in some carbon finance projects.*

### "Doing no harm": Evaluating IFC's environmental effects in investment projects

The evaluation of the results of IFC's "do no harm" approach is based on an ESE indicator, designed to measure—with a four-point rating scale (unsatisfactory, partly unsatisfactory, satisfactory, and excellent)—project performance in meeting IFC's requirements and Performance Standards according to the 1998 and 2006 policies and guidelines, as well as their environmental and social impacts. IFC selects its investment projects based on their potential for high development outcomes that incorporate projects' business performance, economic sustainability, and support for private sector development, together with ESE. IEG's assessment of the environmental effectiveness of IFC investments is based on 604 randomly selected mature investment projects evaluated from 1996 to 2006 (chapter 2 and appendix A describe the methodology for evaluating ESE in further detail).

An ESE rating of satisfactory indicates material fulfillment of IFC requirements and IFC Performance Standards[9] at the time of appraisal, and demonstration of positive impacts. A rating of excellent means that the project also met IFC policies and standards in place at the time of the evaluation (presently, the 2006 Performance Standards on Social and Environmental Sustainability), that an excellent Environmental and Social Management System (ESMS) was effectively implemented, and that IFC could use the project as a model for positive ESE. The relative number of projects showing satisfactory and excellent ratings within a given project category or grouping is here defined as *success rate.*

The information available allows for sectoral and Regional comparisons. The database also permits a careful look at the importance of establishing and operating good ESMS and an opportunity to assess IFC work quality.

*IEG assessed the environmental and social effect of 604 mature investments.*

Two-thirds of all projects met IFC's requirements and standards for acceptable environmental and social performance (table 4.2). Of the remaining 33 percent of projects, 26 percent were rated partly unsatisfactory and 7 percent were unsatisfactory. Partly unsatisfactory projects did not meet IFC requirements and Performance Standards, but deficiencies were addressed through ongoing or planned actions. Earlier underperformance does not appear to have resulted in substantial or permanent environmental damage. Finally, the 7 percent of all projects that were rated unsatisfactory did not meet Performance Standards, and mitigation prospects were uncertain or unlikely.

*Sixty-seven percent of all projects met IFC environmental and social requirements and performance standards.*

The ESE success rate of projects evaluated by IEG has ranged between 60 and 77 percent. This variation reflects not only actual performance but also the introduction of stricter requirements, the growing number of issues examined in environmental and social assessments and evaluations, varying complexity, and ESHS and industry sector risks of evaluated projects. The ESE success rate of FI projects has been slightly lower than that of other (real sector) projects—66 percent versus 68 percent. Although Category A projects by definition involve potentially significant environmental and social impacts, their ESE rate of satisfactory or above has been

**Table 4.2: ESE Success Rate, by Year, for 632 Evaluated IFC Investment Projects**

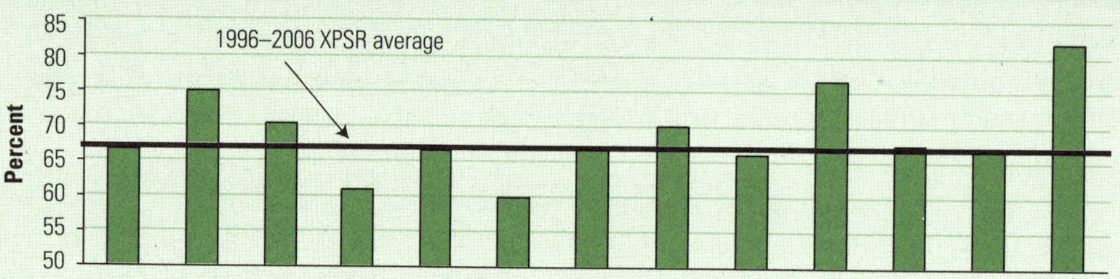


| Evaluation year | 1996 IAR | 1997 IAR | 1998 IAR | 1999 XPSR | 2000 XPSR | 2001 XPSR | 2002 XPSR | 2003 XPSR | 2004 XPSR | 2005 XPSR | 2006 XPSR | XPSRs total | Case study | XPSRs total (%) | 2006 Case study (%) |
|---|---|---|---|---|---|---|---|---|---|---|---|---|---|---|---|
| ESE success rate (%) | 67 | 75 | 70 | 61 | 67 | 60 | 67 | 70 | 66 | 77 | 68 | 67 | 82 | | |
| Non-FIs' ESE success rate | 80 | 81 | 64 | 53 | 72 | 59 | 71 | 71 | 67 | 74 | 73 | 68 | 81 | | |
| FIs' ESE success rate | 40 | 57 | 81 | 74 | 58 | 63 | 60 | 68 | 64 | 81 | 60 | 66 | 100 | | |
| Excellent | 10 | 6 | 7 | 6 | 2 | 8 | 9 | 7 | 3 | 5 | 4 | 67 | 3 | 12 | 11 |
| Satisfactory | 10 | 15 | 31 | 30 | 30 | 34 | 38 | 40 | 38 | 28 | 21 | 315 | 20 | 55 | 71 |
| Partly unsatisfactory | 8 | 6 | 15 | 19 | 14 | 24 | 19 | 12 | 15 | 9 | 8 | 149 | 4 | 26 | 14 |
| Unsatisfactory | 2 | 1 | 1 | 4 | 2 | 4 | 4 | 8 | 6 | 1 | 4 | 37 | 1 | 7 | 4 |
| No opinion possible | | | | 2 | 7 | 7 | | | 4 | 6 | 10 | 36 | | 6 | 0 |
| Total | 30 | 28 | 54 | 61 | 55 | 77 | 70 | 67 | 66 | 49 | 47 | 604 | 28 | | |

*Source:* IEG-IFC database.

*Note:* The average ESE success rate (82 percent versus 67 percent) in the case study sample is explained by the factors used to select countries and sectors for this study. IAR = Investment Assessment Report; XPSR = Expanded Project Supervision Report.

*Management comment:* If the factors mentioned are not properly qualified, IEG's note undermines the high ESE success rate of the case study sample and therefore the success of the work IFC is doing in the countries of the sample. By the same token, the results of each XPSR year need to be qualified based on country and sectoral selection, which has not been an IEG practice in the past.

70 percent, above the overall average of 67 percent.

***Performance by industry sector***

The highest ESE success rate (89 percent satisfactory or above) was in the information technology and publishing sector (figure 4.1). Fourteen of 25 evaluated projects in this sector were in the mobile telephone subsector, where ESHS risks are moderate and usually related to right-of-way alignment and site selection (to ensure that antenna towers do not disturb neighbors and the environment). Projects in the transportation and warehousing sector also achieved a high ESE success rate (85 percent), involving 31 port terminal, shipping, road construction, aviation, and warehouse projects that posed varying environmental, social, and health and safety risks.

*The highest ESE success rates were in the information technology and publishing, transportation and warehousing, and electric power sectors.*

The 26 projects in the electric power sector likewise scored well (with an ESE success rate of 85 percent). These included hydropower plants requiring resettlement and land acquisition, heat- and power-generation plants needing to control emissions, and power-distribution and -transmission projects.

One project in China had an unusually broad impact and demonstration effect. IFC's corporate loan for this project supported investments in combined heat and power plants, as well as in power-generating facilities that would use municipal solid waste in addition to their primary fuel. These investments replaced small, inefficient boilers without emission control; greenhouse gases were reduced through enhanced energy efficiency, improvements in air quality through pollution control, and better waste management and recycling.

Operations in the tourism sector had the lowest ESE success rate (50 percent); they comprised mostly hotel projects. Of 32 hotel projects, 16 had a less than satisfactory rating, including 9 projects in Africa. An IEG evaluation of one hotel project in Africa found it to be noncompliant

**Figure 4.1: ESE Success Rate of IFC Projects, by Industry Sector**

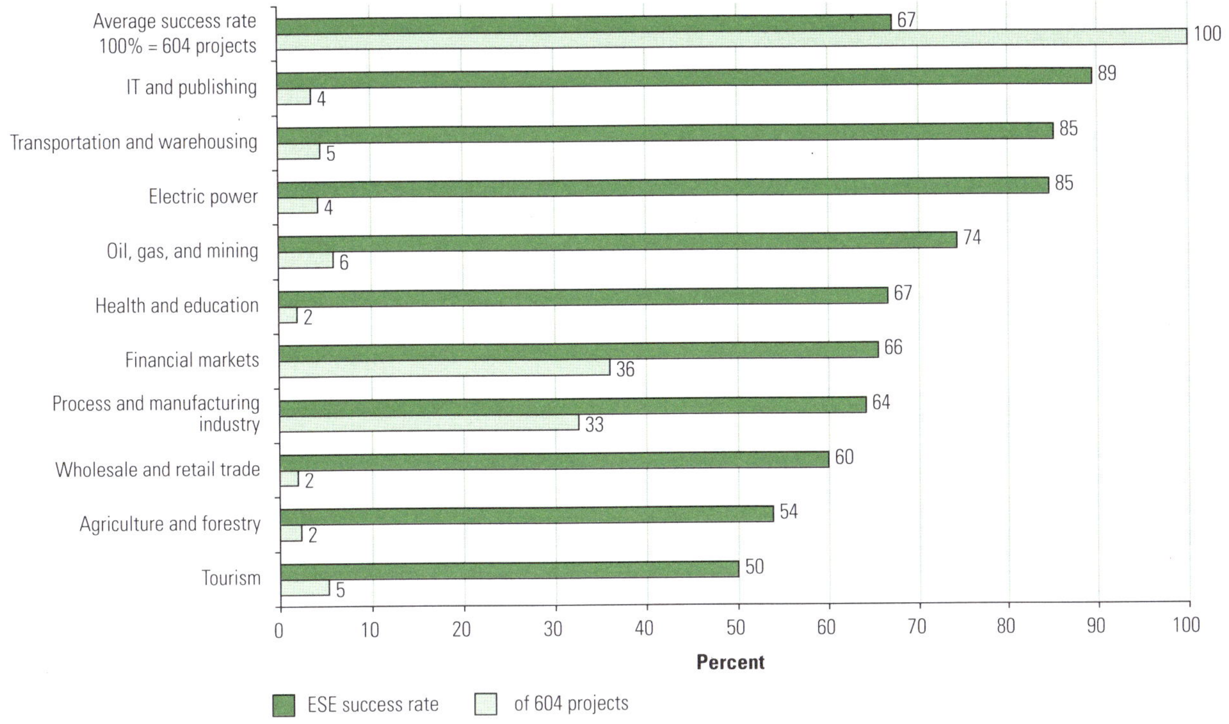


*Source:* IEG database.
*Note:* The upper bar represents the sector's ESE success rate and the lower bar the sector's percentage of all 604 evaluated projects.

with the requirements in the Environmental Review Summary because the fire safety installation had not been completed. Furthermore, no monitoring information was available to confirm performance of the water and wastewater treatment systems. Other hotel projects also had problems with fire safety, effluent discharges, and inadequate reporting.

IFC oil, gas, and mining projects involve a multitude of risks related to pollution, mine closure, dam safety, worker health and safety, land acquisition, and reclamation. Often these projects require carefully designed community programs. They also include the largest share of Category A projects (29 percent). These operations nonetheless had an ESE success rate of 74 percent, suggesting good client commitment and careful IFC appraisal and supervision.

A mining project visited by IEG for this evaluation demonstrated good management of pollution, waste, and worker health and safety. IFC played a key role in introducing ESHS standards, an efficient EMS, and a development plan that addressed community grievances. However, IFC could have carried out greater capacity building and training for environmental management. IFC does not restrict its finance for fossil fuel extraction, transport, refining, and power and heat-generation projects, as such projects provide opportunities to address social and environmental aspects better than they would without IFC involvement. IFC seeks to mitigate greenhouse gas emissions by improving the projects' energy efficiency, carbon finance, and sometimes by using Advisory Services and funding from environmental funds and GEF[10] for energy studies, market transformation, and improved process technology.

*The tourism sector had the lowest ESE success rate.*

*The high-risk oil, gas, and mining sector had an above-average success rate of 74 percent.*

The ESE success rate in the process and manufacturing industry, representing 51 percent of evaluated real sector and 33 percent of all evaluated projects, was 64 percent, just below the overall average of 67 percent. The main concerns in these industries are risk of pollution, fuel and hazardous materials storage, asbestos, polychlorinated biphenyls, greenhouse gas emissions, and worker health and safety.

As a part of the process and manufacturing industry, the chemical and nonmetallic mineral sectors—mainly cement and glass manufacturing plants—scored comparatively well, with about an 80 percent success rate. However, textile, food and beverage, and primary metal industries (44, 53, and 56 percent success rates, respectively) did not comply with IFC requirements for effluent discharges, air emissions, or worker health and safety.

Only six projects were evaluated in the plastics and rubber subsector. One successful chemical industry project was a good practice carbon black manufacturing project in Egypt. At the time of evaluation, that project met the environmental objectives established six years earlier at appraisal and was excellent in the following aims: meeting national and Bank Group requirements; setting up an ESMS, including exemplary control and monitoring of air emissions and recycling and treatment of wastewater; and management, segregation, and storing of solid wastes and storage of hazardous materials and fuels, as well as occupational health and safety provisions. The company also operated a community program and demonstrated best practice in the industry sector.

*Textile, food and beverage, and primary metals did not comply with some IFC requirements.*

The ESE success rate of agribusiness projects has been below average (54 percent), mainly because of pollution from processing plants and agrochemicals. In Brazil, IEG visited and evaluated two controversial IFC investments in working capital and storage facilities for the same client. Previously, NGO concerns about the potential impacts of the project in pushing the agricultural frontier toward virgin rainforests prompted senior management to ask the Office of the CAO to audit the environmental categorization of this investment. The CAO found that, although IFC followed its procedures in categorizing the project, it did not seek sufficient evidence that the company's EMS was effectively implemented when the project was classified Category B rather than Category A. The CAO concluded that the Category B rating could not be justified without the above conditions having been met.

*Pollution from processing plants and agrochemicals has resulted in a below-average ESE success rate for agribusiness projects.*

IEG's subsequent evaluation agreed with the CAO's finding. It also credited the client company for its community engagement at appraisal; for environmental practices on its own 11 farms; and for establishing a system to identify, mitigate, and monitor environmental health and safety risks and prohibit illegal deforestation on about 600 farms that received credit from the company to purchase fertilizers and seeds. At the same time, the company purchased about 40 percent of soy for further processing from the open market; thus the company had a potential indirect impact on the expansion of soy farming in the region. IFC helped the company develop social and community engagement programs and an ESMS.

However, IEG found during its site visit in 2007 that IFC's Corrective Action Plan was not properly supervised and that pollution from some facilities exceeded IFC limits. IEG concluded that projects of this type would benefit from the preparation of more detailed, up-front studies on agrochemical use and impacts on the environment—and on broader regional aspects of deforestation. Also, sustainability of the supply chain needs to be ensured through certification schemes and third-party monitoring.[11]

With a 66 percent overall ESE success rate, FIs had gaps in performance, especially regarding subproject performance in meeting Bank Group guidelines and reporting. Although IFC has greater control over environmental and social assessment and performance in direct investment projects, in FI projects with many subprojects IFC relies on the EMS of the FI to ensure that its Performance Standards are met.

Although IFC's potential reputational risk in many FI projects is modest because it has no financial ownership in most FI subprojects, such projects provide an opportunity for IFC to multiply its environment-related influence by helping to improve performance of vast numbers of FI subprojects. Small and medium-size enterprise clients of FIs often do not have funds to invest in pollution control and waste management and recycling systems. Even if a small percentage have medium or high ESHS risks, their aggregate impact could be significant. Studies have shown that small industries not only produce more waste per unit of output, but they also, at an aggregate level, account for at least as much if not more pollution than their large-scale counterparts (Nagesha and Subrahmanya 2006). In particular, small microfinance loans, such as those to retail shops and street kitchens, generally do not pose environmental concerns but may have significant positive social effects by providing job opportunities and gender-oriented lending programs. [12, 13]

In the recent IEG-IFC study (IEG-IFC 2007), 11 of 65 subprojects had less than satisfactory ESHS performance. Although these subprojects complied formally with environmental and health and safety laws, enforcement of environmental laws had failed to identify obvious shortfalls such as contaminated soil and groundwater at small workshops and gasoline stations and discharge of untreated effluents from tanneries.

#### *Performance by Region*

The highest ESE success rate was in Europe and Central Asia (76 percent). Rates in the Middle East and North Africa, Latin America and the Caribbean, and Asia were close to the overall average, with rates of 71, 68, and 67 percent, respectively. However, the rate for Sub-Saharan Africa (43 percent) was significantly below average (figure 4.2).

Based on an assessment of several projects in Sub-Saharan Africa, reasons for low performance, such as not meeting IFC pollution control and health and safety requirements, were similar to those in unsatisfactory investment projects in other Regions. In order of priority, those reasons were (1) poor company management commitment to environmental management; (2) insufficient IFC client skills and resources to identify, mitigate, and monitor environmental and health and safety risks; (3) missing or poor environmental management procedures; and (4) poor environmental law enforcement. In response, IFC strengthened its supervision program in Africa, with a 30 percent increase in supervision visits from fiscal 2007 to 2008.

*FIs had a success rate close to the average, but there were gaps in performance.*

IEG also identified success rates for projects in each of the case study countries. Altogether, 126 investment projects were evaluated in IEG's previous XPSR evaluation program and 28 projects were visited for IEG country case studies.[14] Because of the small number of all evaluations in Uganda (3), Kenya (3), and Ghana (4), the aggregate informative value of the ESE ratings in these countries is low (table 4.3).

The project success rate was higher than average in Egypt, Russia, and India, but lower in China and Brazil. The success rate of 69 percent in these 126 XPSR projects was close to the average (67 percent) of all 604 evaluated XPSR projects, but the success rate in 28 case study projects visited was high (82 percent), which is explained by the purposeful sampling.[15]

#### *Performance in meeting project-level criteria*

In 2004 IEG began to benchmark projects in meeting performance criteria established at appraisal, and in 2006 it developed an evaluation framework using the new Performance Standards. Using these new criteria, 106 real sector and 51 FI projects were evaluated. The findings of these evaluations are presented here.[16]

The performance criteria most often found in real sector project appraisal documents were labor and working

*The environmental and social success rate was lowest in Sub-Saharan Africa.*

## Figure 4.2: ESE Success Rate of IFC Projects, by Region

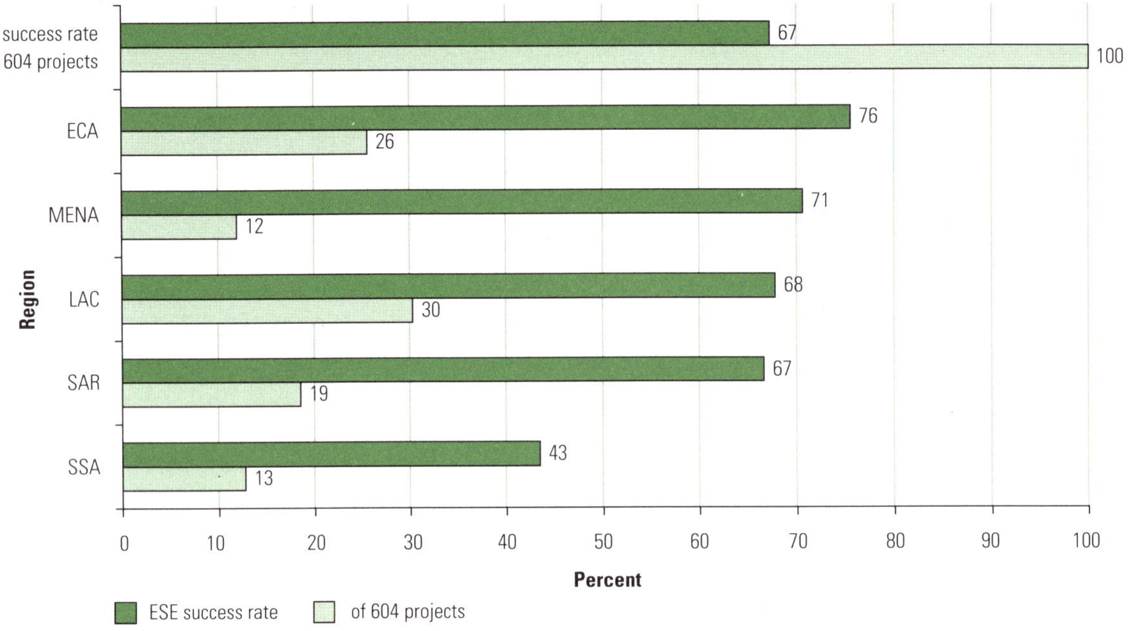


*Source:* IEG database.
*Note:* ECA = Europe and Central Asia; ESE = environment and social effects; LAC = Latin America and the Caribbean; MENA = Middle East and North Africa; SAR = South Asia; SSA = Sub-Saharan Africa.

conditions, including health and safety (present in 92 percent of the projects); ESMSs[17] (81 percent); and pollution prevention (87 percent), including solid waste management, wastewater discharges and air emissions, and emergency preparedness.

These criteria are typical for process and manufacturing industries,[18] which represent 51 percent of evaluated real sector projects. The criteria for land acquisition and involuntary resettlement were present in 37 percent of the sample, but criteria for biodiversity, indigenous

## Table 4.3: ESE Success Rates in IFC XPSR Projects

| | | | Rating | | | | ESE |
|---|---|---|---|---|---|---|---|
| Country | NOP | U | PU | S | E | Total | Success rate (%) |
| Egypt, Arab Republic of | 1 | | 1 | 6 | 4 | 12 | 91 |
| Russian Federation | 2 | 1 | 3 | 11 | 3 | 20 | 78 |
| India | | 1 | 6 | 17 | 6 | 30 | 77 |
| Uganda | | | 1 | 2 | | 3 | 67 |
| Kenya | | 1 | | 2 | | 3 | 67 |
| Brazil | 3 | 1 | 12 | 14 | 7 | 37 | 62 |
| China | 1 | | 7 | 7 | 2 | 17 | 56 |
| Ghana | | 1 | 2 | 1 | | 4 | 25 |
| Total | 7 | 5 | 32 | 60 | 22 | 126 | 69 |

*Source:* IEG database.
*Note:* E = excellent; NOP = no opinion possible; PU = partially satisfactory; S = satisfactory; U = unsatisfactory.

people, and cultural heritage were present in fewer than 7 percent of projects, reflecting the weight in the IFC real sector portfolio of process and manufacturing industry projects, which rarely include these environmental aspects.

The projects evaluated have been largely successful (90 percent success rate) in meeting IFC requirements and Performance Standards related to the development of acceptable ESMS and resettlement of affected communities, and reasonably successful in fulfilling requirements and standards to prevent pollution (83 percent success rate) and protect worker health and safety (76 percent success rate).

IFC's requirements for FIs varied according to the investment type—that is, depending on whether IFC finance was targeted either to the FI (FI type 1) or to its subprojects (FI types 2 and 3).[19] The success rate by different performance criteria and percentage of evaluated projects in the sample of 51 FI projects is shown in figure 4.3.

The performance of FIs was good in terms of meeting IFC's requirement to avoid industries on the exclusion list and ensuring that subproject companies complied with host country laws by obtaining a valid environmental permit. Most of the FIs evaluated also had satisfactory EMSs and adequately trained staff. However, the success rate for reporting on the environmental management process and performance of subprojects was less satisfactory (49 and 52 percent). Annual Environmental Performance Reports were either missing or presented incomplete information, especially on subproject performance. Performance of FI type 2 clients (those that use IFC funds to finance subprojects directly) in meeting Bank Group guidelines was also low.

**Figure 4.3: Success Rates by Performance Criteria in FI Projects**

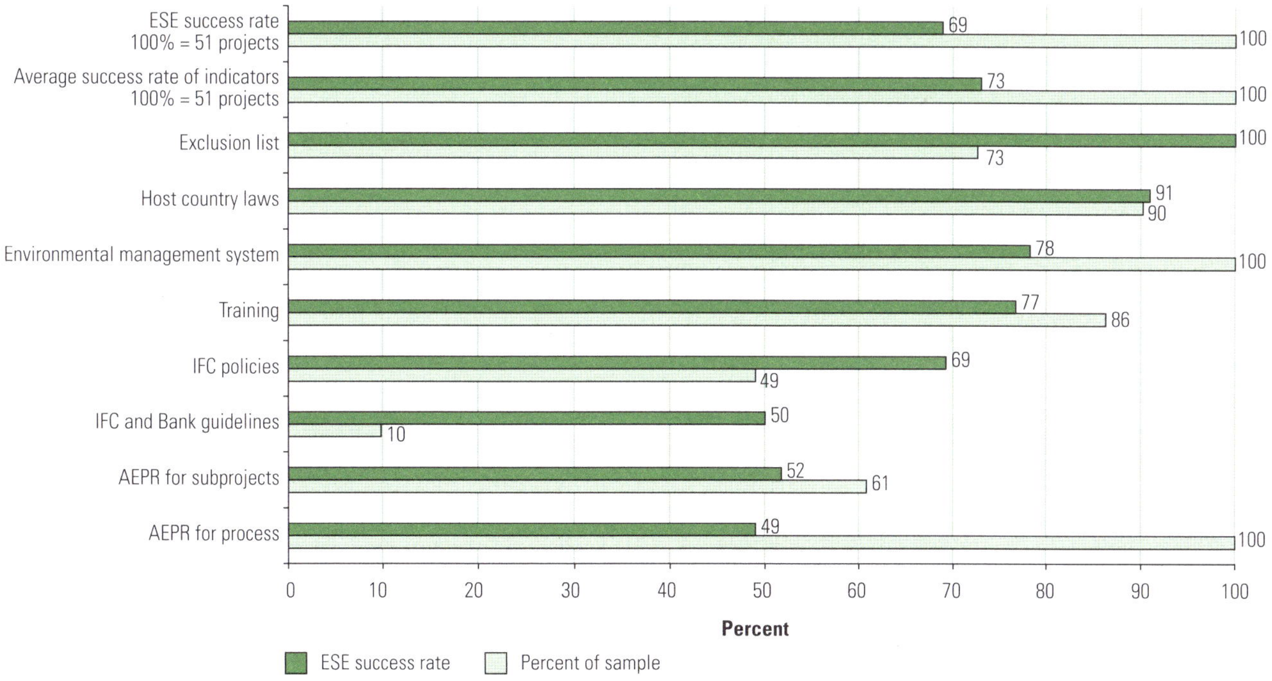


*Source:* IEG database.

*Note:* The upper bar represents performance criterion's success rate and the lower bar its percentage of all 51 evaluated projects. ESE success rate (69 percent) is the overall evaluative success rate, and average success rate (72 percent) is the arithmetic average of eight indicators. AEPR = Annual Environmental Performance Report; ESE = environmental and social effects; FI = financial intermediary.

***Enhancement of environmental and social management systems***

*FIs comply well with the exclusion list requirements but less well with reporting on EMS and subproject performance.*

IFC requires each client to develop an ESMS.[20] Most IFC clients now demonstrate satisfactory ESMS frameworks, reflecting the minimum requirements for a policy statement, organizational structure, and responsibilities.

The importance of a strong ESMS is evident. The share of IFC's project finance has decreased over the past few years[21] and, with a growing share of corporate loans and equity investments, IFC is increasingly exposed to the environmental and social risks faced by the entire company, not just specific project investment risks. In short, IFC support to clients to develop good ESMSs that aim to identify and mitigate companywide ESHS risks is strategic for the institution.

*Most IFC clients demonstrate a satisfactory ESMS framework.*

IEG found a high correlation[22] between quality of ESMS and ESE success rates in real sector projects. In the 81 evaluated projects, high ESMS framework quality (excellent or satisfactory) was positively associated with a high ESE rating in 78 percent of the sample. The correlation was also strong in FI projects.

*There is a correlation between a formal ESMS and ESE success rate in real sector projects.*

However, there is a poor association between certified ISO (International Standards Association) 14001 EMSs and ESE success rates. Although the correlation with the ESMS rating was better, it was still not very strong. None of the projects with ISO 14001 certification had a low rating (unsatisfactory or partly unsatisfactory) for its ESMS quality. This suggests that ISO 14001 certification contributes to good ESMS quality but not necessarily to a good ESE success rating, which entails compliance with other IFC requirements as well.[23] In some cases, export customers required ISO 14001 certification, but IEG found that implementation of the standard had deteriorated.

*ISO 14001 certification contributes to a good ESMS, but not necessarily to ESE success.*

Currently, emissions in client ESMS frameworks and reports are expressed in concentrations (such as milligrams per liter). This does not provide sufficient information on pollution loads, as it is important to understand specific and annual emission levels—for example, kilograms of sulfur dioxide ($SO_2$) and carbon dioxide ($CO_2$) per ton of product, and tons per year. It is especially important to track $CO_2$ emissions in IFC portfolio projects to gauge their impact on climate change and assess carbon shadow costs. IFC has recently started a $CO_2$ tracking program, but its results are not yet available. IFC and the World Bank Group should also develop procedures to valuate ecosystems with cost/benefit analysis and make use of life cycle assessments in appraising critical projects.

***IFC's environmental work quality at appraisal and supervision***

Ratings of ESHS work quality are available for 118 non-FI and 56 FI projects (based on XPSR evaluations and case study sample projects). Analysis of these ratings shows that IFC's environmental appraisal was good for both groups, but supervision quality of the FI portfolio was much lower.[24] The questions used for the ESHS work quality evaluation are shown in appendix A.

Ratings for IFC work quality at appraisal were high (a success rate of more than 80 percent) for FI projects, mainly because the generic requirements for those projects are straightforward and usually have been diligently translated to project documents. The data show a downturn in the supervision quality of FI projects after 2004; that hit a low point (47 percent) in fiscal 2006. A potential contributing factor to this was the substantial growth in the volume of FI business without a corresponding increase in environmental and social review capacity.

Until 2006, IFC had only one environmental specialist dedicated to FI supervision. This has now changed, and IFC has improved its review and supervision procedures and increased its supervision resources to visit more FIs and their high-risk subprojects.[25]

***Lessons drawn from investment projects***

There appear to be five main reasons to explain high ESE success rates:

- IFC's role and contribution in helping real sector and FI clients develop and implement good ESMSs[26]
- Client commitment to good environmental management
- Advanced technology, often provided by international sponsors
- Export to markets that demand "green" products and environmental certification
- Good local ESHS laws and regulations and their proper enforcement.

Based on the evaluation of the ESE of IFC investment projects, five key lessons emerge:

- It is important to stress the need for clients, especially in the FI sector, to develop and implement a solid ESMS based on the principle that sustainability is a part of their business success.
- It is essential to develop solid baseline and feasibility studies and establish performance indicators to better address project impacts.
- It is necessary to promote an early integration of process and pollution control system design and community engagement to provide environmentally, socially, and economically sound solutions.
- It is advisable to stress the need for independent environmental audits as an important part of the project completion tests.
- It is important to design good reporting templates, which help clients better benchmark project and FI subproject performance against IFC requirements and best industry practices and improve monitoring of environmental impacts. Only a limited number of clear and practical performance indicators is needed, to avoid irrelevant reporting.

***"Doing good": Evaluating IFC's stewardship in the private sector***

IFC's investment projects include "doing good" aspects, especially where they have achieved excellent ESE ratings, improved clients' environmental management and worker health and safety, reduced pollution loads, significantly reduced resource and energy use, demonstrated leadership in an industry sector, or moved a market toward sustainability and achieved positive impacts beyond the project boundaries, as in the previously mentioned carbon black manufacturing project in Egypt.[27]

*IFC's environmental work quality at appraisal was good, but the supervision quality of FI projects was insufficient.*

IFC has developed Advisory Services over the past five years in the areas of environmental and social sustainability. In 2002, it also launched three Sustainable Business Assistance Program (SBAP) facilities that were transferred to the Sustainable Business Innovator team in 2006.[28] In addition, IFC has partnered with the Equator Banks and GEF (for which it has administered projects since 1992) and has cooperated with donors in environmental Advisory Services and carbon finance projects. Given their recent implementation, evaluation evidence on these initiatives is limited, but some preliminary findings can be advanced.

***IFC Advisory Services***

With regard to the effectiveness of IFC Advisory Services, the midterm evaluation of the three SBAP facilities by an external consulting company (Triple Line Consulting 2005) in 2004 was generally positive. Results concerning project impact, however, were mixed. The review noted that all the facilities engaged in various forms of capacity building, with the Sustainable Financial Markets Facility (SFMF) providing a good model. SFMF demonstrated that capacity building starts by raising awareness, followed by training through the development of local partners and identification of local service providers.

*Five factors generally account for higher ESE success rates.*

The challenge for innovative programs is to remain focused and relevant to mainstream activities without losing a strategic approach to rapidly evolving markets. Where there was direct collaboration with Private Enterprise Partnership programs, results were good.

*A midterm evaluation of SBAP facilities was positive, but impact was mixed.*

This review found that SBAP facilities were effective at innovating and developing new services. Examples include support for the creation of the BOVESPA sustainability index to track the corporate social responsibility performance of Brazilian firms; the sustainable energy programs with innovative financing products that were mainstreamed into the Investment Department; and IFC clients starting from Hungary in 1998 (the Commercializing Energy Efficiency Finance Program) and expanding thereafter to the Baltic countries, Czech Republic, Slovak Republic, Russia, and China.

The transfer of SBAP to the Sustainable Business Innovator team is expected to lead to greater emphasis on projects that better fit IFC's business strategy, but keep in mind donor requirements. As with other Advisory Services, SBAP facilities have sought to report on ESHS impacts but with varying results, as project objectives were not consistently established at the design stage.

The new 2006 procedure for environmental and social review of projects requires review and monitoring of Advisory Service projects when requested by the IFC Advisory Services Department. This addresses the information gap found in the external evaluation of SBAP projects.

IEG's 2007 pilot evaluation of 198 IFC Advisory Services projects with sufficient information for development effectiveness evaluation and ratings included 24 environmental and social sustainability business line projects with total funding of $3 million. The development effectiveness success rate of these projects was 63 percent, lower than the average 69 percent for all evaluated Advisory Services projects. It was difficult to assess their impacts.

*An IEG evaluation of 24 environmental and social business line Advisory Services projects found a 63 percent development effectiveness success rate and difficulties with assessing impacts.*

The pilot evaluation made an overall assessment of development effectiveness based on strategic relevance, efficiency, output achievement, outcome achievement, and impact achievement. The evaluation used a four-point rating scale (unsatisfactory, partly unsatisfactory, satisfactory, and excellent), and the success rate indicated the share of satisfactory and excellent ratings. The objectives in 24 environmentally and socially sustainable business line projects with sufficient information for development effectiveness evaluation were scattered and included development and implementation of environment-oriented training programs and energy programs, environmental assessments, various technical and economical feasibility studies and market assessments to support potential investments, and environmental products and services. In most cases (22 of 24), it was too soon or impossible to assess projects' impacts and rate them.

#### *Global sustainability—GEF-funded projects*

IFC collaboration with the GEF provides mutual benefits: (1) direct access through IFC to FIs; (2) use of IFC's private sector expertise; and (3) the potential for replication of successful business models within IFC investment departments. IFC works closely with the GEF to increase private sector involvement in GEF projects. These projects support IFC's strategic priorities and permit IFC to explore innovative solutions with a view to mainstreaming proven methodologies and business cases.

In 2005, IFC commissioned a consulting group to review its GEF program. The consultant's report (le Groupe-conseil baastal Group 2006) included a review of 21 GEF-funded projects with commitments greater than $15 million, approved since January 2000. Project effectiveness was assessed on the creation of environmentally sustainable private sector investment, development of commercially viable environmental products and services, reduction of risk for private sector participation in environmentally friendly businesses, and global environmental benefits.

The review concluded that the overall effectiveness and achievement of objectives of IFC/GEF initiatives was satisfactory, with mixed project outcomes.[29] Regarding effectiveness of GEF projects' design and implementation process, a GEF Evaluation Office study (GEF 2006) revealed internal inefficiencies in the GEF activity cycle.

The average elapsed time from pipeline entry to approval (effectiveness) in all IFC projects from 1991 to January 2006 was very long—35 months—and the activity cycle was not cost-effective.[30]

IFC's experience in photovoltaic market initiatives demonstrates constraints in sustainable technology transfer and market transformation toward renewable energy. IFC has invested in the photovoltaic market since 1989 and managed five GEF-funded solar photovoltaic initiatives.[31] Although these programs have been responsible for the installation of more than 80,000 solar home systems, they have been less successful from a financial standpoint, because they have not resulted in significant market transformation or a sizeable number of financially sustainable businesses.

For example, in one Photovoltaic Market Transformation Initiative (PVMTI) project in Kenya, fewer than 100 solar home systems of a planned 10,000 were installed because of market constrains and inefficient project design and financing structure.[32] However, with 24 solar photovoltaic initiatives in more than 20 developing countries, the World Bank Group has gathered ample experience and learned lessons to improve future performance. With rising oil prices, photovoltaic is increasingly attractive compared, for example, with diesel generators and kerosene lamps.[33]

#### *Partnership with the Equator Principle FIs*

IFC has made a significant effort to initiate and develop the Equator Principles[34] to be used in project finance activities of international commercial banks in emerging markets. It is too early to evaluate the impact of these efforts. The number of Equator Principle financial institutions (EPFIs) has increased steadily from 10, reaching 60 in March 2008. Among these are many banks from emerging markets, including four in Brazil and one in South Africa.

The Equator Principles have introduced consistent requirements that are generally easier to implement, saving time and costs on sensitive projects. For EPFIs, the incentive for sponsors to shop for loans based on differing environmental and social criteria should now be much reduced. Over time, EPFIs could help raise project environmental and social performance globally and move other agencies and publicly funded financiers to adopt them.

*An IFC review of its GEF programs found satisfactory effectiveness overall, but with mixed project outcomes.*

IFC worked closely with the Export Credits and Guarantees Working Group of the OECD to harmonize standards used in private sector, limited recourse projects. Through the new common approaches announced in June 2007, the 32 export credit agencies of the OECD countries now benchmark projects against IFC's Performance Standards and the new environmental health and safety (EHS) guidelines.

*The principles are advantageous for sponsors and for banks and may help raise environmental and social performance.*

The potential leveraging power of the Equator Principles is substantial. One journal article observed that total Equator Principle debt financing in emerging markets in the first half of 2006 was $28 billion (93 percent of a $30 billion total; "First Half Review" 2006). This was achieved by EPFI financing of $10 billion, together with $18 billion leveraged from non-Equator banks. The implication is that most project financing to the private sector is now being carried out in some form under the Equator Principles.

Increasingly, EPFIs report their actions and provide information on their Web sites, but no independent evaluation has yet been reported on performance in meeting IFC Performance Standards. According to a BankTrack report (BankTrack 2007), of the 47 EPFIs that had adopted the Equator Principles more than one year before the survey, 9 institutions (19 percent) met the minimum requirements and 19 (40 percent) exceeded them. A total of 19 institutions (40 percent) did not meet the minimum requirements. Because there is no formal control of actual performance, adoption of the Equator Principles may result in free-rider problems. Thus, good implementation is crucial for the reputation of the principles.

*Most project financing to emerging markets now appears to be carried out under the Equator Principles.*

Although IFC is not an enforcing agency of the Equator Principles, it acts as a resource institution to the EPFIs and provides guidance on sustainability practices, including through an annual community of learning event hosted by IFC. Based on discussions among EPFIs and with IFC on reporting and governance issues, a number of changes have been made (for example, a new reporting guideline that an EPFI should follow within two years of Equator Principle adoption, and more transparency on the Equator Principle governance structure). Third-party assurance of Equator Principle implementation is currently optional among EPFIs, though leading EPFIs use external assurance companies in the process of finalizing their sustainability reports.

### Conclusion

Assessing the impact of IFC's operations on the environment over the past two decades is difficult and complex. One part of this task is assessing the performance and impacts at the project level using the IEG methodology that was established in 1996 and further developed since 2003. In this respect, this evaluation shows positive findings both in investment and Advisory Service projects and in other areas of concern. However, important performance gaps persist in investment projects in Africa and in some industry sectors, and there is still insufficient information on achieving expected impacts with some environment-oriented Advisory Services.[35]

*IFC faces challenges with its decentralization, with FI projects, and with implementing more effective safeguards and supporting good regulations and governance.*

IFC also faces challenges in successfully implementing the new Global/Local Strategy, helping FIs improve sustainability in subprojects with environmental and social risks, and establishing and implementing more effective safeguards. It also faces challenges related to supporting good regulations and governance—together with the Bank—in large, high-biodiversity regions that have weak environmental governance, as in the Brazilian Amazon region, Indonesia, and parts of Africa.[36]

*MIGA hired its first environmental specialist in 1998 and, in 2002, adopted its own versions of safeguard policies.*

The Equator Principles have the potential to promote positive environmental and social impacts in private sector finance to the developing world. However, to understand and evaluate the actual effects of this initiative, the EPFIs will need to show greater transparency and better reporting, which are also a fundamental factors for their credibility.[37]

The more difficult but extremely relevant part of evaluating the impact of IFC operations on the environment is monitoring and assessing the aggregate and systemic impact of IFC-supported investments, clients, and Advisory Services on local and national environmental sustainability. This demands that longer-term analysis and strategic implications of its operations in relation to the environment be clearly set out and understood to ensure that IFC and the World Bank Group as a whole—as well as their clients—comprehend the broader, systemic, and longer-term consequences of individual interventions and try to avoid potentially dangerous directions.

## Assessing MIGA Performance

MIGA's Convention and Operations Regulations require it to support projects consistent with the host country's laws, regulations, and stated development priorities. The agency's policies and guidelines require that all the investments it facilitates through its guarantee program be carried out in an environmentally responsible manner. To this end, projects that it insures must comply with applicable MIGA environmental guidelines and safeguard policies and guidelines.

Since its inception in fiscal 1990, MIGA used World Bank safeguard policies to assess its projects and used IFC staff for the environmental review of its projects.[38] MIGA hired its first environmental specialist in fiscal 1998, and soon thereafter, the Board approved its Environmental Assessment and Disclosure Policies (1999). In 2002, MIGA adopted—on an interim basis—its own versions of the issue-specific safeguard policies, adapted to its business.

MIGA adopted the new Policy on Social and Environmental Sustainability and Performance Standards in 2007. These new standards superseded its 1999 policy, which capitalized on the work done by IFC and was intended to minimize client confusion working with Bank Group entities. Although supportive of MIGA's formal incorporation of social and environmental sustainability in its core business, IEG recognizes the challenges of implementing the new policies. They require certain MIGA clients to do a baseline assessment and periodic monitoring of impacts on local communities for projects where such impacts are expected to be significant. For the first time, the policies also cover environmental performance of MIGA's financial sector projects.

MIGA also requires compliance with EHS guidelines (as prepared by IFC), linked to implementation of Performance Standards 2, 3, and 4, as well as compliance with the relevant IFC Industry and Sector Guidelines. MIGA needs to ascertain that each project it insures complies with or will comply with the more stringent guidelines, whether they are the host country's or MIGA's.

### *MIGA guarantee portfolio*

Between fiscal 1990 and 2007, MIGA issued guarantees for 510 projects, for a total exposure of $16.7 billion (this is a total figure, not referring to the environment per se). The volume of new guarantees increased until 2001 and has leveled off since.

*MIGA adopted performance standards and a new disclosure policy in 2007.*

Latin America and the Caribbean and Europe and Central Asia have attracted the highest number of guarantees (figure 4.4). The countries where MIGA has had the largest cumulative exposures are (in order of importance) Brazil, Russia, Argentina, Peru, and Turkey.

One-third of MIGA projects (35 percent of exposure) have been in the financial sector (figure 4.5). Of the productive sector projects, the largest share has been for infrastructure (23 percent of projects, or 32 percent of exposure), followed by manufacturing (20 percent of projects and 11 percent of exposure). Oil, gas, and mining together have accounted for 8 percent of projects and 14 percent of exposure.

More than two-thirds of MIGA's nonfinancial sector projects have been Category B (see box 4.2 or the glossary for an explanation of risk categories). Fewer than 15 percent have been Category A. Of the 115 nonfinancial sector projects active in MIGA's portfolio as of June 30, 2007, 19

*More than two-thirds of nonfinancial sector projects have been Category B, fewer than 15 percent Category A.*

**Figure 4.4: MIGA Portfolio Composition, by Region**

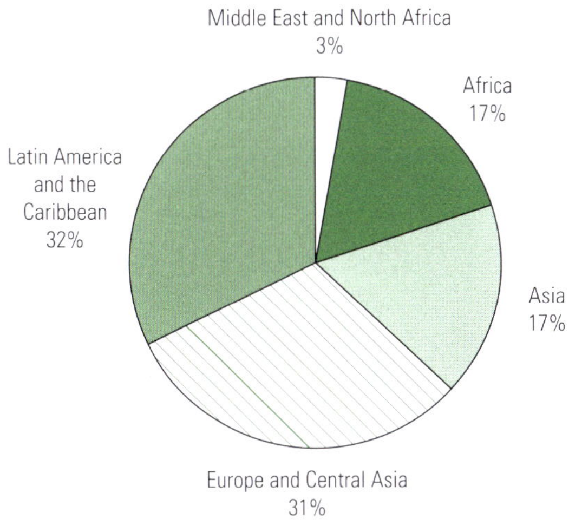


*Source:* MIGA database.

**Figure 4.5: MIGA Portfolio Composition, by Sector**

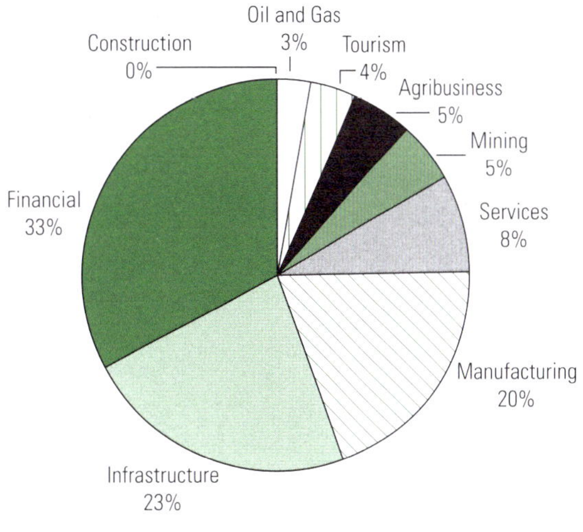


*Source:* MIGA database.

*IEG assessed project outcomes for 29 projects.*

were Category A, 78 Category B, and 18 Category C. The Category A projects were mostly in infrastructure (9 projects), extractive industries (7), and a few large manufacturing projects (3). In addition, all regular financial sector projects have been Category C in the past.[39] According to MIGA policies, Category C projects in the financial sector do not require further appraisal or monitoring, apart from an initial screening.

### "Doing no harm": Environmental standards for guarantee projects

IEG has evaluated the environmental and social effects of a sample of guarantee projects by assessing their performance in meeting applicable MIGA environmental and social requirements and standards at both the time of Board approval and evaluation. A set of criteria reflects safeguard policy requirements and the steps involved in meeting them. The criteria differ between approval and evaluation. For example, at approval, IEG assesses the adequacy and appropriateness of an EMS, and at evaluation it assesses the implementation of the EMS. The findings are based on a sample of 69 guarantee projects approved by MIGA's Board between 1989 and 2006.[40]

**Figure 4.6: Comparison of Performance Ratings at Approval and Evaluation (MIGA Category A and B projects)**

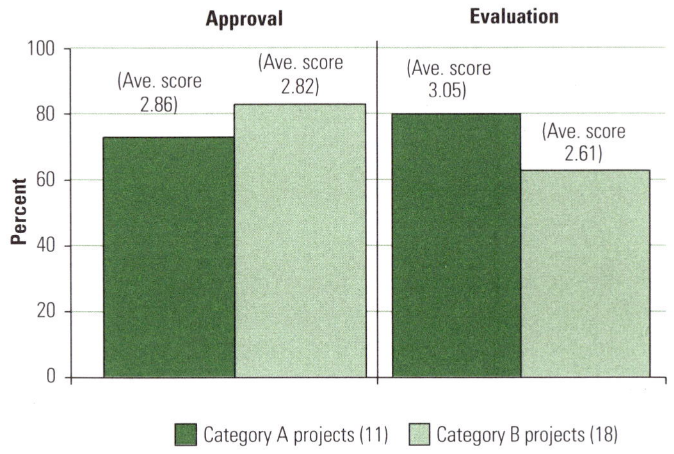


*Source:* IEG database.

Project outcomes were reviewed for 29 projects; 18 mature projects were evaluated ex post[41] and 11 were reviewed for the previous IEG extractive industries evaluation (IEG-World Bank, -IFC, and -MIGA 2003). These 29 projects were in the following sectors: infrastructure (8); oil, gas, and mining (11); and agribusiness, manufacturing, and tourism (10). Eleven of the projects were classified as Category A[42] and 18 as Category B (see box 4.2).[43] In addition, IEG reviewed 14 nonfinancial sector projects underwritten between 1993 and 2006 for the Russia country case study. All projects were evaluated in reference to MIGA's 1999 environmental assessment policy and 2002 issue-specific safeguard policy and current guidelines. (See appendix A for a summary of IEG-MIGA's methodology.)

### Performance of MIGA projects at Board approval and evaluation

Performance in meeting applicable requirements and standards varies significantly between Category A and B projects. Among evaluated Category A projects, 73 percent were substantially consistent with MIGA's performance requirements regarding the quality of EAPs when evaluated at the time of approval, compared with 83 percent of evaluated Category B projects (figure 4.6). However, at evaluation (or during implementation), 80 percent of Category A projects met MIGA's performance requirements in implementing the EAPs, compared with 63 percent of Category B projects.

Most of the Category A projects (especially in extractive industries) are complex and highly visible. Therefore, the guarantee holder, its senior lenders, or the bilateral financing or guarantee agencies typically are more sensitive to the need to identify and mitigate environmental and social impacts. For the most part, Category A projects also received greater attention from MIGA.

Category B projects are less homogeneous in the nature, scale, and complexity of the environmental and social issues involved. Thus, although many MIGA Category B projects can have quite significant local impacts, they do not attract the same attention as the larger projects. EAPs are generally in accordance with MIGA's requirements at the time of appraisal, but their implementation sometimes falls short of plans. In addition, most Category B projects are not on the list of sensitive/risky operations that would normally be visited by MIGA environmental staff.[44]

#### Key issues at Board approval for Category B projects

Almost all 16 Category B projects[45] had adequate EAPs at the time of Board approval (94 percent), but only 56 percent implemented those plans (figure 4.7). Areas of weakness for Category B projects at Board approval included inadequate analysis of feasible project alternatives, inadequate attention to setting up of an ESMS, and deficiencies in the way the issue-specific safeguards were applied.

#### Key issues at evaluation for Category B projects

For Category B projects with shortcomings in meeting MIGA policies and guidelines at evaluation, environmental and social requirements seemed to be unclear to guarantee holders, as were many of the issue-specific safeguards. This may have been because investor-clients were less likely to be involved in management of their investment projects. Lack of requirements for public consultation and disclosure for Category B projects under the previous policies (disclosure requirements changed in the new MIGA Policy on Social and Environmental Sustainability) meant that people affected by a project had fewer opportunities to voice concerns. Only 61 percent of evaluated projects set up an EMS by the time of Board approval; this figure increased to 88 percent at evaluation. One evaluated project in the extractive industries showed that the early establishment of such a system is critical to help reduce potential conflicts with communities and adverse environmental impacts at the start of the project. These are areas where investors seek substantive advice from MIGA.

*Performance varies significantly between Category A and Category B projects.*

Shortcomings in meeting MIGA's Environmental Health and Safety and Pollution Prevention Guidelines and host country environmental standards have been the greatest weakness in

*Performance suffered in Category B projects when guarantee holders were unclear about the requirements.*

**Figure 4.7: Selected Safeguard Performance Criteria at Approval and Evaluation (Category B projects)**

| Criterion | Applicable to (no. of projects) | Addressed substantially or higher (% of projects) | |
|---|---|---|---|
| Environmental health and safety guidelines or host country regulations comprehensively addressed | 16 | Approval | 88 |
| | | Evaluation | 50 |
| Adequate Environmental Action Plan proposed and implemented | 16 | Approval | 94 |
| | | Evaluation | 56 |
| Project investor's environmental management system adequate | 16 | Approval | 61 |
| | | Evaluation | 88 |

*Source:* MIGA data.

*The most common weakness was in meeting EHS Pollution Prevention and Health Safety Guidelines.*

safeguard performance at evaluation (affecting half of the Category B projects; see figure 4.7). Weak implementation of Environmental Management Plans (EMPs) or EAPs (only 61 percent of projects) is also an issue at evaluation. In some cases, MIGA was unaware that projects failed to meet its guidelines, because there were no requirements in its former policies or procedures (or in most Contracts of Guarantee) to report annually on implementation of EMPs/EAPs or on environmental or social performance.[46]

*Most recent projects adhered to requirements at entry.*

*Quality at entry of recent MIGA projects.* In recent projects assessed by IEG for quality at entry (underwritten by MIGA between January 2005 and June 2006), the environmental and social review during underwriting (or approval process) conformed to MIGA requirements. Eighty-six percent of assessed projects conformed to MIGA's review procedures to a satisfactory level at entry (100 percent of Category A and C projects, but only 82 percent of Category B projects were adequately assessed). All infrastructure and agribusiness, manufacturing, and services projects (other than those underwritten under the Small Investment Program) were adequately processed by MIGA with regard to EHS issues during underwriting.

*There were shortcomings in the EHS assessment of projects under the Small Investment Program.*

Small Investment Program projects are required to adhere to the same MIGA policies and review procedures for their environmental category as regular MIGA guarantee operations, but only 70 percent of them met MIGA requirements to a satisfactory level at Board approval.[47] IEG found that there is room to improve MIGA's monitoring, especially for Category B projects.

#### *"Doing good": Stewardship, environmental governance, and sustainability*

MIGA does not have a strategy or business line to actively promote free-standing environmentally beneficial guarantee projects. It has only recently begun to move toward environmental stewardship. The 2007 Policy and Performance Standards are an important milestone, as they spell out MIGA's vision to implement sustainability in its operations. IEG evaluated MIGA's portfolio in Russia[48] to examine the agency's potential to address issues beyond safeguard performance and to provide answers to questions regarding improvement in environmental quality through stewardship, environmental governance, addressing global environmental sustainability, and effectiveness of partnerships with other stakeholders.

#### *Improving environmental quality: Stewardship*

The environmental stewardship mandate expressed in MIGA's policy aims to add value by helping private sector clients go beyond the strict interpretation of MIGA's safeguard policies and guidelines to demonstrate best practice. It aims to influence other investors and financial institutions to follow MIGA clients' example or to work with investors and other financial institutions committed to "doing good" and going beyond MIGA's safeguards. This also requires that MIGA allocate its limited resources to projects without the participation of multilateral or bilateral development partners. MIGA also has an opportunity to work within the Berne Union (the association of investment insurers and export credit agencies) as a standard setter in environmental requirements within the investment insurance industry.

Examples from MIGA's portfolio in Russia illustrate the beneficial impacts it can have on projects it guarantees when it or its investor-clients take a stewardship approach. MIGA's forestry safeguard policy was instrumental in ensuring that timber for a pulp and paper mill was obtained from forests managed in a sustainable way and not from protected and ecologically sensitive areas. The mill involved is among Russia's largest pulp and paper mills, so the impact of its actions was expected to have a positive demonstration effect throughout the national forest industry.

#### *Promoting environmental governance*

In cooperating with development partners, MIGA ensures that (1) its clients have established and adequately trained staff for their Environmental

Health and Safety Management Systems for project construction and operation; (2) contractors working on the project also have such systems in place to implement EMPs and EAPs under the environmental assessment policy; (3) clients provide periodic monitoring reports to MIGA on safeguard compliance; and (4) in extractive industry projects, clients report on payments to host governments and continue consultation with stakeholders affected by the project.

***Global environmental sustainability***

In addition to its commitment to implement international conventions for ozone-depleting substances, persistent organic pollutants, transboundary movement of hazardous wastes, and so forth, and as the World Bank Group increases its focus on issues such as climate change, MIGA needs to consider steps to ensure that global greenhouse gas issues are addressed in its guarantees. It can do this by (1) promoting and providing guarantee support to Clean Development Mechanism and Joint Implementation project investors in its member countries under the Kyoto Protocol; (2) evaluating incremental greenhouse gas emissions from investments guaranteed by MIGA and refusing to provide guarantee support if these are not in line with or better than industry standards; and (3) advising its investors to join voluntary schemes to monitor and report their greenhouse gas emissions.

A few evaluated MIGA projects in Russia have demonstrated their potential to support global environmental sustainability. One project had a corporate strategy to reduce greenhouse gas emissions from its operations worldwide and is promoting initiatives to improve energy efficiency in cooling and refrigeration systems and to switch from hydrofluorocarbon refrigerants and ammonia to "natural refrigerants" such as $CO_2$. Another project, initiated in 1997, insures investments intended to reduce greenhouse gas emissions from pulp and paper mills, such as by using waste wood in boilers instead of natural gas, improving energy efficiency, and reducing water consumption. An aluminum recovery project also potentially reduced greenhouse gas emissions, as energy use in secondary aluminum production is only 5 percent of that for primary aluminum production. One MIGA guarantee project would now qualify for carbon revenues if the processed steel slag had been reused as a substitute for cement in cement/slag mixtures.

*As a matter of policy, MIGA aims to encourage its clients to go beyond strict interpretation of its safeguard policies and guidelines.*

***Partnerships with other stakeholders***

Since MIGA began operating in Russia, it has done so in consonance with priorities identified in the Bank Group's Russia CAS. Moreover, several MIGA guarantee projects have been undertaken jointly with IFC and the European Bank for Reconstruction and Development (EBRD). Half of the projects in Russia that were reviewed for this evaluation have involved other multilateral or bilateral development partners such as IFC, EBRD, and the Overseas Private Investment Corporation.

*MIGA projects in Russia demonstrate the potential of guarantees to support global environmental sustainability.*

Although MIGA carries out due diligence on EHS matters at the project approval stage, it may rely heavily on an environmental impact assessment and other documentation submitted to other development partners.[49] In the past, MIGA has also relied on its development partners to monitor project compliance with its safeguard policies and EHS guidelines or similar standards (such as those of the European Union in the case of the EBRD) and on the host government to monitor performance with regard to its EHS standards.

Until recently, MIGA required a guarantee holder to report on project compliance in only a few cases. MIGA's view traditionally has been that its Contract of Guarantee covers its EHS obligations by stipulating that the project must meet relevant MIGA and/or host country standards and that a contract can be cancelled if those conditions are not met. IEG-MIGA has indicated in recent annual reports and special studies[50] that MIGA has scaled up project compliance monitoring since 2005, but more effective monitoring is required. In ex post evaluations IEG

*Half of the projects reviewed in Russia involved other multilateral or bilateral partners.*

has found that some projects have been out of compliance with MIGA EHS requirements for most of their duration.

The key partner for MIGA in all its projects was a majority equity investor, which in most cases is the guarantee holder. Where the guarantee holder is a minor partner or a third-party financier, MIGA holds little leverage over the major investor to ensure that the project meets MIGA safeguard policies and EHS guidelines. In all but one of the projects in Russia, the guarantee holder was a major foreign investor. Where other multilateral or bilateral agencies were involved, majority investors were responsive to their demands to meet EHS requirements. In one case MIGA made special requirements prior to project approval beyond those necessary to meet host country or shareholder demands. The results were positive and showed that MIGA can directly influence EHS outcomes to the benefit of the investor and the general public.

### Implementation of previous IEG recommendations

Previous IEG-MIGA evaluations have identified 12 areas in which MIGA needed to improve its environmental and social performance.[51] During the 2007 quality-at-entry review, which covered 33 projects underwritten between January 2005 and March 2007, IEG assessed MIGA's implementation record on each of these issues covered by the recommendations where they were applicable.[52] In relation to IEG's past recommendations, analysis of environmental issues in the majority of recent projects met requirements adequately. In particular, MIGA has made substantial progress in strengthening the upstream inclusion of environmental and social issues in underwriting; requiring field visits to Category A projects during due diligence; ensuring that projects had prepared and agreed on resettlement and community development plans before Board approval of the guarantee; making more effective use of its Contract of Guarantee to identify applicable safeguard policies and guidelines, and requirements for remedial action (for example, EMPs and Indigenous Peoples Plans).

*MIGA has made progress on implementing previous IEG recommendations.*

Areas of continuing and important concern were setting up EMSs prior to Board approval, including reporting requirements on environmental and social issues in MIGA's Contract of Guarantee, and harmonizing MIGA environmental and social polices for Category B projects with those of IFC. Appendix B shows the level of implementation for the 12 areas.

### Conclusions

MIGA's main product with an impact on the environment is its guarantee against political risks for private sector investments. This review of the environmental soundness of MIGA projects—according to performance in meeting policies and guidelines—shows that performance differed between Category A and B projects. At Board approval, 73 percent of Category A projects and 83 percent of Category B projects met the requirements and Performance Standards. At evaluation, 80 percent of Category A projects and only 63 percent of Category B projects did. Gaps were observed mainly in comprehensively addressing MIGA environmental and social guidelines and in implementing adequate EAPs.

Although MIGA does not have a business line to support projects intended to benefit the environment, it has the potential to improve environmental quality by assisting private sector clients to demonstrate best practice and to work with investors committed to "doing good." MIGA can promote environmental governance by ensuring that its clients establish and train staff for EMSs. Given the increasing focus on the impacts of growth on the environment, MIGA may also need to address issues of global environmental sustainability, including the promotion of environmentally beneficial projects.

MIGA needs to continue to make progress in (1) fully implementing the harmonization of assessment and monitoring requirements of Category B projects with those of IFC; (2) including EHS reporting requirements in Contracts of Guarantee; (3) requiring investors to set up an EMS on a timely basis, as appropriate in a project cycle; and (4) moving beyond safeguard performance to promoting sustainability in its projects. MIGA's 2007 Policy and Performance Standards are consistent with these concerns.

IEG encourages MIGA's full incorporation of social and environmental sustainability in its core business and recognizes that the challenges lie in the implementation of the new policies. Finally, while recognizing the progress in assessing and monitoring project-level environmental implications, MIGA needs to develop the means to assess, monitor, and evaluate the impacts of its projects on the broader systematic and longer-term consequences of individual interventions.

# Chapter 5

## Evaluation Highlights

- A clear mission, strong authorizing environment, and adequate operational capacity are essential for effective development aid.
- Among other factors that act as external constraints on the effectiveness of Bank Group and other donor environment-related support are inadequate knowledge, poor capacity, and lack of political will on the part of the client.
- Internal constraints include poor knowledge, inadequate capacity, and insufficient coordination on environmental challenges within the Bank Group.
- Greater effectiveness of Bank Group support for the environment requires better understanding of these constraints and firm action to overcome them.

Parched soil near the White Nile, in Khartoum, Sudan. Photo by Arne Hoel, courtesy of the World Bank Photo Library.

# Enhancing Bank Group Effectiveness

This evaluation finds that Bank Group support for the environment since 1990, although impressive in many ways and increasing over time, has had mixed results. The World Bank Group has positively influenced how client countries set their environmental priorities and how private firms address internal environmental management.

But the Bank Group has been less able to help countries address these priorities, in part because of the scale and complexity of the problems involved and varying client interest in receiving Bank Group support. Compliance efforts in both the public and private sectors still encounter political and capacity constraints and other hurdles. Mainstreaming has progressed over the past five years but has not yet fully occurred, and there have been shortfalls ranging from priority setting and compliance to helping public and private sector clients achieve sustainable results. Some of the reasons for this are under the control of the World Bank Group, but many are not.

## External Constraints on Effectiveness

Effective development support requires well-designed interventions and the willingness and ability to implement them. Regarding capacity, including with respect to the enabling environment for private investment, adequate knowledge of the problems to be addressed and their underlying causes and sufficient legal, financial, technical, and other means to address them are needed. Beyond these essentially political, knowledge, and capacity constraints in the country context, other exogenous factors can significantly limit a country's ability to achieve its environmental goals.

Even when actions to improve the environment have a positive impact, they can be overwhelmed by other forces, with a net effect on environmental quality that may be negligible or even negative. The Bombay Sewage Project in India is an example. Even though the submarine outfall built by the project did not adversely affect water quality at its end point, water quality along the beach continued to be poor because much of the population remained unconnected to the sewer system and continued to use storm drains running directly into the sea to dispose of domestic waste.

A second illustration is in Brazil. Even though the World Bank, using grant resources, has helped the Brazilian government put another 600,000 square kilometers of rainforest under stronger legal protection, deforestation in the Amazon region has continued at a high rate because of a combination of powerful market forces and only partially effective government enforcement.

These examples demonstrate two types of problems. In Mumbai, the implemented solution addressed only part of the problem. In Amazonia, the placement of a large additional area under protection did not alter the fundamental economic drivers of deforestation (cattle and soybean expansion in response to rising foreign and domestic demand). In short, even assuming that the political will, knowledge, and institutional capacity exist to address them, exogenous factors will limit both government and donor ability—including that of the Bank Group—to resolve tough environmental problems. In addition to population growth, economic expansion, and poverty, external factors such as market, governance, and institutional failures, as well as political instability and civil unrest in fragile states, contribute to environmental degradation or its perpetuation and are generally beyond donor control, at least in the short run.

*Important pressure factors on the environment include population expansion, economic growth, and poverty.*

### Knowledge and capacity limitations

Understanding the nature and causes of environmental problems is a precondition for effective solutions. Bank ESW and research have helped countries identify environmental challenges. The Bank has also made significant efforts to disseminate knowledge on the nature and causes of environmental problems at the country, Regional, and global levels, including many publications, workshops, and seminars, and several relevant WDRs. However, there seems to be some risk that the Bank's ability to continue this service may be declining.

Another significant effectiveness factor is country capacity for environment-related policy making and management at both the national and subnational levels. Experience in the case study countries reveals that such capacity is often uneven both among and within countries, especially large ones such as Brazil, China, India, and Russia. Most of the case study countries now possess good legal and regulatory frameworks for ENRM. Many also have reasonable levels of financial resources, in part because of support from external donors that have provided technical assistance for environmental governance as well, although this has often been less effective than desired.[1]

*Generation and dissemination of environment-related knowledge can help overcome the effects of these factors.*

But this raises questions of both sustainability and ownership—that is, what will happen when donor resources are no longer available or when they decrease significantly? And how strong is government commitment to address national environmental problems?

IFC and MIGA can help strengthen environmental performance in the projects they support through appraisal and monitoring of compliance with their own and host country policies and standards. However, in many developing countries, governments have limited budgets and difficulty enforcing environmental laws and regulations, establishing and collecting adequate fees and penalties for polluters, and fighting corruption. In this area where public and private sectors meet, a significant opportunity remains for more effective collaboration among the Bank, IFC, and MIGA.

Capacity is usually weaker in smaller and poorer developing countries and at the subnational level, especially in large federated countries.[2] In addition, Bank efforts to help countries build environmental management capacity have had uneven results. One reason is that capacity building is a long-term process, so it is unrealistic to expect a single five-year operation to be sufficient. In this regard, the Bank's approach to environmental institutional development in Brazil, Ghana, Madagascar, Russia, and Uganda through one or several operations over a 10-to-15-year period, although by no means problem-free, has been appropriate, especially when coupled with investments to protect and/or enhance environmental assets.

Country efforts to build capable ENRM institutions normally require a longer time horizon, so the Bank needs to support this process for an extended period.[3] In the case study countries, examples of wavering Bank support over time and shifting instruments (such as abandoning lending in favor of AAA in India in the late 1990s and early 2000s and switching from investment projects to PRSCs and other forms of budget support in Sub-Saharan Africa during the first part of the current decade) seem to indicate uneven Bank commitment to its approach. Responding to country demand, the Bank appears to have applied this lesson best in China, where the government has a clear sense of its priorities with respect to the environment[4] and the large number of follow-on projects is noteworthy.[5]

### Political commitment

Even with a reasonable level of institutional capacity, government efforts to address environmental priorities are unlikely to be effective if they are not backed by strong political support.[6] The critical importance of this factor cannot be overemphasized. The case study countries appear to fall along a continuum of central government commitment to environmental improvement objectives, with China at one end and Russia at the other. These differences are noteworthy because neither of these countries currently needs World Bank financial support, although both have increasingly turned to IFC and MIGA.[7]

India's situation is similar to China's: it is growing very rapidly,[8] which is increasing pressures on its environment and natural resource base and those of its neighbors.[9] The Indian government is aware of the need to confront environmental problems more effectively but seems less capable of doing so. This inability may be caused by a combination of institutional capacity limitations and insufficient political ability to resolve certain issues, such as cross-state water allocation and water quality concerns, which are becoming increasingly serious (World Bank 2005c). Civil society in India, on the other hand, is more proactive than in China and has had a positive impact on enforcement of environmental legislation, especially in relation to urban air quality. But civil society is becoming more active in China as well (Turner and Zhi 2006).

Brazil is growing less rapidly than the other three large countries. Despite rising public awareness and strong civil society support for improved environmental governance, federal and state government effectiveness in addressing issues such as deforestation has been weaker than in China and India, as suggested by aggregate indicators on forest cover change over the past 15 years.

*Capacity development involves a long time horizon, but wavering Bank support and shifting instruments may have detracted from such efforts.*

The same is true for all four of the Sub-Saharan African case study countries; in Uganda and Ghana the deforestation rates were particularly high.[10] More generally, Egypt and the four Sub-Saharan African case study countries also appear to fall in the intermediate range in terms of commitment, with Madagascar and Uganda presently toward the more active end, and Ghana and Senegal at the other.

In all five countries, however, promoting growth is clearly the top priority and there is strong interest in attracting foreign investment from both other countries (especially China, but also India in the case of Sub-Saharan Africa [see Broadman 2007]) and the private sector. This can result in significant (perceived and actual) tradeoffs between growth and the environment.

*Country ownership is as essential as adequate knowledge and institutional capacity.*

## Internal Constraints on Effectiveness

Capacity (including knowledge) and authorizing environmental constraints also condition effectiveness within the World Bank Group, assuming that the institutional mission in relation to the environment is well understood and accepted by all relevant internal stakeholders. However, even this is not necessarily the case, either within or across the different parts of the Bank Group. Different sector groupings may pursue different agendas in the same country, and these may or may be not fully consistent with an overall World Bank Group environmental assistance strategy for that country. Or, as is more often the case, no such cross-sectoral or institution-wide strategy exists or has full buy-in from the various units that would need to help implement it.[11]

*Knowledge, capacity, and authorizing environment constraints exist within the Bank Group as well.*

Although the 2001 Environment Strategy refers mainly to the actions of the World Bank, IFC and MIGA are mentioned in the sections on the private sector and environment. The preface acknowledges, however, that the different parts of the World Bank Group "are legally and financially independent and have different sets of owners and clients, structures and mandates, staffs and toolkits. Accordingly, specific operational and institutional implications differ and need to be spelled out separately" (World Bank 2001b, preface) These differences are reflected in the fact that IFC and MIGA were not active participants in formulation of the 2001 Strategy and thus have been guided more by their clients' needs and their own internal goals and strategies than by the strategy itself.

### Knowledge and capacity constraints

One challenge for the Bank Group is to properly understand environmental problems and their causes. In seeking to do this, the Bank needs to clearly comprehend the ecological, institutional, social, economic, and political context in which its operations are being implemented, which has not always been the case.[12]

*The Bank Group has not always understood the context of some of the projects it has supported.*

There is also a persisting need for the World Bank Group to better incorporate what it has learned from its own experience into its new lending operations and analytical and policy-related activities. And it needs to make a greater effort to learn from the experience of development partners and other agencies that are engaged in environment-related activities. Both internal knowledge networks (communities of practice and so forth) and interchanges with external partners should be strengthened in this regard.

*Internal knowledge dissemination has not been sufficient, perhaps contributing to repetition of less effective approaches.*

Dissemination of relevant experience across operational Regions appears to have been problematic in some cases. Even though the Bank has had successful land and watershed management projects in several Regions, the approach has not been adequately incorporated into its rural development operations in Sub-Saharan Africa, where natural capital accounts for a relatively large share of national wealth (World Bank 2006f). A second example involves the use of credit lines for industrial pollution abatement, the relative ineffectiveness of which in environmental terms[13] has led to their discontinuation by the Bank in Brazil, China, and India. Yet this mechanism continues to be used in Egypt.[14]

Why does the Bank continue to follow this approach? One possible explanation is that the unsatisfactory experience in other Regions has not been conveyed sufficiently well.

IFC and MIGA have similar gaps in their knowledge about project and company performance in meeting environmental requirements and standards. IFC did not systematically establish environmental, social, health, and safety objectives at appraisal for advisory service projects until 2006, nor did it supervise or evaluate these projects from an ESHS perspective. Reporting on environmental performance is particularly problematic for IFC's FIs and for projects in Sub-Saharan Africa. MIGA's analysis of environmental issues during appraisal in most recent projects met its requirements during underwriting. But IEG also found cases where MIGA was unaware that operations were out of compliance. In addition, apart from initial screening, MIGA does not appraise or monitor Category C projects, which in the past included all financial sector operations.

### Moving beyond the country and sector levels

Another internal constraint is the way in which the Bank has tended to approach environmental problems. The most common approaches to ENRM challenges are not always sufficiently holistic or strategic. This has both a sectoral and a spatial dimension and is associated in part with the way the Bank is structured into country management units (CMUs) and sector departments.

CMUs understandably focus on a particular country or countries. However, environmental problems are often transboundary in nature. To be fully effective in such cases, Bank support requires cooperation across CMUs. This is not always easy, however, because cross-boundary issues are less likely to be high on the priority list of either the CMU or the country. They are also frequently more difficult to address institutionally and politically than problems that fall entirely within domestic or CMU spans of control.[15]

As a result, these issues are often addressed through Regional or global programs that are not always well implemented, in part because of weak ownership in the affected countries and the respective CMUs (IEG-World Bank 2004, 2007a). The Bank needs to find better ways of working across CMUs to somewhat offset its strong country focus in order to develop and implement more effective transboundary solutions.[16]

An increasingly important transboundary concern is how to address the international environmental impacts of rising agricultural and natural resource trade and the growing illegal timber trade. The sustained, rapid growth of some developing economies is generating significant demand for natural resources, and rising shares of these resources are being supplied from Sub-Saharan Africa, South America, and elsewhere, as well as from neighboring countries. Along with the gains in trade, these trends, in the absence of accompanying actions, can result in large and significant environmental impacts.

The environmental footprint of these and numerous OECD countries now extends well beyond their national boundaries. Although the Bank has attempted to address some of these issues—for example, through the FLEG initiative (see chapter 3)—little has yet been done to deal with their implications, and awareness about them among CMUs seems to be low. IFC has attempted to address trade sustainability issues to the extent that trade finance transactions follow exclusion list requirements.

More generally, given the demand-driven nature of the Bank's programs at the country level, both local and, especially, global public goods such as environmental quality and sustainability tend to receive insufficient priority. This key finding of an earlier IEG evaluation of Bank experience with global programs (IEG-World Bank 2004)[17] is reinforced by the present assessment, particularly with regard to the integration of Regional and global environmental concerns into country programs. Addressing this continuing constraint will require strong leadership at the corporate, Regional, and country levels.

*The way environmental problems are often approached should be revisited.*

Issues and constraints regarding cross-sector management unit collaboration are similar. The 2006 merger of two former networks—Environmentally and Socially Sustainable Development and the infrastructure portions of the former Finance, Private Sector, and Infrastructure Network—has the potential to help better integrate the environment both in the new anchor departments and in the Regions, although management of such large units will be a significant challenge. But there is also a risk that environmental concerns—with the exception of climate change—may become less visible in the Bank now that those primarily responsible for them are part of a much larger network. In any case, breaking down the old silos will require adjustments in attitudes and behaviors by managers and staff, many of whom may continue to approach their work from a largely sectoral perspective.[18]

*Addressing transboundary issues is a challenge given the Bank's strong country focus.*

Although the recent experience in elaborating the Bank's Clean Energy Investment Framework is a good example of successful joint work across families (that is, those for energy and environment) within the new Sustainable Development Network, a persisting cross-sectoral challenge is the need for better collaboration between the Sustainable Development and Poverty Reduction and Economic Management and Human Development Networks. This is especially the case with respect to preparation of Poverty Assessments, studies of pro-poor growth, PRSCs, and Bank support for borrower-prepared PRSPs.

*Addressing the rapidly growing environmental footprints of countries requires special attention.*

*Better cross-network collaboration is needed regarding poverty-environment and health-environment linkages.*

Effectiveness of World Bank Group assistance for both the environment and poverty reduction is likely to improve when linkages between renewable natural resource access, quality, use, management, and sustainability and rural livelihoods are better integrated into these instruments. The same applies to greater integration of environmental aspects into Bank work in the health sector and its efforts to help countries reduce their vulnerability to natural disasters.

Internal arrangements, methodologies, and skill requirements for key analytical and strategic instruments need to be adjusted to better incorporate environment-poverty, environment-health, and environment-vulnerability linkages. Implementing these changes is primarily a question of making better use of existing resources and guidance materials[19] rather than acquiring new expertise—although some is needed—or starting from scratch in elaborating guidelines. But it does require modifications in how the Bank prepares some core products, how staff in different networks work together, and the way administrative budget resources are allocated for such tasks.

*Better use of existing resources and changes in methodologies, attitudes, and budget allocation procedures are also needed.*

An approach that seeks to further mainstream the environment will require more multisectoral teams, including environmental and natural resource specialists working directly with country clients as well as Bank sector staff to better understand the causes of specific environmental problems; define the desired outcomes to be achieved; and help identify—and then support implementation of—the policy, institutional, legal, regulatory, and investment interventions needed to attain those results.

Where such cross-sectoral and area-focused approaches have been taken (for example, land and watershed management operations in Brazil, China, and India; metropolitan environmental projects in Brazil and China; and multipurpose river basin management projects in China), environmental and other benefits have been substantial and the outcomes have generally been sustainable. Substantially improved monitoring and reporting of environmental outcomes and impacts of World Bank Group interventions are also required.

*Staff skills, including operational ones, need to be strengthened.*

Another internal constraint involves staff skills. Within the World Bank, for example, the concern is in relation to two things. First, analytical and technical capabilities need to be kept current and cutting edge—to identify and implement innovative financial mechanisms and technical and institutional solutions to help country clients address climate change adaptation needs, for example. Second is the operational skills and experience of staff responsible for helping borrowers to prepare and implement ENRM projects. One CMU director identified the latter as the main constraint on his ability to deliver a more robust environmental program.

In contrast, Bank managers responsible for environmental activities stated that lack of a stronger environmental lending program was primarily caused by insufficient support from senior country managers. Greater effectiveness of Bank Group support for the environment requires both.[20] The various parts of the Bank Group should consider undertaking systematic skills needs assessments in light of evolving corporate priorities and client demand (such as for clean energy and climate change mitigation and adaptation).

### Authorizing environment

The authorizing environment within the World Bank Group has several levels, starting with the Bank and IFC Boards of Directors through the policies, country strategies, and projects they approve; then there is senior management, as manifested in part in Regional and sector operational strategies (World Bank 2007f). Finally comes the country program level, mainly through country strategies, which are elaborated in consultation with client governments and other national stakeholders. For IFC and MIGA the authorizing environment includes corporate policies, ESHS guidelines, and Performance Standards intended to mitigate or avoid adverse environmental impacts and identify opportunities for improved sustainability.[21]

At each level and all three Bank Group institutions, differing priorities compete for the use of scarce budgetary, human, and other resources to produce lending and nonlending services.

The Bank president, together with the managing directors and the executive vice presidents of IFC and MIGA, sets and publicly presents the World Bank Group agenda. That includes the relative importance of the environment and sustainable development in relation to other corporate priorities, as well as among different areas of environmental significance. This can at times be strongly affected by outside influences, including from the Bank's major shareholders, as with the growing focus on climate change that responds in part to a 2005 request by G-8 countries for greater Bank Group international leadership.

Within the World Bank, country directors largely control three important assets at the country level: policy dialogue with national stakeholders, definition of the lending and nonlending services presented in the multiyear CAS or Country Partnership Strategy, and allocation of the administrative budget to the sector management units. In response to competing demands, the relative priorities set by CMUs determine much of the authorizing environment for other Bank staff in terms of the attention given to environmental versus other concerns in the country work program. The degree of interest in the environment on the part of country directors and other pertinent managers varies across countries and over time and reflects both client demand and internal capacity constraints.

Compared with the situation in 1990, or even 2001, the country case studies and other assessments suggest that many CMU directors have become increasingly concerned with the environment. This is clearly the case in China and India. As recent experience in Russia shows, however, what the Bank Group can do is ultimately limited by what governments want to borrow or seek policy advice for, even in countries facing serious environmental problems.[22] CMUs are nonetheless encouraged to identify strategic entry points in their programs (perhaps in critical sectors such as energy) to help advance the Bank Group's corporate environmental sustainability objectives.

*Ownership of the environment mission is as important a key to effectiveness within the Bank Group as it is for borrowers.*

In the Bank, within the limits set by these constraints, Regional vice presidents and country directors set the tone and allocate the resources for Bank task teams. Thus, it is important that they are fully aware of and support the World Bank Group's mission in relation to the environment, which itself needs to be clearly defined. Because they control the Bank's country work program and budget, Regional vice presidents and CMUs are in the best position to insist that sector management units collaborate and ensure that the right skills are brought to bear on Bank lending and nonlending activities. They are also well positioned to insist that further mainstreaming of environmental concerns occurs and that applicable evaluation findings and other relevant knowledge are adequately reflected in new lending and nonlending services.

*Country managers need to firmly buy into the Bank Group's environmental mission.*

### Taking a longer-term view

As the 2003 WDR stressed, adequately integrating environmental concerns—and those associated with sustainable development more generally—into national development strategies and associated actions requires a medium- and a long-term perspective. This is especially clear in relation to climate change, but it is true for many other aspects of national and global environmental governance as well.[23]

*Country willingness to borrow constrains potential Bank actions.*

This evaluation concludes that the need for greater focus on the longer term also applies to many World Bank Group approaches and programs. Especially at the country and Regional levels, the Bank Group currently lacks the instruments to do this. Even though they often support longer-term national objectives, CASs and Country Partnership Strategies have a five-year time horizon at most and are generally limited to three years. Regional strategies normally have similar time frames.

The Bank Group does not clearly possess a mechanism to situate its short-term assistance and partnership strategies in the context of longer-term national, Regional, or global development needs and challenges, many of which are environmental in nature (CEAs, if properly oriented, can serve this function in part). Thus, the Bank Group should consider more systematically developing and periodically updating flexible medium- and longer-term country and Regional assistance frameworks (not strategies per se), at least for its largest clients.

Such frameworks, which are particularly important for the largest countries and those facing environmental challenges of global significance, should reflect the emerging development problems and opportunities they are likely to face over a longer time horizon, taking emerging demographic, socioeconomic, political, institutional, and associated environmental (including pressures on natural resources) trends into account. Such exercises should have at least a 5-to-10-year and perhaps longer time horizon and be developed and updated in close collaboration with the countries themselves.

### *Bank leadership on the environment*

Over the past decade, many outside the institution have increasingly looked to the World Bank Group for intellectual leadership in relation to the environment. This reflected a strong economics research program on the environment and the presence of high-level specialists, including a chief scientist who was formerly chair of the Nobel Prize-winning Intergovernmental Panel on Climate Change.

*The Bank should attempt to regain its international leadership in relation to the environment.*

Over the past several years, the team that produced much of the Bank's economics research on environmental issues and other prominent senior managers and staff, including the aforementioned chief scientist, have retired or departed to pursue other opportunities. Thus, the Bank now needs to recruit additional senior-level specialists to help lead its work on climate change in particular, and the environment more generally. This would also help the Bank Group regain its former international preeminence in this regard.[24]

## Coordination within the World Bank Group

A final constraint on more effective World Bank Group support for the environment is the extent to which the Bank, IFC, and MIGA are coordinated in their strategies and interventions at both the corporate and country levels. This is important for a number of reasons.

For IFC and MIGA to operate effectively in client countries, and for healthy private sector development more generally, an adequate national legal and regulatory framework needs to be in place and to be sufficiently enforced. This depends on government policy and practices, where IFC and MIGA have less influence than the Bank. The feasibility of many private investments may also depend on adequate infrastructure, including wastewater treatment and waste management and recycling services being in place. In many countries, such infrastructure and services are still nonexistent, poorly organized, or provided by public utilities and other government agencies that are often World Bank clients. By the same token, achievement of the objectives of many Bank strategies, including its Environment Strategy, depends in part on private sector performance—to minimize environmental damage on the part of productive enterprises, for example—where IFC and MIGA can play an important role.

Good IFC-Bank coordination has been evident in some countries in the water and waste management and power sectors. IFC and the Bank appear to have collaborated successfully in India, for example, where IFC has its largest portfolio in the power and water sectors, followed by China and Brazil. Slow progress on the privatization of environmental infrastructure utilities, however, has impeded greater IFC investment in other case study countries. But IFC is increasingly working with the public sector in advising on regulatory issues and public-private partnership projects and promoting private sector sustainability and corporate social responsibility. IFC is also developing new project structures to increase opportunities for public-private partnership financing.

Where such cooperation has been successful, it has often involved a two-step process. Initially, the Bank has created opportunities for private sector participation through preparatory infrastructure investments and/or dialogue with a government to implement structural reforms facilitating public-private partnerships. After this step, IFC has sought partners for joint financing and implementation of specific investment projects. However, in some cases, private sector projects are being financed ahead of Bank policy interventions, and IFC's experience has been used to alert the Bank of the need for policy intervention or government participation in the same or similar projects. Drivers for collaboration have varied and depended on the extent of private investment opportunities for environmental utilities, government strategies to borrow from the World Bank Group, and how well IFC and Bank staff have worked together.

But there have been occasions when IFC and the Bank have pursued different approaches and priorities and/or may have missed opportunities for greater collaboration. For example, the divergence in approaches with respect to project environmental requirements and differing approaches to development in the Brazilian Amazon is a situation that has reportedly changed over the past two years. Looking forward, moreover, it is important that proposed new IFC and World Bank–supported investments (for example, power plants in India and elsewhere)[25] meet the same environmental Performance Standards and seek to avoid producing significant new greenhouse gas emissions.[26]

Following broad internal World Bank Group and public consultations, IFC adopted its new Policy and Performance Standards on Social and Environmental Sustainability in 2006. MIGA adopted a similar approach in October 2007.[27]

The Bank continues to follow a safeguards approach, initially adopted in the late 1980s, with later modifications. The most significant of these occurred in the late 1990s, when the operational policy for environmental assessment was converted into an operational directive. IFC participated in this process.

*IFC and MIGA require a propitious investment climate, which the Bank's work can help create.*

At that time, a significant effort to harmonize the approach to environmental and social due diligence both within the Bank Group and among all the multilateral development institutions also took place. The 2001 Environmental Strategy, moreover, called for "improving the safeguards and compliance system, including strengthening compliance with policies and a comprehensive review of the safeguards policy framework to fit the needs of a changing Bank." This occurred in part through creation of the Quality Assurance and Compliance Unit, efforts to rely increasingly on country systems, and a revision of the approach to environmental due diligence in policy-based lending.

IFC's and MIGA's Performance Standards on Social and Environmental Sustainability have a more private sector focus than the Bank's safeguard policies. Thus, differing approaches to addressing potential environmental impacts of World Bank Group operations are now being followed. The new IFC-MIGA approach has broader coverage, but the key question concerns the environmental impact of the alternative approaches in the field. Thus, it will be important to closely monitor and evaluate the effects of these approaches even though, given that both IFC's and especially MIGA's application of the Performance Standards has occurred only within the past two years, it is too early to assess their results.

*With the adoption of IFC's and MIGA's new policy and Performance Standards, the approaches of the World Bank Group to environmental due diligence have diverged.*

A second example concerns differing Bank and IFC approaches to development in the Brazilian Amazon, where environmental sustainability and private sector development are both important—but potentially conflicting—objectives. Efforts to

*It is too early to assess the effects of these differing approaches.*

harmonize these approaches since 2005—and in the recent IFC Brazilian Amazon Initiative and Bank Group Brazil Country Partnership Strategy for the Region—need to be evaluated with respect to their environmental impact.

The experience with two recent IFC agribusiness projects will provide crucial lessons for future directions. Bank ESW and other work have identified increased cattle ranching and expanded soybean production as the principal causes of deforestation in the Region (Margulis 2004). These projects assume that IFC participation in targeted private sector investments is important to transform markets toward greater sustainability in regions where public policy capacity is low. In the absence of IFC support, private sector activities would result in greater adverse environmental impacts.

But although some NGOs have cooperated with the soy industry, aiming at avoidance of deforestation, other NGOs have raised concerns about the potential indirect and cumulative impacts of such interventions. In both cases, given the global importance of the region, there is a need to look beyond the confines of the project to the broader long-term and possibly irreversible environmental impacts.

Thus, although there are recent examples of positive collaboration among the various parts of the World Bank Group from an environmental perspective, there have also been important differences in the past. The consultations inside the World Bank Group and with external stakeholders around the new Performance Standards and the joint initiatives are encouraging, but the need remains for greater coordination of strategies, approaches, and interventions at both the corporate and country levels. Welcome Bank-IFC coordination is presently happening with respect to climate change, where it is particularly important that the Bank Group have a unified approach. But this coordination should also be applied to updating the 2001 Environment Strategy and other areas.[28]

In conclusion, better understanding of the constraints on effectiveness of Bank Group support for environmental sustainability is a necessary first step. Although the ability of the World Bank Group to affect external constraints is limited, especially in the short term and in the largest client countries, it can proactively seek to overcome internal ones. These include both limitations that affect the Bank, IFC, and MIGA individually and those that refer to coordination within the Bank Group as a whole.

# Chapter 6

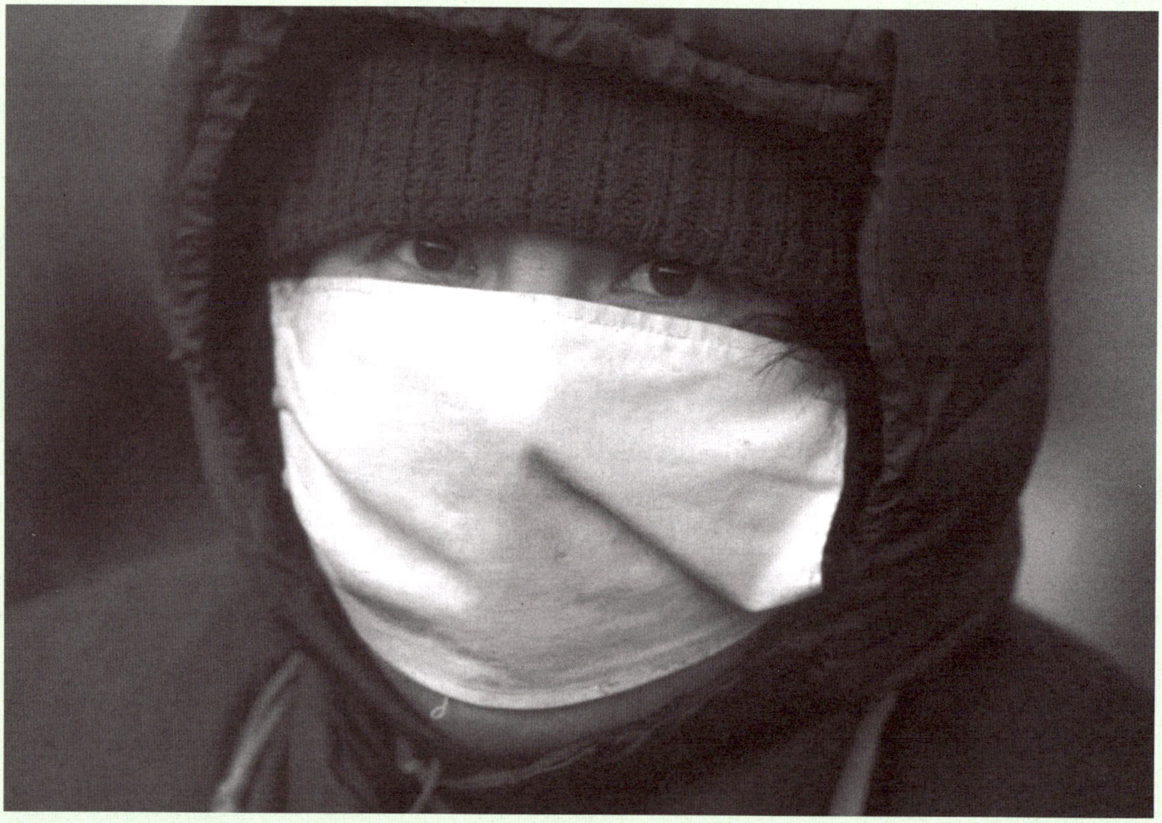

Many people in Asia wear masks because of the pollution. Photo by Curt Carnemark, courtesy of the World Bank Photo Library.

# Conclusions and Recommendations

## Conclusions

### *The World Bank*

**The World Bank has made progress in including environmental concerns in its strategies, lending, and nonlending activities, but the operational significance and impact of these efforts have varied over time and across themes, countries, and issues.**

In terms of lending, for example, the portfolio analysis and country case studies show that some instruments, such as Montreal Protocol and GEF grants to reduce ozone-depleting substances, have contributed to positive environmental outcomes. Other Bank-supported interventions—such as rural land and watershed management projects, as in Brazil, China, and India; community-based forest management projects, as in India; and biodiversity projects, as in Brazil, China, Ghana, India, Madagascar, Russia, and Uganda—have generally also met their objectives. But use of dedicated credit lines to abate industrial pollution in several countries has not proven to be the most effective approach from an environmental perspective, while attempts to strengthen capacity for environmental management have made progress in some countries, such as Brazil and China, but not in others, such as India and, initially, Madagascar. Such operations have generally been more effective when actions to strengthen institutions were combined with investments to protect environmental assets.

**Bank financial commitments for the environment and natural resource management have increased since the 2001 Strategy was adopted.**

The overall increase in commitments in recent years, however, is explained in part by greater use of DPLs in Latin America (Brazil, Mexico, and Colombia), although their results in terms of environmental improvement have not yet been assessed. Investment lending for environmental issues, although imprecisely measured, seems to have remained low, as these concerns have not been as high operational priorities for Bank financial assistance in many client countries. The volume of GEF grants and funding for the global environment more generally has also increased over this period,[1] which has helped leverage financing from other sources, including the Bank and IFC. Increasing support has also been given for carbon finance to help address climate change issues. However, Bank-administered GEF grants declined both in number and funding volume in fiscal 2006–07.

**Bank nonlending activities for the environment have also been important.**

Economic and sector work has increased in recent years, including CEAs and Strategic

Environmental Assessments (SEAs), among other forms of AAA. Some of these activities have had an important influence on national policies and institutions. One example is the technical cooperation provided to Brazil, China, India, Indonesia, Mexico, the Philippines, and elsewhere on the role of public disclosure in industrial pollution management.

**Environmental problems are a rapidly growing concern in middle-income countries, but the results of Bank support have varied greatly,[2] while Bank performance in environmental and natural resource management projects has been weaker in lower-income countries, especially in Sub-Saharan Africa.**

In the case of Africa, while experience across countries varies and despite considerable support for elaboration and implementation of national EAPs, Bank financial support for the environment in Ghana, Madagascar, and Uganda has largely focused on technical assistance for capacity building and biodiversity conservation (and there has been even less activity in Senegal). While these concerns are not insignificant, much less attention has been given to the urban environment and, more importantly, considering the essential role of natural resources for both environmental sustainability and rural livelihoods, to land, watershed, river basin, and forest management.

### *IFC*

**IFC's support has been moderately satisfactory in meeting its due diligence requirements and standards at the project level. But gaps were found in investment projects in Africa and in some industry sectors, and in achieving expected impacts with some environment-oriented Advisory Services.**

The environmental and social effects success rate of projects evaluated by IEG was 67 percent. Thus, one in three projects did not fully meet IFC requirements. Inadequate performance was especially evident in Sub-Saharan Africa and in the textile, food and beverage, tourism, and agriculture and forestry sectors. IFC helped its clients develop environmental and social management systems to better address those aspects of their operations and has also rapidly developed its environment-related Advisory Services over the past five years. The services that have been evaluated have been generally positive, but findings concerning project impact in three dedicated environmental facilities were mixed, and impacts in the Environment and Social Sustainability business line projects are difficult to assess.

**The quality of IFC's environmental work at project appraisal has been good overall, but the quality of environment-related supervision of FI projects is a concern.**

This is explained in part by limited in-house resources to visit FI projects. Even though the percentage of subprojects with environmental or social risks in the FI portfolio appears to be small, the aggregate impacts of a large number of subprojects may be significant, especially when FI clients lack resources to ensure proper mitigation of pollution. IFC has recognized this gap and has increased supervision resources and improved review processes for such operations.

**Despite recent progress, IFC faces substantial environment-related challenges.**

IFC has developed a Policy on Social and Environmental Sustainability and Performance Standards, launched sustainable business initiatives, geared its Advisory Services more toward sustainability, and enhanced its systems to identify, monitor, and evaluate performance criteria for both investments and Advisory Services. It has also increased its potential to indirectly influence environmental and social impacts of private sector activities by launching the Equator Principles, which now cover the majority of large-scale project financing in the developing world. But, in addition to it being too soon to evaluate the results of these recent changes, three challenges are especially noteworthy:

- ***Implementation of the Global/Local Strategy.*** The strategy is to move environmental specialists closer to clients. However, maintaining the coherence and knowledge base of IFC's more decentralized environmental staff will be a challenge. The strategic focus on frontier markets, especially in Sub-Saharan Africa, requires that IFC develop and intensify its environmental investment support and Advisory Services. In addition, corporate finance is increasing and involves greater environmental risks compared with project finance, making development of more effective environmental and social management systems even more important for IFC and its clients.

- ***Improve sustainability of financial intermediary subprojects with environmental and social risks.*** FIs often do not have legal obligations to the host country to ensure sustainability of their subprojects, lack environmental management capacity, and are unwilling to hire external consultants because of the associated costs in a competitive market situation. There is thus a need for IFC to expand its own environmental supervision resources; nurture consultancies and partnerships to help FIs identify, monitor, and mitigate ESHS risks; and provide adequate capacity building and incentives for FIs and their clients to improve environmental performance.
- ***Introduce more effective safeguards in environmentally sensitive regions that have weak environmental governance, such as the last large areas of tropical biodiversity.*** Indirect, induced, and cumulative environmental impacts are difficult to identify and mitigate, especially when governance or political will in the public sector is weak. Better up-front environmental and social assessment and stronger mitigation efforts are required in similarly complex situations.

**To consider the performance of IFC and MIGA as part of the World Bank Group's contributions, a shift is needed to focus on issues beyond those of individual projects to include the aggregation of impacts in the affected sector or region of a country.**

Individual project performance is confined mainly to compliance with standards at the company level, but the evaluation of IFC and MIGA as parts of the World Bank Group must also consider the sectorwide or regionwide effects. This is a direction that both self-evaluation and independent evaluation must take.

### *MIGA*

**For a sample of MIGA projects, performance in meeting requirements and standards differed between Category A and Category B projects.**

At Board approval, 73 percent of Category A projects and 83 percent of Category B projects met the requirements and standards for an acceptable EAP. At evaluation, 80 percent of Category A projects met MIGA's performance requirements in implementing the EAP, but only 63 percent of Category B projects did. This was mainly because MIGA environmental and social guidelines were not comprehensively addressed or EAPs were not adequately implemented.

**Although MIGA does not have an explicit business line to support environmentally beneficial projects, it can contribute to improved environmental quality by helping private sector clients demonstrate best practice and by working with investors committed to "doing good."**

MIGA can promote environmental governance by ensuring that its clients establish and train staff to effectively implement EMSs. Given the increasing focus on the impacts of development on the environment, MIGA may also need to address issues of global environmental sustainability—by promoting environmentally beneficial projects, for example.

**MIGA needs to continue to make progress in several areas.**

These include fully implementing the harmonization of assessment and monitoring requirements of Category B projects with those of IFC; including environmental health and safety reporting requirements in Contracts of Guarantee; requiring investors to set up EMSs on a timely basis, as appropriate to a project cycle; and moving beyond safeguard compliance to promote sustainability. MIGA's new Policy and Performance Standards are consistent with these remaining concerns. IEG is supportive of MIGA's formal incorporation of social and environmental sustainability in its core business and recognizes that the real challenges lie in the implementation of the 2007 policies.

### *World Bank Group*

**Environmental problems in developing countries remain serious and are increasing in many places, reflecting both the Bank Group's limited ability to affect larger—including market—forces that have an impact on the environment and the need for greater attention to these concerns by the countries themselves and the donor community as a whole.**

Even though the Bank has provided considerable lending for urban sanitation and environmental management in China and elsewhere, poor water and air quality continue to generate serious public health problems in megacities and other urban areas. Global greenhouse gases continue to rise, especially in China and India (as well as in some developed countries), and the Bank has only recently stepped up its efforts to help the most vulnerable nations in South Asia, Sub-Saharan Africa, and elsewhere adapt to the likely impacts of climate change. Finally, despite Bank-supported interventions in support of sustainable development in the Brazilian Amazon over the past several decades, deforestation continues at high rates and could further accelerate, depending on the evolution of international and domestic demand for beef, soybeans, timber, and ethanol, together with government infrastructure and private agribusiness investments. While the Bank Group cannot be expected to address all environmental priorities, and ultimately is limited by what its clients want it to do, it can nonetheless be more proactive in its efforts to help them address local and global environmental challenges, both through its own support and by working more effectively with partner institutions that share the same objectives.

**The world has changed considerably since 2001. The role of the private sector in international financial flows—and of IFC and MIGA operations within the World Bank Group—has sharply expanded, while global environmental challenges, especially climate change and transnational environmental footprints, have become increasingly important and visible. In this context, and in view of its efforts to promote inclusive and sustainable globalization, the World Bank Group's strategy for the environment needs to be updated.**

It is crucial that the World Bank Group have a clear definition of its role in support of its clients' efforts to achieve greater environmental sustainability in the years ahead. Consultations carried out during this evaluation revealed that a broad range of external stakeholders, including the private sector and civil society, are looking to the World Bank Group for this definition. Representatives of the private sector have indicated, moreover, a desire to continue to engage actively, not only with IFC and MIGA in relation to environmental sustainability concerns, but more directly with the World Bank as well.

**Strengthening coordination and collaboration in relation to the environment within the World Bank Group, at both the corporate and country levels, should be a central part of the updated strategy.**[3]

This is particularly important for countries where the Bank Group has its largest portfolios and whose environmental management challenges have the most significant global implications. It also reflects a broader need for more effective public-private partnerships in countries where the Bank Group operates, as well as for greater transfers and development of appropriate technologies, and support for environmentally friendly market transformation more generally. Stronger intra-World Bank Group collaboration is needed across the board, including in work with its clients to improve environmental performance of small and medium-size enterprises, as well as with larger firms and financial intermediaries, through better supply chain management and capacity building, among other measures.

**The evaluation confirms that partnerships can—and often do—play a vital role in enhancing the effectiveness of Bank Group support for environmental sustain-**

**ability. But it has also shown that these partnerships have not always been as effective as they might have been, and thus could—and should—be enhanced.**

This is especially important given the growing scale and seriousness of many environmental problems at both the national and global levels. The Bank Group's existing environment-related partnerships with other U.N. agencies (especially UNEP and UNDP), with programs such as the GEF, with major international environmental NGOs, and with the private sector should thus be strengthened. The Bank Group should also collaborate with MDBs to promote the use of IFC Performance Standards and engage with more financial institutions to adopt Equator Principles, while helping them to improve their compliance reporting. Partnerships in the public and private sectors should also be a central theme in updating the World Bank Group environment strategy, a process that should include active consultations with such partners. All of this, however, including future joint activity in relation to climate change, must continue to occur in the context of the Bank Group's overriding poverty reduction and sustainable development mission. Environmental issues, while increasingly important, are only part of the dialogue. World Bank Group clients also face many other challenges, and the Bank Group must grapple with other demands as well.

**While helping clients address climate change (including responding better to both mitigation and adaptation needs) is critical, it is equally important to ensure that other persisting environmental challenges—such as biodiversity conservation, water resource management, and local pollution abatement—continue to receive adequate priority and attention.**

In updating the strategy, the economic benefits of environmental investments and the need to avoid the costs of inaction should also be brought out, together with the links to poverty reduction and growth in both the short and longer term.

**The Bank Group, particularly the World Bank, needs to strengthen its information base regarding the environmental aspects, results, and impacts of its interventions.**

This evaluation has found shortcomings in this regard at both the individual project and portfolio levels. Better tracking of the environmental effects of Bank Group advisory and other nonlending services would also be desirable. Monitoring, evaluation, and reporting need to be enhanced at all levels, as does environment-related research and knowledge generation and dissemination more generally, both within the World Bank Group and in conjunction with external collaborators. The Bank Group can and should learn more from the experience of other organizations, including its major development and country partners. In short, the World Bank Group's role as a knowledge bank on matters related to the environment and sustainable development needs to be reinforced.

## Recommendations

**1. Increase the attention to environmental sustainability in the World Bank Group by ensuring that environmental issues enter fully into discussions of its strategic directions and Regional and country assistance programs.**

Promotion of environmental sustainability (including, but not limited to, addressing climate change) should be a central pillar of the World Bank Group's strategic directions in its efforts to support inclusive and sustainable globalization. The Bank Group should jointly reformulate and update the 2001 Environment Strategy in light of the new international realities—including the increasingly important role of the private sector, technology transfer to developing countries, global public goods, and transnational environmental footprints—and emerging Bank Group corporate priorities.

In close collaboration with its client countries, the World Bank Group should also consider both medium-term (5–10 year) and longer-term (10–20 year) approaches to strengthening environmental sustainability at the Regional and national levels and should incorporate short-term (3–5 year) environmental programs into country assistance and partnership strategies where feasible, especially for countries with large investment portfolios and environmental challenges of global significance.[4,5]

Such approaches and programs should also seek to identify opportunities for intra-Bank Group cooperation in helping clients address key national and global environmental challenges, including pollution reduction and long-term (for periods up to 50 years) goals for greenhouse gas abatement and adaptation to climate change. Areas of joint activity could include promotion and development of public-private partnerships for the provision of environmental sanitation and environmentally responsible power and energy projects (hydropower, clean coal, energy efficiency, alternative energy sources, and the like). Project selection and nonlending support, including IFC Advisory Services, should seek to maximize environmental benefits, especially by helping market transformation toward sustainability.

The World Bank should continue to work closely with its development partners to help countries address environmental problems. Wherever possible CEAs and SEAs should be used for this purpose at the national, policy, sectoral, and subnational levels. Institutional capacity building should be viewed as a means rather than an end, and thus be linked to attainment of observable environmental outcomes. Greater attention should also be given to improving the performance of projects that focus primarily on environmental policy and institutions, as well as to that of environment and natural resource management projects in Sub-Saharan Africa more generally.

IFC and MIGA should further encourage the adoption and use of the Equator Principles as global environmental standards in private sector investments in the developing world and IFC Policy and Performance Standards on Environmental and Social Sustainability by MDBs, and seek to extend their use among public financiers. The results of application of these mechanisms should be carefully monitored, reported, and evaluated—for example, by using external assurance companies.

IFC should continue to develop systems with its Community Learning Initiative to improve accountability and transparency among Equator Principles signatories. It should also encourage and support environmental consultants and develop and institutionalize market-driven training to help them master IFC's Policy and Performance Standards on Social and Environmental Sustainability. IFC should focus its Advisory Services and capacity building efforts on Regions and sectors with low environmental performance, especially Sub-Saharan Africa and the textile, food and beverage, tourism, and agriculture sectors. IFC should continue supporting market transformation toward sustainability with its Advisory Services and direct and financial intermediary investments, emphasizing technology transfer and development in clean production, energy efficiency, and sustainable supply chain management.

MIGA should move beyond safeguard compliance to promote sustainability consistent with MIGA's new Policy and Performance Standards. It should proactively expand its environment-related technical assistance to clients, which should enable it to be more effective in helping the private sector to meet its new Performance Standards, especially in Sub-Saharan Africa.

**2. Move to more cross-sectoral and spatially oriented approaches to environmental support and strengthen staff skills.**

The World Bank Group should help its clients adopt more cross-sectoral and spatially focused (including area-based) approaches to environmental challenges. While the Bank Group should be responsive to client demand in its policy advice and lending, it can still be proactive in analyzing environmental issues and seeking to identify strategic entry points in countries with significant environmental concerns. For example, it should seek to be more proactive on a variety of environmental concerns, including adaptation to, as well as mitigation of, climate change, but not at the expense of other local and global environmental priorities. It also needs to better integrate environmental, health, and labor issues under its sustainability agenda in the short and longer terms.

In the World Bank, this applies to efforts by country departments and Regions to help address problems that cross national and regional boundaries, as well as to increasingly serious environmental and carbon footprint concerns, which should receive greater analytical and operational attention across the World Bank Group. The Bank should also seek to strengthen its Poverty Assessments, PRSCs, and analytical work on pro-poor growth, as well as its support to countries for preparation of PRSPs, by giving greater emphasis to linkages between poverty and the environment. Greater attention is also needed with respect to environmental health issues in both rural and urban areas, which will require stronger collaboration among those responsible for health, water supply and sanitation, energy, transport, urban development, and environment. This also applies to those working on vulnerability issues, including issues related to the impacts of climate change.

World Bank Group staff skills should be strengthened in a number of technical and operational areas, including adaptation to climate change, carbon finance, and the ability to deliver environment-related investment and policy reform projects. This requires improvements in training and selective recruitment of experienced staff, including in areas related to climate change and alternative financing mechanisms. While some additional resources may be required, priority should be given to using existing human and budget resources more effectively.

IFC and the Bank should better coordinate policy dialogue with governments to enhance structural reforms aimed at public-private partnerships in the water; wastewater; and waste management, reuse, and recycling sectors, and ensure that industry views in these and other environmentally relevant and sensitive sectors are represented in the national and sectoral policy dialogues.

In implementing their Environmental and Social Performance Standards, IFC and MIGA should stress the need for clients, especially financial intermediaries, to develop and implement solid ESMSs in recognition that sustainability is key to their business success; ensure that engineering and pollution control system design and community engagement are integrated in the early project stage to provide environmentally, socially, and economically sound solutions; and use more independent environmental audits as part of project completion tests. IFC should also emphasize the potential for environmental benefits in its marketing and selection of projects. MIGA's engagement with projects should provide advice on environmental (and social) issues to help bring clients closer to best practices in the industry.

**3. Improve the Bank Group's ability to assess its support for the environment and to monitor and evaluate the results of its environment-related interventions.**

The World Bank Group needs to do a better job of measuring the environmental performance and impacts of its activities. The Bank needs to improve monitoring, evaluation, and reporting of environmental aspects and results of lending operations at both the project and portfolio levels. While IFC has recently developed new tools to track and analyze environmental performance indicators at the project level, and MIGA has scaled up it assessment and monitoring of project environmental and social performance, both institutions need to further improve their attention to baseline environmental assessments for better identification of performance indicators, especially those regarding specific and annual emissions. IFC and MIGA should also be concerned with and measure more fully the aggregate impact —beyond individual project compliance—of projects with large environmental impacts, such as those in energy and agribusiness.[6] The Bank Group needs to develop and apply methods to assess environmental impacts. Together with agencies such as UNEP and UNDP, it needs to help quantify progress toward the achievement of Millennium Development Goal 7 for environmental sustainability, a goal that is not being tracked adequately.

The World Bank should improve the way it determines how much of its total financing has supported environmental improvement. It should also revise its preparation guidelines for Implementation Completion Reports to require a more systematic review of project environmental dimensions and results—including, but not limited to, application of and compliance with environmental safeguards—as it already does for poverty, gender, and social development aspects of projects. Existing IFC and MIGA systems to identify, track, and evaluate project environmental performance and impacts could provide a starting point for better monitoring by the World Bank. A mechanism to track the influence of Bank nonlending services on environment-related policies and institutions in client countries is also desirable. Results of such assessments should be considered in the periodic country assistance/partnership strategy implementation review and updating process.

Reporting and monitoring of performance criteria in IFC projects should include specific emissions and mass flows in addition to the present system that monitors pollutant concentrations. These indicators should be determined before and assessed afterward for all relevant projects to track their impacts on such matters as the abatement of effluent discharges and dust and greenhouse gas emissions. For environmentally sensitive IFC agriculture and forestry projects, especially in areas of high biodiversity, carefully designed baseline studies should be done to identify indirect, induced, and cumulative (as well as direct) environmental and social impacts. Adequate plans to mitigate any negative effects should be designed, implemented, and carefully monitored. Sustainability of supply chains with certification schemes and third-party monitoring should also be enhanced.

MIGA should fully implement the harmonization of assessment and monitoring requirements of Category B projects with those of IFC. It also should make a sustained effort with its clients to improve performance of projects on its environmental and social policies on a timely basis, as appropriate in a project cycle. Investor clients should be required to establish environmental and social project management systems at a sufficiently early stage to effectively monitor impacts, including during construction. MIGA's Contracts of Guarantee should consistently incorporate provisions for regular reporting of safeguard performance during project implementation.

**4. Improve coordination among the Bank, IFC, and MIGA and between the World Bank Group and external partners (public and private) in relation to the Bank Group's environmental mission and ensure consistent and effective implementation at the corporate and country levels.**

Mechanisms should be established to promote and monitor coordination across the Bank, IFC, and MIGA with respect to environment-related policies, strategies, and instruments. Areas where specific interventions are recommended include the following:

- Bank Group strategy for the environment, including climate change, should actively involve IFC and MIGA, starting with the updating of the 2001 Environment Strategy and monitoring and evaluation of its implementation.
- Environmental aspects of World Bank Group country assistance and partnership strategies— especially for countries with large or rapidly growing portfolios and those facing significant environmental challenges—should be identified jointly by the Bank, IFC, and MIGA and mitigation of adverse impacts should be planned, monitored, evaluated, and reported in a coordinated and timely manner.
- The various parts of the World Bank Group should increase efforts to share experience in the up-front assessment, monitoring, evaluation, and reporting of environmental aspects, results, and impacts of their lending and non-

lending activities at both the corporate and, where pertinent, country levels.
- Application and results of environmental due diligence policies and procedures (safeguards and Performance Standards) should be systematically monitored and evaluated by all three parts of the World Bank Group.

Furthermore, strengthening external partnerships with both the public and private sectors should be a central theme in an updated World Bank Group environmental strategy. Effective partnerships will be essential to success in addressing the world's urgent environmental concerns.

MIGA should improve coordination with global programs, such as the GEF and the Bank's Carbon Finance Group, and other entities to identify potential partners whose clients might benefit from MIGA guarantee support.

Cement factory in the Dominican Republic. Photo courtesy of Jouni Martti Eerikainen.

# Appendixes

A farmer plants cassava on ground cleared by fire. Photo reproduced by permission of Michael K. Nichols/National Geographic Image Collection.

# APPENDIX A: EVALUATION METHODOLOGY

The World Bank, IFC, and MIGA portions of this evaluation employed different methodological approaches, reflecting their different roles in the World Bank Group and different information constraints. This appendix describes these methodological approaches in further detail.

## Assessing World Bank Group Effectiveness

The purpose of this evaluation is to assess the effectiveness of World Bank Group assistance for the environment since 1990. More specifically, its objective is to determine how the Bank Group has attempted to assist its clients in setting and addressing their environmental priorities in both the public and private sectors and how effective those interventions have been. Ideally, effectiveness would be measured in observed improvements in ambient environmental quality resulting directly from Bank Group activities but, as noted in chapter 2, this is not possible at present owing to problems with information, time horizon, countervailing factors, and attribution.

The "information problem" refers to the fact that the information base for environmental results—let alone the impacts on ambient environmental quality—of most International Bank for Reconstruction and Development/International Development Association lending and nonlending activities is extremely poor and, in many cases, is nonexistent. This situation reflects poor monitoring, evaluation, and reporting requirements and practices for Bank operations in relation to the environment. Current Bank guidelines for Implementation Completion Reports (issued in August 2006 and last updated in June 2007) do not require systematic reporting on project environmental outcomes or impacts, although there is such a requirement for other cross-cutting themes such as poverty, gender aspects, and social development.

While there is a requirement to "summarize key safeguard and fiduciary issues in the operation, compliance with the Bank policy and procedural requirements, and any problems that arose and their resolution, as applicable"—including "any significant deviations or waivers from the Bank safeguard/fiduciary policies"—there is no requirement that the application results of such policies during project implementation be systematically reported. In short, there is no requirement that the implementation results of project environmental management plans—or even the extent of implementation—be reported in completion reports. As a result, information regarding project environmental results and impacts in Implementation Completion Reports, even for the most sensitive Category A projects (see glossary for definitions of categories), is uneven at best. Similarly, there is no systematic way of gauging the influence of Bank environment-related economic and sector work (ESW) and research on client country policies and institutions. These serious shortcomings need to be corrected if the Bank is to have a better sense of the effectiveness of its lending assistance in relation to the environment.

The "time horizon problem" refers to the fact that environmental outcomes and impacts often take considerable time to become apparent. This problem was also cited in the most recent Sector Strategy Implementation Update, discussed by the Executive Board's Committee on Development Effectiveness in September 2007, which partly focused on the progress to date of the 2001

Environment Strategy. More specifically, the Sector Strategy Implementation Update affirmed: "environmental outcomes are complex and take effect in a much longer timeframe than that of Bank strategies. Air-quality deterioration, for instance, takes 20 years to be reversed even after suitable interventions in energy and transport are implemented. And activities designed to address long-term ecological processes in protected areas take considerable time to have effects" (World Bank 2007f). This is not a valid reason not to monitor and report on project environmental outcomes and impacts, although it does mean that monitoring, evaluation, and reporting of such outcomes and impacts should be carried out over an extended period after such interventions occur. In consideration of this problem, however, the present evaluation has deliberately taken a comparatively long time horizon (from 1990 to the present), which also allows it to capture how Bank Group approaches to environmental and natural resource management have evolved over time, both at the individual country level and more generally.

The "countervailing factors problem" is mainly a constraint in terms of assessing the ultimate impact of Bank-supported interventions in terms of ambient environmental quality. It refers to the fact that, even when Bank-assisted actions have positive environmental outcomes (such as reduced emissions from certain industries or reduced effluents as the result of a wastewater treatment plant), they may be partially or completely offset by other factors (for example, emissions from other sources, including industries that did not benefit under the Bank project, or untreated effluents flowing into the same body of water) that contribute to ambient air or water quality in the same locations. This is especially important where Bank Group–supported interventions only address part of a broader environmental problem or where rapid economic growth or urbanization means that overall pollution loads and other pressures on natural resources are increasing, as is clearly the case in China, India, and the Brazilian Amazon, for instance.

The "attribution problem" is by no means unique to environment-related interventions, but may complicate efforts to determine cause-and-effect relationships, especially when it comes to influencing policies and institutions. More specifically, in the case of the environment, many other donors and domestic stakeholders—including nongovernmental organizations (NGOs), the media, the court system, different parts of government, as well as the Bank—are involved, making it virtually impossible to separate out the Bank's influence from that of other actors. This problem is well described in the completion report for the China Country Assistance Strategy for 2003–05, presented as an annex to the new Country Partnership Strategy for 2006–10, which observed that:

> *Although the China portfolio is one of the Bank's largest, it is small in relation to China's economy (less than 0.2 percent of total investment over the [Country Assistance Strategy] period). Hence, the Bank's impact is felt through the demonstration effects of lending projects, and the influence of analytical work on policy reforms. When the Bank is successful, it contributes to development impacts that reach far beyond the direct outputs of the [analytical and advisory assistance] and projects that it supports, but, given the presence of other change agents in China, it is rarely the case that the Bank is the only contributor at the start of the causal chain that leads to a given result. In most cases, other (domestic and external) agents have also contributed, and these multiple inputs have led to a unique approach that no change agent fully presented as such at the outset of the reform process. Determining the effectiveness of the Bank's work in China is necessarily an exercise in judgment.* [World Bank, IFC, and MIGA 2006, pp. 57–58.

This observation applies to the influence and impact of Bank interventions in other countries as well, especially large ones such as Brazil, India, and Russia, and countries that are assisted by a large number of other donors, such as Egypt, Ghana,

Madagascar, Senegal, and Uganda. In short, especially in view of the problems mentioned above with respect to poor information, the fact that environmental outcomes and impacts frequently take considerable time to fully manifest themselves, and that countervailing factors often override positive impacts of Bank-supported interventions, assessing effectiveness is truly an exercise in judgment. Moreover, performance cannot be readily quantified.

Quantifying performance is particularly problematic in the case of environmental and natural resource management because it is not specifically assessed at the project level. Furthermore, overall Bank project outcome ratings are also of limited usefulness because three-fourths of the projects with environmental and natural resource management-related objectives or content (as identified during the project thematic coding process by their task team leaders), and more than 90 percent of the total commitments in such operations are mapped to sector boards other than that for environment and, therefore, have a broad range of sectoral purposes, against which their overall performance is primarily rated. Even among the minority of environmental and natural resource management projects mapped to the Environment Sector Board, overall performance ratings do not necessarily speak directly to environmental outcomes. Such is the case with many environmental capacity-building projects and the recent set of fast-disbursing Development Policy Loans (nominally for the environment and sustainable development) for which impacts on the environment have not been assessed afterward.

Given these constraints, the World Bank portion of this evaluation has combined a more general literature review with qualitative country case studies in order to: (1) survey the various ways (strategic, nonlending, and lending instruments) the Bank has provided environmental and natural resource management–related assistance to governments and the private sector; and (2) assess how effective this assistance has been across these various instruments and over time. The case study countries were selected to include: (1) the Bank Group's largest clients—in terms of the volume of lending and nonlending support provided since 1990—which are also among the most important non-OECD (Organisation for Economic Co-operation and Development) countries in their global environmental importance, especially with respect to climate change, biodiversity, and the production and consumption of ozone-depleting substances (that is, China, India, Russia, and Brazil); and (2) one or more countries from each of the Bank's six operational Regions, including Egypt in the Middle East and North Africa Region, and Ghana, Madagascar, Senegal, and Uganda in the Sub-Saharan Africa Region, in addition to the four already mentioned.[1]

Egypt was selected both because of its importance for the Nile River and Mediterranean Basins and because it is a major recipient of bilateral development assistance, especially from the United States, which has an impact on the Bank's leverage relative to that of other donors. Sub-Saharan Africa is a Bank Group priority Region and particular attention was given to the selection of case study countries there, to reflect the diversity in geographic and ecological situations and a broad range of development challenges and aid effectiveness experience, as well as to ensure that both Anglophone and Francophone countries were represented. The rich biodiversity of Madagascar, an island, and landlocked Uganda were also a consideration, as were the coastal locations of Ghana and Senegal.

The case study countries in the Sub-Saharan Africa Region and the Middle East and North Africa Region were selected following consultations with Regional managers and staff. Conversations concerning country case studies were also held with Bank managers and staff in the other Regions on the basis of other possible cases (including Colombia, Indonesia, Kazakhstan, Mexico, Romania, Turkey, and Vietnam). Given resource constraints, however, it was decided to select just one country in each of the Bank's operational Regions other than Sub-Saharan Africa, and to focus on countries that were of greatest importance from a global environmental standpoint. In all cases, except

Russia, they were also the Bank's largest borrowers in their respective Regions.

In short, other countries in each of the Bank's Regions could have been selected had the resources permitted, and the experience in each one would have been somewhat different. Therefore, it is important to keep in mind that the findings of this evaluation with respect to the effectiveness of World Bank support are primarily based on experiences in the case study countries, all of which were visited by IEG staff and consultants in the course of this evaluation. It should also be kept in mind, especially in the case of the larger countries, that these field visits were carried out largely to obtain the views of stakeholders in the government, private sector, academia, and other parts of civil society (including both national and international NGOs and the media) regarding the nature and effectiveness of Bank Group assistance for the environment since the early 1990s. However, due to resource constraints, no formal stakeholder surveys were attempted. The field visits allowed IEG staff to conduct new performance assessments of roughly 20 environment-related Bank lending operations (listed in appendix E).

In view of the impossibility of assessing the impact of Bank Group–supported activities on ambient environmental quality, the approach followed was to organize the evaluation partly around the "lenses" provided by the Bank's fourfold environmental agenda of the 1990s—safeguards, stewardship, mainstreaming, and global sustainability. This agenda continues to be highly relevant and was also the approach taken in IEG's earlier assessment of Bank environmental performance, which was also based in part on country case studies (IEG-World Bank 2002).[2] The thematic "lenses" of the 2001 Environment Strategy were added to the agenda—poverty and livelihoods, health, vulnerability, governance, the private sector (IFC and MIGA), and local aspects of global sustainability.

Finally, the evaluation sought to consider an important aspect of the Bank Group's assistance for the environment that did not receive attention in the earlier evaluation: the role of partnerships. This was done mainly by meeting with selected key partners, including other United Nations or multilateral agencies such as the Food and Agriculture Organization, International Fund for Agricultural Development, Organisation for Economic Co-operation and Development, United Nations Development Programme, and United Nations Environment Program; regional development banks, including the Asian Development Bank and European Bank for Reconstruction and Development; selected bilateral donors and assistance agencies, including the United Kingdom's Department for International Development, Germany's GTZ and KfW, Japan's JICA, and others at the country level, such as Denmark's DANIDA and the United States' USAID in Egypt, and Sweden's and Finland's bilateral assistance in Russia; and international environmental NGOs and think tanks at their headquarters in North America (Conservation International; Heinz Center for Business, Science, and the Environment; Worldwatch Institute; World Resources Institute; World Wildlife Fund–U.S.) and in Europe (International Institute for Environment and Development, International Union for the Conservation of Nature, and World Wildlife Fund International) or in the field (Conservation International in China and Madagascar, Greenpeace in Russia, International Union for the Conservation of Nature in Russia and Senegal, and World Wildlife Fund in Brazil, Madagascar, and Russia).

IEG, likewise, met with prominent national environmental NGOs such as Friends of the Environment, in Alexandria, and the Egyptian Water Partnership, in Cairo; Advocates Coalition for Development and Environment, and Greenwatch Uganda, in Kampala; the Socio-Ecological Union, and Biodiversity Conservation Center, in Moscow, and the Baltic Fund for Nature, and Public Organization for Ecology and Business, in St. Petersburg; the Centre for Science and Environment, and Confederation of Indian Industries, in New Delhi; and Amigos da Terra, and Instituto Socio-Ambiental, in São

Paulo, and Instituto para Sociedade, Populacao, e Natureza, in Brasilia. These and other organizations provided valuable insights into the effectiveness of World Bank assistance for the environment, as perceived by actual partners and other key local stakeholders. However, the evaluation did not attempt to assess the effectiveness of individual partnerships, in and of themselves.

## Assessing IFC Effectiveness

The objectives of the IEG-IFC evaluation were to:

- Evaluate how effectively IFC's projects and environmental investment support and finance have contributed to improving environmental and social sustainability (through enhanced health and safety for workers, efficient resource use and biodiversity conservation, as well as the prevention and reduction of pollution and other adverse environmental, social, health, and safety [ESHS] impacts), and to protecting natural resources and the quality of the regional and global commons. What have been the impacts at the project, regional/country, and industry-sector levels? What have been the cumulative impacts on the upstream/downstream supply chains of IFC's projects, especially with regard to indigenous people and biodiversity issues in agricultural projects, and to labor and working conditions, including child labor, in manufacturing industry projects?
- Evaluate IFC's role and impact in enhancing clients' management of environmental risks and introducing additional environmental improvements, such as carbon trading, energy efficiency, and biodiversity programs.
- Assess the environmental impact and effectiveness, and the extent of coordination with the International Bank for Reconstruction and Development, in IFC's financing of sustainable public and private sector infrastructure projects with significant environmental benefits. Such projects would comprise, for example, renewable energy and sustainable forestry projects, and public-private partnership projects to develop and finance water and wastewater treatment, waste and hazardous waste management, and recycling enterprises and utilities that would serve households and industrial enterprises on a cost-effective basis in urban areas.
- Assess how IFC could help develop the local environmental consultant capacity that could serve IFC's present and future clients in environmental appraisal, monitoring, and studies. A special part of the assessment is of the local ESHS consultancy service industry, which could assist financial intermediaries that IFC finances.
- Evaluate to what extent and how IFC's Advisory Services and other nonlending services have been strengthened and with what benefits to clients and other stakeholders.
- Evaluate to what extent and how IFC has used its partnerships with other key development stakeholders (multilateral development banks, the Global Environment Facility (GEF), and bilateral donors) and companies to enhance the effectiveness of its assistance to private sector clients, with respect to environmental management and sustainability—for example, in launching industry sector initiatives, such as the Equator Principles for international commerce and the Bank's project finance activities in emerging markets.

## IEG-IFC Evaluation Methodology

Each project's environmental, social, health, and safety impacts were assessed using templates (shown at the end of this section) for nonfinancial intermediary (non-FI) and financial intermediary (FI) operations. Because performance on each of these aspects is considered as part of an aggregate environmental and social effects (ESE) indicator, the results reported in this evaluation cover all dimensions of IFC environmental and social due diligence performance.

The evaluation of IFC-financed investment projects was based on the results of previous IEG evaluations, site visits, a literature review, and structured interviews with project sponsors, governmental and regional environmental authorities, consultants, NGOs, and Bank Group staff in Washington, DC, and in country offices. IFC's environmental and social programs and activities that were not related to IFC investment projects, and environmental and social Advisory Services that supported investment projects, were both evaluated using literature surveys, interviews, and a meta-evaluation, which synthesized available program evaluations.

The source material for evaluating IFC investment projects comprised 632 project evaluations: IEG visited 28 projects, purposively sampled, in nine case study countries (the case study sample), and used the results of 604 randomly sampled Expanded Project Supervision Reports (XPSRs)[3] from 1996 to 2006. Eight projects scheduled for XPSRs were visited and evaluated with the same methodology used for the case study sample, bringing the number of visited projects to 36. Because the case study sample was purposively selected to cover a wide range of industry sectors with varying potential environmental and social impacts, the environmental screening category's distribution (see endnote 6) was somewhat different from the XPSR population for 1996–2006. In proportion, the case study sample included more real sector (non-FI) projects than FI projects and no Category C projects. The case study sample, therefore, cannot be directly compared with the IEG-IFC statistically generalizable sample in XPSR evaluations (table A.1).

The effectiveness of IFC investment projects was assessed with IEG's Environmental and Social Effects Indicator, which covers the project's performance in achieving IFC's requirements and objectives for the environment, and the project's actual environmental impacts. ESE as well as business performance, economic sustainability, and private sector development are evaluated and rated on a four-point scale (unsatisfactory, partly unsatisfactory, satisfactory, and excellent) in the XPSRs. These ratings are then synthesized as an evaluative (not mathematical) summary into an overall development outcome rating.[4] The XPSRs are self-evaluations made by operations staff. IEG then reviews the ratings and their justifications. XPSR evaluations are done on about 50 percent of those projects having five years' maturity after IFC commitment. Each year, a randomly selected and representative sample of projects at early operational maturity is made, and the operational staff complete XPSR evaluations. To assess project impacts in the field and, if ESHS information for desk evaluation is not available, IEG-IFC environmental specialists visit the projects. Since 2005, about 10–15 projects have been visited annually. IEG-IFC uses a generic ESHS review template to review the ESE in XPSR projects. For this study, the template was modified to also include ESHS success factors, wider impacts, the use of consultants, as well as key issues for successful Advisory Services and capacity building (see template below). The "ESE success rate" was calculated as a percentage of excellent and satisfactory ratings and presented separately for the XPSR projects and the case study sample.

The International Standards Organization (ISO) defines "environmental impact" as any change to the environment resulting from an organization's environmental aspects (ISO standard 14001). To capture impact, assessment of "environmental performance" (measurable results of an organization's management of its environmental aspects, ISO standard 14001), including environmental condition at appraisal and at the time of evaluation

**Table A.1: Distribution of Environmental Category in XPSRs and the Case Study Sample**

| | Environmental screening category | | | | | | | | | |
|---|---|---|---|---|---|---|---|---|---|---|
| | A | | B | | C | | FI | | Total | |
| Sample | No. | % | No. | % | No. | % | No. | % | No. | % |
| 2006 case study | 2 | 7 | 24 | 86 | 0 | 0 | 2 | 7 | 28 | 100 |
| 1996–2006 XPSRs | 32 | 5 | 337 | 56 | 83 | 14 | 152 | 25 | 604 | 100 |

*Source:* IEG database on XPSR project reports.
*Note:* For the environmental screening category, see endnote 6.

is needed. Project baselines are usually well established in environmental impact assessments of Category A projects, but in many Category B projects it was difficult to evaluate the changes and impacts because of missing baseline and performance information.

IFC selects its investment projects based on their potential for high development outcomes. The potential to achieve good ESE is not the only criterion for project selection, of course. Other important criteria are a project's business performance, economic sustainability, and contribution to private sector development. The selection of investment projects based on the potential for positive environmental impacts is not addressed in this evaluation, but projects that met IFC's requirements and achieved high positive environmental impacts are credited with high ESE ratings.

IFC investment projects comprise investments in the form of loans and equity that go directly to private sector clients (known as "real sector" or "non-FI" projects) and indirectly to financial intermediaries ("FI projects"), which are the commercial banks, funds, and leasing or insurance companies providing finance to their clients with IFC proceeds. Of the 604 evaluated XPSR projects *with ESE ratings*, 385 were non-FI (real sector) and 219 were FI projects. The case study sample of 28 projects consisted of 26 real sector and 2 FI projects. The 604 XPSR projects represent 35 percent of 1,738 projects that were appraised during 1990–2002 and required environmental supervision (A, B, and FI categories, see endnote 3).

The methodology applied in investment projects was to evaluate the project against specific requirements described in the Environmental and Social Clearance Memorandum, which clears the project for Board consideration, and in the Environmental Review Summary, which is agreed upon with the sponsors of Category B projects and is published after Board approval. The evaluation also takes into account environmental covenants in the legal documents, as well as IFC's procedures, guidelines, and policies—both current and at the time of appraisal and evaluation. The "at-appraisal" requirements for the case study sample comprise the 1998 Procedure for Environmental and Social Review of Projects, Bank Group industry sector guidelines, the Bank Group's 1998 *Pollution Prevention and Abatement Handbook* (World Bank Group with UNEP and UNIDO 1999), as well as operational policies and directives.

All projects in the case study sample and the XPSR 2006 projects were also evaluated against IFC's 2006 Procedure for Environmental and Social Review of Projects and 2006 Policy and Performance Standards. For FI projects, the requirements depend on whether IFC invested in the FI or provided finance directly for specific FI subprojects.

IEG started to produce ESHS review reports and evaluate ESHS work quality in 2003. Since 2004, all XPSR projects have been evaluated based on their ESHS work quality at appraisal and supervision, and on IFC's role and contribution. IFC's work quality has been evaluated for 148 XPSR projects and the case study sample. The checklists and issues addressed in the project evaluations are described further in the ESHS review template below.

The countries selected for this study covered the most significant IFC client countries in terms of their global environmental importance—Brazil, China, and India. Given both their global and Regional significance, Russia and Egypt were selected from the Europe and Central Asia Region and Middle East and North Africa Region, respectively. In considering the Bank Group's priority attention to Africa, the corresponding case studies focused on three countries—Ghana, Kenya, and Uganda. IEG also visited IFC's South Africa office in Johannesburg to discuss environment-oriented Advisory Services in Africa, which are managed from that office. These nine countries represent a broad range in terms of demographic and territorial size, income levels, recent economic growth rates, political systems, and environmental challenges, and are drawn from all six IFC operational Regions. However, in Africa, the IEG-IFC country selection differed somewhat from the

IEG-World Bank selection (Ethiopia, Ghana, Madagascar, Senegal, and Uganda), because IFC has very limited exposure in Ethiopia, Madagascar, and Senegal. The selected countries are presented below by Region:

- ***Africa:*** Ghana, Kenya, South Africa (Private Enterprise Partnerships–Africa projects only), Uganda
- ***Asia:*** China, India
- ***Europe and Central Asia:*** Russia
- ***Latin America and the Caribbean:*** Brazil
- ***Middle East and North Africa:*** Egypt

## IEG-IFC Environmental and Social Review Template and Evaluation Questions

***Environmental and Social Effects***

**Ratings:** Unsatisfactory, partly unsatisfactory, satisfactory, excellent

**Evaluation questions:** Environmental screening category, ESHS impacts, risks and mitigation, ESHS opportunities, FI portfolio projects and categorization, environmental management system (EMS), commitment, compliance with ESHS objectives and IFC's present and at-appraisal policies and standards, ESHS impacts, the "extra mile" (client has achieved beyond compliance performance), community programs, and demonstration effects.

The rating should be based on analysis of the project's key environmental performance indicators and objectives, including operational performance indicators, for example, pollution loads; management performance indicators; environmental condition indicators; (see ISO standard 14031), and social, health, and safety indicators. In FI projects, the rating is based on (1) the project's environmental performance in meeting IFC's requirements; and (2) the project's actual environmental impacts through its subprojects.

***Project Screening and Appraisal, IFC's Work Quality (ESHS only)***

**Ratings:** Unsatisfactory, partly unsatisfactory, satisfactory, excellent

**Evaluation questions:** Effectiveness of implementing IFC's at-approval procedure for environmental appraisal and site visit(s). Identification of the key environmental risks of the project (subproject portfolio in FI projects) in the screening of the environmental category and determining it and the key ESHS requirements. Translation of IFC's environmental procedures, policies, guidelines, and performance standards to the requirements in the Environmental Review Summary or Environmental and Social Clearance Memorandum and legal documents. Ensuring adequacy of the EMS and eventual Corrective Action Plan and trained staff to implement them. Appropriateness of the baseline study and Environmental Impact Assessment and disclosure according to IFC's procedures in Category A projects. Addressing cumulative impacts, area of influence, role of third parties and community engagement. Addressing the environmental improvements and costs and integration in process design in feasibility studies. Assessment of the adequacy of policies or supervision standards of the local environmental authority. Training needs and procedural adjustments. Addressing relevant lessons from other operations. Addressing the issues or concerns raised at appraisal—for example, in IFC's review process, by the Bank, civil society, or other stakeholders.

***Supervision, IFC's Work Quality (ESHS only)***

**Ratings:** Unsatisfactory, partly unsatisfactory, satisfactory, excellent

**Evaluation questions:** Reappraisal of the project and the environmental category with new, appropriate requirements if the project concept and environmental risks (portfolio risks in FI projects) changed during implementation; adequacy of the Environmental Impact Assessment and Environmental Audit Reports and Corrective Action Plans and submission for IFC's approval; ESHS site visits and correspondence. Quality of the Annual Monitoring Report or Annual Environmental Performance Report reviews, identification of potential deficiencies, with requests for corrective actions and submission to the investment officer and the company.

Implementation of the corrective actions. Appraisal and monitoring of FI's Category A and B subprojects by IFC or the FI, or by using environmental consultants when appropriate.

***Role and Contribution, IFC's Work Quality (ESHS only)***

**Ratings:** Unsatisfactory, partly unsatisfactory, satisfactory, excellent

**Evaluation questions:** IFC's role and contribution at appraisal and supervision, and in enhancing client's environmental management, identification and mitigation of environmental risks, and introducing training and additional environmental improvements such as carbon trading, energy efficiency, biodiversity programs, and Advisory Services.

***ESHS Success Factors and Wider Impacts***

- Project's wider impacts to improve environmental management of the client, reduce pollution loads, and enhance livelihoods.
- Impact in the Region and country and in the industry sector (demonstration effect).
- IFC's contribution in reaching wider environmental and social impacts.
- What have been the cumulative impacts on upstream/downstream supply chains of IFC's projects, especially with regard to indigenous people and biodiversity issues in agricultural projects, and to labor and working conditions, including child labor, in manufacturing industry projects?

***Cooperation with Consultants and Future Needs for Environmental Appraisal, Monitoring, and Studies***

- How many times have environmental consultants been used in the past five years?
- Domestic/international consultants?
- For what purposes (appraisal, monitoring, environmental studies)?
- For what reasons (skills, experience, measuring equipment, lack of staff time)?
- Were the experiences useless or useful?
- Price/quality and output? FI's satisfaction?
- Future needs?
- Overall need in the country/Region (demand/supply situation)?
- Would the client use consultants if costs were partly/fully covered by Advisory Services?

## Ratings on Compliance with ESHS Objectives for Non-FI Projects

- **Excellent (E):** The project has either: (1) maintained the company's excellent environmental management or materially improved the company's overall environmental performance (for example, through training and addressing environmental, social, cultural, and community aspects, as well as labor and working conditions, or by introducing an environmental management system (EMS) or corporate program for environmental and social responsibility broader than IFC's requirements); or (2) raised the environmental performance of local companies (for example, by raising industry standards and serving as an example of good practice for regulators). In addition, the project has consistently met IFC's at-approval requirements and its environmental effects are deemed acceptable in view of IFC's current requirements. IFC should be able to use projects rated excellent as a role model for positive environmental effects.
- **Satisfactory (S):** The project is, and was during its lifecycle, in material compliance with either IFC's current or at-approval requirements, including Bank Group environmental, health, and safety policies and guidelines.
- **Partly unsatisfactory (PU):** The project is not in material compliance with either IFC's current or at-approval requirements, but deficiencies are being addressed through ongoing and/or planned actions; or earlier noncompliance (since corrected) resulted in environmental damage.
- **Unsatisfactory (U):** The project is not in material compliance with either IFC's current or at-approval requirements, and mitigation prospects are uncertain or unlikely; or earlier noncompliance (since corrected) resulted in substantial and permanent environmental damage.
- **No opinion possible (NOP):** After best efforts, the relevant information to establish material compliance (or lack thereof) cannot be obtained, for example, because of insufficient or missing Annual Monitoring Reports (AMRs). Use of the NOP rating should be a last resort, after reasonable effort has been made to obtain the necessary information. A sponsor's failure to report should result in a partly unsatisfactory or unsatisfactory rating only if the sponsor has repeatedly refused to cooperate on this issue.
- **Not applicable (NA):** If the project was classified as Category C (no impact) and that categorization has remained valid over the lifecycle of the project so far (and is likely to remain going forward), then the correct rating is not applicable. If, despite its Category C classification, the project has had actual or potential environmental and social impacts, then it should be rated accordingly.

| | U | PU | S | E | NOP | NA | |
|---|---|---|---|---|---|---|---|
| **Summary on Compliance with At-Appraisal Objectives** | | | • | | | | |
| 1. Objective at appraisal. *Add from environmental review.* | | | • | | | | |
| 2. Environmental and social management system | | | | | | | |
| 3. Air emissions | | | | | | | |
| 4. Waste waters | | | | | | | |
| 5. IFC at-appraisal policies | | | | | | | |
| 6. Bank Group at-appraisal environmental guidelines | | | | | | | |
| 7. Annual Monitoring Reports (AMRs) | | | | | | | |

| | U | PU | S | E | NOP | NA | |
|---|---|---|---|---|---|---|---|
| **Summary on Compliance with Current Performance Standards** | | | • | | | | |
| 1. Environmental and social assessment and management system | | | • | | | | |
| 2. Labor and working conditions | | | | | | | |
| 3. Pollution prevention and abatement | | | | | | | |
| 4. Community health, safety, and security | | | | | | | |
| 5. Land acquisition and involuntary resettlement | | | | | | | |
| 6. Biodiversity conservation and sustainable natural resource management | | | | | | | |
| 7. Indigenous people | | | | | | | |
| 8. Cultural heritage | | | | | | | |

**Role model and issues beyond compliance**

## Ratings on Compliance with ESHS Objectives for FI Projects

- **Excellent (E):** The project has maintained the FI's EMS or materially improved the efficacy of the FI's overall environmental risk management (for example, through training and introduction of a well-functioning EMS) and the environmental performance of portfolio companies. In addition, the FI has provided transparent and detailed reports on time, verifying that the project (and subprojects, as applicable) has consistently met IFC's requirements at approval and its environmental effects are deemed acceptable in view of IFC's current requirements. IFC should be able to use projects rated excellent as role models for positive environmental effects.
- **Satisfactory (S):** The project meets either IFC's at-approval requirements or IFC's current requirements, and its environmental effects are deemed acceptable overall. For all FI project types, trained staff implement an appropriate EMS that has been functioning over the project lifecycle (as also reflected in acceptable environmental standards being applied to projects financed by the FI). The subprojects are and have been in substantial material compliance with IFC's requirements for the duration of the project.
- **Partly unsatisfactory (PU):** The project does not meet IFC's requirements, but the shortfalls are either being corrected or negative impacts are moderate. For example, the FI's EMS is adequate, but some subprojects have resulted in environmental damage, or the subprojects visited have acceptable environmental standards, but the EMS is materially inadequate; or an FI (type 1) initially had no EMS, but has recently introduced a functioning one.
- **Unsatisfactory (U):** The project does not meet IFC's requirements and substantial negative effects are known or likely, for example, the FI's EMS is completely inadequate and nothing is known about subproject performance; the EMS has material shortcomings and some subprojects have negative environmental effects; while the EMS appears adequate, a significant portion of subprojects have negative environmental effects; or some subprojects have resulted in substantial and irreversible environmental damage.
- **No opinion possible (NOP):** After best efforts, the relevant information to establish material compliance (or lack thereof) cannot be obtained, for example, because of insufficient or missing Annual Environmental Performance Reports. Use of the NOP rating should be a last resort, after reasonable effort has been made to obtain the necessary information.
- **Not applicable (NA):** If the project was classified as Category C (no impact) and that categorization has remained valid over the lifecycle of the project so far (and is likely to remain so going forward), then the correct rating is not applicable. If, despite its Category C classification, the project has had actual or potential environmental and social impacts, then it should be rated accordingly.

**Requirements for FI type T1, T2, and T3 projects, according to the 1998 Environmental and Social Review Procedure (ESRP) and 2006 ESRP, are given below. The 2006 ESRP has no requirements for FIs investing in retail operations.**

| | U | PU | S | E | NOP | NA |
|---|---|---|---|---|---|---|
| **Summary on Compliance with At-Appraisal Objectives** | | | • | | | |
| 1. Process (policy, procedure, responsible staff) | | | • | | | |
| 2. IFC training | | | | | | |
| 3. General Exclusion List (T2 and T3)/ Microfinance Exclusion List (T1 MF) | | | | | | |
| 4. Host-country laws | | | | | | |
| 5. IFC policies (> 0.5 US$ million) | | | | | | |
| 6. Category A subprojects meet applicable guidelines | | | | | | |
| 7. Category B subprojects meet applicable guidelines | | | | | | |
| 8. IFC clearance, public consultation, and environmental assessment of Category A subprojects | | | | | | |
| 9. IFC clearance of each subproject | | | | | | |
| 10. Annual report (AEPR) on process (EMS, appraisal, screening) | | | | | | |
| 11. Annual report summarizing subprojects' performance | | | | | | |
| | **U** | **PU** | **S** | **E** | **NOP** | **NA** |
| **Summary on Compliance with 2006 ESRP** | | | • | | | |
| 1. Environmental and social policies and procedures, skills and competence in ESHS | | | • | | | |
| 2. Training and awareness of investment, legal, and credit officers | | | | | | |
| 3. Exclusion list for (i) all FIs and (ii) MF, trade finance, and listed equities | | | | | | |
| 4. Host-country laws | | | | | | |
| 5. IFC performance standards | | | | | | |
| 6. Mobilizing additional resources | | | | | | |
| 7. Annual report (AEPR) | | | | | | |

**Role model and issues beyond compliance**

## Assessing MIGA Effectiveness

IEG-MIGA assesses the extent to which evaluated projects were (and are) consistent with MIGA's safeguard policies and environmental, health, and safety (EHS) guidelines.[5] IEG focuses on the consistency with environmental and social safeguards and EHS guidelines (collectively described below as "safeguards") at two phases in the project cycle.

- ***At Board approval (and when the contract of guarantee is signed):*** To what extent did a guaranteed investment comply with the requirements of MIGA safeguard policies and guidelines at the time of Board approval? (Any significant differences between the guidelines applicable at approval and current guidelines are highlighted in the evaluation of each project.)
- ***At evaluation (typically three to four years after the guarantee is issued):*** To what extent did a project fulfill or conform to the conditions and requirements of the safeguard policies and guidelines during project implementation (and at evaluation) and adequately implement the safeguard management/action plans that were identified at approval?

IEG evaluation criteria reflect key safeguard policy requirements and the necessary steps involved in meeting them. The criteria differ between approval and evaluation (for example, at approval, IEG assesses the adequacy and appropriateness of an EMS, while at evaluation it assesses the implementation of the EMS). The criteria are based on MIGA's own environmental assessment and disclosure policies and procedures (1999), as well as on MIGA's interim issue-specific safeguards (2002).[6] Consistency with host-country environmental, health, and safety standards is also assessed.

IEG used MIGA's policies, in effect between 1999 and 2007, and current guidelines as the basis for evaluation for all projects in the sample (MIGA's 1999 environmental assessment and disclosure policies and procedures, and 2002 interim issue-specific safeguards).

## IEG-MIGA Environmental, Social, Health, and Safety Review Checklist

The requirements for each criterion of safeguard policy compliance were rated according to the following scale:

- ***Excellent:*** The requirements were fully met, or are expected to be fully met, with no shortcomings.
- ***Satisfactory:*** The requirements generally were met, or are expected to be met, with only minor shortcomings.
- ***Partially satisfactory:*** The requirements were met, or are expected to be met, but with significant shortcomings.
- ***Unsatisfactory:*** The requirements were not met, or are expected not to be met, due to major shortcomings.

(For a list of requirements assessed by IEG at approval and at evaluation, see tables A.2 and A.3)

**Table A.2: MIGA Safeguard Policies—Criteria for Consistency at Approval**

| Criterion | Ratings | | | |
|---|---|---|---|---|
| | Excellent | Satisfactory | Partially satisfactory | Unsatis-factory |
| Comprehensive environmental assessment | | | | |
| Adequate analysis of feasible alternatives | | | | |
| EHS guidelines or host country's regulations adequately addressed | | | | |
| Comprehensive environmental and social baseline survey | | | | |
| Adequate Environmental Action Plan or Environmental Management Plan proposed | | | | |
| Project sponsor's EMS adequate | | | | |
| Public disclosure/consultation addressed | | | | |
| Comprehensive and implementable resettlement plan/ community development plan prepared | | | | |
| Comprehensive and implementable indigenous peoples plan prepared | | | | |
| Natural habitats protected or offsets provided | | | | |
| Comprehensive dam safety measures proposed | | | | |
| Cultural property protection proposed | | | | |

*Note:* EHS = environmental health and safety; EMS = environmental management system.

**Table A.3: MIGA Safeguard Policies—Criteria for Consistency at Evaluation**

| Criterion | Ratings | | | |
|---|---|---|---|---|
| | Excellent | Satisfactory | Partially satisfactory | Unsatis-factory |
| Environmental Action Plan or Environmental Management Plan fully implemented | | | | |
| Environmental and social monitoring implemented | | | | |
| Sponsor's project implementation EMS effective | | | | |
| Continuing public disclosure and consultation | | | | |
| Full compensation of project-affected people | | | | |
| Resettlement plan/community development plan fully implemented | | | | |
| Indigenous peoples plan fully implemented | | | | |
| Natural habitats protected or offsets provided | | | | |
| Dam safety measures implemented | | | | |
| Cultural property protected | | | | |
| Contract of guarantee for implementation of safeguard policies/ guidelines adequate | | | | |
| Reporting on safeguard policies by sponsor adequate | | | | |

*Note:* EMS = environmental management system.

A gold separation facility in Ghana is an example of a sustainable operation. Photo courtesy of Jouni Martti Eerikainen.

# APPENDIX B: RELEVANT FINDINGS FROM PREVIOUS IEG EVALUATIONS

In 2001, IEG evaluated the World Bank's effectiveness in relation to the environment during the 1990s, specifically considering its performance on environmental safeguards, stewardship, mainstreaming, and global sustainability. A more recent IEG assessment examined Bank experience regarding natural hazards, and there have also been previous evaluations of MIGA's environmental and social due diligence processes. The main findings of each of these evaluations, many of which continue to be relevant, are summarized below.

## Previous IEG Findings Regarding Environmental Assessment

- Environmental assessment (EA) policies and objectives are generally sound, but environmental assessments are often not completed soon enough in the project cycle to have much impact on project design. The criteria for application of environmental assessment standards have not been consistently applied across Regions and countries. Delays in making environmental assessments available to the public have contributed to external criticism. Heavy reliance on external consultants has undercut environmental assessment effectiveness and has not contributed to the building of local capacity.
- Compliance shortfalls in highly visible operations have cast doubt on the integrity of the quality assurance process. Guidelines for the application of policies have not been fully internalized by many task managers and staff, partly because the provisions are not always clear.
- Supervision of environmental aspects of Category A and particularly Category B projects (see glossary for definitions of categories) has been weak, and monitoring of action plan implementation has been spotty. Hence, it is nearly impossible to verify the effectiveness of mitigation measures and, once the Bank's involvement ceases, there is no regular program for monitoring the implementation and sustainability of environmental measures during the lifecycle of the project.
- Adjustment (now called development policy) lending was largely excluded from the environmental assessment process, even though several NGOs and internal studies had clearly identified the impacts that such lending can have on the environment, and recommended methods to assess such effects.

## Previous IEG Findings Regarding Stewardship

- The Bank's program to support national environmental action plans and environmental ESW put the environment on the policy agenda, but the documents themselves were of mixed quality and follow-up has not been consistent.
- Integration of the environment into country assistance strategies was limited, even when International Development Association (IDA) deputies stressed such inclusion.
- Environmental ESW was declining compared with the early 1990s, in both numbers of studies and budgetary allocations.
- Bank projects included many successful examples both of direct environmental lending and of operations that had mainstreamed the environment into other operations.
- Bank treatment of the environment as a sector, rather than a cross-cutting priority, was reflected in the difficulty in getting environmental projects into country programs and environmental components into sectoral projects; the

current structure pitched environmental units against other sector units in a competition for funds and slots in country lending programs.
- The Bank's long-term engagement with client countries needs to ensure continued focus on permanent vulnerability reduction.

## Previous IEG Findings Regarding Mainstreaming

- Despite indications of progress, many difficulties were faced in introducing mainstreaming activities. Sector reviews were completed but their recommendations were not followed up, and environmental capacity developed but was then lost when environmental specialists moved elsewhere. Real commitment from borrowers, demonstrated by adequate budgets and the accountability of managers, was often lacking.
- Bank staff often faced the reluctance of countries to borrow for environmental projects, especially when bilateral grant resources were available, and/or used relatively scarce International Bank for Reconstruction and Development/International Development Association funds for other priorities. This led to environmental concerns being deemphasized in some Bank country strategies.
- Performance on mainstreaming the environment into other sectors and what is now called development policy lending was harder to measure. Although it was widely agreed by both management and staff that an integrated approach was desirable, lack of clear objectives, insufficient means of monitoring, and lack of internal incentives pushed in the opposite direction.
- After having identified the pervasive aspects of environmental issues, recorded their importance to poverty alleviation, and confirmed that mainstreaming is essential to achieving environmental objectives and commitments, in practice the Bank had done little institutionally to promote, monitor, or otherwise make mainstreaming happen.

## Previous IEG Findings Regarding Global Sustainability

- The Bank prepared GEF projects to address biodiversity, ozone depletion, and international waters issues, but these were sometimes isolated operations in response to the global mandate, and were not integrated into coherent national strategies. In other cases, they failed to contribute to larger environmental objectives or to help Bank efforts to mainstream.
- The Bank's emphasis on global issues should not detract from addressing regional environmental issues, which are very important to member countries. Many environmental issues involve watersheds or ecosystems that span national borders. Cooperation among countries is needed and the Bank has the potential to facilitate greater cooperation than has been the case so far. Although the Bank has encouraged members to take these issues into account, it has not undertaken projects to address multicountry environmental issues because its strong country and sectoral orientation has impeded such activities.
- Considering resource constraints, the Bank's efforts to address global issues in its own research and analysis have been satisfactory. It has also begun working with international agencies and NGOs on global issues. This approach has proven partially effective in bringing attention to global issues in country dialogues, but it has not made much progress in gaining borrower support. Bank efforts have been satisfactory neither in mitigating the local impacts of climate change nor in addressing regional issues, but the Bank is beginning to expand its work in the former.

## Previous IEG Findings Regarding Bank Assistance for Natural Disasters

(This section draws on IEG-World Bank 2006c)

- The development community needs to engage with disaster-stricken borrowers earlier and stay engaged longer.
- Bank lending in response to natural disasters has been increasing over time because the incidence of weather-related events, such as flooding and severe tropical storms, appears to be increasing.
- Economic and social impacts of natural disasters are very large in developing countries.

- Human actions that contribute to the destructiveness associated with natural disasters need to be addressed.
- Emergency preparedness studies are typically completed too late and are used too little. While attention to mitigation measures is improving, it too often lacks borrower ownership.
- In general, disaster responses have tended toward the reactive and tactical, when instead a proactive and strategic approach would have had longer-term benefits.
- Natural-hazard risks are highly concentrated. Ten countries, including Brazil, China, India, and Madagascar, account for close to 40 percent of the Bank's portfolio of projects fully or partly focused on natural disasters. Special attention therefore needs to be given to planning ahead for disaster and reducing long-term vulnerability in these countries.

## Previous IEG Findings Regarding Implementation of IEG-MIGA Recommendations on Environmental and Social Aspects

IEG has made several recommendations related to the social and environmental compliance of MIGA projects in its annual reports and in its report on extractive industries. The performance standards adopted in 2007 are expected to address many of these recommendations. Because these standards have been in place for only a short time, the following summary is a progress report based on findings (from the 2007 IEG quality-at-entry [QAE] review)[1,2] of MIGA guarantees, issued during fiscal 2005 and 2006, which predate the recent policy.

- ***Adequacy of security arrangements.*** The 2007 QAE review found that one extractive industry's project investor had taken this concern seriously and was planning to implement best international practice in managing its security arrangements to protect the rights of individuals who may come into contact with its security personnel.
- ***Preparation of resettlement plans, community development plans, and indigenous peoples plans prior to Board approval.*** Seventy-five percent of MIGA's projects involving resettlement or community development have had plans prepared and agreed to with communities prior to Board approval or contract signing.
- ***Support to investors to improve environmental, health, and safety (EHS) issues prior to Board approval.*** The QAE review found that MIGA had not provided financial or external technical assistance to improve EHS issues in any of the 25 reviewed projects.
- ***Setting up of an EMS prior to Board approval.*** The QAE review found that only 8 percent (2 projects) had set up an EMS prior to Board approval, and that in only 32 percent (8 projects) had investors provided adequate documentation in support of their proposed EMS. Therefore, in almost 70 percent of its projects, MIGA cannot be certain that its EHS standards are adequately addressed by its guarantee holders.
- ***Adequacy of community consultation on Category A projects.*** All of the Category A projects reviewed for QAE were found to have followed adequate community consultation arrangements, indicating a substantial improvement in this area of MIGA's due diligence.
- ***Reporting requirements included in contracts of guarantee.*** In 28 percent of the Category A and B projects underwritten between January 2005 and June 2006 and reviewed for QAE, MIGA required annual or key milestone reporting in meeting its EHS requirements in the contract of guarantee, a significant improvement over the past.
- ***Field visits by MIGA's environmental, health, and safety staff for Category A projects.*** Each of the Category A projects in the QAE review was visited by an environmental or social specialist. Two of the Category B projects were visited by an environmental specialist and one Category B project was visited by both environmental and social specialists. One each of the Category A and B projects would have benefited from the involvement of a social specialist in addition to the environmental specialist. Two of the Category B projects should have been visited by both environmental and social specialists.

- ***Improvements in EHS assessments of Category B projects.*** The QAE review found that in 2 projects (9 percent), MIGA improved the EHS performance through its due diligence. One involved a site visit by both an environmental and a social specialist, in which MIGA was able to assist the investor with a resettlement issue and to reduce the environmental impact of an urban development project. In the other case, MIGA identified a potential site contamination issue that was not resolved, but it at least alerted the investor to the potential risk.
- ***Better use of contracts of guarantee.*** Fifty-four percent of projects reviewed for QAE showed better use of contracts of guarantee to refer to appropriate MIGA safeguards and guidelines. The expectation is that with this improved trend, it will become routine to fully incorporate substantive EHS provisions in contracts of guarantee.
- ***Beyond safeguard compliance to "doing good."*** In 3 of the 26 projects reviewed for QAE, the project sponsors went beyond the strict requirements of safeguard policies and guidelines to "doing good." However, only in one case was MIGA directly responsible for encouraging this initiative. The other projects that went beyond MIGA safeguards and guidelines were encouraged to do so by the European Bank for Reconstruction and Development, United States Agency for International Development, and the Bank.
- ***Coordination with other development partners.*** The 2007 QAE review noted that MIGA cooperated effectively with development partners on all of the projects in which such partners were involved. The quality of the EHS work carried out by such partners is often far better than on projects where MIGA is the sole development agency involved in the project.

**Figure B.1: Implementation of IEG-MIGA Environmental and Social Recommendations**

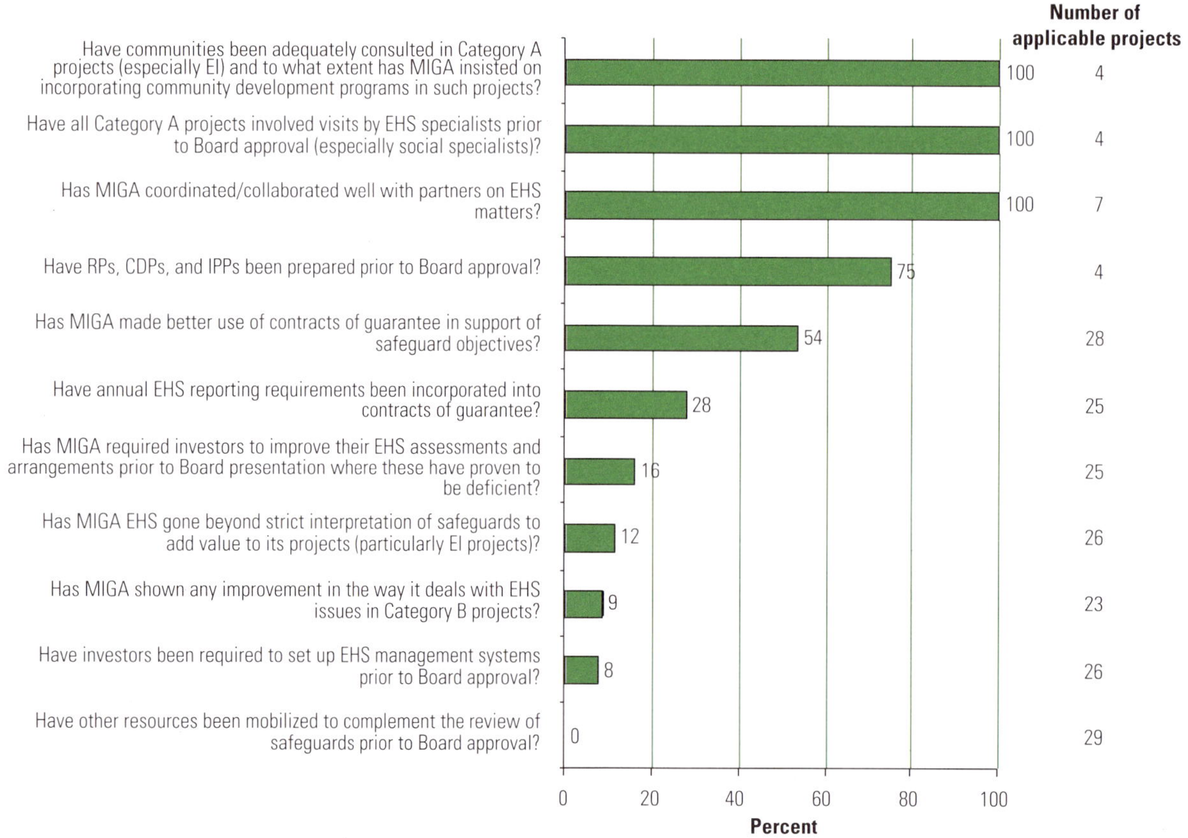


*Note:* Not all categories are shown in this figure. RP = resettlement plan, CDP = community development plan, IPP = indigenous peoples plan.

The countries selected as cases for this evaluation include some of the Bank Group's oldest (Brazil and India) and largest clients in terms of both territory and support levels (Russia and China), as well as five smaller borrowers (Egypt, Ghana, Madagascar, Senegal, and Uganda). Each country is distinct in many ways, not only ecologically, historically, and culturally, but also in some of their basic demographic and economic characteristics. Most of the countries are of regional and/or global environmental significance. The effectiveness of Bank Group support for the environment within their boundaries is of great relevance nationally as well as at the regional and global levels.[1]

## Basic Demographic and Economic Characteristics

The nine case study countries, taken together, account for 41 percent of the total land area of all lower- and middle-income countries,[2] and accounted for 53 percent of the combined population and 45 percent of the combined gross domestic product (GDP) in this category in 2004.[3] On average, this sample is slightly less urbanized than the set of lower- and middle-income countries as a whole (38 percent urban in the former, as compared with 43 percent urban in the latter) and somewhat poorer in per capita GDP ($1,320 in the sample, compared with $1,566 in this category as a whole). In both cases, this reflects the important weight of India (29 percent urban, $640 per capita GDP) among the sample countries, together with those in Sub-Saharan Africa, where urbanization levels ranged from a very low 12 percent (Madagascar) to just over 50 percent (Senegal), and where per capita GDP ranged from only $243 to $684 (respectively, in the same two countries). The basic physical, demographic, and economic characteristics of the case study countries are summarized in table C.1.

The averages presented in table C.1 mask significant variations in case study country characteristics. Three of the countries—Brazil, China, and Russia—are among the five largest in the world in terms of territory, and China and India alone account for 37 percent of the world's total population. China is also rapidly becoming one of the world's largest economies, although Brazil and Russia still have per capita GDP figures more than two times that of China, roughly three times that of Egypt, five times that of Senegal and India, eight times that of Ghana, and nearly 12 times that of Uganda and Madagascar. The four Sub-Saharan African countries are much smaller than the other countries in the sample in terms of geography, population, and economic size.

Other important differences exist among these countries as well. Rural population densities in relation to arable land vary significantly from just 32 and 52 persons per square kilometer in Russia and Brazil, respectively, at one extreme, to 1,409 persons per square kilometer in Egypt, at the other extreme (reflecting the very limited amounts of arable land in a country constituted largely of desert). China (554 persons per square kilometer), India (475), Uganda (453), and Madagascar (438) fall in the middle, followed by Ghana (277) and Senegal (228).

Urbanization levels also vary widely and are roughly correlated with per capita GDP, with Brazil (84 percent) and Russia (73 percent) at one end, and Uganda (12 percent), Madagascar (27 percent), and India (29 percent) at the other. China, Egypt, Ghana, and Senegal fall in the 40 to 50 percent range. Finally, there are notable differences in population growth rates in the sample, with the four Sub-Saharan African countries

**Table C.1: Physical, Demographic, and Economic Characteristics of the Case Study Countries, 1990–2003**

| Country | Area (thousand km²) | Population (million) | Annual population growth, 1990–2003 | Urban population (%) | Rural population density (per km²) | GDP (US$ billion) | GDP per capita (US$) |
|---|---|---|---|---|---|---|---|
| Brazil | 8,459 | 183.9 | 1.4 | 83.6 | 52 | 604.0 | 3,284.4 |
| China | 9,327 | 1,296.2 | 1.4 | 40.6 | 554 | 1,931.7 | 1,490.3 |
| Egypt, Arab Republic of | 995 | 72.6 | 1.9 | 42.2 | 1409 | 78.8 | 1,085.4 |
| Ghana | 228 | 21.7 | 2.3 | 45.8 | 277 | 8.9 | 410.1 |
| India | 2,973 | 1,079.7 | 1.7 | 28.5 | 475 | 691.2 | 640.2 |
| Madagascar | 582 | 18.1 | 2.9 | 26.8 | 438 | 4.4 | 243.1 |
| Russian Federation | 16,889 | 143.4 | −0.3 | 73.3 | 32 | 432.9 | 3,018.8 |
| Senegal | 193 | 11.4 | 2.6 | 50.3 | 228 | 7.8 | 684.2 |
| Uganda | 197 | 25.3 | 2.9 | 12.4 | 453 | 6.3 | 249.0 |
| **Subtotal (case study countries)** | **39,843** | **2,852.3** | | **38.2** | | **3,766.0** | **1,320.3** |
| Total (developing countries) | 96,6450 | 5,360.8 | 1.5 | 43.3 | 503 | 8,395.2 | 1,566.0 |
| **Subtotal (case study countries as a share of developing countries, in percent)** | **41.2** | **53.2** | | | | **44.9** | **84.3** |
| **World** | **129,663** | **6,365.0** | **1.4** | **48.4** | **492** | **41,290.4** | **6,487.1** |

(especially Madagascar and Uganda) having rates exceeding 2 percent a year. Population in India is growing at an annual rate of about 1.7 percent, and in Brazil and China at 1.4 percent, while the Russian population is declining in absolute terms, registering a −0.3 annual growth rate between 1990 and 2003.

Recent economic growth rates, productive structures, and rural land use, likewise, vary tremendously. Between 1990 and 2003, for example, GDP in China grew at a rate of 9.6 percent a year, following an average annual growth of 10.3 percent in the 1980s. GDP in India expanded at an average rate of 5.9 percent per year during the most recent period and at 5.7 percent between 1980 and 1990. Rapid growth in both countries continued in 2003–04, at 9.4 percent a year in China and 7.8 percent in India. In contrast, GDP growth in Brazil was only 2.6 percent a year between 1990 and 2003, down slightly from 2.7 percent in the 1980s, and continued at 2.5 percent in 2003–04. Economic growth in Russia was negative (−1.8 percent a year) between 1990 and 2003, but accelerated sharply in 2003–04 (to 7.2 percent a year), owing in good measure to rising international oil and gas prices. The experience among the African countries was mixed, with GDP in Uganda growing at a comparatively high average rate of 6.8 percent annually between 1990 and 2003, while Egypt and Ghana expanded at 4.5 percent and 4.3 percent a year, respectively, and Madagascar and Senegal grew at an annual average of just 2.1 percent. All of these countries, except Madagascar and Uganda, grew more rapidly during the 1980s than in the years after.

Important structural differences likewise characterize the economies of the various sample countries, with industry accounting for 52 percent of GDP in China in 2003, but only 15 percent in Madagascar. Industry also accounted for comparatively low shares of total GDP in Brazil (19 percent), Senegal, and Uganda (21 percent each) in 2003, and relatively higher shares in Russia and Egypt (34 percent each), with India (27 percent) and Ghana (25 percent) falling in between. Agriculture accounted for a high of 36 percent of GDP in Ghana, followed by 32 percent in Uganda, and 29 percent in

Madagascar in 2003, compared with just 5 percent in Russia and 6 percent in Brazil, two countries where the service sector clearly predominates (accounting for 61 percent and 75 percent of GDP, respectively).

Similarly, there were sharp differences in rural land use, with agricultural land prevailing in Ghana (65 percent), Uganda (63 percent), India (61 percent), and China (59 percent)—which, together with Egypt, were also the sample countries that had the highest rural population densities—and forest land representing the largest shares in Brazil (57 percent, mainly due to Amazonia), Russia (48 percent), and Senegal (45 percent). Egypt was at the other extreme in this respect, with nearly 97 percent of its land area being desert and only 3 percent in agricultural use. Reflecting severe climate constraints as well, just 13 percent of Russia's land area was in agriculture, compared with 47 percent in Madagascar, 42 percent in Senegal, and 31 percent in Brazil. Significant climate differences—particularly water availability—also help to explain the much larger relative shares of cropland under irrigation in Egypt (almost 100 percent), China (35 percent), India (33 percent), and Madagascar (31 percent) as compared with Uganda (0.1 percent), Ghana (0.5 percent), Russia (3.7 percent), Brazil (4.4 percent, mostly in the semiarid northeast), and Senegal (4.8 percent).

## National Wealth and Genuine Savings

The recent Bank publication, *Where Is the Wealth of Nations?* (World Bank 2006f), provides useful information on the case study countries. The publication compares countries on two basic variables, "genuine savings" and national wealth, which refer more specifically to the impact of natural resource and environmental degradation on national incomes and natural capital asset stocks, respectively. In relation to national wealth estimates, for example, per capita wealth in 2000 was highest in Brazil ($86,992), followed by Russia ($38,709), and Egypt ($21,879), and lowest in Madagascar ($5,020), followed by India ($6,820), China ($9,387), Senegal ($10,167), and Ghana ($10,365).[4] In terms of the relative importance of natural capital to total wealth, the case study countries ranked as follows: Russia (44.5 percent of total wealth, primarily in the form of subsoil resources, such as oil, gas, coal, and minerals), Madagascar (33.5 percent), India (28.3 percent), China (23.7 percent, mainly cropland, followed by subsoil assets), Egypt (14.8 percent), Ghana (12.9 percent), Senegal (12.5 percent), and Brazil (7.8 percent).[5]

Rates of "genuine savings" ranged from a high of 25.5 percent in China to a low of –13.4 percent in Russia, with India (12.9 percent), Brazil (7.2 percent), and Ghana (5.6 percent) at the higher end and Madagascar (2.9 percent), Uganda (3.4 percent), and Egypt (3.6 percent) at the lower end.[6] Finally, with regard to changes in wealth per capita, four countries recorded positive figures (China with a per capita wealth increase of $200, followed by Brazil at $64, India at $16, and Russia at $4), and four have negative changes in wealth (Madagascar at –$56, Egypt at –$45, Senegal at –$27, and Ghana at –$18). This clearly suggests that countries on the African continent are not becoming wealthier in per capita terms when natural resource depletion is taken into account. Also, Russia's barely positive change in per capita wealth may reflect its absolute loss of population, at least as much as its real accumulation of wealth, which, based on a negative genuine savings rate, may not have grown at all in real terms in 2000.

## Regional and Global Environmental Significance

Most of the countries are very significant from a global environmental perspective, especially China and India with respect to climate change;[7] China, India, and Russia with regard to ozone-depleting substances; and Brazil, China, India, Madagascar, and Russia with respect to biodiversity.[8] Several of these countries participate in major Bank-supported regional or other special environmental programs, such as Egypt in the Mediterranean Technical Assistance Program for the Environment,[9] the Red Sea and Gulf of Aden Program,[10] and the Nile Basin Initiative; Uganda in the Nile Basin Initiative[11] and the Lake Victoria Environmental Management Program;[12] Senegal in the Senegal River Basin Project;[13] Brazil in the

Guarani Aquifer Project[14] and the G-7 Pilot Program to Conserve the Rainforests; and Russia in the Baltic,[15] Black,[16] and Caspian Seas[17] Environmental Programs.

## Country Environmental Indicators

A suggestive cross-country comparison is also provided by the pilot 2006 Environmental Performance Index, compiled by the Yale Center for Environmental Law and Policy and the Center for International Earth Science Information Network at Columbia University. While this index is not universally regarded as a true measure of environmental performance, [18] it nevertheless gives an idea as to how different countries presently rank according to one set of aggregate criteria. The index centers on two broad environmental protection objectives: reducing environmental stresses on human health and promoting ecosystem vitality and sound natural resource management. These two dimensions are gauged using 16 indicators tracked in six policy categories: environmental health,[19] air quality, water resources, productive natural resources, biodiversity and habitat, and sustainable energy. The overall Environmental Performance Index values for all 133 countries surveyed range from a high of 88.0 (New Zealand) to a low of 25.7 (Niger). The IEG case study countries cover a wide range of index scores, with Russia (77.5) and Brazil (77.0) ranked fairly high (32nd and 34th, respectively)—achieving scores not too different from that for the United States (78.5, ranked 28th)—and India (47.4, ranked 118th), Madagascar (48.5, 116th), Senegal (52.1, 107th), and China (56.2, 94th) at the lower end of the spectrum. Ghana (63.1, 72nd), Uganda (60.8, 78th), and Egypt (57.9, 85th) fall in between. More specific figures also exist for each case study country; they indicate considerable variation across the various dimensions considered (see table C.2).

## World Bank Lending Commitments and IFC Exposure

Finally, most of the countries selected have been long-time and significant Bank Group clients. India is, by far, the Bank Group's largest client (although MIGA does not operate there), with 525 World Bank lending and grant operations, involving total commitments of $66.1 billion through June 2006. China (which only began borrowing in the early 1980s) and Brazil are the second and third largest clients, with 382 Bank operations involving $42.4 billion in commitments in China, and 395 Bank operations with commitments of $38.3 billion in Brazil.[20] While Russia has only been a member of the Bank Group since 1992, it received Bank commitments totaling $13.9 billion in 84 operations (many of which were for adjustment) through June 2006. As the data in table C.3 show, Brazil, China, India, and Russia are all countries where

**Table C.2: Environmental Performance Index Values for Selected Variables, by Country**

| Country | Air quality | Water resources | Productive natural resources | Sustainable energy | Biodiversity and habitats | Environmental health |
|---|---|---|---|---|---|---|
| Brazil | 64.0 | 97.7 | 80.9 | 80.6 | 50.5 | 79.3 |
| China | 22.3 | 49.6 | 66.2 | 50.8 | 68.1 | 61.0 |
| Egypt, Arab Republic of | 14.8 | 71.5 | 38.9 | 57.2 | 23.9 | 74.6 |
| Ghana | 87.3 | 99.4 | 76.5 | 83.3 | 50.1 | 48.8 |
| India | 28.4 | 67.6 | 62.1 | 59.7 | 39.8 | 43.8 |
| Madagascar | 74.7 | 88.8 | 83.3 | 82.7 | 39.5 | 23.3 |
| Russian Federation | 55.6 | 98.0 | 83.3 | 15.5 | 61.0 | 92.3 |
| Senegal | 52.9 | 52.0 | 72.1 | 77.6 | 67.6 | 39.9 |
| Uganda | 98.0 | 92.7 | 93.0 | 92.4 | 73.6 | 31.7 |

*Source:* Pilot 2006 Environmental Performance Index.

IFC presently has significant exposure; Egypt is also in the top 15.

Total Bank commitments to date (mostly in the form of IDA credits) have been considerably lower in the African countries, ranging from $2.7 billion for Senegal and $3.1 billion for Madagascar, at one end, to $7.8 billion for Egypt at the other, with Ghana ($5.3 billion) and Uganda ($4.7 billion) in between. However, all five of these countries have had more than 100 total Bank operations, ranging from 102 in Madagascar to 147 in Ghana. Uganda (127), Egypt (135), and Senegal (137) fall in between. The Bank Group therefore has had substantial experience in all of the case study countries over the past four decades. A more detailed breakdown of Bank loans, IDA credits (in all countries except Brazil), and grant funding to the countries in the sample is presented in table C.3.

**Table C.3: Total IBRD/IDA Commitments and IFC Exposure, in Selected Countries**

| Total IBRD/IDA commitments, 1947–2006 | | | | Total IFC commitments, current exposure | |
|---|---|---|---|---|---|
| Country | Number of loans/credits | Number of grants | Total commitments (US$ million) | Country | Total commitments (US$ million) |
| India | 496 | 30 | 65,988.8 | Brazil | 3,714.7 |
| China | 328 | 54 | 42,398.6 | Mexico | 2,810.4 |
| Brazil | 356 | 42 | 38,236.0 | India | 2,786.4 |
| Mexico | 239 | 35 | 38,074.5 | Argentina | 2,704.8 |
| Indonesia | 349 | 32 | 31,617.1 | Russian Federation | 2,672.4 |
| Turkey | 173 | 9 | 25,372.4 | Turkey | 2,669.9 |
| Argentina | 149 | 19 | 23,008.4 | China | 2,198.0 |
| Pakistan | 242 | 18 | 16,930.3 | Indonesia | 1,674.9 |
| Korea | 121 | 1 | 15,697.8 | Pakistan | 1,271.4 |
| Russian Federation | 73 | 11 | 13,880.7 | Colombia | 1,051.7 |
| Colombia | 207 | 19 | 13,672.3 | Thailand | 1,040.8 |
| Philippines | 206 | 31 | 12,296.1 | Philippines | 1,036.7 |
| Nigeria | 135 | 15 | 9,154.3 | Egypt, Arab Republic of | 922.3 |
| Egypt, Arab Republic of | 124 | 11 | 7,814.0 | Nigeria | 745.8 |
| Peru | 120 | 13 | 6,684.4 | | |
| Ethiopia | 112 | 12 | 5,573.4 | | |
| Ghana | 136 | 11 | 5,297.3 | | |
| Uganda | 111 | 16 | 4,720.9 | | |
| Chile | 87 | 17 | 4,054.6 | | |
| Madagascar | 99 | 3 | 3,039.3 | | |
| Senegal | 124 | 13 | 2,681.3 | | |

*Source:* World Bank database.

Brazilian factory. Photo by Jim Pickerell, courtesy of the World Bank Photo Library.

# APPENDIX D: SUMMARY OF COUNTRY CASE STUDY FINDINGS: ENVIRONMENTAL PRIORITIES AND BANK SUPPORT

The following matrixes, one for each of the nine case study countries, are intended to provide a summary overview of country environmental priorities[1] and the extent to which the Bank has attempted to address these priorities in its country strategies, analytical and advisory activities (AAA), and other nonlending activities and lending and grant operations since 1990 in each country. The environmental problems considered are: urban air quality, indoor air pollution, water quality, water scarcity/resource management, land degradation/soil erosion, deforestation/forest resource management, biodiversity loss, energy efficiency/alternative energy, greenhouse gas emissions/climate change, ozone depletion, and institutional capacity.

Three types of Bank instruments are considered: Country Assistance Strategies and Country Partnership Strategies (CAS/CPS), ESW and other AAA, and lending (including IDA credits) and grant operations. In the Sub-Saharan African cases, country-prepared (but often Bank-assisted) Poverty Reduction Strategy Papers (PRSPs) are also rated in terms of the relative intensity of Bank attention to each issue in the CAS/CPS and PRSPs, and the relative use of ESW/AAA and loans/grants to help countries address each issue.

Problem severity is ranked as high, medium, low, or nonexistent. In some cases a change is indicated over time, divided into two periods—before and after 2000. These ratings are based on several sources including borrower National Environmental Action Plans (NEAPs) and Bank Country Environmental Strategy Papers, Bank costs of environmental degradation studies, and Country Environmental Analyses (CEAs)—where they exist—and other relevant Bank ESW, together with the Yale/Columbia country environmental indicators presented in appendix C, and the judgments of the respective IEG country case study team leaders. In one case (India), these have been slightly modified, based on specific comments on the preliminary draft of this report received from Bank management.

The fact that a particular priority for any given country is listed as high, medium, or low, while the relative ratings for the attention it has received in Bank strategies, nonlending activities, and/or lending and grant operations over time differ from the same, should not be interpreted to mean, in any sense, that IEG is indicating that Bank performance was inadequate in this regard. Neither does it reflect an assumption on the part of IEG that the Bank should (or could) have been engaged in all environmental priority areas; the extent of Bank involvement ultimately depends on the countries and national governments themselves.

The intention of the matrixes is to indicate, in a more systematic way for each of the country case studies, where the relative emphasis of Bank strategies, nonlending activities, and financial support has been over time, both across the various themes and in relation to one another. In short, it is intended as a way of "mapping" some of the case study findings more clearly in a country-specific way.

**Brazil: Country Matrix**

The ratings in the matrix below are shown for (before 2000) / (after 2000). Where a single rating is given, attention at the level indicated was relatively uniform both before and after 2000.

| Theme/ instrument | Problem severity | CAS/CPS |
|---|---|---|
| **Urban air quality** | **Medium**<br>A serious problem in the São Paulo Metro region, Baixada Fluminense, Goiania, Cubatão, and other locations, but average in most other large cities. | **Medium**<br>Air pollution issues discussed consistently throughout the evaluation period. |
| **Indoor air pollution** | **Medium**<br>A problem in some rural areas, although the extent of the problem is unknown. | **Low**<br>Not prioritized in the face of other brown issues. |
| **Water quality** | **Medium**<br>A problem in urban areas due to industrial and domestic pollution. | **Medium**<br>Water pollution figures regularly in CAS documents as an ongoing problem. |
| **Water scarcity/ resource management** | **Medium**<br>Water supplies are highly variable regionally and for urban versus rural areas. | **Medium**<br>Water resource management emphasized since 2000 in the northeast especially. |
| **Land degradation/ soil erosion** | **High**<br>A serious problem in the Paraguay-Pananá basin; is on the increase in Amazonia. | **Medium**<br>Discussed in connection with environmental management in Amazonia. |
| **Deforestation/ forest resource management** | **High**<br>Deforestation is an increasingly serious problem in the Amazon. | **Medium/high**<br>Conservation and sustainable development have been heavily prioritized since 1990. |
| **Biodiversity loss** | **Medium**<br>Not yet a serious problem, but of growing concern as rates of deforestation rise in Amazonia. A serious issue in the Atlantic Rainforest, cerrado, and semiarid interior of the northeast. | **Medium/high**<br>A growing problem in Amazonia. |
| **Energy efficiency/ alternative energy** | **Medium**<br>Some concern over energy consumption rates in Brazil despite high tariffs. | **Low**<br>Barely mentioned in view of the seriousness of other issues. |
| **Greenhouse gas emissions/ climate change** | **High**<br>The importance of greenhouse gas emissions from Amazonian deforestation is now recognized. | **Low/medium**<br>Climate change and carbon-trading are now acknowledged. |
| **Ozone depletion** | **Low**<br>Not treated as a major issue. Many companies have phased out chloroflurocarbons voluntarily, with no assistance from government or Montreal Protocol. | **Absent**<br>Not discussed. |
| **Institutional capacity** | **High**<br>A major challenge across all sectors at federal, state, and municipal levels, although this varies by state. | **Medium**<br>Discussed regularly as a major bottleneck to effective implementation. |

*Source:* IEG.

| ESW/AAA | Lending/grants |
|---|---|
| **Medium/low**<br>Some analysis of pollution (brown) issues in mid-1990s, but these were not followed up. | **Low**<br>Analysis in this area was not matched by project lending. |
| **Low**<br>Other urban pollution issues were prioritized. | **Absent**<br>Other urban pollution issues were prioritized. |
| **Medium**<br>A few Bank studies address this issue. | **Medium**<br>Water quality and pollution control projects have been limited. |
| **Medium**<br>Bank AAA work has had a formative policy influence on the water resources management (blue) agenda. | **High**<br>Significant institutional support and water resource management projects have been implemented. |
| **High**<br>A major theme in analysis and policy advice around rainforest conservation. | **High**<br>Closely associated with renewable natural resource (green) agenda's prioritization of forest conservation; and in southern Brazil. |
| **High**<br>Several landmark studies have been produced on Amazonia, deforestation, and rainforest policy. | **High**<br>Green issues have enjoyed a high profile in lending and grant-making since the 1990s. |
| **Medium/high**<br>A fundamental issue in connection with analyses of the impacts of deforestation and loss of environmental services. | **Medium/high**<br>Conservation of biodiversity figures in a host of forest policy-related projects. |
| **Low**<br>Relatively little emphasis given. | **Low**<br>Little weight given in funding. |
| **Low/high**<br>Importance of Brazil in climate change and environmental service provision is now firmly on the research and policy agenda. | **Low/medium**<br>A growing number of projects are addressing carbon trading, climate change, and global implications. |
| **Absent**<br>Not discussed. | **Absent**<br>There was a Montreal Protocol Project during the 1990s and early 2000s, but it closed after a frustrating implementation experience. |
| **High**<br>Discussed regularly as a major bottleneck to effective implementation. | **Medium**<br>Many Bank-funded projects contain important institutional strengthening components. |

## China Country Matrix

The ratings in the matrix below are shown for (before 2000) / (after 2000). Where a single rating is given, attention at the level indicated was relatively uniform both before and after 2000.

| Theme/ instrument | Problem severity | CAS/CPS |
|---|---|---|
| **Urban air quality** | **Medium/high**<br>Fueled by strong economic growth, urbanization, and industrialization, gradually increased in importance throughout the evaluation period. | **High/high**<br>Addressed consistently in NEAP (1994), CASs (1995, 1997, 2003), and CPS 2006, with increasing emphasis in later years. |
| **Indoor air pollution** | **High/high**<br>Problem has been consistently high, though not studied as much as outdoor air pollution. | **Low/low**<br>Indoor air pollution issues receive significantly less attention compared with wider air pollution issues. |
| **Water quality** | **High/high**<br>Fueled by strong economic growth, urbanization, and industrialization, gradually increased in importance throughout the evaluation period. | **Medium/high**<br>Addressed consistently, especially for urban areas and, to a lesser extent, for coastal zones in NEAP (1994), CASs (1995, 1997, 2003), and CPS (2006). |
| **Water scarcity/ resource management** | **High/high**<br>High-priority issue in most parts of China. | **Medium/high**<br>Holistic approach to water scarcity improved in CAS 2003 and CPS 2006. |
| **Land degradation/ soil erosion** | **High/high**<br>High-priority issue in most parts of China. | **High/high**<br>Addressed consistently in CASs 1997, 2003 and CPS 2006, though NEAP (1994) accorded relatively less priority. |
| **Deforestation/ forest resource management** | **High/high**<br>High-priority issue in most parts of China. | **High/high**<br>Addressed prominently in CASs 1997 and 2003, though NEAP (1994) accorded relatively less priority. |
| **Biodiversity loss** | **High/high**<br>Recognized as high-priority issue in most parts of China, though it has not been studied to the same extent as blue or brown issues. | **High/high**<br>Addressed prominently in CASs 1997 and 2003. |
| **Energy efficiency/ alternative energy** | **High/high**<br>Recognized as a high-priority issue, especially due to large share of coal use as well as continuing need to adopt clean production technologies. | **Medium/high**<br>Addressed prominently in CAS 1995 as well as in CPS 2006, with the latter emphasizing policy options. Emphasis on alternative energy increased after 2000. |
| **Greenhouse gas emissions/ climate change** | **Medium/high**<br>Recognized as an issue of growing importance due to increasing energy, and need to adopt clean production mechanisms. | **Medium/high**<br>Essentially similar to the pattern for energy efficiency. |
| **Ozone depletion** | **High/high**<br>High priority as recognized by the Montreal Protocol. | **Medium/high**<br>Addressed consistently since CAS 1997. |
| **Institutional capacity** | **High/high**<br>Mismatch between capacity at the national level and adequate decentralization and capacity at state and lower levels. | **High/high**<br>Strong emphasis since CAS 1995, beginning with the countrywide institutional framework and moving on to the sectoral level, especially water and energy. |

*Source:* IEG.

*Note:* ALW = China: Air, Land, Water—Environmental Priorities; CES = China Environment Strategy; CUESM = China Urban Environmental Service Management; CWBS = Clear Water Blue Skies; GEF = Global Environment Facility; WRAS = Water Resources Assistance Strategy.

| ESW/AAA | Lending/grants |
|---|---|
| **High/high**<br>Covered well by CES (1992) and raised to high priority by CWBS (1997). | **High/high**<br>Together with water pollution, the most frequently occurring objective in projects before and after 2000. |
| **Low/medium**<br>Not as prominent as wider air pollution issues. Recent work by Energy Sector Management Assistance Program (2006) puts specific focus on this issue. | **Low/low**<br>Not prominent throughout the period covered by the evaluation. |
| **Medium/high**<br>Addressed increasingly by CES (1992), CUESM (1994), CWBS (1997), with greater emphasis on institutional issues in ALW (2001). | **High/high**<br>Together with air pollution, the most frequently occurring objective in projects before and after 2000. |
| **Medium/medium**<br>Holistic emphasis grew from CES (1992) to CWBS (1997) and addressed more directly by WRAS (2002). | **High/medium**<br>Strong emphasis before year 2000, but relatively lower project activity after 2000. |
| **Medium/medium**<br>Received relatively less attention in ESW before and after 2000. | **Medium/medium**<br>Together with deforestation, project activity has been very significant throughout, but lower relative to the brown agenda. |
| **Medium/medium**<br>Received relatively less attention in ESW before and after 2000. | **Medium/medium**<br>Together with land degradation/soil erosion, project activity has been very significant throughout, but lower relative to the brown agenda. |
| **Medium/medium**<br>Received relatively less attention in ESW before and after 2000. | **Low/low**<br>The number of projects directly addressing biodiversity issues was low. |
| **High/high**<br>Received strong coverage in ESW throughout the evaluation period. | **Medium/high**<br>Energy efficiency was indirectly covered in several energy projects, and directly by GEF projects promoting boiler efficiency. There were two dedicated renewable energy projects during the evaluation period. |
| **High/high**<br>Received strong coverage in ESW throughout the evaluation period. | **Medium/high**<br>Greenhouse gas emissions were indirectly covered in several energy projects and GEF projects targeting boiler efficiency. |
| **High/high**<br>Received significant coverage in ESW throughout the evaluation period. | **High/high**<br>A series of four ozone phase-out projects provided consistent attention to this area. |
| **High/high**<br>Received strong coverage throughout the evaluation period. ALW (2001) put strong emphasis on institutional issues at all levels. | **High/high**<br>There was one major project dedicated to the national institutional framework for environment, and the vast majority of projects have significant institutional components. |

**Egypt, Arab Republic of: Country Matrix**

The ratings in the matrix below are shown for (before 2000) / (after 2000). Where a single rating is given, attention at the level indicated was relatively uniform both before and after 2000.

| Theme/ instrument | Problem severity | CAS/CPS |
|---|---|---|
| **Urban air quality** | **High**<br>Serious problem in Cairo, limited data for other cities. | **High**<br>Mentioned in all CASs. |
| **Indoor air pollution** | **Low**<br>Limited data, not likely to be a severe problem due to limited use of solid fuels. | **Absent** |
| **Water quality** | **High**<br>A major health threat in both rural and urban areas. | **High**<br>Mentioned as a priority environmental issue in most CASs. |
| **Water scarcity/ resource management** | **High**<br>Major vulnerability factor for the country, fueled by unsustainable subsidies. | **High**<br>Mentioned as a priority environmental issue in most CASs. |
| **Land degradation/ soil erosion** | **High**<br>Mainly associated with poor irrigation practices. | **Medium**<br>Reference in the 2001 CAS as a main problem. |
| **Deforestation/ forest resource management** | **Not available** | **Absent** |
| **Biodiversity loss** | **Low**<br>Limited mainly to coral reefs and associated tourism pressure. | **Absent** |
| **Energy efficiency/ alternative energy** | **Medium**<br>Mostly associated with distorted policy incentives. | **Medium**<br>Some reference to pricing policies, subsidies. |
| **Greenhouse gas emissions/ climate change** | **High**<br>Extreme vulnerability to sea-level rise in the Nile Delta. Emissions not globally significant. | **Absent** |
| **Ozone depletion** | **Low**<br>Limited data, not major contributor. | **Absent** |
| **Institutional capacity** | **High**<br>Major legislative gaps, very weak enforcement, weak local capacity, poor coordination. | **High**<br>All CASs make reference to the need to strengthen capacity. |

*Source:* IEG.

| ESW/AAA | Lending/grants |
|---|---|
| **Medium**<br>One study associated with pollution abatement project. | **High**<br>Major focus of both pollution abatement projects. |
| **Absent**<br>Very brief reference in above study. | **Absent** |
| **Medium**<br>Limited monitoring and addressed mainly as part of water resource management studies. | **Medium**<br>Mostly as part of water resource management projects, but not main focus. |
| **High**<br>In association with other donors and as part of project preparation. | **High**<br>Main area of assistance, mostly infrastructure-oriented; regional projects. |
| **Medium**<br>In support to rural and agricultural projects; mostly agricultural perspective. | **Medium**<br>Two rural/regional development projects; mostly agricultural perspective. |
| **Absent** | **Absent** |
| **Low**<br>Essentially limited to coastal zone management. | **Low**<br>Limited to one coastal zone management operation. |
| **High**<br>Focus of Bank-funded studies, attention to subsidies. | **Medium**<br>Part of various infrastructure projects and small GEF grants. |
| **Medium**<br>Mostly as part of clean development mechanism and energy-related studies. Nothing on adaptation to climate change. | **Low**<br>Small portfolio, mostly GEF projects and regional projects. |
| **Absent** | **Absent** |
| **Medium**<br>In support to Pollution Abatement Project and ongoing policy dialogue. | **Medium**<br>Mainly as a component of pollution projects. Absent from sector projects. |

## Ghana: Country Matrix

The ratings in the matrix below are shown for (before 2000) / (after 2000). Where a single rating is given, attention at the level indicated was relatively uniform both before and after 2000.

| Theme/ instrument | Problem severity | CAS/CPS |
|---|---|---|
| **Urban air quality** | **Low** | **Absent** |
| **Indoor air pollution** | **Low** | **Absent** |
| **Water quality** | **Medium**<br>Chronic around Accra and within and downstream of opencast gold mining. | **Modest/modest**<br>Reduced with the increased focus on governance, private sector development, and budget support instruments. |
| **Water scarcity/ resource management** | **Medium**<br>Mostly in the north as a result of desert encroachment and poor watershed management. | **Modest/modest**<br>Sidelined with the increased focus on governance, private sector development, and budget support instruments. |
| **Land degradation/ soil erosion** | **High**<br>Primarily the result of the insecurity of traditional land tenure arrangements and rural poverty, which leads to soil resource mining and agricultural extension in forested areas. | **High/modest**<br>Reduced focus with the increased emphasis on governance, private sector development, and budget-support instruments. |
| **Deforestation/ forest resource management** | **High**<br>Of the 8 million hectares of forest cover at the start of the twentieth century, only about 1.4 million hectares remained by 2000. By the early 1990s, between 50 and 70 percent of the total area of reserve forests in western Ghana had been illegally encroached, primarily for timber extraction, cocoa plantation, or mining activities. | **High/high**<br>From being a direct concern through lending, it now has reduced attention because direct attempts at sector reform and improved governance have proved elusive. Institutional issues are now being addressed through a greater focus on governance and international trade agreements. |
| **Biodiversity loss** | **High**<br>The result of deforestation and human pressure and the breakdown of traditional authority to regulate access. | **Medium/low**<br>From direct to indirect: better governance may safeguard forests while measures to reduce rural poverty will reduce need for predation. |
| **Energy efficiency/ alternative energy** | **High**<br>Wood fuel is the major source of energy for domestic use and demand for charcoal is growing fast. | **Medium/high**<br>Critical priorities include completing the power sector expansion of generating capacity to meet demand growth. |
| **Greenhouse gas emissions/ climate change** | **Modest**<br>As a result of forest conversion to charcoal and its combustion. | **Absent/absent** |
| **Ozone depletion** | **Low**<br>Not seen as an issue by most stakeholders. | **Absent/absent** |
| **Institutional capacity** | **High**<br>The major challenge, particularly for environment and forest management. Poor forest governance is a major source of environmental degradation. | **High/high**<br>This remains the largest challenge. |

*Source:* IEG.

| ESW/AAA | Lending/grants |
|---|---|
| **Low/modest**<br>Included in the recent CEA. | **Absent** |
| **Low/modest**<br>Included in the recent CEA. | **Absent** |
| **Modest/modest**<br>Included in the recent CEA. | **Modest/modest**<br>Primarily through extension and upgrading of water supply and sanitation, and components for better mining governance and efficiency. |
| **Modest/high** | **Low/low** |
| **Modest/high**<br>Links to poverty alleviation have been highlighted in recent ESW. | **Modest/modest**<br>Earlier modest lending is now being replaced by budget support. It is expected that the direct involvement of partners and GEF will be facilitated through partnership agreements. |
| **High/high**<br>Given increasing prominence in the latest ESW and its impact on longer-term gross domestic product. | **High/modest**<br>The earlier direct lending has now ceased with the change to budget support. It is expected that the direct involvement of partners and GEF will be facilitated through partnership agreements. |
| **Not available** | **Modest/low**<br>No direct lending, but GEF support facilitated. |
| **Modest/high**<br>This is now receiving greater attention both in terms of improving rural access and exploring linkages to regional power grids. | **Modest/high**<br>Increased emphasis on private sector provision. |
| **Low/low** | **Absent** |
| **Low/low** | **Absent** |
| **High/high** | **High/high**<br>Increased lending in partnership to redress. |

**India: Country Matrix**

The ratings in the matrix below are shown for (before 2000) / (after 2000). Where a single rating is given, attention at the level indicated was relatively uniform both before and after 2000.

| Theme/ instrument | Problem severity | CAS/CPS |
|---|---|---|
| **Urban air quality** | **High**<br>The third most serious problem according to Bank ESW. | **Low/medium**<br>Increasing attention over time, but not identified as a high priority. |
| **Indoor air pollution** | **High**<br>At least as serious as urban air pollution from a public health standpoint in rural areas. | **Absent/medium**<br>Similar story to outdoor air pollution. |
| **Water quality** | **High**<br>The most serious problem in terms of (health-related) degradation costs, according to Bank ESW. | **Low/medium**<br>Not a significant priority, despite findings of Bank ESW. |
| **Water scarcity/ resource management** | **High**<br>Increasingly serious as drawdown increases, but politically very sensitive. | **Medium**<br>Given some attention, particularly safeguard aspects, especially with Narmada. |
| **Land degradation/ soil erosion** | **High**<br>The second most serious problem, according to Bank ESW. | **Low**<br>Not identified as a priority, despite Bank ESW. |
| **Deforestation/ forest resource management** | **Medium** | **Medium**<br>Present more as social than environmental concern. |
| **Biodiversity loss** | **High** | **Medium**<br>GEF identified as a partner. |
| **Energy efficiency/ alternative energy** | **Medium** | **Low**<br>Not identified as a priority, but again GEF identified as a partner. |
| **Greenhouse gas emissions/ climate change** | **High**<br>Especially due to heavy coal use. | **Low/medium**<br>But likely to increase in the future. |
| **Ozone depletion** | **Medium** | **Medium**<br>Montreal Protocol identified as a partner. |
| **Institutional capacity** | **Medium**<br>Good legal/regulatory frameworks; capacity and political will vary by state. | **Medium**<br>Some attention following the NEAP. |

*Source:* IEG.
*Note:* Based on Yale/Columbia index values, NEAP, CEAs, and Bank costs of environmental degradation estimates and other ESW.

| ESW/AAA | Lending/grants |
|---|---|
| **Low/high**<br>Mainly with a focus on health impacts and what others have done. | **Absent**<br>Although a concern in selected industries (not necessarily in urban areas) in 1990s. |
| **Absent/high**<br>With a focus on both health and poverty impacts—several Energy Sector Management Assistance Program studies. | **Absent** |
| **Low/medium**<br>Somewhat more attention in recent years because of health impacts. | **Low**<br>Except in Mumbai and selected industries in 1990s, but had been a greater focus of lending in the 1970s and 1980s. |
| **Medium/high**<br>Strong focus of Bank ESW, especially in recent years. | **Medium**<br>But only within states, whereas most serious problems are interstate (e.g., Narmada, Ganges) and also in multiple states through watershed management programs. |
| **Absent** | **Medium**<br>In watershed/sodic lands projects. |
| **Medium**<br>Forest management is a consistent ESW focus. | **Medium**<br>Community forestry projects. |
| **Absent** | **Medium**<br>Both through IDA and GEF projects. |
| **Absent** | **Low**<br>Small GEF renewable energy projects were largely unsuccessful. |
| **Low**<br>Some workshop activity related to clean coal technologies. AAA in process addressing low carbon growth, vulnerability, and adaptation. | **Medium**<br>Some lending in hydropower and transmission; modest portfolio in carbon finance; little attention to adaptation. |
| **Absent** | **High**<br>Through a series of Montreal Protocol projects. |
| **Medium**<br>Focus declined in early 2000s but renewed attention in most recent ESW and CEAs. | **Medium/low**<br>One specific, not very successful, project; no new lending after the late 1990s. Two lending projects under preparation for industrial pollution and coastal zone management. |

**Madagascar: Country Matrix**

The ratings in the matrix below are shown for (before 2000) / (after 2000). Where a single rating is given, attention at the level indicated was relatively uniform both before and after 2000.

| Theme/ instrument | Problem severity | CAS/CPS |
|---|---|---|
| **Urban air quality** | **Low** | **Not available** |
| **Indoor air pollution** | **Low** | **Not available** |
| **Water quality** | **Not available** | **Not available** |
| **Water scarcity/ resource management** | **Medium** | **Medium** Lack of irrigation. |
| **Land degradation/ soil erosion** | **Medium** | **Medium** Lack of irrigation. |
| **Deforestation/ forest resource management** | **High** | **High** Maintenance of the level of forest and reforestation is a strategic goal of the CAS. |
| **Biodiversity loss** | **High** | **Not available** |
| **Energy efficiency/ alternative energy** | **Low/medium** | **Not available** |
| **Greenhouse gas emissions/ climate change** | **Low** | **Not available** |
| **Ozone depletion** | **Not available** | **Not available** |
| **Institutional capacity** | **High** | **High** Low capacity of the Ministry of Environment. |

*Source:* IEG.
*Note:* CAS/CPS: from the 2007–11 CAS; PRSP: from the 2005 PRSP progress report.

| PRSP | ESW/AAA | Lending/grants |
|---|---|---|
| **Not available** | **Low**<br>One urban sector review (1991). | **Not available** |
| **Not available** | **Not available** | **Low**<br>Pollution was one component of Tana Plain Development project in 1990. |
| **Not available** | **Not available** | **Not available** |
| **Medium**<br>See subprogram environment, water, and forest. | **Medium/high**<br>Rural and environment sector review. | **Medium**<br>Small-Scale Rural Water Supply and Sanitation Project in 1998 and Irrigation II in 1995. |
| **Not available** | **Low**<br>ESW done on land titling and land property rights but nothing on degradation or soil erosion. | **Low/medium** |
| **High**<br>See priority (ii) on protected areas and conservation sites and subprogram on environment, water, and forest. | **Medium**<br>Rural and environment sector review. | **Medium**<br>Forest management has been neglected, more attention to reducing rates of deforestation through assistance to protected area systems. |
| **High**<br>Priority for protected areas and conservation sites. | **Medium**<br>Rural and environment sector review (2003) | **High**<br>Addressed through Environmental Projects 1, 2, and 3. |
| **Medium**<br>Energy subprogram. | **Medium**<br>Issues and options in the energy sector ESW done in 1987 and Energy Sector Management Assistance Program study on wood fuels. | **Low**<br>One energy sector development project in 1996 and an oil supplemental credit in 2000. |
| **Not available** | **Not available** | **Low**<br>Environmental Project 3 is the only project with a climate change component. |
| **Not available** | **Not available** | **Not available** |
| **High**<br>See priority (i) on good governance and accountability. | **Not available** | **High**<br>Ten projects, out of 28, have institutional components. |

**Russian Federation: Country Matrix**

The ratings in the matrix below are shown for (before 2000) / (after 2000). Where a single rating is given, attention at the level indicated was relatively uniform both before and after 2000.

| Theme/ instrument | Problem severity | CAS |
|---|---|---|
| **Urban air quality** | **Very high**<br>Particularly in industrial areas, near mines, smelters, steam generators, and power plants. | **Medium**<br>CAS 1992 foresees environmental improvements from the closing of inefficient industries. CAS 1999 and 2002 target issue. |
| **Indoor air pollution** | **Low**<br>This is apparently not a serious issue in Russia, except perhaps for the question of secondary smoke from cigarettes. | **Absent**<br>Not discussed. |
| **Water quality** | **High**<br>Many rivers, lakes, and estuaries in Russia are polluted by fertilizer and pesticide runoff, industrial effluents, and oil spills. | **Medium**<br>CAS 1999–2001 discusses water-quality data, mentions flood risks. CASs 1999, 2002, and 2006 target issue. |
| **Water scarcity/ resource management** | **Medium**<br>Water is not generally scarce in Russia, but good-quality water is. Many watersheds lack comprehensive management plans. | **Low**<br>Mentioned in several CASs but not a major focus. |
| **Land degradation/ soil erosion** | **Medium**<br>Studies indicate that erosion is an extensive problem in Russian agriculture. Industrial waste disposal, oil spills, and radiation from nuclear facilities have degraded many large areas. | **Low**<br>CAS 1999–2001 presented detailed soil data, but no lending is recommended. |
| **Deforestation/ forest resource management** | **Medium**<br>Enforcement of forestry regulations and effective management of forest resources have declined since 1991. Siberian forests are being logged to supply East Asian markets. | **Low**<br>CAS 1993 targets unsustainable logging, especially in Taiga forest. CAS 1999 mentions issue, and CAS 2001 reinforces the issue. |
| **Biodiversity loss** | **Medium**<br>Many of Russia's biomes are threatened by logging, mining, oil spills, and the like. Effective protected area management has declined since 1991. Less than 3 percent of national territory is protected. | **Low**<br>The issue is mentioned in some CASs. |
| **Energy efficiency/ alternative energy** | **High**<br>Russia has high energy loss from oil and gas fields, pipelines, and industrial plants. | **Medium**<br>CAS 1993 identifies need for rehab of oil/gas production and pipelines. CAS 1993 identifies need for regulatory reform. |
| **Greenhouse gas emissions/ climate change** | **High** | **Medium**<br>While not targeting greenhouse gases, CAS 1993 targets measures that would result in lower emissions. CAS 2003 focuses on Kyoto as an opportunity to upgrade industrial infrastructure. |
| **Ozone depletion** | **Low**<br>The Russian ozone program is regarded as a model of success. Most ozone-depleting substances have been phased out in industry and consumption. | **Low** |
| **Institutional capacity** | **Medium** | **Medium**<br>CAS 1995 identifies need for institution building. |

*Source:* IEG.

*Note:* The Russia Ozone Abatement Program is regarded as one of the most successful. It succeeded in virtually eliminating ozone-depleting substances in production and consumption.

| ESW/AAA | Lending/grants |
|---|---|
| **High**<br>The problem has received attention in sector work related to energy efficiency, but has not merited specific attention. | **Low**<br>Bank lending contributed indirectly to improving air quality in selected areas by increasing the efficiency of district heating plants, closing inefficient coal mines, and reducing losses in oil and gas pipelines. |
| **Absent**<br>Not discussed. | **Absent**<br>Not discussed. |
| **Low**<br>Discussed in environmental management ESW 2004. | **Medium**<br>Several Bank loans were aimed at improving water supply and the quality of water in supply systems. |
| **High** | **Low**<br>Relatively little investment in watershed management, storage, flood control, and the like. |
| **Absent**<br>Not mentioned in ESW other than general references. | **Absent**<br>No lending in this area. |
| **Medium**<br>ESW (1996 and 1997) diagnosed the ills of Russian forestry and recommended strengthening policy and regulatory frameworks. | **Medium**<br>The Bank made one substantial forestry loan that is still under implementation. |
| **Medium**<br>A study in 1997 laid out the basis for the GEF Biodiversity Project. | **Medium**<br>GEF Biodiversity Project had mixed success, mainly in the area of protected-area conservation. A multicountry study (1996) recommended decentralization, local participation, and better incentive structure. |
| **High**<br>A 1993 study on structural reform emphasized the need for allowing mining and other industries to reduce inefficient or environmentally damaging practices. Regional ESW (2000) focused on inefficiencies in district heating schemes. | **Medium**<br>Several large loans for reducing losses in oil and gas fields, rehabilitating parts of the pipeline network, and increasing efficiency in district heating plants. The Bank also contributed to the rationalization of the coal industry and the privatization of coal mining. |
| **Medium**<br>ESW (2004) concludes that meeting Kyoto targets will not necessarily reduce growth. | **Medium**<br>Russia has only recently acceded to Kyoto Protocol. No grants from Bank Group yet. |
| **Absent**<br>No specific ESW. | **High**<br>The Bank was the key donor among several that contributed over US$200 million to the phase-out of the production and consumption of ozone-depleting substances. |
| **Medium**<br>Several studies identified weaknesses in the regulatory system. | **Medium**<br>The Bank's main thrust in this area was the Environmental Management Project, which has been very slow in disbursing, with mixed success. |

**Senegal: Country Matrix**

The ratings in the matrix below are shown for (before 2000) / (after 2000). Where a single rating is given, attention at the level indicated was relatively uniform both before and after 2000.

| Theme/ instrument | Problem severity | CAS |
|---|---|---|
| **Urban air quality** | **Medium/high** | **Medium**<br>CAS refers to the Urban Mobility Project, which deals directly with urban air quality by having established an air-quality monitoring center. |
| **Indoor air pollution** | **Not available** | **Not available** |
| **Water quality** | **High**<br>Dams and the development of irrigated agriculture In Senegal River valley threaten the lagoon water quality. | **Low** |
| **Water scarcity/ resource management** | **High**<br>Construction of the Diama Dam, changes in the lake's water quality and ecosystem, together with increased use, triggered a need for improved management. | **Medium** |
| **Land degradation/ soil erosion** | **High** | **Low** |
| **Deforestation/ forest resource management** | **High**<br>There is a high correlation between the need for enhanced sustainable forest management and poverty in Senegal. | **Low** |
| **Biodiversity loss** | **High** | **Medium**<br>Coastal and riverine environment are both only rated as "moderate" priorities, but the Intergrated Marine and Coastal Resources Management Project supports a framework for protected areas and biodiversity management. |
| **Energy efficiency/ alternative energy** | **High** | **Low** |
| **Greenhouse gas emissions/ climate change** | **Not available** | **Not available** |
| **Ozone depletion** | **Not available** | **Not available** |
| **Institutional capacity** | **Low** | **Not available** |

*Source:* IEG.

*Note:* AAA = analytical and advisory activities; CAS = Country Assistance Strategy; CESP = Country Environmental Strategy Paper; ESW = economic and sector work; PRSC = Poverty Reduction Strategy Credit; PRSP = Poverty Reduction Strategy Paper.

| PRSP/PRSC | ESW/AAA | Lending/grants |
|---|---|---|
| **High**<br>PRSC II recognizes pollution of poorly regulated industries, mainly around Dakar, as one of Senegal's main environmental threats. | **Low**<br>A World Bank study found that motorized transport was responsible for over 90 percent of particulate matter and petroleum fuel emissions in Dakar. | **Medium**<br>The Clean Air Initiative in Sub-Saharan African Cities has improved air quality management in Senegal, mainly through the phase-out of leaded gasoline. Also, IFC funds will install a new state-of-the-art environment-friendly cement production line. |
| **Not available** | **Not available** | **Not available** |
| **Low** | **Not available** | **Not available** |
| **Medium** | **Low**<br>See ESW associated with the Long-Term Water Sector Project, and the discussion of managed floods and other water resource management issues in the 1994 CESP. | **Medium**<br>Senegal River Basin Water and Environmental Management Project (GEF 2003); the Long-Term Water Sector Project. |
| **High**<br>PRSC II identifies soil degradation as the first environmental challenge in Senegal. | **Not available** | **Not available** |
| **Low** | **High** | **High**<br>The Sustainable and Participatory Energy Management Project was highly relevant but too small in scope and not scaled up in a second phase. |
| **High**<br>One of PRSC II main environmental threats. | **Low** | **Low**<br>Integrated Marine and Coastal Resources Management Project only. |
| **Low** | **Medium**<br>See World Bank 2006a. | **Medium**<br>Sustainable Participatory Energy Management Project; Electricity Services for Rural Areas Project. |
| **Not available** | **Not available** | **Not available** |
| **Not available** | **Not available** | **Not available** |
| **Not available** | **Not available** | **Low**<br>One Institutional Development Fund grant: a US$200,000 grant for the Superior Council for the Environment, charged with overseeing the National Environmental Action Plan process, which has since been disbanded. |

## Uganda: Country Matrix

The ratings in the matrix below are shown for (before 2000) / (after 2000). Where a single rating is given, attention at the level indicated was relatively uniform both before and after 2000.

| Theme/ instrument | Problem severity | CAS/CPS |
|---|---|---|
| **Urban air quality** | **Medium**<br>Moderate automobile and industrial pollution in Kampala but not nationwide. | **Low**<br>Air pollution mentioned but not high priority. |
| **Indoor air pollution** | **Medium**<br>A problem in poorer rural areas, but not well documented. | **Low**<br>Not priority for 1990-2002 CAS. |
| **Water quality** | **Medium**<br>Problem in urban areas due to industrial and domestic pollution. Some agricultural runoff issues in rural areas and lakeside. | **Low**<br>Urban water quality issues not highlighted in strategies up to 2000. Water supply is primary focus. |
| **Water scarcity/ resource management** | **Medium**<br>Problem is high in northern Uganda, but less so in other parts of the country. | **Medium**<br>CAS 1995–2004 priority to rural water supply. |
| **Land degradation/ soil erosion** | **High**<br>Serious issue in the north. Poor agricultural practices elsewhere. | **High**<br>CAS prior to 2002 focused on natural resource management and land degradation. |
| **Deforestation/ forest resource management** | **High**<br>Rates are high in unprotected areas and management of forests not fully effective. | **High**<br>Focus of CAS support for NEAP and Uganda Wildlife Authority based on priority improving natural resource management and arresting deforestation. |
| **Biodiversity loss** | **High**<br>Persistent loss in protected areas slowing but still high. | **High**<br>Biodiversity loss emphasis in NEAP cited consistently in CAS 1995–2005. |
| **Energy efficiency/ alternative energy** | **Medium**<br>Increasingly important as country continues to grow faster than hydropower investments. | **Low**<br>Bank strategies of 1990–2002 mention but do not highlight. |
| **Greenhouse gas emissions/ climate change** | **Medium**<br>Deforestation is the driver, more than industrial or automobile emissions. | **Low**<br>Passing mention in early 1995–2002 CAS as part of natural resource management/deforestation discussion. |
| **Ozone depletion** | **Low**<br>Not regarded as notable problem at country level. | **Absent**<br>Not identified as an issue. |
| **Institutional capacity** | **High**<br>Environment and resources management institutions face financial and staffing constraints at national and local levels. | **High**<br>Focus of environment in CAS 1995–2004 on building capacity for natural resource/environment management. |

*Source:* IEG.
*Note:* EMCB = Economic Managing Capacity Building; LVEMP = Lake Victoria Environmental Management Projects; PAMSU = Protected Area Management and Sustainable Use.

| PRSP | ESW/AAA | Lending/grants |
|---|---|---|
| **Low** Issue of air pollution mentioned, but is not focus of Poverty Reduction Strategies in 2002–07. | **Low** Not specific subject of analysis. | **Low** No specific lending. PRSC focus primarily rural, but would allow for expenditures for public health. |
| **Low** Issue mentioned as poverty related, but not highlighted as serious. | **Absent** No specific analysis carried out on urban or rural issue. | **Low** Addressed indirectly through PRSC funding for rural development, but not specific focus of lending. |
| **Low** PRSP approach: water quality in context of rural/urban water supply. PRSP approach: primarily rural focus. | **Low** Discussed in water supply ESW, but coverage is primary focus. | **Low** Early rural pre-2000 water supply lending and included and eligible PRSC. |
| **Medium** PRSP 2002 onward: focus on rural including water supply and resource management. | **Medium** ESW underlying water supply projects. | **Medium** Lending for water supply; natural resouces management through PRSC. |
| **High** PRSP underscores importance of reversing land degradation and erosion to promote rural development and increasing agricultural incomes. | **Medium** Not extensive, but some analysis of relationship of soil nutrient depletion and crop productivity in 2005. Planning land management support. | **Medium** Primarily indirect support through PRSC. |
| **High** PRSP link to deforestation and natural resources management related to rural development, not conservation priority. | **Low** Little direct analytical work on natural resources management/forestry; carried out through other research centers. | **Low** Lending 1995–2006 for National Environment Management Authority, PAMSU/GEF/Bwindi grant primary source; no major forestry initiative. |
| **Low** Loss of biodiversity barely mentioned in PRSP as central to increasing rural incomes. | **Low** Limited to preparatory work for PAMSU/GEF/Bwindi pending land management initiatives. | **Medium** Early 1995–2004 support for GEF/Bwindi; PAMSU; Lake Victoria; not highlighted in PRSC. |
| **Low** Little emphasis in context of poverty reduction. | **Medium** Treated in context of power sector reform and analysis of options for rural sector grid. | **Low** No lending specifically for this; GEF/United Nations Development Programme rural solar project. |
| **Low** Environmental challenge linked to soil erosion and desertification in the north; not prioritized. | **Absent** No direct analytical work. | **Absent** No direct lending. |
| **Absent** Not identified as issue. | **Absent** No analytical work on theme. | **Absent** No direct or indirect lending/grants. |
| **Medium** PRSP identifies as central issue across-the-board, including agriculture/rural development/environment sector. | **Medium** Preparatory work for EMCB/PAMSU/Lake Victoria in pending sector environmental assessment and local natural resources management | **High** Centerpiece of Bank support for environment in Uganda: EMCB/ PAMSU/LVEMP until in 2006, mentioned in PRSC as direct Bank lending, new initiatives programmed for sectorwide approaches. |

Power plant in Egypt. Photo courtesy of Jouni Martti Eerikainen.

# APPENDIX E: WORLD BANK ENVIRONMENTAL PROJECTS ASSESSED FOR THIS EVALUATION

In addition to the country case studies, this evaluation included performance assessments for completed environment projects in Brazil, China, Ghana, India, Madagascar, Russia, and Uganda. Earlier IEG Project Performance Assessment Reports (PPARs) and Implementation Completion Report reviews for environmental and natural resource management (ENRM) projects in these countries, together with Egypt and Senegal, were also used as important inputs for the case studies and the overall evaluation. The new Project Performance Assessment Reports undertaken during this evaluation were:

- Brazil—Water Quality and Pollution Control Project (São Paulo and Paraná)
- Brazil—Espírito Santo Water Coastal Pollution Management Project
- China—Environmental Technical Assistance Project
- China—Second Loess Plateau Watershed Rehabilitation Project
- China—Nature Reserves Management Project (GEF)
- China—Tarim Basin II Project
- China—Xiaolangdi Multipurpose Project
- China—Second Xiaolangdi Multipurpose Project
- Ghana—Coastal Wetlands Management Project (GEF)
- Ghana—Environmental Resources Management Project
- Ghana—Natural Resource Management Project
- India—Ecodevelopment Project (International Development Association/GEF)
- India—Environmental Management Capacity Building Technical Assistance Project
- India—Industrial Pollution Control Project
- India—Industrial Pollution Prevention Project
- Madagascar—Environment Support Program, Phase II (International Development Association/GEF)
- Russia—Biodiversity Conservation Project (GEF)
- Uganda—Bwindi Impenetrable National Park and Mgahinga Gorilla National Park Conservation Project (GEF)
- Uganda—Environmental Management and Capacity Building Project.

Coal mines outside Samaca, Colombia. Photo by Scott Wallace, courtesy of the World Bank Photo Library.

The World Bank's ENRM portfolio is composed of all projects approved between fiscal 1990 and 2007, in which the task team leaders indicated that the project at least partially contained one or more of the following subthemes:

(1) Biodiversity
(2) Climate change
(3) Environmental policies and institutions
(4) Land administration[1] and management
(5) Pollution management and environmental health
(6) Water resources management
(7) Other environment and natural resources management.

As a cross-cutting theme (and not a sector like education, health, and transport), ENRM projects are "mapped" to many different sector boards, including one specifically for environment. This review considers both the broader ENRM and much smaller environment portfolios. It should be noted at the outset that different Regions map projects to sector boards in different ways. As a result, similar projects can be mapped to different sector boards, depending on the originating Region.

## ENRM Portfolio Characteristics

From fiscal 1990 through 2007, a Bank database recorded 6,792 projects with various sources of funding (loans, credits, grants, and the like). Of this number, 2,401 are included in the ENRM portfolio, representing 35.4 percent of the total; 563 were in the environment portfolio,[2] representing 8.3 percent of the total and 23.4 percent of the ENRM subtotal. Therefore, less than one-quarter of all ENRM projects were mapped to the Environment Sector Board.

Both the environment and ENRM portfolios are comparatively younger—that is, they had higher shares of all projects still under implementation (46 percent and 41 percent, respectively) at the end of fiscal 2007—than that for the Bank as a whole (36 percent). This reflects the fact that Bank financial support for ENRM purposes is comparatively more recent than that for many other themes or sectors. This is especially the case for grant operations for global environmental purposes and carbon finance projects.

Commitments for projects in the ENRM portfolio approved from fiscal 1990 through 2007 were $140.1 billion, representing 34.9 percent of the total in all Bank projects during this period. The vast majority of ENRM commitments were in the form of International Bank for Reconstruction and Development (IBRD) loans and International Development Association (IDA) credits (95.3 percent), followed by regular GEF grants (1.8 percent), with Bank guarantees, carbon finance projects, Montreal Protocol operations, and other small grant projects accounting for the rest. Commitments in Bank-administered GEF projects between the early 1990s and the end of fiscal 2007 were estimated to be $4 billion, while those for carbon-offset operations were about $1.1 billion—dominated by a single $931 million operation in China, approved in fiscal 2006—and those for Montreal Protocol projects were $500 million.

The share of ENRM commitments was greatest, by far, in East Asia and Pacific at 28.3 percent, followed by Latin America and the Caribbean at 19.8 percent, and South Asia at 16.9 percent. Shares were lowest in the Middle East and North Africa at 6.7 percent of the total, followed by Europe and Central Asia at 13.3 percent, and Sub-Saharan Africa at 15 percent.

The East Asia and Pacific Region (mainly China) accounted for 88.5 percent of all commitments for carbon offsets through fiscal 2007, while Latin America and the Caribbean had just 7.4 percent and Europe and Central Asia had the remainder. In contrast, Latin America and the Caribbean (with 25.4 percent) had a slightly larger share of total commitments in regular GEF projects than East Asia and Pacific (24.7 percent), followed by Africa (20.6 percent), Europe and Central Asia (18.8 percent), and, at a considerable distance, the Middle East and North Africa (5.7 percent) and South Asia (3.7 percent). More than half of all Montreal Protocol commitments, in turn, were in East Asia and Pacific (53.4 percent)—again, most notably in China—followed by South Asia (34.8 percent)—mainly in India—and Latin America and the Caribbean (9.6 percent).

ENRM operations were mapped to 16 different sector boards, but were mainly concentrated in 6 (see table F.1 below), which collectively accounted for 86.7 percent of all such projects and 87.5 percent of total commitments in these operations. This wide distribution of ENRM projects across a number of sector boards suggests that considerable mainstreaming of environment-related investments—a major objective of both the 2001 Environment Strategy and the earlier fourfold agenda of the 1990s—has, in fact, occurred over the past two decades. ENRM projects mapped to the Environment Sector Board, however, are much smaller in terms of commitments ($20.3 million), on average, than those mapped to other sector boards ($70 million).

ENRM operations were both investment and policy-based (including Adjustment Loans and Poverty Reduction Support Credits), with investments accounting for roughly 90 percent of total commitments. Altogether, 132 policy-based operations were coded by their task team leaders as being at least in part ENRM in nature. The bulk of these were in Africa (43.9 percent), followed by Latin America and the Caribbean (22 percent) and Europe and Central Asia (14.4 percent),[3] and included a number of Poverty Reduction Support Credits—more specifically, 15 in Africa, 3 each in East Asia and Pacific and Latin America and the Caribbean, 2 in Europe and Central Asia, and 1 in South Asia (Sri Lanka).[4]

Only a small number of all Development Policy Loans that reportedly had some ENRM content were primarily for environmental purposes. These were mainly in Latin America and the Caribbean (one for Brazil and two each for Colombia and Mexico). Only eight such operations (6.1 percent) were mapped to the Environment Sector Board,

**Table F.1: Distribution of ENRM Projects by Sector Board, Fiscal 1990–2007**

| Sector Board | ENRM projects | Share of total projects (percent) | Share of total commitments (percent) |
|---|---|---|---|
| Environment | 563 | 23.4 | 8.2 |
| Agriculture & Rural Development | 531 | 22.1 | 21.9 |
| Energy and Mining | 362 | 15.1 | 20.1 |
| Water Supply & Sanitation | 351 | 14.6 | 12.5 |
| Urban Development | 225 | 9.4 | 12.1 |
| Transport | 150 | 6.2 | 12.7 |
| Others[a] | 219 | 9.1 | 12.5 |
| Total | 2,401 | 100.0 | 100.0 |

*Source:* World Bank.

a. Among the remaining 339 ENRM operations (13.3 percent), the largest number were mapped to the Social Protection Board (85), followed by the Private Sector Development (51), Economic Policy (46), Public Sector (42), Social Development (24), and Health (21) Sector Boards. The remainder was mapped to the Financial Sector (17), Education (16), Poverty Reduction (15), and Global Information/Communications Technology (1) Sector Boards.

indicating that relatively little use has been made to date of policy-based loans and credits for the purpose of advancing ENRM objectives. Most of the operations that have attempted to do so have been quite recent, with six of the operations mapped to the Environment Sector Board being approved between fiscal 2005 and 2007, and all of them since fiscal 2000.

## Environment Portfolio Characteristics

ENRM projects mapped to the Environment sector board differed from those mapped to other sector boards in that IBRD/IDA operations accounted for just 28.4 percent of the total. Regular and mid-size GEF grants represented a much larger share, 39.8 percent, while very small Institutional Development Fund (IDF) grants constituted 14.9 percent and Montreal Protocol, carbon offset, and Brazil Rainforest Trust Fund operations accounted for 5.5 percent, 5.2 percent, and 1.4 percent, respectively. Taken together, GEF, Montreal Protocol, carbon finance, and Rainforest projects represent more than half of all operations mapped to the Environment Sector Board, a share that rises to nearly two-thirds when IDF grants are excluded. The preponderance of grant-funded projects also explains why average commitments are much lower for ENRM operations mapped to environment than those mapped to other sector boards.[5]

The Regional share of total (including IDF and GEF mid-size) operations mapped to the Environment Sector Board was highest in Latin America and the Caribbean (35.7 percent) and lowest in South Asia (5 percent), with Europe and Central Asia (21 percent), Africa (20.4 percent), East Asia and Pacific (12.1 percent), and the Middle East and North Africa (5.7 percent) falling in between. Latin America and the Caribbean's relative shares of carbon-offset projects (62.1 percent) and GEF mid-size grants (45.3 percent) were particularly striking, but Latin America and the Caribbean also led the Bank both in IBRD/IDA operations mapped to the Environment Sector Board (35 percent, followed by Africa with 25 percent) and regular GEF projects (30 percent, again followed by Africa with 28.8 percent, then Europe and Central Asia with 26.3 percent). It should be recalled, however, that many of the same types of IBRD/IDA operations mapped to the Environment Sector Board by the Latin America and the Caribbean Region were mapped to different sector boards by other Regions, especially East Asia and Pacific and South Asia.[6]

Latin America and the Caribbean's predominance in the environment portfolio is even higher in terms of commitments, where it accounted for 41 percent of the total from fiscal 1990 through 2007. East Asia and Pacific was second, with 23.4 percent.[7] These two Regions were followed at a distance by South Asia (12.4 percent of total commitments), Africa (10.7 percent), Europe and Central Asia (8.9 percent), and the Middle East and North Africa (3.3 percent). Latin America and the Caribbean and East Asia and Pacific alone accounted for nearly two-thirds of total commitments in projects mapped to the Environment Sector Board.

## ENRM Portfolio Performance

Outcome ratings for all closed (and evaluated) ENRM and environment projects approved between fiscal 1990 and 2007 can likewise be compared. They can also be broken down by lending/grant source (IBRD/IDA, GEF, Montreal Protocol, and so on), Sector board mapping,[8] Region, and subtheme (see the final section of this appendix). Altogether, there were 1,014 such projects, of which 89.3 percent were financed with IBRD and/or IDA funds, 7.5 percent with GEF resources, and the rest with funds from other sources.[9] In Regional terms, Africa, Latin America and the Caribbean, and East Asia and Pacific together accounted for more than three-fifths of the total.[10]

Overall, 75.6 percent of all evaluated ENRM projects were rated satisfactory on completion. The average for all IBRD/IDA-financed ENRM projects (74.9 percent satisfactory) was slightly below that for all ENRM operations, compared with 100 percent satisfactory for the handful of Montreal Protocol and Brazil Rainforest Pilot Projects that were rated.[11] Closed full-sized GEF projects also had an above-average success rate (82.9 percent). Therefore, operations devoted to global environmental improvement have performed better in terms of overall outcome ratings, on average, than the ENRM portfolio as a whole.

The same percentage of satisfactory projects (75.6 percent) was found for the much larger universe of all completed and evaluated Bank operations approved from fiscal 1990 through 2007 (2,815). However, there were some fairly minor differences among these projects when considered according to their environmental assessment classification, with Category A projects performing slightly less well, on average (74.5 percent satisfactory), than Category B (75.5 percent) and Category C operations (75.8 percent).[12]

In terms of sector board mapping, the highest share of satisfactory ENRM projects was recorded by the Transport Sector Board (89.9 percent), followed by those mapped to the Rural Development (76.1 percent), Energy (74.2 percent), Environment (74 percent), other (74.1 percent), and the Urban Development and Water Sector Boards (73 percent each). With the sole exception of operations mapped to the Transport Sector Board, performance of ENRM projects mapped to various sector boards was close to the average for the portfolio as a whole (and to one another).

There is considerably greater variation across Regions, however, with the highest share of satisfactory projects in Europe and Central Asia (84.6 percent) and the lowest in Africa (66.8 percent). Two other Regions—Latin America and the Caribbean (with 79.8 percent) and East Asia and Pacific (78.1 percent)—were also above the average, while the Middle East and North Africa (72 percent) and South Asia (70.8 percent) were not.[13] These figures are consistent with project performance differences across Regions more generally.

Finally, even though relatively few operations approved after fiscal 1998 had been evaluated by the end of fiscal 2007, and there are some notable year-to-year variations, there appears to be a clearly improving trend in ENRM project performance over time, which is consistent with the trend for Bank operations as a whole. The lowest average outcome ratings were recorded for projects approved in fiscal 1990 (56.3 percent satisfactory), 1991 (69.6 percent), and 1994 (71.3 percent). ENRM project performance was much better, on average, for those approved in the latter part of the 1990s and first half of the 2000s than in the early to mid-1990s.

## Environment Portfolio Performance

The above ratings do not necessarily convey much about project environmental performance, especially for infrastructure and many rural development operations. Unfortunately, as noted in appendix A, project environmental performance is not systematically evaluated at the time of completion. However, there is more likely to be a close association between overall project performance and the environment for the approximately 15 percent of all completed ENRM operations mapped to the Environment Sector Board. But even here there may be exceptions, because actual project environmental impacts are frequently not assessed in Bank Implementation Completion Reports.

Overall performance of completed environment projects differs both by funding source and Region. By funding source, 100 percent of the small numbers of Montreal Protocol (9), Rainforest Pilot Program (1), and special financing (1) projects were rated satisfactory, as were 81.3 percent of all regular GEF projects (48). However, just 68.4 percent of those financed with IBRD/IDA resources (95) were rated satisfactory, compared with 74.9 percent for all IBRD/IDA-funded projects in the ENRM portfolio as a whole.

Regional performance differences are also noteworthy, with Europe and Central Asia having the highest percentage of satisfactory projects (88.9 percent) and Africa the lowest (60.7 percent), thereby mirroring the situation with the ENRM portfolio overall. However, there were differences in this regard for the other Regions, with South Asia (86.7 percent satisfactory) and the Middle East and North Africa (81.8 percent) performing comparatively better when environment and ENRM project outcomes are compared, and Latin America and the Caribbean

(69.4 percent) and East Asia and Pacific (66.7 percent) doing less well.[14] There were also performance differences among the case study countries.[15]

The vast majority (80 percent) of unsatisfactory projects mapped to the Environment Sector Board were approved between fiscal 1992 and 1997, with the largest number (7) approved in fiscal 1994.[16] Among all unsatisfactory environment projects, the highest shares were in Latin America and the Caribbean (38.5 percent) and Africa (28.2 percent), followed by East Asia and Pacific (12.8 percent) and Europe and Central Asia (10.3 percent). More than three-quarters (31) were IBRD or IDA operations and the remainder (9), including three of the five unsatisfactory projects approved after fiscal 1997, were GEF-financed. Many of the unsatisfactory projects, especially in Latin America and the Caribbean and Africa, were institutional development operations for environmental management, although some involved natural resource management and biodiversity conservation. Country political and economic factors affected performance in a number of these operations.[17]

Finally, as with the ENRM portfolio as a whole, environment project performance was better among those approved in the late 1990s and (thus far) in the first half of the present decade, than those approved in the first half of the 1990s; the worst years were fiscal 1992 (when just 45.5 percent of the total were rated satisfactory) and 1994 (61.1 percent). As was the case for the larger ENRM portfolio, GEF and Montreal Protocol projects performed better than IBRD/IDA operations throughout the period.[18] The improving trend over time suggests that the Bank has learned from its ENRM and environment project experience, which is reflected in the discontinuation (for the most part) of design approaches that have proven less successful.

## Performance by ENRM Subtheme

In accordance with the Bank's current coding system, each project can have from one to five subthemes, which, in turn, fall under broader single or multiple themes. Altogether, there are 11 themes[19] and 70 subthemes, including the 7 for ENRM identified at the beginning of this appendix. Among all projects approved by the Bank between fiscal 1990 and 2007, ENRM subthemes were indicated 3,051 times in a total of 2,281 projects (excluding IDF grants). Many projects, therefore, had two or more ENRM subthemes.

Table F.2 shows the relative importance of the various ENRM subthemes, with the first subtheme generally receiving the highest weight, followed by the second subtheme, the third, and so on. In some cases, however, more than one subtheme was given the same weight, in which case the relative ranking is somewhat arbitrary. This information nonetheless gives a fairly good picture of the relative importance of the various subthemes within the ENRM portfolio.

**Table F.2: Thematic Composition of Bank ENRM Projects, Fiscal 1990–2007 (number of projects)**

| Subtheme | First | Second | Third | Fourth | Fifth | Total |
|---|---|---|---|---|---|---|
| Biodiversity conservation | 220 | 73 | 36 | 19 | 21 | 369 |
| Climate change | 144 | 50 | 40 | 46 | 30 | 310 |
| Environmental policy and institutions | 125 | 255 | 129 | 104 | 50 | 663 |
| Land administration and management | 101 | 87 | 62 | 70 | 50 | 370 |
| Pollution management/environmental health | 179 | 203 | 156 | 83 | 54 | 675 |
| Water resource management | 122 | 129 | 106 | 72 | 30 | 459 |
| Other ENRM | 59 | 51 | 44 | 37 | 14 | 205 |
| Total | 950 | 848 | 573 | 431 | 249 | 3,051 |

*Source:* World Bank database.

In terms of total mentions, the most significant subthemes were pollution management/ environmental health (22.1 percent) and environmental policy and institutions (21.7 percent), followed by water resource management (15 percent), land administration and management, and biodiversity conservation (12.1 percent each), climate change (10.2 percent), and other ENRM (6.7 percent). However, among projects whose highest-ranking subtheme was ENRM-related, the largest shares were in projects involving biodiversity conservation (23.2 percent), pollution management/ environmental heath (18.8 percent), and climate change (15.2 percent).[20]

Examined another way, nearly three-fifths (59.6 percent) of all ENRM projects having biodiversity conservation as a subtheme identified it as the primary one, the same being true for 46.5 percent of all projects with climate change as a subtheme. These subsets largely consisted of GEF and carbon-offset operations, respectively, while those under the other five ENRM subthemes (that is, projects not focused primarily on global environmental concerns) were largely funded by IBRD loans or IDA credits.[21] In contrast with the biodiversity and climate change subsets, many of those involving environmental policy and institutions, pollution management/environmental health, and water resource management indicated that these were more important as secondary than as primary subthemes.[22]

The shares of commitment amounts, by ENRM theme, for all projects for which one of these subthemes is identified as the primary one can also be determined, together with total commitments for all ENRM-related purposes in these projects. Doing so highlights the numerous cases in which multiple ENRM subthemes were identified for the same operation. These figures (see table F.3) reveal that, among the 950 projects in which ENRM subthemes were the highest ranking, the largest aggregate commitments were for pollution management/environmental health ($3 billion) and water resource management ($2.7 billion), followed by climate change ($2.2 billion) and environmental policy and institutions ($1.9 billion). As previously noted, however, the climate change subset contains one very large carbon finance project in China that accounts for a substantial share of this total. Similarly, the environmental policy and institutions category includes seven Development Policy Loans[23] (which, if excluded from the calculations, would reduce the overall commitment amount for this subtheme from $1.9 to $1.4 billion, and the total ENRM commitments among this subset of projects from close to $4.2 to just under $3 billion).[24]

**Table F.3: Commitment Amounts and Averages, by ENRM Subtheme, Fiscal 1990–2007**

| Subtheme | Subtheme amount ($ millions) | ENRM amount ($ millions) | Total commitments ($ millions) | Average subtheme commitments ($ millions) | Average total project commitments ($ millions) |
|---|---|---|---|---|---|
| Biodiversity conservation | 775.0 | 1,823.9 | 2,583.7 | 3.5 | 11.7 |
| Climate change | 2,224.8 | 3,594.7 | 4,995.7 | 15.5 | 34.7 |
| Environmental policy and institutions | 1,885.8 | 4,175.5 | 5,908.9 | 15.1 | 47.3 |
| Land administration and management | 1,467.9 | 2,135.8 | 4,179.2 | 14.5 | 41.4 |
| Pollution management/environmental health | 3,019.0 | 5,865.8 | 7,892.0 | 16.9 | 44.1 |
| Water resource management | 2,697.8 | 5,036.1 | 8,314.4 | 22.1 | 68.2 |
| Other ENRM | 560.8 | 1,024.1 | 1,604.0 | 9.5 | 27.2 |
| Total | 12,640.1 | 23,655.8 | 35,477.9 | 13.3 | 37.3 |

*Source:* World Bank database.

When including the seven Development Policy Loans, however, projects in which environment policy and institutions was the first-ranking ENRM subtheme accounted for 17.7 percent of all ENRM-related commitments among the 950 projects considered. This is exceeded only by the subsets for pollution management/ environmental health (24.8 percent of the total) and water resource management (21.3 percent). The smallest shares of such commitments were for "other ENRM" projects (4.3 percent), followed by those focusing on biodiversity conservation (7.7 percent); land (including watershed) management–related (9 percent) and climate change (15.6 percent) projects fell in between.

The overall outcome ratings of the 355 completed and evaluated projects of which the highest-ranking subthemes were ENRM ones can also be compared.[25] Table F.4 indicates that project subsets that had pollution management/environmental health, land administration and management, and water resource management as their first ENRM subthemes had above-average overall satisfactory outcome ratings. In contrast, projects focusing on environment policy and institutions had, by far, the lowest such rating, followed by those focusing on biodiversity.[26] Projects concentrating on climate change and "other ENRM" activities performed slightly below the average for all evaluated ENRM operations.

Several observations should be made in relation to theses patterns, however. Some thematic portfolios are comparatively much less evaluated than others, reflecting the fact that these subsets are still relatively new (that is, a relatively larger share of their total operations was approved in more recent years and, therefore, is still under implementation). This is particularly evident with respect to the climate change subset, in which less than 14 percent of all projects approved since fiscal 1990 (in recent years most have been operations under the Prototype Carbon Fund) have been completed and evaluated. But it is also the case to a lesser extent for the biodiversity subset.

Each subtheme may contain projects with quite different objectives, designs, and/or emphases, many of which also have different outcomes. A case in point is the pollution management/ environmental health subset, which includes 21 Montreal Protocol and 5 GEF operations designed to help countries phase out ozone-depleting substances. Thirteen (or 50 percent) of these projects have been evaluated, all with satisfactory outcome ratings. Separating out these projects from the total for this subtheme would reduce its share of satisfactory projects from 80.2 percent to 76.7 percent. In short, the non-ozone-related pollution management/environmental health projects performed less well, on average. Six industrial pollution control projects (two in

**Table F.4: Overall Outcome Ratings, by ENRM Subtheme**

| Subtheme | Percent satisfactory | Percent unsatisfactory | Number of projects evaluated | Percent of projects evaluated |
|---|---|---|---|---|
| Biodiversity conservation | 71.2 | 28.8 | 66 | 30.0 |
| Climate change | 75.0 | 25.0 | 20 | 13.9 |
| Environmental policy and institutions | 64.8 | 35.2 | 54 | 43.2 |
| Land administration and management | 80.0 | 20.0 | 45 | 44.6 |
| Pollution management/environmental health | 80.2 | 19.8 | 86 | 48.0 |
| Water resource management | 79.7 | 20.3 | 64 | 52.5 |
| Other ENRM | 75.0 | 25.0 | 20 | 33.9 |
| Total | 75.5 | 24.5 | 355 | 37.4 |

*Source:* World Bank database.
*Note:* Ratings shown are for evaluated projects approved since fiscal 1990.

India and one each in Algeria, Brazil, China, and Egypt), for example, also fall under this subtheme; half were rated unsatisfactory.[27]

Performance trends over time and space should also be considered. In the biodiversity subset, for instance, all but one of the 20 projects assessed as unsatisfactory, to date, were approved before fiscal 1998, and all but six of them before fiscal 1996. Therefore, biodiversity project performance has improved significantly over time—as has that for the Environment Sector Board and larger ENRM portfolios more generally—suggesting that learning has taken place from the uneven performance of the first generation of such operations approved in the early and mid-1990s.

Finally, it is important to consider where unsatisfactory projects are located. In the biodiversity subset, eight of these projects were in Sub-Saharan Africa (40 percent), four in Latin America and the Caribbean, three in East Asia and Pacific, two in the Middle East and North Africa, and one in Europe and Central Asia. Five countries—Kenya (four projects), Algeria, Brazil, Indonesia, and Malawi (two each)—accounted for 60 percent of the unsatisfactory biodiversity projects, suggesting that country, as well as project design and implementation, factors may have played a role in their poor performance.[28] All of the above comments suggest that a case-by-case assessment of the elements associated with good and poor project performance— whether in terms of environmental results or overall outcomes—is also desirable, but such an assessment is beyond the scope of the present review.

## Advisory Panel Statement

1. Director general of the International Union for the Conservation of Nature, represented at the Advisory Panel meeting by Dr. Erich Vogt, Senior Multilateral Policy Advisor.

2. President of the World Business Council for Sustainable Development.

3. Head of the Program of Country Environmental Performance Review, Organisation for Economic Co-operation and Development.

4. Advisor, Fundación Futuro Latinoamericano.

5. Assistant administrator and director of development policy, United Nations Development Programme.

## Management Response

1. IEG observes that the methodologies used to analyze results of World Bank, IFC, and MIGA operations are well known and well accepted. By including all three organizations, the evaluation was able to look at World Bank Group effectiveness.

2. IEG observes that the case studies, which were handled consistently across countries and which covered a large share of the Bank's environmental work, were complemented by a portfolio review of all Bank environment and natural resource management projects and more than 600 IFC project evaluations, together with a broad literature review. Triangulating evidence from various sources in this way is a common and widely accepted approach in sector and thematic evaluations.

3. IEG's view is that the evaluation recognizes that the responsibility for assessment of, and design and implementation of mitigation measures for, potential environmental and social impacts of IFC-supported projects rests fully with the sponsor.

4. IEG observes that the evaluation covers World Bank Group experience from 1990 to 2006 (with the portfolio analysis extended through June 2007). Recent activities in the Bank, IFC, and MIGA (for example, IFC's Sustainability Business Innovator Program) are therefore not covered by this evaluation.

## Chapter 1

1. Other key messages from the report: environmental degradation threatens all aspects of human well-being; environmental sustainability (Millennium Development Goal number 7) is critical to attainment of the other Millennium Development Goals; some progress toward sustainable development has been made since the 1987 World Commission on Environment and Development report, but some institutional negotiations have stalled over questions of equity and responsibility sharing; effective policy responses are needed at all levels of governance; and society has the capacity to make a difference in the way the environment is used to underpin development and human well-being.

2. The *Global Monitoring Report* affirms, for example: "Urgency of action to accelerate and broaden progress toward the development goals [that is, the MDGs] is paralleled by urgency of action to combat climate change that threatens the well-being of all countries, but particularly that of poor countries and poor people. Development and environmental sustainability are fundamentally complementary objectives (although in the short term they may appear as trade-offs). Environmental sustainability is essential for continued economic growth and poverty reduction. . . . Economic growth and development in poor countries in turn can contribute to environmental sustainability by improving their access to modern energy and cleaner and more efficient technologies and reducing reliance on activities, such as cutting forests, that are detrimental to the environment" (World Bank and IMF 2008, p. 3).

3. This phenomenon has been called the "environmental Kuznets curve," whereby pollution levels, initially fairly low, rise as national income increases up to a certain point, then begin to decline with further economic growth as cleaner technologies are adopted and envi-

ronmental sanitation infrastructure investments begin to catch up with expanding local needs.

4. The various relationships between economic growth and environment are detailed in the 1992 WDR, which suggests in one chapter heading that development and environment are a false dichotomy. In this regard, one of the WDR's most important messages is "the protection of the environment is an essential part of development. Without adequate environmental protection, development is undermined; without development, resources will be inadequate for needed investments, and environmental protection will fail" (box 1, p. 2).

5. A Center for Global Development report cited in "World's Power Plant Emissions Detailed: US Appears to Be Worst Carbon Dioxide Polluter, but China Is Catching Up Fast," *Washington Post,* November 15, 2007, identifies the principal national contributors to $CO_2$ emissions: the United States, 2,790 million tons; China, 2,680 million tons; Russia, 661 million tons; India, 583 million tons; Japan, 400 million tons; and Germany, 356 million tons. According to the same article, a single U.S. power plant in South Carolina emits more $CO_2$ than the entire power sector in Brazil.

6. On Polonoroeste, see Wade 1997. It was also specifically cited in then-President Barber Conable's speech to the World Resources Institute in May 1987, when he announced the establishment of the Bank's Environment Department and other environment-related measures. The adverse environmental and social impacts of Polonoroeste, Narmada, and the Transmigration Program, among other Bank-supported projects, are also discussed in Rich 1994.

7. Operational Manual Statement (OMS) 2.36.

8. The Environmental Assessment Operational Directive was first revised in October 1991 and further revised and reissued as an Operational Policy in January 1999. It was last revised in August 2004 and updated in March 2007 to reflect other policy changes.

9. The Bank also issued guidance materials, including an *Environmental Assessment Sourcebook,* published in 1991 (World Bank 1991a), and a *Pollution Prevention and Abatement Handbook,* prepared in collaboration with the United Nations Industrial Development Organization and UNEP, in July 1998 (World Bank Group, UNEP, and UNIDO 1999).

10. The report averred that environmental problems that damaged the health and productivity of the poor had received inadequate attention. To address them, policies were required to build on the positive linkages between development and environment and to break the negative ones. The former included: removing subsidies that encouraged excessive use of natural resources and energy; clarifying property rights to natural resources; accelerating provision of environmental sanitation and related services; and educating and empowering farmers, local communities, indigenous peoples, and women. The WDR pointed out that tradeoffs between income and environmental quality should be carefully assessed, environmental standards and policies need to be "realistic and consistent with the monitoring and enforcement capacity and administrative traditions of the country," and that environmental policies should "work with the grain of the market rather than against it, using incentives rather than regulations where possible." At the same time, governments needed to build "constituencies for change—to curb the power of vested interests, to hold institutions accountable, and to increase the willingness to pay the costs of protection." In this regard, local participation "in setting and implementing environmental policies and investments" was expected to yield high results (p. 3).

11. The Environmentally and Socially Sustainable Development Network was merged with Infrastructure in 2006 to form a new Vice Presidency for Sustainable Development, with parallel organizational changes in each of the six Operational Regions.

12. The protocol was first adopted in 1987 and became binding international law in 1998. The Bank agreed in July 1991 to help channel resources to developing countries for the phase-out of ozone-depleting substances.

13. Restructured as a full-scale global funding mechanism in March of 1994, the GEF has focal areas for biodiversity, climate change, ozone depletion, international waters, land degradation, and persistent organic pollutants.

14. IFC's Environmental and Social Advisory Programs are Biodiversity, Carbon Finance, Cleaner Technologies, Environmental Business Finance Program, Gender Entrepreneurship Markets, Social Responsibility, Sustainable Energy, and Sustainable Investing.

15. This agenda consisted of: (1) assisting countries with environmental stewardship by helping them define national environmental strategies and action plans, Bank lending for environmental management, and expanding and disseminating knowledge; (2) assessing and mitigating adverse impacts of Bank-financed projects through environmental and social assessment; (3) building on positive synergies between development and environment

by investing in people and promoting efficient resource use; and (4) addressing global environmental challenges, particularly through the GEF. The third item was relabeled "mainstreaming the environment" in 1995 (World Bank 1995a). The corresponding report for fiscal 1994 was entitled *Making Development Sustainable.* This series was discontinued after fiscal 2004 and replaced with the periodic publication *Environment Matters at the World Bank,* which has been issued annually just before the Annual Meetings since 1999.

16. The preface to the strategy affirmed that "the four World Bank Group institutions [including IDA] are aligned with the core mission of poverty reduction—and, therefore, the overall vision, strategic framework, and objectives of this strategy." It also states: "members of the World Bank Group, however, are legally and financially independent and have different sets of owners and clients, structures and mandates, staffs and toolkits. Accordingly, specific operational and institutional implications differ and need to be spelled out separately." (World Bank 2001b, pp. x–xi) In practice, the private sector's role in the context of environmental sustainability was seen from the Bank's perspective, and IFC and MIGA did not feel strictly bound to implement the strategy as defined primarily by the Bank.

17. The World Resources reports began in 1986. They have been produced by the World Resources Institute, initially in collaboration with the International Institute for Environment and Development in London. The 1988–89 publication was also done in collaboration with UNEP, and that for 1990–91 with both UNEP and UNDP (although not with the International Institute for Environment and Development ). The 1996–97 report, which focused on the urban environment, was the first in which the Bank also participated, and it has been involved in all of the subsequent reports (1998–99, 2000–01, 2003–04, and 2005), as have UNEP and UNDP, with the World Resources Institute taking the lead. The last three of these reports focused on people and ecosystems, environmental governance (formally subtitled *Decisions for the Earth: Balance, Voice, and Power* [UNDP and others 2003]), and managing ecosystems to fight poverty, respectively.

18. Expanding on the 2001 Environment Strategy, it affirmed that "associated challenges are to improve livelihoods on fragile lands, transform institutions on agricultural lands, get the best from cities, strengthen national coordination, and better integrate global problems and local concerns, especially with regard to conserving biodiversity and maintaining ecosystems, on the one hand, and mitigating and adapting to climate change, on the other." See also World Bank 2004c for a post-Johannesburg view of the sustainable decelopment challenges Bank clients face. More specifically, the 2003 WDR concluded that "given the social and environmental stresses caused by past development strategies, the goal for raising human well-being worldwide must be pursued through a development process that does better—a poverty-eliminating growth path that integrates environmental and social concerns in pursuit of the goal of sustained improvements in well-being" (p. 3).

19. Background papers for the World Bank Group strategy covered such topics as poverty and environment, health and environment, natural resource management, urban air quality management, and mainstreaming the environment in country strategies, as well as preparation of a sourcebook on poverty, environment, and natural resources for PRSPs, and more than 30 consultations were held with a wide variety of stakeholders in different parts of the world. Another important input was *The World Bank and the Global Environment: A Progress Report* (World Bank 2000c).

20. Acknowledging that past achievements had "fallen short" of the Bank's own high expectations and those of others, even bearing in mind that, by itself, "the Bank can never stem the tide of global environmental change," the 2001 Strategy accepted IEG's recommendations that the World Bank Group should: (1) build on its comparative advantage and analytical capacity to demonstrate the environment's critical role in sustainable poverty reduction; (2) review its safeguard oversight system and processes to strengthen accountability for compliance; (3) continue to update the policy framework, adapting it to changing practices and new Bank instruments and take account of recent experience; and (4) help implement the global environmental agenda by concentrating on global issues that involve local and national benefits (chapter 5).

21. This varies from country to country, however. For instance, in 2004, China received total overseas development assistance in the form of commitments for loans, grants, and other official flows of US$5 billion, comprised primarily of contributions from Japan (US$1.3 billion), the Asian Development Bank (US$1.3 billion), the World Bank (US$1.2 billion), and European Union countries (US$1.0 billion). The share of this total for the environment was estimated by OECD to be roughly 10 percent.

22. Russia, at least at the central-government level, for example, currently is not interested in Bank support for the environment, while such assistance appears to be a high priority for China, although it does not need the Bank's financing per se. Other countries, such as Turkey, while concerned about the environment, prefer other donors, such as the European Union, to the Bank in this regard.

23. Although IFC is a relatively small player compared with other sources of private capital for the developing world, it is the largest multilateral source of finance for the private sector, accounting for 29 percent of all such investments in developing countries over the 1991–2006 period.

## Chapter 2

1. Two recent Bank papers on the same subject are Sundberg and Gelb 2006 and DRG 2005. For another important dimension to this question in Africa, which also focuses on the often vexing donor coordination challenge, see Pomerantz 2004. The paper argues that "improving knowledge about these links and how they contribute to development outcomes is helping reshape the prevailing aid model based primarily on two elements: (1) country ownership of the development strategy, around which donors need to align; and (2) aid allocation based primarily on monitorable results (governance as well as outcome indicators)" (p. 11). For our purposes, environment can be substituted for development in the first item, while the emphasis on country ownership can be seen as referring to the national authorizing environment for the environmental improvement mission.

2. For project coding purposes within the Bank, ENRM has seven subthemes: biodiversity, climate change, environmental policies and institutions, land administration and management, pollution management and environmental health, water resource management, and other ENRM. These subthemes map to five main environmental agendas: brown—pollution management and environmental health; green—land administration and management and other environmental and natural resource management; blue—water resource management; institutional and policy—environmental policies and institutions; and global—biodiversity, ozone depletion, and climate change.

3. Starting in November 2001, the Bank required that projects be classified by both theme and sector based on a number of subthemes and subsectors. Sectors included: agriculture, fishing, and forestry; education; energy and mining; finance; health and other social services; industry and trade; information and communications; law, justice, and public administration; transportation; and water, sanitation, and flood protection. Themes included: economic management; ENRM; financial and private sector development; human development; public sector governance; rule of law; rural development; social development/gender/inclusion; social protection and risk management; trade and integration; and urban development. Projects can be coded in up to five subsectors and five subthemes, in many cases involving different sectors and themes. Projects are also mapped to different sector boards by Regions, in a process that is not necessarily fully consistent with their thematic coding, especially in the case of ENRM operations.

4. IEG has recently assessed World Bank (but not IFC and MIGA) support in both middle-income countries and fragile states, although the latter did not give specific attention to environmental aspects. See IEG-World Bank 2006b, 2007b.

5. This is the case even for Category A projects, which have the most potential for significant adverse environmental impacts. Even for these projects, moreover, there is no requirement that ICRs indicate whether the Environmental Management Plans included as part of project design were actually carried out—and with what results—during implementation.

6. Argentina, Indonesia, Mexico, Pakistan, South Korea, and Turkey, all of which have been Bank borrowers for much longer, also rank ahead of Russia in total Bank commitments. The countries selected for the case studies also account for considerable shares of both the Bank's ENRM portfolio and IFC and MIGA operations (with the exception of India in the case of MIGA, which is not active there). The case study countries, particularly in Sub-Saharan Africa, were identified in consultation with World Bank Regional staff as those where the Bank had been significantly involved in ERNM activities since 1990 (and even before in the case of Madagascar, which was the first country for which a National Environmental Action Plan—NEAP—was prepared with substantial Bank assistance).

7. According to the most recent United Nations Habitat Global Report on Human Settlements (UN-Habitat 2007), populations in these megacities in 2005 were as follows (in millions): Beijing, 10.9; Cairo, 11.1; Calcutta, 14.9; Delhi, 15.3; Moscow, 10.7; Mumbai, 18.4; Rio de Janeiro, 11.5; São Paulo, 18.3; and Shanghai, 12.7.

## Chapter 3

1. The environment has been a significant pillar in successive strategy documents for Brazil and China; its significance declined then rose again in India. It has been up and down in many Sub-Saharan African countries and has decreased substantially in the recent strategy for Russia.

2. This pioneering experience, together with that in other parts of Sub-Saharan Africa, is described in Falloux and Talbot (1993).

3. The Bank's assessment of experience with national environmental strategies and action plans in the early 1990s provided a number of key lessons for policymakers, including (in addition to the need to set priorities) the need to (1) balance analysis and participation; (2) involve the right national stakeholders; (3) clarify the objectives of any such strategy or action plan; (4) ensure "quick victories" to help build and sustain support; (5) insist on donor coordination; and (6) closely monitor and evaluate the results (World Bank 1995c).

4. PRSPs are generally prepared by cross-cutting planning teams, and weak national environmental institutions may not be well equipped to have a strong input. However, good analytical work on the environment, together with client country institutions, may help improve the situation.

5. Nonlending services include AAA, such as ESW, informal policy and technical advice, and direct technical support to country agencies by operational staff. Relevant AAA includes surveys of environmental problems and potential measures to address them at the national and subnational levels, both for the full range of such problems and specific issues such as pollution or deforestation; use of standard Bank diagnostic tools such as Country Economic Memoranda and newer instruments such as CEAs and SEAs; research and outreach by the Development Economics and Environment departments; capacity building by the World Bank Institute and Legal Department; and evaluation work by IEG.

6. The Environment Sector Board reached the same conclusion more generally in Acharya, Dyoulgerov, and Tsutsui (2005).

7. Egypt is just one of the countries in the Middle East and North Africa Region for which pioneering costs of environmental degradation studies were done by the Bank. The Bank has even published a trilingual training manual (Bolt, Ruta, and Sarraf 2005) on how to undertake such assessments in Arabic, French, and English.

8. Both the Consultative Group for Agricultural Research system, which has been an environmentally significant instrument for enhancing global environmental productivity over the past 40 years, and the Critical Ecosytems Partnership Fund, which is jointly financed by the GEF, Conservation International, and the Japanese government but was launched in part by a multiyear Development Grant Facility grant, have previously been the subject of IEG assessments.

9. For a recent example, see ADB (2006).

10. For a more general discussion of these reviews, see OECD (2001). One of the most recent of these assessments was for China (OECD 2007). However, similar performance evaluations have been carried out for Chile, Korea, Mexico, Poland, Russia, Turkey, and other Bank Group client countries, as well as for more developed ones, including G-7 countries.

11. IEG found during its mission to India that a highly consultative CEA process had been undertaken. As the CEA report affirms, "From the outset, the main value added of this exercise was seen not so much in producing new knowledge or new analytical results, as in helping to develop a commonly shared vision on the way forward, reconciling different perspectives by diverse stakeholders" (World Bank 2006b).

12. These were formerly known as Adjustment Loans and include PRSCs for low-income borrowers, which are based on country-prepared PRSPs. The environmental impacts of adjustment are the subject of several non-Bank evaluations (such as Reed 1992).

13. CEAs were originally intended to overcome some of the deficiencies of the earlier NEAPs through more rigorous analysis of country environmental priorities and environmental management capacity. CEAs today are used for a variety of purposes and need to be tailored accordingly to respond to the objectives of the analysis.

14. Guidance on CEAs was initially provided by the Environment Sector Board in two reports (Segnestam and others 2003; Pillai and Lunde 2006), which were only partially based on actual Bank experience.

15. There is clearly some degree of overlap between these themes. Biodiversity conservation, for example, can be considered a part of both the green and the global agendas; reduction of greenhouse gas emissions and ozone-depleting substances can fall under both the brown and global agendas. For purposes of this evaluation—especially because Bank-supported interventions to help address global environmental issues such as biodiversity loss, climate change, and ozone depletion are not financed primarily through IBRD loans and

IDA credits, but through alternative financing mechanisms such as GEF and Montreal Protocol grants and carbon offsets—the green and brown agendas will refer mainly to those natural resource management and pollution-related activities not covered under the global agenda.

16. For earlier reviews of parts of this portfolio, see Redwood, Robelus, and Vetleseter (1998), Keck (1998), Margulis and Vetleseter (1999), and World Bank (2004b). Bank operational Regions have also carried out portfolio reviews (for example, World Bank 1998d; Crooks and others 1999; Margulis and others 2006).

17. Although the share of DPLs in total commitments for ENRM purposes has varied considerably over the period under review, it was highest in fiscal 2005, when such operations accounted for more than 25 percent of the total.

18. An IEG assessment of the Environmental Structural Adjustment Loan in Mexico, which was designed to be the first of three DPLs for environment-related purposes, found that the loan had been satisfactory in terms of putting the anticipated processes in place, but, as no specific environmental quality targets had been set for the first operation, it was not possible to determine what its actual impact on the environment had been at this stage of the program (World Bank 2005e ).

19. To give just a few examples from the case study countries, $194.4 million (or 33 percent) of a $589.0 million loan for improvement of the Grand Trunk Road in India was reportedly for ENRM purposes, as was $125.7 million (33 percent) of a $381 million loan for the Gujarat Highways Project, $117 million (26 percent) of a $454.6 million loan for the Second Powergrid Project, and $70.5 million (13 percent) of a $542 million loan for the Mumbai Urban Transport Project. In Russia, in turn, commitments reportedly for ENRM purposes included $158.6 million (26 percent) out of a $610 million loan for the first Oil Rehabilitation Project, $165 million (33 percent) of a $500 million loan for the second Oil Rehabilitation Project, $132 million (33 percent) for a $400 million housing project, and $112 million (14 percent) of the $800 million Second Coal Sector Adjustment Loan. Other examples could be given for China and Brazil, as well as for non-case study countries such as Turkey, Mexico, and the Philippines.

20. ENRM commitments in China account for more than 16 percent of all such commitments Bank-wide. This is nearly as much as those for South Asia and Africa.

21. There are also important differences across countries. In China, 28 percent of the ENRM portfolio is mapped to Rural Development, 19 percent each to Energy, Mining, and Telecommunications and Water Supply and Sanitation, and 12 percent to Transport, compared with just 12 percent to the Environment Sector Board. In Brazil, 36 percent (including projects for water resource management) were mapped to the Environment Sector Board, 21 percent to Rural Development, and 10 percent each to Transport and Water Supply and Sanitation.

22. IEG-World Bank (2002), based on Boisson de Chazournes (2000) and International Union of Conservation of Nature and Natural Resources (IUCN 2000). Regional and country reviews reinforce the findings of the Bank-wide surveys. An assessment for Sub-Saharan Africa found that environmental assessments had positively influenced the design, quality, and sustainability of Bank-financed projects but were insufficient in use of environmental economics, attention to public health, participation, and analysis of alternatives (Mercier 1995).

23. IEG-World Bank (2002) also concluded that Inspection Panel reports had "highlighted a significant problem with the implementation of environmental assessment policy in the Bank due to perceived ambiguities in the scope, intent, and requirements of the policies among staff responsible for their implementation and among senior management."

24. Case study country projects for which full inspections were carried out are Rondonia Natural Resource Management Project (Planafloro) in Brazil; Itaparica Resettlement and Irrigation Project in Brazil; National Thermal Power Generation Project in India; Ecodevelopment Project in India; Western Poverty Reduction Project in China; Coal Sector Environmental and Social Mitigation Project in India; Third Power Project, Fourth Power Project, and (proposed) Bujagali Hydropower Project in Uganda; and Mumbai Urban Transport Project in India.

25. This compares with 29 requests involving alleged noncompliance with supervision policies, 23 regarding policies on involuntary settlement, and 20 involving indigenous peoples.

26. SEA has been defined as "a systematic process for evaluating the environmental consequences of proposed policy, plan, or programme initiatives in order to ensure that they are fully included and appropriately addressed at the earliest appropriate stage of decision making or on a par with economic and social consid-

erations" (Dalal-Clayton and Sadler 2004; Conor and Dovers 2004). Alternatively, "A participatory approach for upstreaming environmental and social issues to influence processes for development planning and decisionmaking, and implementation at the strategic level" is discussed in Ahmed, Mercier, and Verheem (2005).

27. See, for example, World Bank 2005d. Though drawing largely on experience in Part I countries, this review was based in part on case studies from Argentina, Colombia, the Czech Republic, the Slovak Republic, and South Africa. See also Sanchez-Triana and Enriquez (2005).

28. More specifically, the Quality Assurance Group review found that several systemic problems in implementing environmental safeguards could be traced to "oversights in preparation," including (1) inadequate analysis of institutional capability/organization, particularly weaknesses in coordination across sectors; (2) fragile institutional arrangements, often based on an expectation that a "champion" (individual or technical body) was judged secure enough to sustain the relevant functions in an unstable institutional environment; (3) underappreciation of the complexity of and constraints on the legal and planning process and a poor monitoring and evaluation framework; (4) lack of guidance for supervision (such as absence of a supervision plan), including designated use of specialists; (5) synergy with "neighboring" projects (both spatially and temporally) not recognized, and thus insufficient attention given to cumulative impacts; and (6) inexperience of task team members in environmental planning and management and sustainable development. There were also "major" deficiencies during supervision: absence or insufficient use of environmental specialists; a need for earlier interventions to help modify or restructure poorly performing components, especially with respect to institutional arrangements and responsibilities; a need to sharpen baseline studies and reorder management priorities; reluctance to reshape supervision requirements (such as team composition); failure to coordinate the preparation of supervision objectives with borrower agencies; and variable support from both the borrower and Bank management.

29. See World Bank 2007h, which concludes that "only modest progress has been made to date with the use of country systems, and that for real progress to be made it will be necessary to move beyond the project-by-project approach adopted for the Safeguards pilot when it was approved in March 2005."

30. The most recent specific Environment Department review of Bank environmental assessment experience was for fiscal 1996–2000 (see Green and Raphael 2000). The previous such evaluation by the Environment Sector Board was *The Impact of Environmental Assessment: A Review of World Bank Experience* (World Bank 1997b), and the only evaluation of Bank environmental safeguards by IEG-World Bank (then OED) was issued in June 1996 (IEG-World Bank 1996).

31. Satisfactory projects are those that received an IEG project outcome rating of highly satisfactory, satisfactory, or moderately/marginally satisfactory.

32. There was also comparatively little difference in overall outcome ratings for completed projects approved between fiscal 1990 and fiscal 2005 by environmental assessment category, although Category A operations performed slightly less well (74.5 percent satisfactory) than Category B (75.5 percent) and C (75.8 percent) projects. See the glossary for a description of environmental risk categories.

33. One possible reason for the better performance of GEF, Montreal Protocol, and Rainforest Pilot Program projects than those financed with IBRD loans and IDA credits may be the generally greater complexity of and implementation difficulties faced by the latter than the former, especially in Sub-Saharan Africa. However, there may be other important reasons as well that merit further investigation.

34. One explanation is that strong differences exist in the way projects have been mapped to different sector boards by the Regions, with many fewer ENRM operations mapped to the Environment Sector Board in East Asia and Pacific than in the other Regions.

35. Experience, in short, has been mixed, with the least successful operations being those focusing more exclusively on technical assistance (Bolivia, Honduras, Malawi, Mexico, Morocco, Trinidad and Tobago, Zambia, India, and Madagascar). Other countries, especially those with significant investment components and stronger institutional capacity to begin with (Brazil, Chile, China, and Poland), have proven more successful (see Margulis and Vetleseter 1999; Ruthenberg and others 2001).

36. Each project can have from one to five themes, environmental and other. In some cases, the same percentage is assigned to more than one theme. To avoid multiple counting of the same operations, this table refers only to the top-ranked theme for each project as

specified in a Bank database. Although this is somewhat arbitrary, it is generally indicative of actual performance differences.

37. When the 13 ozone projects are removed, the percentage of satisfactory projects in this category falls from 80.2 percent to 76.7 percent.

38. Although decreasing Bank attention to the environment in Russia largely reflects its declining priority for the central government, elsewhere (in Africa, for example) shifts over time seem to be due more to changes in Bank approach, priority, or instruments of choice—such as policy-based lending and budget support versus traditional investment projects.

39. This evaluation did not systematically assess the reasons for these observed differences, but, based on those projects examined in detail in the case study countries, the factors that seem to have contributed to these results (in no particular order of importance) included (1) the "win-win" nature of many blue and green projects in terms of both private economic and environmental benefits, especially those for watershed management and community forestry; (2) stronger government ownership and institutional capacity in such operations, especially at the subnational level, than in pure capacity-building ones; (3) relatively ineffective approaches to pollution abatement in projects primarily relying on directed lines; (4) insufficiently comprehensive approaches to pollution management in both industrial and many urban projects (including in China, where the experience was relatively better than elsewhere); and (5) the role of local community involvement and beneficiary participation in many blue and green projects.

40. Three examples: In India, the Bank identified water pollution as the most serious problem in terms of environmental degradation costs, yet almost totally withdrew from the urban water supply and sanitation sector—and urban development more generally—over the past two decades. In Egypt, the same has occurred in relation to air quality, which is particularly serious in metropolitan Cairo. In Sub-Saharan Africa, land degradation and natural resource management have not received adequate attention despite their importance for both environmental sustainability and rural poverty reduction.

41. More specifically, the report affirms "achieving results in a sector often requires that constraints in other sectors be identified and removed as well."

42. Global environmental issues fall into two categories. The first consists of global commons issues "directly related to maintenance of major components of the Earth's systems," including climate change, ozone depletion, accumulation of persistent organic pollutants, and loss of certain biodiversity elements, such as migratory species that cross national borders and globally important genetic resources. The second involves natural resource degradation on a global scale. This includes most other biodiversity concerns, degradation of international waters and marine ecosystems (including coral reefs), land degradation and desertification, and degradation and loss of forest resources (World Bank 2001b).

43. The strategy affirmed, for example, that "a poverty-focused environmental agenda will require an increased emphasis on the local aspects of global environmental challenges, on reducing the impacts of the degradation of the global environmental commons on developing countries, and on interventions that are carefully targeted to benefit developing countries and local communities."

44. This has been documented in a recent assessment by the GEF Evaluation Office (GEF 2006).

45. The evaluation did not attempt to assess the effectiveness of specific environment-related partnerships per se, but rather sought to consider the nature of their role in Bank efforts to support environmental sustainability in a general sense, especially in the case study countries, and to obtain views, based on interviews, from selected institutions with which the Bank was engaged in varying ways in matters related to the environment. These interviews told how the institutions regarded the Bank as a partner in such activities of mutual interest. These interviews were carried out by IEG both during the field visits for the individual country case studies and through meetings at the headquarters of some of the institutions involved, including both other multilateral and bilateral donors and several international environmental NGOs.

46. The Environment Strategy specifically refers to "constructive partnerships" with the GEF, Montreal Protocol, and Prototype Carbon Fund to help implement major international conventions. The strategy further states that "applying the principles of the Comprehensive Development Framework, partnerships at the country level are aimed at increasing development effectiveness and reducing transaction costs through coordination led by the countries and through harmonization of operational policies and practices of development partners" and with international envi-

ronmental NGOs such as the International Union for Conservation of Nature and Natural Resources (IUCN), a key actor in connection with the World Commission on Dams; the World Wildlife Fund, which is implementing an innovative Forest Alliance with the Bank; Conservation International, which is executing the Critical Ecosystems Partnership Fund with Bank and GEF grant support; and the World Resources Institute (WRI), which issues periodic World Resources Reports. Key environment-related partnerships also exist with other United Nations agencies and programs, including the Food and Agricultural Organization, which helps prepare and supervise Bank agriculture, rural development, and environmental projects. They also include UNDP, United Nations Environment Programme, United Nations Industrial Development Organization, and the World Health Organization (World Bank 2001b).

47. The authors are grateful to Nancy McPherson, Special Advisor for Performance Assessment at IUCN, for referring us to two helpful papers on evaluation of partnerships (IUCN 2005; Lusthaus and Milton-Feasby 2006).

48. Personal communication from two senior UNDP officials interviewed by IEG in New York in March 2007. Similarly positive views of Poverty-Environment Partnerships and less positive ones of TerrAfrica were expressed by representatives of DFID, the International Institute for Environment and Development, the German Federal Ministry for Economic Cooperation and Development, IUCN, and World Wildlife Fund International in April–May 2007.

49. It should be pointed out, however, that it is only natural that the field presence of environmental specialists should be larger in Brazil, China, and India—Indonesia providing a similar example—given the size and complexity of operations in those countries.

50. Although the periodic visits of Bank specialists from Headquarters are appreciated by government counterparts and other domestic stakeholders, there tends to be less coordination with donors and country-based NGOs.

51. The relationships between poverty and environment were further set out in a background paper for the Environment Strategy, using the framework developed in the 2000/2001 WDR (World Bank 2001c; also see Bucknall, Kraus, and Pillai 2001). See also Mink (1993) and DFID and others (2002).

52. Enhancing the sustainability of natural resource management is a main pillar of the latter, which gives specific attention to soil fertility, watershed development, community natural resource management, community forests, and fisheries (World Bank 2003b).

53. A Bank publication that assesses the role of natural resources in economic growth in Latin America also fails to consider the links between natural resources and rural poverty reduction (Lederman and Maloney 2007).

54. This report states, "Africa will be under severe pressure from climate change. Many vulnerable regions, embracing millions of people, are likely to be adversely affected by climate change, including the mixed arid-semiarid systems in the Sahel, arid-semiarid rangeland systems in parts of eastern Africa, the systems in the Great Lake regions of eastern Africa, the coastal regions of eastern Africa, and many of the drier zones of southern Africa" (Stern 2006, p. 120).

55. The 2003 WDR's approach entailed an assessment of sustainable development challenges from different spatial perspectives, specifically to improve livelihoods on "fragile lands"; transform institutions on (commercially viable) agricultural land; "get the best from cities"; strengthen national-level coordination; and address "global problems and local concerns."

56. See, for example, World Bank 2004a. Similar analyses were issued in separate reports for Honduras and Nicaragua at the same time.

57. A background paper on this subject was issued in April 2000, a revised version of which was later published by the Environment Department (Lvovsky 2001; Listorti and Doumai 2001).

58. See, for example, the aforementioned CEA for Colombia, which contained specific chapters on waterborne diseases and indoor air pollution, which is described as "a silent killer" (Sanchez-Triana, Ahmed, and Awe 2007).

59. A combination of water resource development, population growth, and migration has resulted in the spread of disease to previously nonendemic areas. This is the case in the Senegal River Basin, where increased intensity of schistosomiasis was directly associated with physical-chemical changes in the aquatic environment resulting from dam construction the late 1980s. Despite this, just one of Senegal's six health-related projects approved since 1990 has attempted to address environment-related diseases (World Bank 2004d). The situation in Uganda has been similar, with only one of five health sector projects providing environmental health-related funding.

60. Other countries included in this pilot program are Mexico, the Philippines, and Tanzania. The project

sought to link family planning and other health interventions with natural resource management activities in Fianarantsoa Province, which contains some of the country's most important national parks and a "500 km long moist forest corridor harbor[ing] extraordinary biodiversity."

61. Mogelgaard and Patterson (2006) noted that "increasingly in Fianarantsoa and across Madagascar, cross-sectoral approaches are being incorporated into broader development approaches and local planning efforts." They also affirmed that "a growing number of practitioners in the environment and health sectors have indicated . . . that they support and promote these initiatives because they believe that coordination can yield better results and provide more benefits to communities than when the services are provided separately."

62. These challenges are described in considerable detail in Stern (2006), part II (Impacts of Climate Change on Growth and Development).

63. The 2001 Strategy did not use the expression "environmental governance" per se, but this is essentially what it was referring to in its sections on improving the quality of growth. Thus, there is no standard Bank definition of this concept. However, this was also the central topic of the *World Resources 2002–2004: Decisions for the Earth,* cosponsored by WRI, the United Nations Environment Programme, UNDP, and the Bank. This report describes governance in general as being "about decisions and how we make them" and identifies seven key elements of environmental governance: institutions and laws; participation rights and representation; authority level (local, regional, national, or international); accountability and transparency; property rights and tenure; markets and financial flows; and science and risk (UNDP and others 2003).

64. This is discussed in greater detail in a parallel IEG-World Bank review of Bank experience with implementation of its 2002 Forest Strategy and forest-related global initiatives.

65. A new Bank-IFC strategy, presented to the Board in May 2008 and entitled the "Amazon Partnership Framework," reportedly incorporates lessons of past Bank experience and proposes a "new model" for the Region in seeking to reconcile economic development with conservation. One of the lessons of past experience reflected in this new approach is recognition that the WBG required a comprehensive regional framework for its support to development initiatives in the Amazon.

## Chapter 4

1. IEG has recently recommended a stronger institutional country focus to complement the sectoral and regional approach. Parallel to the Global/Local Initiative, IFC is moving in this direction.

2. *Management comment:* IFC's instruments and investment work should not be characterized as "do no harm." The Environmental and Social (E&S) Performance Standards applied to IFC's business are designed to help companies improve and do good by doing well. More significantly, the report does not deal with the fact that in IFC, environmental and social work is integrated in risk and opportunity dimensions. Therefore, the report does not examine sustainability in its full context at IFC and misses the significance of sustainability as a business driver.

3. *Management comment:* The report simply quotes findings from previous Advisory Services evaluations and audits. There is no new IEG analysis of IFC's Advisory Services, nor is there a comprehensive evaluation of all the environmental and social advisory activities and groundbreaking innovation work that IFC has undertaken, on its own or in partnership with others, over the last 10 years, including renewable energy/energy efficiency investments and carbon finance, among other things. Furthermore, the report does not mention IFC's standard-setting work or its role in generating and sharing good practice so that private goods generated by IFC enter the public domain.

4. The 10 Operational Policies (OPs) and Operational Directives (ODs) were: OP 4.01, Environmental Assessment; OP 4.04, Natural Habitats; OP 4.09, Pest Management; OP 4.36, Forestry; OP 4.37, Safety of Dams; OP 7.50, International Waterways; OP Note 11.03, Cultural Property; IFC Policy Statement on Forced Labor and Harmful Child Labor; OD 4.20, Indigenous Peoples; and OD 4.30, Involuntary Resettlement.

5. The main changes have been made in Performance Standards 1, 2, and 4. The Guidance Notes for Performance Standard 1 define a project's area of influence, third-party roles, global and cumulative impacts, supply chain management, vulnerable groups, and gender issues. In Performance Standard 2 the objectives are to establish, maintain, and improve the relationship between workers and management, to promote fair treatment, nondiscrimination, and equal opportunities for workers and compliance with national labor and employment laws. Performance Standard 4 addresses a project's impacts on community health, safety, and se-

curity. Performance Standards 2 and 4 expand IFC's role in labor issues and community engagement.

6. "CAO Review of IFC's Safeguard Policies" (IFC 2003) included a gap analysis and recommendations for an integrated corporate approach, stakeholder engagement, revamping the policies, social policy, supervision system, and support to FIs. A CAO review of the draft Policy and Performance Standards in December 2005 revealed that recommendations relating to policy are reasonably well reflected in the new policy framework.

7. For this evaluation, IFC's industry sectors were regrouped based on their typical ESHS risk factors. The Industrial and Consumer Products, Nonmetallic Mineral Product Manufacturing, Textiles, Apparel and Leather, Pulp and Paper, Primary Metals and Plastics and Rubber Sectors in IFC's Global Manufacturing Department and Food and Beverage Sector in IFC's Agribusiness Department and Global Manufacturing Department—as well as the Chemicals Sector in IFC's Oil, Gas, Mining, and Chemicals Department—pose several risks that usually concern effluent discharges, air emissions and wastes, and workers' health and safety. These industry sectors were combined under a generic "process and manufacturing industry."

8. Through two Dutch-funded carbon facilities, IFC will purchase carbon credits for the benefit of the government of the Netherlands. These facilities are the IFC-Netherlands Carbon Facility (INCaF), operating under the rules of the Clean Development Mechanism, and the Netherlands European Carbon Facility (NECaF), operating under the rules of the joint implementation mechanism and managed jointly with IBRD. Of the $145 million available for INCaF, about $50 million has been committed in six projects; the balance is expected to be fully committed by the end of fiscal 2008. IFC has fully committed its NECaF obligation of $40 million in two projects. The partnership with the Netherlands has enabled IFC to gain experience in the carbon market and to develop new value-added financial products that will help mitigate risks in the carbon market by leveraging its own ability to take long-term project and credit risk in emerging markets. IFC, which is given a triple-A credit rating, now offers a Carbon Delivery Guarantee for credits from projects in developing countries; this product will service those who need credits for compliance and channel a higher value to qualifying projects in developing countries. Four projects using this product have been approved by the Board; the first deal was committed in December 2007.

9. Compliance with World Bank Group industry sector guidelines means compliance with "good industry practices" and measures that the World Bank Group considers "acceptable for financing."

10. For example, GEF and IFC launched the Earth Fund on the margins of the United Nations Climate Change conference in Bali in December 2007. The fund will use a wide array of financial instruments that reward environmental innovation in areas such as second-generation biofuels and clean energies.

11. *Management comment:* IFC has a different view on the CAO findings on this particular project, especially in relation to the development of the EMS. The impacts of ESMS, which was under development during the CAO review and is a major positive contribution of the investment, were not captured. Some elements of the system were being successfully implemented at the time, such as those related to the project's prefinanced suppliers. The ESMS was instrumental in identifying where environmental improvements were needed. In addition, NGO concerns were not validated, and some major NGOs did not oppose the investment and actually worked with the sponsors. The CAO review did not find any evidence that the project was encouraging deforestation of "virgin rainforests."

The report does not mention IFC's early efforts to bring NGOs and the private sector together, which over time led to the Roundtable for Responsible Soy, of which the company and a number of NGOs (such as World Wildlife Fund) are founding members. The Roundtable today is the principal multistakeholder dialogue group that is developing best practice for the soy sector. The company was also a founding member of the Amazon soy moratorium, working with Greenpeace, TNC, World Wildlife Fund, IPAM, and others to ensure that soy is not coming from newly deforested areas in the Amazon forest biome. All these efforts advanced significantly as a result of the company's ESMS efforts. In fact, the lessons of the Soy Roundtable have been applied in other commodity roundtable programs where IFC has put its energies, including the Roundtable on Sustainable Palm Oil and the Better Cotton Initiative.

12. *Management comment:* The high-volume FI activities are focused in very low-impact sectors, such as consumer loans, education, low-income housing, and the like. FI financing of projects where there is a higher potential of environmental and social risks would be captured through the FI categorization and the needs for subprojects to meet national law and, in some cases,

meet the full requirements of IFC's environmental and social Performance Standards, where the impact assessment is comprehensive and includes potential cumulative effects. The risk-based approach therefore appears to provide a useful framework to differentiate among the FIs and the basis from which to look out for potential cumulative impacts. The potential scenario of cumulative impacts raised in the report therefore appears to be rather speculative.

13. *Management comment:* IFC has gone to some length to explain IFC's policy and procedural approach to managing and mitigating risk in our FI investments under the management system introduced in 2006. If IEG disagrees that our risk-based approach is appropriate, IFC suggests that this be stated together with the rationale, as opposed to implying that IFC does not appraise or supervise its FIs projects. The high priority given to improving the EHS standards of all IFC projects, including those through MSME FIs, was the rationale behind the comprehensive policy changes brought about by the IFC Sustainability Policy Framework that has been implemented since May 2006. The Sustainability Policy Framework includes a risk-based appraisal and supervision of FIs. This risk-based approach allows IFC to be more effective in its resource allocation by spending more time on high-risk projects than on taking a one-size-fits-all approach. The risk-based approach entails an analysis of the FI's portfolio. This is carried out during appraisal to establish the risk level of the FI's operation. The results of the portfolio analysis and the performance of the FI's social and environmental management system are captured in an Environmental and Social Risk Rating measure that is established at appraisal and is tracked and updated by IFC during project supervision. Additionally, the supervision plan includes a systematic portfolio review to identify and address performance and knowledge gaps that are expected to result in substantial portfolio rationalization and improvements in overall portfolio performance. The staff capacity issue related to the delivery of the supervision plan is being addressed. IFC has more than doubled the team that supports FI-related investments and intends to further add to this team in headquarters and in country offices in fiscal 2009.

*IEG reply:* IEG agrees and supports IFC in the risk-based approach for FI supervision. See notes 20 and 25.

14. South Africa was excluded, as IEG evaluated only Poverty-Environment Partnership Africa projects and no investment projects in that country.

15. *Management comment:* See comment in table 4.2.

16. Because information is available only for projects evaluated after 2004, the 28 case study projects were added to the XPSR evaluation sample.

17. Before the 2006 Performance Standards, ESMS was not required for all projects.

18. The process and manufacturing industry projects include investments of IFC's Global Manufacturing; Agribusiness; Oil, Gas, Mining; and Chemicals business departments.

19. For all FIs, including FI type 1 operations in which IFC does not directly finance subprojects, the FIs must do the following: (1) develop an EMS; (2) train responsible environmental staff; (3) provide Annual Environmental Performance Reports; and (4) ensure that subprojects comply with host country laws and, for microfinance subloans, with the IFC Microfinance Exclusion List that describes sectors that IFC does not finance. In addition, when IFC funds are used to directly finance subprojects (FI type 2) or when IFC is the lender of record on subprojects (FI type 3), FI subprojects must comply with IFC's General Exclusion List, IFC environmental and social policies, and Bank Group industry sector guidelines when applicable, and IFC must clear all Category A subprojects. IFC's approach in the 1998 ESRP consisted of both procedural requirements that the FI had to fulfill and ESHS requirements for the subborrower (subproject of FI).

20. IFC's requirement that its clients develop ESMSs dates back to a 1993 environmental analysis and review of projects. With its 1998 Operational Policy 4.01 on environmental assessment, IFC also required clients to strengthen their institutional capacity or retain qualified outside expertise. The 1998 ESRP required clients to produce a summary of the management systems (including staffing and training); ensure safe project design, construction, and operation; and maintain the effectiveness of emergency equipment and response plans. FIs were likewise required, where relevant, to establish ESMSs and ensure that operational activities complied with host country environmental, health, and safety requirements. The first 2006 Performance Standard requires the project sponsor to establish and maintain an ESMS appropriate to the nature and scale of the project and commensurate with its level of social and environmental risks and impacts. This system must incorporate social and environmental assessment, management program, organizational capacity, training,

community engagement, monitoring, and reporting. Performance Standard 1's purpose is to generate an integrated assessment to identify (1) project social and environmental impacts, risks, and opportunities; (2) effective community engagement through disclosure of project-related information and consultation with local communities on matters affecting them directly; and (3) client management of social and environmental performance throughout the life of the project. For FIs with investments having potentially significant environmental and social impacts, IFC reviews the client's ESMS for gaps and identifies actions the client may need to take.

21. In 2006, only 28 percent of IFC investments were targeted to project finance.

22. Chi-squared test significance level p was below 0.001 percent ($p<0.001\%$); below 5 percent usually is regarded as high correlation or dependence.

23. ISO 14001 helps clients structure their ESMS and define environmental organizations and responsibilities, but it does not guarantee that all IFC requirements are met, especially in relation to health and safety standards. Site inspections of some ISO 14001–certified clients, for example, found obsolete, absent, or non-use of personal protection equipment that led to a downgraded project ESE rating.

24. *Management comment:* See note 13.

25. In February 2007, IFC had 254 FI projects with reporting requirements, but until 2006 only one environmental specialist had been fully dedicated to FI supervision. CES had allocated most supervision resources to Category A and those Category B projects with high risks. As a result, IFC had no intention and not enough staff to visit some lower-risk Category B projects and most FI projects (see also IEG-IFC 2007), which were considered to have potentially fewer ESHS risks. IFC has recognized the need to improve FI supervision and has hired new professionals since 2006, bringing the environmental team working on FI projects to four full-time staff. In addition, short-term consultants are used to support supervision. IFC's Environment and Social Development Department's (CES's) fiscal 2008–10 strategy is to visit Category B projects with low environmental or social risks (good or satisfactory environmental and social risk rating) every three years and FI projects that have a high-risk profile or deficiencies in their EMSs. ESMS deficiencies may be addressed without a site visit. The intensified supervision for FI and real sector projects resulted in a drop in the aggregate ESHS knowledge gap in the IFC portfolio, from 38 percent to 24 percent over six months. To complement the capacity of CES to supervise projects across all sectors, an initiative was undertaken to train investment officers to mainstream accountability for ESHS compliance. Investment departments are now required to follow up immediately with clients that are late in providing Annual Monitoring Reports so that CES can review them to reduce ESHS knowledge gaps. CES also suggested in June 2007 that the monitoring data entry system be improved and that Investment Department scorecards include environmental and social issues.

26. *Management comment:* Under the 2006 Sustainability Policy Framework, IFC actively engages with the client FI up front during the appraisal stage, and a time-bound social and environmental management system plan is committed to and included in the covenants of the investment agreement between the client FI and IFC. This new approach is a significant improvement over the 1998 policy, in which the client was required to establish an EMS after attending training conducted by IFC. IFC's ability to conduct training for clients was limited by staffing, resource, and geographical constraints. IFC now makes available one-on-one guidance to high-risk clients. IFC is in the process of developing a comprehensive FI client-support service portal, which will include tools and guidance for clients to develop social and environmental management systems.

27. *Management comment:* There are numerous IFC-supported projects that have both direct and indirect environmental and social benefits, even if they are not classified as "environment projects." "Examples include energy efficiency lines of credit, energy-efficient housing finance loans, high energy efficient cement projects, and so forth.... These projects are inherently environmental by the very nature of their scope and design, and not by the overlay of environmental due diligence requirements. In fiscal 2008 only, and as of the end of December 2007, IFC had invested $66 million in clean energy components in 11 projects. In fiscal 2007, IFC invested $484 million in clean energy components in 27 projects. Also on the Advisory Services side, the statement fails to account for the significant amount of Advisory Services dedicated to environment: $1 billion in GEF projects, $185 million in Carbon Finance, $208 million in ESS BL, totaling 24 percent of IFC's Advisory Services funding.

28. In 2006, IFC organized its center of environmental finance under the Sustainable Business Innovator to provide loans, equity investments, grants for project cofinancing, advisories, and capacity building focusing on

three areas: (1) incubating innovative business initiatives that deliver environmental and social benefits; (2) demonstrating their commercial attractiveness; and (3) encouraging their independent replication in the private sector in emerging markets. In July 2006, the Sustainable Business Innovator received the Corporate Citizenship Facility (CCF), Environmental Opportunities Facility (EOF), and remaining activities from Sustainable Financial Markets Facility (SFMF). The Sustainable Business Innovator programs include Biodiversity, Carbon Finance, Cleaner Technologies (formerly EOF), Environmental Business Finance, Gender Entrepreneurship Markets, Social Responsibility (formerly CCF), Sustainable Energy, and Sustainable Investing (formerly SFMF).

29. The July 2006 review of the GEF program concluded that the renewable energy project portfolio was moderately effective at attracting cofinancing and at leveraging IFC and private sector investment. To a modest extent, these projects created commercially viable environmental products and services. An example of a successful energy efficiency project was the Efficient Lighting Initiative, which developed a quality mark now applied to more than 200 efficient lighting products. The project achieved significant reductions in the product prices, improvements in quality, and increases in sales. Preliminary project monitoring and evaluation data suggest that Efficient Lighting Initiative reduced energy consumption by 2,590 gigawatts and carbon dioxide emissions by 2 million tons over 2000–03 across seven countries. With global replicability, effectiveness is high. The effectiveness of the biodiversity project portfolio was considered too new to assess, as most projects were at an early stage of implementation.

30. *Management comment:* The GEF story is not complete. The specific comments on IFC's GEF portfolio simply summarize the conclusions of an earlier evaluation IFC commissioned and include no new information or recommendations. As the evaluation is limited to projects up to and including fiscal 2006, it doesn't refer to any of the significant developments during the past two years:

In July 2006 IFC received approval from the GEF Council for four new projects, PADGO (distributed generation—Sri Lanka), BACP (global), Lighting Africa (Kenya and Ghana), and Philippines Sustainable Energy Finance. The first three have so far received endorsement and come under management. All four reflect lessons of previous projects in attempting to be more programmatic and transformational, less targeted to specific technologies, and more financially leveraged. Each of these projects has also involved varying degrees of partnerships as a means of expanding influence and sharing risks.

A further step toward assuring learning of lessons from previous GEF projects was the compilation and publication of reports on experience with two of the largest subjects in IFC's GEF portfolio, solar energy and energy efficiency finance. The first of these reports, "Selling Solar" (http:// www.ifc.org/ifcext/ enviro.nsf/ Attachments-ByTitle/p_SellingSolar/$FILE/Selling Solar.pdf.]), was completed in August 2007; the second report, on energy efficiency, is planned for completion in June 2008. These reports are consistent with the conclusion that results have been "mixed"—several projects had to be cancelled, significantly restructured, or terminated prematurely, but this is consistent with undertaking early stage, high-risk projects, and more often donor funds were for the most part not lost but simply could not be spent effectively, risks were cost shared, and lessons were learned and acted on, in that restructured projects have been more successful.

A third significant development was GEF Council approval in June 2007 of a public-private partnership between GEF and IFC, with an initial commitment of $60 million to provide streamlined approval of innovative private sector investments with significant global environmental impact. This program, subsequently named the Earth Fund, was circulated to the Council for endorsement (the final stage prior to management approval) in March 2008 and is expected to be operational later in 2008.

31. IFC's five GEF-funded solar PV initiatives are IFC/GEF Small and Medium-Scale Enterprise Program, Photovoltaic Market Transformation Initiative, Solar Development Group, Renewable Energy and Energy Efficiency Fund, and the grid-tied solar power plant of the Cagayan Electric Power and Light Company.

32. *Management comment:* Photovoltaic Market Transformation Initiative was an experiment to assess what business models are possible and sustainable for promoting PV businesses, and three very different countries were chosen to see what succeeds, what doesn't, and why. The lessons learned from this exercise are key to IFC strategy and future direction in rural electrification, which is an integral part of our climate change strategy; these have been highlighted in the "Selling Solar" study mentioned above and informed both SEF (funds-based approach to investing in small projects) and PADGO (mentioned above) in their design and execution. The Photovoltaic Market Transformation Ini-

tiative was restructured in 2004 with new targets being set (70 percent of commitments being disbursed). The initiative is well on its way to achieving this. In India, Selco, Shell Solar, and SREI have been three successfully incubated projects. There is now market consolidation, with SREI purchasing all of Shell Solar assets in South Asia, and Selco is seeking expansion capital and collaborating with SEWA, a prominent social and microfinance organization, to expand to other technologies. The issue is Kenya is not representative of IFC's experience in the PV initiative, as there were significant macroeconomic, societal, and political issues. It took years for the conditions to become more conducive. The initiative then was restructured to focus on technical assistance for training and establishing standard guidelines. This is proceeding well. The report should have also mentioned other countries' experience and provided a more comprehensive and balanced view.

33. *Management comment:* The GEF story is not complete. The specific comments on IFC's GEF portfolio simply summarize the conclusions of an earlier evaluation IFC commissioned and include no new information or recommendations. As the evaluation is limited to projects up to and including fiscal 2006, it doesn't refer to any of the significant developments during the past two years:

In July 2006 IFC received approval from the GEF Council for four new projects, PADGO (distributed generation — Sri Lanka), BACP (global), Lighting Africa (Kenya and Ghana), and Philippines Sustainable Energy Finance. The first three have so far received endorsement and come under management. All four reflect lessons of previous projects in attempting to be more programmatic and transformational, less targeted to specific technologies, and more financially leveraged. Each of these projects has also involved varying degrees of partnerships as a means of expanding influence and sharing risks.

A further step toward assuring learning of lessons from previous GEF projects was the compilation and publication of reports on experience with two of the largest subjects in IFC's GEF portfolio, solar energy and energy efficiency finance. The first of these reports, "Selling Solar" (http://www.ifc.org/ifcext/enviro.nsf/Attachments-ByTitle/p_SellingSolar/$FILE/SellingSolar.pdf), was completed in August 2007; the second report, on energy efficiency, is planned for completion in June 2008. These reports are consistent with the conclusion that results have been "mixed"—several projects had to be cancelled, significantly restructured, or terminated prematurely, but this is consistent with undertaking early stage, high-risk projects, and more often donor funds were for the most part not lost but simply could not be spent effectively, risks were cost shared, and lessons were learned and acted on, in that restructured projects have been more successful.

A third significant development was GEF Council approval in June 2007 of a public-private partnership between GEF and IFC, with an initial commitment of $60 million to provide streamlined approval of innovative private sector investments with significant global environmental impact. This program, subsequently named the Earth Fund, was circulated to the Council for endorsement (the final stage prior to management approval) in March 2008 and is expected to be operational later in 2008.

34. The 10 Equator Principles are Review and Categorization, Social and Environmental Assessment (Process), Applicable Social and Environmental Standards, Action Plan and Management System, Consultation and Disclosure, Grievance Mechanism, Independent Review, Covenants, Independent Monitoring and Reporting, and Reporting on Implementation by EPFIs. This set of industry-led voluntary principles are applied as follows: (1) to all projects with a total cost greater than $10 million, project finance Advisory Services, and significant expansion and upgrading projects; (2) all projects must undergo social and environmental review and categorization; (3) high-impact projects must include stakeholder consultation and an EMP. IFC Performance Standards and World Bank Group Environmental Health and Safety Guidelines apply to low- and middle-income countries. EPFIs are responsible for implementing internal procedures in a way that makes social and environmental risk management an integral part of the credit control function. The EPFIs rely on independent external experts for Category A and some Category B projects. Each participating bank is responsible for reporting annually on implementation. IFC is not an enforcement agency in this regard, but does play a convening role by providing support to Equator Banks and encouraging other financial institutions, including regional and national ones, to adopt the standards. Several EPFIs have commented that the financial community will now take the lead in continuing to develop these principles and expect them to be applied across most of their lending operations.

35. *Management comment:* As qualified up front in the executive summary in the report: Generally weaker

sponsor capacity and sometimes wavering sponsor commitment to the sustainability agenda make IFC's work more challenging, especially for smaller projects in Africa. The implementation environment is often made even more challenging by the often poor environmental governance capacity. In response, IFC has strengthened its portfolio supervision program during the last two years, following the introduction of the new policy framework implemented since May 2006. In particular, IFC has been successfully implementing its supervision strategy for the Africa Region, with increased supervision visits by 30 percent from fiscal 2007 to fiscal 2008.

36. *Management comment:* As a financial institution working solely in developing countries, IFC faces numerous challenges across the entire operational spectrum, including in high biodiversity areas of the world. IFC is acutely aware of these challenges and risks and engages in projects in such regions with due consideration of the policy environment and operational challenges. On the Brazilian Amazon, the report refers to only one project in Brazil in an incomplete manner. It does not recognize the change in strategy that has underpinned efforts to support economic development in the Amazon or the broad agreement that has emerged among many stakeholders. The Amazon strategy also represents a solid example of Bank-IFC collaboration under a regime of increased World Bank–IFC collaboration overall. The report does not include the broader strategic context and objectives pursued by IFC's engagement in the Amazon or the sector transformations that are pursued through such projects. The project level focus is in fact inconsistent with the fact that IFC has an Amazon strategy, which itself is fully consistent with the Bank Group Amazon Partnership Framework.

37. *Management comment:* The review has not examined the effectiveness or the performance of IFC's decentralization efforts (that is, the Global/Local Strategy) on environmental and social performance or whether projects handled by in-country staff were materially different in quality or outcome. In response to IFC's ongoing decentralization and the setting up of internal delegated decision authority to two Regions, IFC's Environmental and Social Review Procedures were updated and amended to accommodate delegated authority to South Asia and East Asia Regions, a measure that fully supports the decentralization effort. Also, IFC's Sustainability Knowledge Network, in operation since June 2007, focuses on providing a knowledge-based operational platform for IFC's sustainability professionals across the world and in support of IFC's 2010 vision. Key activities of the network include staff onboarding, thematic practice groups, training, enhanced information technology, and communications that improve business process and delivery of IFC's sustainability work. On FIs, see note 13.

*IEG Reply:* It is too early to evaluate the implications of IFC's decentralization efforts (that is, the Global/Local) on environmental and social performance. It is important to note that this issue—localization of environmental specialists—is a positive step but has its challenges. The study does not criticize these efforts.

38. Currently, MIGA's Economics and Policy Group is responsible for the environmental and social review, clearance, and supervision of projects in a manner consistent with the requirements contained in its review procedures.

39. MIGA did not categorize projects prior to 1999, but retrofitted its portfolio with tentative categories. Using these, between 1990 and 2004, 11 percent of projects could have been categorized as Category A, 41 percent as Category B, and 48 percent as Category C projects. Excluding all financial sector projects (mostly C), 18 percent of real sector projects would have been Category A, 63 percent Category B, and 19 percent Category C over that period. Also, note that under the new policy, FI investments can be either Category C or the new Category FI.

40. This sample represents 8.5 percent of MIGA's total nonfinancial sector projects.

41. The 18 ex post evaluated projects consisted of 2 Category A projects and 16 Category B projects. Category C projects, mostly financial sector projects, were excluded because, based on MIGA's environmental assessment policy, beyond screening, no further environmental assessment action is required for Category C projects. To be eligible for ex post evaluation, a project has to meet IEG's maturity criterion (that is, the minimum time period of three to four years under implementation to produce meaningful data to be evaluated). The sample for IEG ex post evaluations is drawn randomly from all active guarantee projects mature enough to derive meaningful outcomes. Similarly, the extractive industries projects evaluated in 2003 were selected randomly from MIGA projects in the mining and the oil and gas sectors.

42. A proposed investment will be classified as Category A if the project is likely to have significant adverse

environmental impacts that are sensitive, diverse, or unprecedented. These impacts may affect an area broader than the sites or facilities subject to physical works.

43. A proposed investment will be classified as Category B if the project's potential adverse environmental impacts on human populations or environmentally important areas (including wetlands, forests, grasslands, and other natural habitats) are less adverse than those of Category A projects. These impacts are site-specific; few, if any, of the impacts are irreversible, and in most cases, mitigating measures can be designed more readily than for Category A projects.

44. Of the projects active on March 2007, 65 percent of Category A projects and 24 percent of Category B had been visited (IEG-MIGA 2007, par. 2.18).

45. The 16 Category B projects come from the sample of 18 mature projects reviewed ex post. Two Category B projects from the extractive industries evaluation were excluded from this analysis because of lack of direct comparability of subcategories.

46. In certain cases, Contracts of Guarantee specified investors to submit these reports to MIGA.

47. Shortcomings noted in Sector Investment Program projects included reliance on outdated environmental audits, environmental impact assessments not covering the full scope of the project, absence of environmental and social assessments, and lack of EMSs.

48. Russia is the second-largest recipient country for MIGA guarantees to date, accounting for 9.8 percent of MIGA's guarantee volume issued between 1990 and 2007. MIGA insured its first project in Russia in June 1993 and has since issued 47 guarantees for foreign investments in 25 projects for a cumulative maximum aggregate liability of $1,630 million. MIGA has supported 9 financial services projects (which, as Category C projects, were not reviewed for this evaluation); 11 manufacturing, agribusiness, and services projects; 4 projects in oil, gas, and mining; and 1 in the infrastructure sector. Although this evaluation reviewed all projects in Russia (except in the financial sector), it relied on a desk study of internal MIGA and publicly available documents. The findings therefore do not refer to results and outcomes, but rather to MIGA's work in appraising the projects and their potential to address issues beyond safeguard compliance.

49. In one project, MIGA relied entirely on IFC's due diligence and did not carry out an independent assessment. Therefore, this case was excluded from this study.

50. The EHS recommendations from these reports are summarized in appendix 16 of IEG-MIGA 2006 annual report (IEG-MIGA 2006).

51. Recommendations were made in the following reports: *2003 Report on Operations Evaluation* (IEG-MIGA 2003); *2004 Review of Development Effectiveness* (IEG-MIGA 2004); and *IEG-MIGA 2006 Annual Report* (IEG-MIGA 2006).

52. Based on an analysis done for the IEG-MIGA *2007 Annual Report* (IEG-MIGA 2007).

## Chapter 5

1. The need for the Bank to revamp its research in this area was also among the conclusions of an independent external evaluation of Bank research led by Angus Deaton that also noted the important contributions of earlier Bank environment-related research, such as that on pollution management (World Bank 2000a) cited in chapter 3.

See Pomerantz (2004) and IEG-World Bank (2005), which concluded that (1) most capacity support remains fragmented; (2) sector-specific capacity building approaches need strengthening; and (3) capacity-building tools and instruments could be more effectively used.

2. In larger nations, such capabilities may be stronger in some states and metropolitan areas than at the central government level. In Brazil, for instance, the state of São Paulo has traditionally had much stronger institutional capacity to address environmental problems than the Brazilian federal government and has even, for all intents and purposes, drafted environmental legislation on behalf of the latter, as in the case of federal vehicle emission controls.

3. The need for sustained assistance to develop solid environmental institutions and help build domestic stakeholder coalitions to support them was a main message of the 2003 WDR.

4. The priority given to environmental improvement, including the specification of targets in relation to major environmental problems, is clearly established in China's most recent Five-Year Plan.

5. The approach used in these operations was highlighted in the completion report for the previous China CAS, which identified the cumulative nature of Bank support involving multiple inputs over several decades as key to effectiveness (World Bank, IFC, and MIGA 2006, p. 58). This report also observes that "because the Bank Group's impact in China depends on its influence on policy and institutional reform impacts are difficult to

identify precisely," thus making the "attribution problem" even more complicated.

6. This can be demonstrated from recent U.S. experience: the Supreme Court has had to require the Environmental Protection Agency to enforce environmental legislation to curb greenhouse gases from vehicles and power plants, against the prior instructions of the federal executive branch, which had sought to limit administrative enforcement of such measures.

7. The central government in Russia has indicated that the environment is not currently a high priority. Illustrative of this, it downgraded the former Ministry of Environment first to a State Secretariat, then to a department within the Ministry of Natural Resources, which is primarily concerned with the productive use of such resources. China, in contrast, appears much more firmly committed to environmental improvement, setting numerical targets for environmental quality in its Five-Year Plan for 2006–10. Both countries identify sustained rapid economic growth as their greatest national priority, but the Chinese government appears to realize that neglect of increasingly serious environmental problems may undermine future economic growth. It thus recognizes that the country's present growth path is unsustainable unless increasing pollution and natural resource degradation trends are reversed. These issues are considered far less pressing by the government of Russia.

8. For a recent Bank publication on economic growth over the past several decades in China and India and its impact on and implications for the global economy, see Winters and Yusuf (2007). One chapter in this book refers specifically to the impact of economic growth in the two countries on air quality and climate change (Shalizi 2007).

9. For an excellent discussion of recent environmental trends and government reactions to them in both India and China, see Flavin and Gardner (2006).

10. According to the Bank's *Little Green Data Book* for 2007 (World Bank 2007d), deforestation declined by an average of 1.7 percent a year in China and 0.4 percent a year in India between 1990 and 2005, while it increased by 1.8 percent a year in Uganda, 1.7 percent a year in Ghana, 0.5 percent a year in Brazil and Senegal, and 0.4 percent a year in Madagascar.

11. Different Bank Regions also approached preparation of their strategies for the environment (in parallel to elaboration of the overall Bank strategy in 2000–01) in different ways. The Latin America and Caribbean Region, for example, established a steering committee chaired by a country director and containing representatives from each of the other sector networks and CMUs in an effort to obtain the broadest possible inputs into and ownership of its strategy.

12. The Bank has sometimes unnecessarily repeated past mistakes, including project design errors, as it did in Planafloro and Prodegro in relation to Polonoroeste in Brazil and the Industrial Pollution Control and Prevention Projects in India. Conclusions, lessons, and recommendations of Bank evaluation work have occasionally been insufficiently absorbed and integrated into ongoing or new operations.

13. Because of the need for industrial sub-borrowers to be creditworthy to receive funding under such credit lines, many of the largest polluters in Egypt, for example, proved to be ineligible for such support; thus the main target was missed. Second, the industries that actually benefited under these projects tended to be widely scattered and not necessarily concentrated in those areas either where industrial pollution was most serious or where it had the greatest adverse human health impacts. Third, although the resulting industrial subprojects may have resulted in reductions in emissions and effluents at the individual plant level, they may have had little, if any, significant impact in terms of ambient air and/or water quality in the specific areas in which they were located because of other pollution sources (both industrial and nonindustrial) that were not simultaneously addressed. This occurred in Brazil, India, and China, as well as Egypt. Finally, some Bank staff have argued, including in ICRs for such projects (for example, those in India), that, as a matter of principle, the Bank should not be providing subsidized credit to private sector industrial polluters so they can meet their legal obligation to cut emissions and effluents even if this approach had been more effective in terms of improving ambient environmental quality. For all these reasons, this approach was essentially abandoned in all but the Middle East and North Africa Region in the late 1990s.

14. IEG's assessment of the experience in the latter country suggests that this instrument has not been substantially more effective there than elsewhere.

15. By the same token, particularly in large countries, environmental and other problems that require cooperation across states or provinces are often more difficult to resolve than those within their administrative boundaries, as the water resource management situa-

tion in India demonstrates. The same tension frequently also exists across municipalities, so managing cross-jurisdictional relations is often a challenge at all levels of spatial aggregation, from local to global.

16. The present evaluation reiterates the recommendations of IEG's recent assessment of World Bank support to multicountry programs (IEG-World Bank 2007a, p. x, chap. 7): (1) establish regional program strategies and integrate them into country strategies; (2) work to strengthen the international architecture for financing Regional development programs; (3) increase the impact of Bank support for Regional partnerships; and (4) strengthen corporate incentives and capacities to provide effective regional program support.

17. More specifically, this evaluation concluded that "Bank performance in global programs is better at the global than at the country level." It further observed that "other partners view the Bank's leadership role, its financial clout, it access to policymakers, its operational support, and its fiduciary oversight as a seal of approval, giving them confidence to invest in global programs, both in-house and externally managed. Even at the global level though, the Bank's performance can be improved, particularly with respect to strategy, independent oversight, and global-country linkages." (IEG-World Bank 2004, p. xxix).

18. Another encouraging sign is the establishment of a new Spatial and Local Development Team in the Sustainable Development Network. The decision for the 2009 WDR to examine spatial disparities offers yet another opportunity, and, building on previous WDRs, it should consider the environmental together with other dimensions associated with such disparities.

19. An example would be the integration of environmental considerations into PRSPs.

20. The country director's position was that, because they have a relatively short (normally 4 to 5 years) tenure and want to provide as many services as possible to their country clients, CMU directors have to be "somewhat opportunistic," and this may mean taking advantage of what can be most readily delivered by the various sector management units.

21. Their activities also are influenced by the local regulatory framework in host countries and related enforcement mechanisms, areas potentially under the purview of the Bank.

22. As one CMU director indicated, because of sensitivities surrounding certain environmental issues on the part of particular governments, some country strategies deliberately understate what the Bank is seeking to achieve to avoid exacerbating client resistance.

23. One of the key messages of the 2003 *World Development Report* is the need to "act now-for long-term problems." It affirms, for example, that although "some problems of sustainability are already urgent and require immediate action . . . another category of issues unfolds over a longer time horizon. The problems may not yet be urgent, but the direction of change is unmistakable. For these it is important to get ahead of the curve and prevent a worsening crisis before it is too costly. Biodiversity loss and climate change are in this category . . . . Similarly, the need to anticipate urban growth by facilitating low-income settlements in safe areas and by setting aside major rights-of-way and spaces for public amenities makes it necessary to act now to avoid greater costs and regrets later" (World Bank 2003d, pp. 10–11).

24. The Bank is seen by some external stakeholders—including various Bank partners interviewed by IEG during the course of this evaluation—as having lost, at least temporarily, much of its earlier intellectual leadership role with respect to the environment.

25. The large coal-fired power plant project in India, approved by the IFC Board in April 2008, is controversial. A major concern of its critics is that the proposed plant is a large facility and uses a nonrenewable energy source that will generate significant amounts of greenhouse gases. However, the supercritical steam technology proposed for use in this project meets World Bank Group emission requirements and offers high energy efficiency (40–45 percent) and less specific greenhouse gas emissions compared with investment in conventional power plants (energy efficiency of 30–35 percent). This controversy must be addressed in the future Bank Group climate change strategy to establish a common World Bank Group approach and to avoid serious reputational and environmental damages.

26. The Bank, IFC, and MIGA have their own due diligence procedures for responding to their different public/private sector clients, business models, and project cycles, but all World Bank Group institutions have broadly used the same industry sector guidelines and *Pollution Prevention and Abatement Handbook* (World Bank Group with UNEP and UNIDO 1999)—for example, to establish emission limit values for their respective industrial projects. These guidelines have been updated recently for most industry sectors, including large power plants, to be jointly used in World Bank Group environmental work.

27. It should be pointed out, however, that MIGA has not adopted the IFC guidelines; instead, it prepared MIGA-specific guidelines based on the earlier approved IFC ones.

28. *Management comment:* It is important to keep in mind that a precursor to IFC investing is often investment climate work done through Foreign Investment Advisory Services, a joint IFC-WB-MIGA function, a good example of coordination and collaboration within the World Bank Group. IFC would welcome an analysis of the areas where the World Bank and IFC are already collaborating, such as climate change and gender. In addition, this argument on proper sequencing of the Bank/IFC interventions is largely out of date and does not necessarily fit today's reality of World Bank Group interventions and client country demands. In some cases, private sector projects are being financed ahead of Bank policy interventions, and IFC's experience is used as feedback to the Bank on the need for policy intervention. In other cases, IFC's investments make way for the Bank to be able to help governments participate in the same or similar projects.

## Chapter 6

1. A single very large ($930 million) carbon offset operation in China in fiscal 2006 has also contributed to this increase.

2. Consistent with the findings of this assessment, IEG's recent evaluation of development results in middle-income countries (IEG-World Bank 2007b) concluded that "meeting environmental challenges in middle-income countries has been problematic." It further affirmed that "the Bank has given some attention to the topic, and most MIC country assistance strategies mention environmental issues. Some country programs, for example, those in Brazil in the review period, have helped to deliver satisfactory progress by positioning environmental issues as integral to the sustainable growth agenda, securing government ownership, and building domestic institutional capacity in the environment field. But this experience has not been widespread." (executive summary, p. xv)

3. *Management comment:* While IFC concurs with the idea that closer collaboration in areas with a specific operational purpose is certainly desirable, it finds the generally stated collaboration argument unsubstantiated. IFC would welcome an analysis of the areas where the World Bank and IFC are already collaborating, such as climate change and gender, among others. Also, this argument on proper sequencing of the Bank/IFC interventions is largely out of date, and does not necessarily fit today's reality of World Bank Group interventions and client country demands. In some cases, private sector projects are being financed ahead of Bank policy interventions, and IFC's experience is used as feedback to the Bank on the need for policy intervention. In other cases, IFC's investments make way for the Bank to be able to help governments participate in the same or similar projects.

4. *Management comment:* IFC's sustainability agenda is first set at the corporate strategic direction level, with sustainability being one of the five strategic pillars of IFC. This is not mentioned in the report. Furthermore, the detailed Regional and sector approaches are set in the Regional and industry department strategies. These are investment strategies with a mid-term (3–5 year) horizon, in view of the rapidly evolving sustainability agenda and IFC's need to meet changing client mix and demand. As a result, it is unrealistic for the evaluation to recommend that IFC set medium (5–10 years) and long-term strategies of 10–20-year horizon together with the World Bank. Enhanced coordination with the CAS team for country strategies, and integrated sector and thematic strategies (e.g., the Strategic Framework on Climate Change and Development) of shorter time horizon would nonetheless be more useful for IFC.

5. *Management comment:* IFC's sustainability agenda is first set at the corporate strategic direction level, with sustainability being one of the five strategic pillars of IFC. Furthermore, the detailed Regional and sector approaches are set in the Regional and industry department strategies. These are investment strategies with a mid-term (3–5 year) horizon, in view of the rapidly evolving sustainability agenda and IFC's need to meet changing client mix and demand. As a result, it is not practical to recommend that IFC set medium (5–10 years) and long-term strategies of 10–20-year horizon. Enhanced coordination with the CAS team for country strategies, and integrated sector and thematic strategies (e.g., the Strategic Framework on Climate Change and Development) of shorter time horizon would nonetheless be more useful for IFC.

6. *Management comment:* IFC already undertakes monitoring and development outcome reporting of its lending operations. Provisions relating to 'area of influence' and 'cumulative impacts' in IFC's Performance Standard 1 (Social and Environmental Assessment and Management Systems) provide the framework for IFC to capture potential environmental and social impacts more effectively, especially for large-scale projects. IFC monitors environmental and social performance of in-

vestments and manages associated risks on an ongoing basis through an environmental and social risk rating for applicable investments since 2000. The rating is given on an annual basis by IFC's environmental and social specialists after review of a company's *Annual Monitoring Report* or site supervision visit. IFC is measuring E&S development impact though a set of monitorable indicators and assessment of environmental and social project performance, which is linked to the environmental and social risk rating.

## Appendix A

1. Ghana, India, and Uganda were also among the 10 largest IDA recipients in fiscal 2006, together with Bangladesh, Democratic Republic of Congo, Ethiopia, Pakistan, Tanzania, Vietnam, and Nigeria.

2. The country case studies for this evaluation were of India, Madagascar, Mexico, Morocco, and Nigeria, although they were not given much attention in the overview report and were not formally published. The present evaluation also draws on and updates the earlier case studies of India and Madagascar.

3. In 1996–98, the project evaluation reports were called Investment Assessment Reports. ESE ratings were available for 604 XPSR project evaluations. From 1996 to 2006, IEG independently evaluated 627 projects across the client countries and sectors, but ESE ratings were not available for 23 projects because they were rated as N/A (that is, having no potential ESHS risks).

4. IEG evaluation methodology and guidelines: http://www.ifc.org/ifcext/ieg.nsf/Content/EvalProcess

5. See the World Bank Group's *Pollution Prevention and Abatement Handbook* (World Bank Group with UNEP and UNIDO 1999) and IFC's supplementary guidelines as listed in: http://www.ifc.org/ifcext/enviro.nsf/Content/EnvironmentalGuidelines.

6. In October 2007, MIGA adopted the new Policy on Social and Environmental Sustainability and a new disclosure policy, which replaced existing policies.

## Appendix B

1. A total of 46 projects (guaranteed from January 1, 2005, to June 30, 2006) were assessed, plus 4 Small Investment Program projects, which were covered until March 2007. These 50 projects include 23 new regular projects, 14 modified contracts of existing projects, and 13 Small Investment Program projects.

2. See IEG-MIGA 2007 for a full analysis of the quality-at-entry assessments.

## Appendix C

1. The quantitative information presented in this section is drawn from the 2005 World Development Indicators (World Bank 2005f) and The Little Green Data Book 2006 (World Bank 2006d).

2. This total includes all countries with per capita gross national incomes of less than $10,066 in 2004.

3. In relation to the entire world, these countries account for 32 percent of the total land area (primarily Brazil, China, and Russia) and 47 percent of the total population (mainly China and India), but only 9 percent of global GDP. As a result, their per capita GDP is just 20 percent of that for the world as a whole, which is heavily biased toward the upper-income OECD (Organisation for Economic Co-operation and Development) countries.

4. Data for Uganda were not available.

5. Data for Uganda were not available.

6. Data for Senegal were not available.

7. In 2005, China was already the second-largest source of greenhouse gas emissions in the world, following the United States, and China is expected to surpass the U.S. as early as 2009. India was the fourth-largest emitter of greenhouse gases, and its emissions are also growing rapidly.

8. The GEF benefits index for biodiversity is a composite measure of biodiversity potential, developed by the GEF, on the basis of the species represented in each country, their threat status, and the diversity of habitat types. The index ranges from zero (no biodiversity potential) to 100 (maximum biodiversity potential). For the countries in the study, in 2005, the index numbers were: Brazil, 100; China, 64.8; India, 43.9; Russia, 37.1; Madagascar, 31.4; Uganda, 3.3; Egypt, 3.2; Ghana, 2.0; and Senegal, 1.3.

9. Founded as a pilot program in 1990, METAP (Mediterranean Technical Assistance Program for the Environment) is funded by the European Investment Bank, the European Commission, the United Nations Development Programme, and the World Bank. It involves most of the countries in the Mediterranean Basin and addresses the need for environmental policy, capacity building, and investments at the regional, national, and local levels. Its four main priority areas are solid and hazardous waste management, integrated water resource management, coastal zone management, and marine pollution.

10. This program involves Jordan and Yemen as well as Egypt, and is partially funded by Saudi Arabia.

11. In addition to Egypt and Uganda, Burundi, Djibouti, Ethiopia, Kenya, Rwanda, Somalia, Sudan, and Tanzania are all members of the Nile Basin Initiative.

12. This program also involves Kenya and Tanzania.

13. This program includes Guinea, Mali, Mauritania, and Senegal.

14. This program also includes Argentina, Paraguay, and Uruguay.

15. Implementation of the Baltic Sea Environment Program is being coordinated by a taskforce under the leadership of the Helsinki Commission. The taskforce includes representatives from the countries in the Baltic Sea drainage basin, including Russia, as well as international financial organizations (including the European Bank for Reconstruction and Development and the World Bank), selected technical organizations, and NGOs. Related investment projects have been undertaken in Estonia, Latvia, Lithuania, and Poland.

16. The Program for Environmental Management and Protection of the Black Sea is intended to provide the coastal countries—Bulgaria, Georgia, Romania, Russia, Turkey, and Ukraine—with a solid basis for developing long-term policies and investment programs. It is jointly funded by the European Bank for Reconstruction and Development, the World Bank, the Global Environment Fund, and several bilateral donors.

17. This program involves Iran, Kazakhstan, Turkmenistan, and Russia.

18. OECD, for example, considers country performance to refer specifically to the achievement of national objectives (both domestic and international commitments) efficiently and effectively, giving attention to the linkages between intentions, actions, and outcomes, rather than ranking well on an index. In addition, the Yale index has been received among OECD country authorities with considerable concern regarding the soundness and credibility of its methodology. OECD, consequently, favors the use of more "meaningful" environmental indicators. (Source: personal communication from Christian Averous, Head of the Environmental Performance and Information Division, Environment Directorate, OECD, April 2008.)

19. "Environmental health" is itself a composite index, which includes values for child mortality, indoor air pollution, drinking water, adequate sanitation, and urban particulates. The values for air quality (which also includes urban particulates), water resources, productive natural resources, sustainable energy, and biodiversity and habitats, together, make up the index for "ecosystem vitality."

20. They are followed, in terms of total commitments, by Mexico ($38.2 billion, 241 operations), Indonesia ($31.8 billion, 352 operations), Turkey ($25.4 billion, 173 operations), and Argentina ($23.4 billion, 152 operations).

## Appendix D

1. This does not necessarily mean, however, that this priority ranking of the severity of each issue currently corresponds to that of the respective national government, but rather is based on information from a variety of sources and professional judgments on the part of the task team leaders of the respective IEG country case studies.

## Appendix F

1. It could be persuasively argued that land administration (as opposed to land management) projects are not really environmental in nature, although they may be of environmental relevance, at least in rural areas, to the extent that they ensure clear property rights over land as a productive resource. For the purposes of this review, however, we will continue to include them as part of the ENRM portfolio.

2. Forty-three (nearly 8 percent) of the 563 projects mapped to the Environment Sector Board were not thematically coded as ENRM projects. Most of these (33) were IDF grants for various purposes, but there were also five small Montreal Protocol projects (two in Mexico and one each in Ecuador, Malaysia, and Thailand), one GEF mid-size grant (in Côte d'Ivoire), the GEF Global Overlays Program (with a total allocation of $25 million), which benefited many countries, and three recipient-executed Trust Fund operations (for the Aral Sea region, the Philippines, and Thailand). These Environment Sector Board projects were added to the ENRM portfolio, as found in the Bank's database.

3. The rest were in East Asia and Pacific (9.8 percent), South Asia (6.1 percent), and Middle East and North Africa (3.8 percent).

4. Interestingly, they also include one GEF operation (Cameroon), one carbon-offset operation (Indonesia), and one Montreal Protocol project (India), as well as a number of economic or disaster emergency recovery loans or credits, again mainly in Africa.

5. Not surprisingly, however, the share of IBRD/IDA projects in total commitments for all operations mapped to the Environment Sector Board is much greater (74.6

percent) than its share in terms of the number of projects (28.4 percent). Regular GEF projects account for the second-largest share of total commitments (11 percent), followed by carbon-offset operations (8.2 percent) and Montreal Protocol projects (4.2 percent). The average commitment size of IBRD/IDA projects mapped to the Environment Sector Board is $53.3 million, compared with $7.9 million for regular GEF projects, $34.2 million for carbon-offset operations, and $15.5 million for Montreal Protocol operations.

6. The reason for this is twofold. The former Environmental and Socially Sustainable Development Departments in East Asia and Pacific and South Asia were divided into two, one for Agriculture and Rural Development and the other for Environment and Social Development. The latter focused mainly on safeguard compliance and technical cross-support and delegating most project management to other departments, including those for Agriculture and Rural Development. This is reflected in the fact that, whereas Latin America and the Caribbean had a total of 56 IBRD/IDA operations "mapped" to the Environment Sector Board, both East Asia and Pacific and South Asia had just 14. This organizational difference (and difference in approaches to project management) across operational regions is even reflected in the number of GEF regular operations "mapped" to the Environment Sector Board, with a total of 48 in Latin America and the Caribbean, compared with just 8 in East Asia and Pacific and only 4 in South Asia. Africa, Europe and Central Asia, and the Middle East and North Africa followed the Latin America and the Caribbean model rather than that of the two Asia Regions.

7. This included 94.2 percent of all funding for carbon-offset operations (again because of the large single project in China) and 54 percent of the total for Montreal Protocol projects (followed by South Asia with 36.2 percent).

8. In terms of sector board mapping, the shares of evaluated projects were as follows, in rank order among the most important boards: (1) Rural Development, 23.5 percent; (2) Environment, 15.2 percent; (3) Energy, 14.9 percent; (4) Urban Development, 11.3 percent; (5) Water, 10.9 percent; and (6) Transport, 7.8 percent. The remaining 16.4 percent were mapped to 10 other sector boards.

9. No carbon-offset projects have been rated in terms of their performance. GEF mid-size projects, IDF grants, and recipient-executed trust fund projects, likewise, have not been rated. None of these sources is therefore considered here.

10. More specifically, the rated projects were distributed as follows: (1) Africa, 22.3 percent; (2) Latin America and the Caribbean, 21.5 percent; (3) East Asia and Pacific, 19.8 percent; (4) Europe and Central Asia, 15.4 percent; (5) South Asia, 16.4 percent; and (6) Middle East and North Africa, 9.9 percent.

11. Only 10 of the 22 completed Montreal Protocol, and 2 of the 10 completed Rainforest projects, were rated, however, compared with 83 percent of all completed IBRD/IDA-financed operations in the ENRM portfolio. It is not clear why 17 percent of the closed IBRD/IDA projects in this portfolio had no performance ratings.

12. Unrated projects performed even better, on average (76.5 percent "satisfactory"). Altogether, there were 176 completed Category A projects for which overall performance ratings were available; 1,037 Category B projects; 1,280 Category C projects; and 289 Category U projects, many of which were Adjustment or Development Policy Loans. There were also much smaller numbers of financial intermediary or Category FI projects (16), with an average satisfactory performance rating at 81.3 percent, and Category D projects (17), with the lowest average performance of all the groups, at just 64.7 percent satisfactory.

13. The nine case study countries are somewhat atypical because not only is the overall average percentage of satisfactory projects (83.3 percent) considerably higher than the average for the whole ENRM portfolio (75.6 percent), but the lowest-ranked country among them—Russia, with just a 50 percent satisfactory rating—is in the highest-ranked Region overall (Europe and Central Asia, with 84.6 percent satisfactory). Also, all four of the African countries are above—and in the cases of Ghana (92.9 percent satisfactory) and Senegal (85.7 percent), well above—the Regional average (66.8 percent). Both China (93.2 percent) and Brazil (90 percent) also have average percent satisfactory outcome ratings well above those for their Regions, while Egypt (at 71.4 percent satisfactory) is the closest to its overall Regional average (72 percent). Madagascar, which also had 71.4 percent of its ENRM projects rated satisfactory on completion, and Uganda, with 76.5 percent satisfactory, were also above the average ENRM project performance rating for Africa. Altogether, there were 240

rated, completed, ENRM fiscal 1990–2007 projects in the nine case study countries, or 23.7 percent of all such projects Bank-wide. The largest numbers were in China (73), India (54), and Brazil (40), and the lowest in Egypt and Senegal (7 each), followed by Ghana, Madagascar, and Russia (14 each), and Uganda (17).

14. It should be noted, however, that there is a significant imbalance in the relative Regional shares of the operations mapped to the Environment Sector Board and ENRM projects more generally, with Latin America and the Caribbean predominating among the former (with 31.8 percent of the total), followed by Europe and Central Asia (23.4 percent), and Africa (18.2 percent), East Asia and Pacific and South Asia (9.7 percent each), and Middle East and North Africa (7.1 percent). Among the ENRM portfolio as a whole, the Regional distribution was as follows: Africa (22.3 percent), East Asia and Pacific (19.8 percent), Europe and Central Asia (15.4 percent), Latin America and the Caribbean (21.5 percent), Middle East and North Africa (9.9 percent), and South Asia (16.4 percent). East Asia and Pacific and South Asia, in particular, but also Africa, had smaller percentages of Environment Sector Board than ENRM projects, while the reverse was true for Latin America and the Caribbean, Europe and Central Asia, and Middle East and North Africa. In the two Asia Regions, as already suggested, this difference primarily reflects the fact that most environment-related projects have not been managed by their respective Environment and Social Development Departments, unlike the situation elsewhere. In the case of South Asia, moreover, it may also reflect the very limited use of GEF resources compared with other Regions, especially Africa, East Asia and Pacific, and Latin America and the Caribbean.

15. The performance of 38 evaluated Environment Sector Board projects in the nine case study countries was better than for the Bank as a whole (78.9 percent satisfactory, compared with 74.7 percent for the total), and for each of the Regions in which they were located, except for Madagascar and Uganda, where just 50 percent of the Environment Sector Board operations were rated satisfactory. In comparison, all Environment Sector Board projects in Egypt, Ghana, Russia, and Senegal were rated satisfactory, but in all six of these countries, there is a "small numbers" problem because there were just four rated projects in Uganda, two each in Egypt, Ghana, Madagascar, and Russia, and only one in Senegal. The satisfactory shares of Environment Sector Board projects in Brazil (72.7 percent), China (83.3 percent), and India (87.5 percent) were also higher than those for their respective Regions, but again the numbers of evaluated projects, especially in the cases of China (6) and India (8) were comparatively small. Altogether, evaluated Environment Sector Board projects in the case study countries represent just 15.8 percent of the evaluated Environment Sector Board total.

16. Although six each were approved in fiscal 1992 and 1995, and five in 1997.

17. Among individual countries, the largest number of unsatisfactory Environment Sector Board projects were in Indonesia (4), Brazil (3), and Kenya (3), followed by Benin, Bolivia, India, Mexico, and Venezuela (with two each). Most of the unsatisfactory GEF projects, in turn, were biodiversity-related (Africa Region, Benin, Ecuador, Indonesia, and Ukraine), although two each were for international waters (Aral Sea and Kenya) or climate-related (Mali and Russia). Unsatisfactory IBRD/IDA projects, in turn, covered a wide gamut, but most were either natural resource management or biodiversity-related (Benin, Brazil, Haiti, Indonesia, Kenya, Pakistan, Paraguay, and Venezuela) or primarily for institutional capacity building for environmental management, especially in Latin America and the Caribbean (Bolivia, Honduras, Mexico, Trinidad and Tobago, and Venezuela), but also in Sub-Saharan Africa (Madagascar, Malawi, and Zambia), Northern Africa (Morocco), and South Asia (India). Recognizing the performance problems with this latter type of operation, this approach was largely abandoned in the late 1990s.

18. The worst (approval) years for IBRD/ IDA projects mapped to the Environment Sector Board were fiscal 1994 (only 44.4 percent "satisfactory") and 1992 (45.5 percent "satisfactory"), followed by fiscal 1995 (58.3 percent). The best year for which there are presently at least 10 closed projects was fiscal 1998 (83.3 percent "satisfactory"). Close to 90 percent of all (9) closed IBRD/IDA projects mapped to the Environment Sector Board that were approved between fiscal 1999 and 2003 have also been rated satisfactory, but the numbers are too small perhaps to be fully reflective of overall performance at this stage.

19. These are: economic management; public sector governance; rule of law; financial and private sector development; trade and integration; social protection and risk management; social development, gender, and inclusion; human development; urban development;

rural development; and environment and natural resource management.

20. Altogether, 31.1 percent of all projects having one or more environment-related subthemes had an ENRM subtheme as its highest-ranking (or primary) one, and 27.8 percent had one such subtheme as its second-highest-ranking one, together representing almost three-fifths (58.9 percent) of the total.

21. Projects mainly involving land administration/management also had this subtheme to a significant extent as their first (27.3 percent) or second (23.5 percent) highest-ranking ones. This was also the case for projects whose first and second themes were coded as "other ENRM."

22. This was especially the case for projects in which environmental policy and institutions was identified as a relevant subtheme (with 38.5 percent indicating it as the second and 19.5 percent as the third subtheme, compared with 18.9 percent as the primary one).

23. These include one Development Policy Loan in Brazil for $502.5 million, and two in Mexico for a combined $402.5 million.

24. Excluding the seven Development Policy Loans, the average commitment size of this subset of projects would also decrease significantly, from $15.1 million to $11.8 million for the environmental policy and institutions theme, and from $47.3 million to $37.8 million for these projects considered as a whole.

25. It would also be interesting to consider those projects that did not have ENRM subthemes as their first ones, but nevertheless indicated that such subthemes were relevant (that is, those projects in which ENRM subthemes ranked from two to five). However, both because of the considerable extent to which double (or triple, quadruple, or even quintuple) counting would occur and because the average overall outcome rating for those projects in which an ENRM subtheme was the first one (75.5 percent satisfactory) is almost exactly the same as that for all evaluated ENRM projects (75.6 percent satisfactory), the remainder of this analysis will focus on those where one of the seven ENRM subthemes ranks in first place.

26. Interestingly, despite the predominance of GEF projects in the Bank's biodiversity portfolio, more than about half (55 percent) of the unsatisfactory projects in this subset were financed with IBRD or IDA resources.

27. An informal review of one of the three projects rated satisfactory (based on their ICR) in connection with the case studies for the present evaluation, moreover, suggests that a more appropriate rating would probably have been moderately unsatisfactory.

28. Macroeconomic and subnational governance problems were clearly a critical element in the poor performance of the two projects in Brazil, for example.

Man drinking from a water pipe in Ecuador. Photo by Edwin Huffman, courtesy of the World Bank Photo Library.

# BIBLIOGRAPHY


Acharya, A., M. Dyoulgerov, and E. Tsutsui. 2005. *Analytical and Advisory Activities in Environmental and Natural Resource Management: A Review of Fiscal 2002–04 Activities.* Environment Strategy Paper No. 10, Environment Department. Washington, DC: World Bank.

ADB (Asian Development Bank). 2006. *Country Environmental Analysis for the People's Republic of China.* Manila: ADB.

Ahmed, K., J.R. Mercier, and R. Verheem. 2005. *Strategic Environmental Assessment: Concept and Practice.* Environment Strategy Note No. 14, Environment Department. Washington, DC: World Bank.

Ahmed, K., Y. Awe, D.F. Barnes, M.L. Cropper, and M. Kojima. 2005. *Environmental Health and Traditional Fuel Use in Guatemala.* Washington DC: World Bank.

BankTrack. 2007. "The Silence of the Banks." http://www.banktrack.org/doc/File/internal%20documents/Gender%20Action/0_071203%20silence%20of%20the%20banks.pdf.

Barrionuevo, A. 2007. "China's Harvest in Brazil." *New York Times,* April 6.

Bedi, T., A. Courdouel, and K. Simier. 2007. *More Than a Pretty Picture: Using Poverty Maps to Design Better Policies and Interventions.* Washington, DC: World Bank.

Bekhechi, M., and J.R. Mercier. 2002. *The Legal and Regulatory Framework for Environmental Impact Assessments: A Study of Selected Countries in Sub-Saharan Africa.* Washington, DC: World Bank.

Bell, A., and P. Shyamsundar. (Unpublished). "An Environmental Review of 2000/2001 Country Assistance Strategies." Environment Department, World Bank, Washington, DC.

Bell, A., P. Shyamsundar, and K. Hamilton. 2002. *Country Assistance Strategies and the Environment—Taking Stock.* Environment Strategy Notes No. 2. Washington, DC: World Bank.

Besley, T., and L. Cord (eds.). 2007. *Delivering on the Promise of Pro-Poor Growth: Insights and Lessons from Country Experience.* New York: Palgrave Macmillan.

Boisson de Chazournes, L. 2000. *Compliance with Operational Policies and Procedures: A Contextual Analysis.* IEG. Washington, DC: World Bank.

Bojo, J., and C.R. Reddy. 2003a. *Poverty Reduction Strategies and the Millennium Development Goal on Environmental Sustainability.* Environment Department Paper No. 92. Washington, DC: World Bank.

———. 2003b. *Status and Evolution of Environmental Priorities in the Poverty Reduction Strategy Papers: An Assessment of Fifty PRSPs.* Environment Department Paper No. 93. Washington, DC: World Bank.

———. 2002. *Poverty Reduction Strategies and the Environment: A Review of 40 Interim and Full Poverty Reduction Strategy Papers.* Environment Department Paper No. 86. Washington, DC: World Bank.

Bojo, J., K. Green, S. Kishore, S. Pilapitiya, and C.R. Reddy. 2004. *Environment in Poverty Reduction Support Papers and Poverty Reduction Support Credits.* Environment Department Paper No 102. Washington, DC: World Bank.

Bolt, K., G. Ruta, and M. Sarraf. 2005. *Estimating the Costs of Environmental Degradation: A Training Manual in English, French, and Arabic.* Environment Department Paper. Washington, DC: World Bank.

Bourguignon, F., and M. Sundberg. 2006. *Aid Effectiveness—Opening the Black Box.* Washington, DC: World Bank.

Broadman, H. 2007. *Africa's Silk Road: China and India's New Economic Frontier.* Washington, DC: World Bank.

Bucknall, J., K. Hamilton, and N. Kishor. 2000. "Sourcebook on Poverty, Environment, and Natural Resources for the Poverty Reduction Strategy Papers." Environment Strategy Background Paper. World Bank, Washington, DC.

Bucknall, J., C. Kraus, and P. Pillai. 2001. "Poverty and Environment: Background Paper for the World Bank Environment Strategy." World Bank, Washington, DC.

CSE (Centre for Science and Environment). 2006. *The Leapfrog Factor: Clearing the Air in Asian Cities.* New Delhi: CSE.

Chomitz, K., P. Buys, G. De Luca, T. Thomas, and S. Wertz-Kanounnikoff. 2007. *At Loggerheads? Agricultural Expansion, Poverty Reduction, and Environment in Tropical Forests.* World Bank Policy Research Report. Washington, DC: World Bank.

Christiaensen, L., and L. Demery. 2007. *Down to Earth: Agriculture and Poverty Reduction in Africa.* Washington, DC: World Bank.

Cleaver, K., and G. Schreiber. 1994. *Reversing the Spiral: The Population, Agriculture, and Environment Nexus in Sub-Saharan Africa.* Washington, DC: World Bank.

Conable, B. 1987. "Address to the World Resources Institute." May 5, World Bank, Washington, DC.

Conor, R., and S. Dovers. 2004. *Institutional Change for Sustainable Development.* Cheltenham, UK: Edward Elgar.

Crooks, R., W. Magrath, G. Morgan, and S. Shen. 1999. *Natural Resources Management: A Strategic Framework for East Asia and the Pacific.* Rural Development Unit (EASRD) and Environment and Social Development Unit (EASES), East Asia and the Pacific Region. Washington, DC: World Bank.

Dalal-Clayton, B., and B. Sadler. 2004. *Strategic Environmental Assessment (SEA): A Sourcebook Reference Guide on International Experience.* London: International Institute for Environment and Development.

Deaton, A., A. Banerjee, N. Lustig, and K. Rogoff. 2006. "Evaluation of World Bank Research 1998–2005." Development Economics, World Bank, Washington, DC.

DFID (Department for International Development, U.K.), European Commission, UNDP, and World Bank. 2002. *Linking Poverty Reduction and Environmental Management: Policy Challenges and Opportunities.* Washington, DC: World Bank.

DRG (Development Research Group). 2005. "Development Aid Effectiveness: What Have We Learned, What Are We Doing, Where Are We Going?" *Knowledge in Development Notes.* Washington, DC: World Bank.

Economy, Elizabeth. 2007. "Great Leap Backward?" *Foreign Affairs* (September): 45.

Esty, D.C., M.A. Levy, T. Srebotnjak, A. de Sherbinin, C.H. Kim, and B. Anderson. 2006. *Pilot 2006 Environmental Performance Index.* New Haven: Yale Center for Environmental Law & Policy.

Falloux, F., and L. Talbot. 1993. *Crisis and Opportunity: Environment and Development in Africa.* London: Earthscan.

Flavin, C., and G. Gardner. 2006. *China, India, and the New Order.* Washington, DC: Worldwatch Institute.

GEF (Global Environment Facility). 2007. *Joint Evaluation of the GEF Activity Cycle and Modalities.* Washington, DC: World Bank.

———. 2006. *The Role of Local Benefits in Global Environmental Programs.* Evaluation Office, Evaluation Report No. 30. Washington, DC: World Bank.

Goodland, R., J.R. Mercier, and S. Mutemba (eds.). 1996. *Environmental Assessment in Africa: A World Bank Commitment.* Proceedings of the Durban World Bank Workshop, June 25, 1995. AFTES. Washington, DC: World Bank.

Green, K., and A. Raphael, 2000. "Third Environmental Assessment Review (FY96–00)." Environment Department, World Bank, Washington, DC.

Le Groupe-conseil baastel ltée. 2006. "Evaluation of the Environmental Finance Group's Global Environment Facility Funded Initiatives." Baastal Group, Gatineau, Quebec, Canada.

IEG-IFC (Independent Evaluation Group–International Finance Corporation). 2007. *Financing Micro, Small, and Medium Enterprises: An Independent Evaluation of IFC's Experience with Financial Intermediaries in Frontier Countries.* Washington, DC: World Bank.

IEG-MIGA (Independent Evaluation Group–Multilateral Investment Guarantee Agency). 2007. *2007 Annual Report.* Washington, DC: World Bank.

———. 2006. *2006 Annual Report.* Washington, DC: World Bank.

———. 2004. *2004 Review of Development Effectiveness.* Washington, DC: World Bank.

———. 2003. *2003 Report on Operations Evaluation.* Washington, DC: World Bank.

IEG-World Bank (Independent Evaluation Group–World Bank). 2007a. *The Development Potential of Regional Programs: An Evaluation of World Bank Support of Multicountry Operations.* IEG Study Series. Washington, DC: World Bank.

———. 2007b. *Development Results in Middle-Income Countries: An Evaluation of the World Bank's Support*. IEG Study Series. Washington, DC: World Bank.

———. 2007c. *Disasters, Climate Change, and Economic Development in Sub-Saharan Africa: Lessons and Future Directions*. Independent Evaluation Group (IEG), Evaluation Brief 3. Washington, DC: IEG-World Bank.

———. 2006a. *2006 Annual Review of Development Effectiveness*. IEG Study Series. Washington, DC: World Bank.

———. 2006b. *Engaging with Fragile States: An IEG Review of World Bank Support to Low-Income Countries Under Stress*. IEG Study Series. Washington, DC: World Bank.

———. 2006c. *Hazards of Nature, Risks to Development: An IEG Evaluation of World Bank Assistance for Natural Disasters*. IEG Study Series. Washington, DC: World Bank.

———. 2005. *Capacity Building in Africa*. IEG Study Series. Washington, DC: World Bank.

———. 2004. *Addressing the Challenges of Globalization: An Independent Evaluation of the World Bank's Approach to Global Programs*. IEG Study Series. Washington, DC: World Bank.

———. 2002. *Promoting Environmental Sustainability in Development: An Evaluation of World Bank Performance*. IEG Study Series. Washington, DC: World Bank.

———. 2001. *The World Bank Forest Strategy: Striking the Right Balance*. IEG Study Series. Washington, DC: World Bank.

———. 1996. *Effectiveness of Environmental Assessments and National Environmental Action Plans: A Process Study*. World Bank, Report No. 15835. Washington, DC: World Bank.

IEG-World Bank, -IFC, and -MIGA. 2003. *Extractive Industries and Sustainable Development: An Evaluation of World Bank Experience. Vol. 4—MIGA's Experience*. Washington, DC: World Bank.

IFC (International Finance Corporation). 2008. *IFC Road Map, FY09–11: Creating Opportunity: Doing Our Part for an Inclusive and Sustainable World*. Washington, DC: World Bank.

———. 2007. *Selling Solar*. Washington, DC: IFC.

———. 2006. "IFC Strategic Directions, FY08–10: Creating Opportunity." IFC, Washington, DC.

———. 2003. "CAO Review of IFC's Safeguard Policies." World Bank, Washington, DC. http://www.cao-ombudsman.org/html-english/advisor-safeguard_091905.htm.

India, MoEF (Ministry of Environment and Forests). 2006. *National Environment Policy 2006*. http://envfor.nic.in/ nep/nep2006e.pdf.

IUCN (International Union of Conservation of Nature and Natural Resources). 2005. *Review of the Implementation of the Red List Programme Agreement*. Montreal: Unversalia.

———. 2000. *Environmental Assessment Policy and Practice at the World Bank*. Report for IEG. Washington, DC: World Bank.

Keck, A. 1998. *Biodiversity in World Bank Projects: A Portfolio Review*. Environment Department Paper No. 59. Washington, DC: World Bank.

Kelly, L. 2004. "The Multilateral Fund for Implementation of the Montreal Protocol." IEG Working Paper. Washington, DC: World Bank.

Kishore, S., and P. Shyamsundar. 2005. *An Environmental Review of 2002–04 Country Assistance Strategies*. Environment Department Paper No. 88. Washington, DC: World Bank.

Lecoq, F., and Z. Shalizi. 2004. "Will the Kyoto Protocol Affect Growth in Russia?" World Bank Policy Research Working Paper No. 3454. Washington, DC.

Lederman, D., and W. Maloney. 2007. *Natural Resources: Neither Curse nor Destiny*. Palo Alto, CA: Stanford University Press.

Lee, J. 1985. *The Environment, Public Health, and Human Ecology: Considerations for Economic Development*. Baltimore, Maryland: Johns Hopkins University Press.

Listorti, J., and F. Doumai. 2001. *Environmental Health: Bridging the Gap*. World Bank Discussion Paper No. 422. Washington, DC: World Bank.

Lusthaus, C., and C. Milton-Feasby. 2006. *The Evaluation of Inter-Organizational Relationships in the Not-for-Profit Sector: Some Observations*. Montreal: Universalia.

Lvovsky, K. 2001. *Health and Environment*. Environment Strategy Paper No. 1. Washington, DC: World Bank.

Mani, M., and A. Sears. 2006. *Implementation of Environment and Natural Resource Aspects in Development Policy Lending: First Year Review*. Environment Department Paper No. 111. Washington, DC: World Bank.

Margulis, S. 2004. *Causes of Deforestation in the Brazilian Amazon,* World Bank Discussion Paper No. 22. World Bank: Washington, DC.

Margulis, S., and T. Vetleseter. 1999. *Environmental Capacity Building: A Review of the World Bank's Portfolio*. Environment Department Paper 68. Washington, DC: World Bank.

Margulis, S., and others. 2006. "A Review of the Africa Region Environment Portfolio (and Elements for a Business Plan)." Draft. World Bank, Washington, DC.

Mercier, J.R. 1995. *Environmental Assessment Review in Sub-Saharan Africa: Building Blocks for Africa 2025*. Paper No. 7, Environmentally Sustainable Development Division, Africa Technical Department (AFTES). Washington, DC: World Bank.

Mink, S. 1993. *Poverty, Population, and the Environment*. World Bank Discussion Paper No. 189. Washington, DC: World Bank.

Mogelgaard, K., and K. Patterson. 2006. *Linking Population, Health, and Environment in Fianarantsoa Province, Madagascar*. Washington, DC: Population Reference Bureau. http://www.prb.org/pdf06/PHEMadagascar2006.pdf.

Moore, M.H. 1995. *Creating Public Value: Strategic Management in Government*. Cambridge, MA: Harvard University Press.

Munasinghe, M. 1994. *Economywide Policies and the Environment: Emerging Lessons from Experience*. Washington, DC: World Bank.

Nagesha, N., and M.H. Bala Subrahmanya. 2006. "Energy Efficiency for Sustainable Development of Small Industry Clusters: What Factors Influence It?" *International Journal of Economic Policy Studies* 1 (October).

OECD (Organisation for Economic Co-operation and Development). 2007. *Environmental Performance Review—China*. Paris: OECD.

———. 2001. *Environmental Performance Reviews: Achievements in OECD Countries*. Paris: OECD.

Pielemeier, J. 2007. *Lessons from the First Generation of Integrated Population, Health, and Environment Projects*. Woodrow Wilson International Center for Scholars. Washington, DC: World Bank.

Pillai, P., and L. Lunde. 2006. *CEA and Institutional Assessment: A Review of International and World Bank Tools*. Environment Strategy Paper No. 11, Environment Department. Washington, DC: World Bank.

Pomerantz, P. 2004. *Aid Effectiveness in Africa: Developing Trust Between Donors and Governments*. Lanham, MD: Lexington Books.

QAG (Quality Assurance Group). 2007. *Quality of Supervision Assessment 7 (QSA7)*. Washington, DC: World Bank.

Redwood, J., R. Robelus, and T. Vetleseter. 1998. *Natural Resource Management Portfolio Review*. Environment Department Paper No. 58. Washington, DC: World Bank.

Reed, D. (ed.). 1992. *Structural Adjustment and the Environment*. London: Earthscan.

Rich, B. 1994. *Mortgaging the Earth: The World Bank, Environmental Impoverishment, and the Crisis of Development*. Boston, MA: Beacon Press.

Ruthenberg, I., K. Ahmed, C. Brandon, J. Dixon, A. Armstrong, G. Espinoza, P. Pisani, L. Sierralta, S. Garcia Opazo, X. Abogabir, J. Dinamarca, and P. Matus. 2001. *A Decade of Environmental Management in Chile*. Environment Department Paper No. 82. Washington, DC: World Bank.

Sanchez-Triana, E., and S. Enriquez. 2005. "Using Strategic Assessments for Environmental Mainstreaming in the Water and Sanitation Sector: The Cases of Argentina and Colombia." Latin America and Caribbean Region, Sustainable Development Working Paper 26, World Bank, Washington, DC.

Sanchez-Triana, E., K. Ahmed, and Y. Awe (eds.). 2007. *Environmental Priorities and Poverty Reduction: A Country Environmental Analysis for Colombia*. Washington, DC: World Bank.

Schramm, G., and J. Warford. 1989. *Environmental Management and Economic Development*. Baltimore, MD: Johns Hopkins University Press.

Segnestam, L., A. Persson, M. Nilsson, A. Arvidsson, and E. Ijjasz. 2003. *Country-level Environmental Analysis: A Review of International Experience*. Environment Strategy Paper No. 8, Environment Department. Washington, DC: World Bank.

Shalizi, Z. 2007. "Energy and Emissions: Local and Global Effects of the Giants' Rise." In *Dancing with Giants: China, India, and the Global Economy*, ed. L. Alan Winters and Shalid Yusuf. Singapore: World Bank and Institute of Policy Studies.

Shyamsundar, P., and K. Hamilton. 2000. *An Environmental Review of 1999 Country Assistance Strategies*. Environment Department Paper No. 74. Washington, DC: World Bank.

Shyamsundar, P., K. Hamilton, L. Segnestam, M. Sarrafet, and S. Fankhauser. 2001. *Country Assistance Strategies and the Environment*. Environment Department Paper No. 81. Washington, DC: World Bank.

Stern, N. 2006. *The Economics of Climate Change.* Cambridge, U.K.: Cambridge University Press.

Sun, P. (ed.). 1994. *Multipurpose River Basin Development in China.* EDI Seminar Series, Economic Development Institute. Washington, DC: World Bank.

Sundberg, M., and A. Gelb. 2006. "Making Aid Work." *Finance and Development* 43:4

Thomas, V., and others. 2000. *The Quality of Growth.* New York: Oxford University Press.

Triple Line Consulting. 2005. "Midterm Review of CCF, EOF, SFMF." UK: Triple Line Consulting.

Turner, Jennifer L., and L. Zhi. 2006. "Building a Green Civil Society in China." In *State of the World 2006: Special Focus: China and India.* Washington, DC: Worldwatch Institute.

UNDP (United Nations Development Program). 2007. *Human Development Report 2007/2008—Fighting Climate Change: Human Solidarity in a Divided World.* New York: Palgrave Macmillan.

UNDP (United Nations Development Program), UNEP (United Nations Environment Programme), World Bank, and WRI (World Resources Institute). 2003. *World Resources 2002–2004: Decisions for the Earth—Balance, Voice, and Power.* Washington, DC: WRI.

UNEP (United Nations Environment Programme). 2007. *Global Environment Outlook (GEO4): Environment for Development.* Malta: Progress Press Limited.

UN-Habitat. 2007. *Global Report on Human Settlements 2007: Enhancing Urban Safety and Security.* London: Earthscan.

Wade, R. 1997. "Greening the Bank: The Struggle over the Environment, 1970–1995." In D. Kapur, J. Lewis, and R. Webb, *The World Bank: Its First Half Century.* Washington, DC: Brookings Institution.

WCED (World Commission on Environment and Development). 1987. *Our Common Future.* Oxford: Oxford University Press.

Winters, L. Alan, and Shalid Yusuf. 2007. *Dancing with Giants: China, India, and the Global Economy.* Washington, DC, and Singapore: World Bank and Institute of Policy Studies.

World Bank. 2008a. *Environmental Health and Child Survival: Epidemiology, Economics, Experiences.* Washington, DC: World Bank.

———. 2008b. *Global Monitoring Report 2008: MDGs and the Environment—Agenda for Inclusive and Sustainable Development.* Washington, DC: World Bank and International Monetary Fund.

———. 2008c. *Sector Strategy Implementation Update: Third Review Part II.* Report No. 42128. Washington, DC: World Bank.

———. 2007a. "Clean Energy for Development Investment Framework: The World Bank Action Plan." Report No. 38994. World Bank, Washington, DC.

———. 2007b. *Cost of Pollution in China: Economic Estimates of Physical Damages.* Washington, DC: World Bank.

———. 2007c. *Healthy Development: The World Bank Strategy for Health, Nutrition, and Population Results.* Report No. 39485. Washington, DC: World Bank.

———. 2007d. *The Little Green Data Book 2007.* Washington, DC: World Bank.

———. 2007e. "Regional Briefing—Latin America and the Caribbean Region." Presentation to the World Bank Board of Directors, March 8, Washington, DC.

———. 2007f. *Sector Strategy Implementation Update.* Operations Policy and Country Services (OPCS). Washington, DC: World Bank.

———. 2007g. "Strengthening Policy Dialogue on Environment: Learning from Five Years of Country Environmental Analysis." Environment Department, World Bank, Washington, DC.

———. 2007h. *Use of Country Systems in Bank-Supported Operations.* Operations Policy and Country Services (OPCS). Washington, DC: World Bank.

———. 2007i. "Regional Integration Assistance Strategy for Sub-Saharan Africa." Report No. 43022. Africa Regional Integration Department, World Bank, Washington, DC.

———. 2007j. "Towards a Strategic Framework on Climate Change and Development for the World Bank Group: Concept and Issues Paper, Consultation Draft." World Bank, Washington, DC. http://siteresources.worldbank.org/INTCC/Resources/SFCCD_Concept_and_Issues_Paper_Consultation_Draft_27March2008sm.pdf.

———. 2006a. "Energy Sector Reform and the Pattern of the Poor: Energy Use and Supply, a Four-Country Study: Botswana, Ghana, Honduras, and Senegal." ESMAP Technical Paper 095, World Bank, Washington, DC.

———. 2006b. *India: Inclusive Growth and Service Delivery: Building on India's Success—Development Policy Review.* Washington, DC: World Bank.

———. 2006c. *India: Strengthening Institutions for Sustainable Growth—Country Environmental Analysis.* Report No. 38292-IN. Washington, DC: World Bank.

———. 2006d. *The Little Green Data Book 2006*. Washington, DC: World Bank.

———. 2006e. "Strengthening Forest Law and Governance: Addressing a Systemic Constraint to Sustainable Development." Report No. 36638-GLB, World Bank, Washington, DC.

———. 2006f. *Where Is The Wealth of Nations? Measuring Capital for the 21st Century*. Washington, DC: World Bank.

———. 2005a. *Environment Strategy for the World Bank in the Asia and Pacific Region*. Washington, DC: World Bank.

———. 2005b. *For A Breath of Fresh Air: Ten Years of Progress and Challenges in Urban Air Quality Management in India, 1993–2002*. Environment and Social Development Unit, South Asia Region (India). Washington, DC: World Bank.

———. 2005c. "India's Water Economy: Bracing for a Turbulent Future." South Asia Region Report No. 34750-IN, World Bank, Washington, DC.

———. 2005d. *Integrating Environmental Considerations into Policy Formulation: Lessons from Policy-Based SEA Experience,* Report No. 32783, World Bank Environment Department. Washington, DC: World Bank.

———. 2005e. "Mexico: Northern Border Environment Project and Environmental Structural Adjustment Loan." Project Performance Assessment Report No. 32690, World Bank, Washington, DC.

———. 2005f. *World Development Indicators*. Washington, DC: World Bank.

———. 2004a. *Drivers of Sustainable Rural Growth and Poverty Reduction in Central America—Guatemala Case Study Report*. Report No. 311191-GT. Washington, DC: World Bank.

———. 2004b. *Ensuring the Future:: The World Bank and Biodiversity—1988–2004*. Environment Department. Washington, DC: World Bank.

———. 2004c. *Responsible Growth for the New Millennium: Integrating Society, Ecology, and the Economy*. Washington, DC: World Bank.

———. 2004d. *Senegal: Epidemic Disease Control Project*. Implementation Completion Report, Report No. No. 30277. Washington, DC: World Bank.

———. 2003a. *Putting Our Commitments to Work: Environmental Strategy Implementation Progress Report*. Report No. 25784. Washington, DC: World Bank.

———. 2003b. *Reaching the Rural Poor: A Renewed Strategy for Rural Development*. Washington, DC: World Bank.

———. 2003c. *Rural Poverty Alleviation in Brazil: Toward An Integrated Strategy*. World Bank Country Study. Washington, DC: World Bank.

———. 2003d. *World Development Report 2003: Sustainable Development in a Dynamic World: Transforming Institutions, Growth, and Quality of Life*. Washington, DC: World Bank.

———. 2002a. *Building a Sustainable Future: The Africa Region Environment Strategy*. Directions in Development. Washington, DC: World Bank.

———. 2002b. *Environmental Strategy for the Latin America and Caribbean Region*. Washington, DC: World Bank.

———. 2002c. "Poverty in India: The Challenge of Uttar Pradesh." Sector Report No. 22323, World Bank, Washington, DC.

———. 2001a. *China: Air, Land, and Water—Environmental Priorities for a New Millennium*. Washington, DC: World Bank.

———. 2001b. *Making Sustainable Commitments—An Environment Strategy for the World Bank*. Washington, DC: World Bank.

———. 2001c. *World Development Report 2000/01—Attacking Poverty*. Washington, DC, and New York: World Bank and Oxford University Press.

———. 2000a. *Greening Industry: New Roles for Communities, Markets, and Governments*. World Bank Policy Research Report. Washington, DC: World Bank.

———. 2000b. *India: Policies to Reduce Poverty and Accelerate Sustainable Development*. Report No. 19471-IN. Washington, DC: World Bank.

———. 2000c. *The World Bank and the Global Environment: A Progress Report*. Environment Department. Washington, DC: World Bank.

———. 1999. *Environment Matters at the World Bank: Toward Environmentally and Socially Sustainable Development*. Washington, DC: World Bank.

———. 1998a. *Brazil: Managing Pollution Problems: The Brown Environmental Agenda*. Report No. 16635-BR. Washington, DC: World Bank.

———. 1998b. "Environmental Assessment Sourcebook and Updates." World Bank, Washington, DC. http://web.worldbank.org/WBSITE/EXTERNAL/TOPICS/ENVIRONMENT/EXTENVASS/0,,contentMDK:20282864~pagePK:148956~piPK:216618~theSitePK:407988,00.html.

———. 1998c. "India: Country Strategy Paper." World Bank, Washington, DC.

———. 1998d. *The World Bank and the Environment in Central and Eastern Europe and the Commonwealth of Independent States, 1995–1998*. Report No. 18557. Europe and Central Asia Region. Washington, DC: World Bank.

———. 1997a. *Clear Water, Blue Skies: China's Environment in the New Century*. Washington, DC: World Bank.

———. 1997b. *The Impact of Environmental Assessment: A Review of World Bank Experience*, World Bank Technical Paper No. 363.

———. 1996. *Toward Environmentally Sustainable Development in Sub-Saharan Africa: A World Bank Agenda*. Washington, DC: World Bank.

———. 1995a. *Mainstreaming the Environment: The World Bank Group and the Environment since the Rio Earth Summit*. Washington, DC: World Bank.

———. 1995b. *Middle East and North Africa Environmental Strategy*. Report No. 13601-MNA. Washington, DC: World Bank.

———. 1995c. *National Environmental Strategies: Learning from Experience*. Environment Department. Washington, DC: World Bank.

———. 1994. *Making Development Sustainable*. Washington, DC: World Bank.

———. 1993. *The World Bank and the Environment—Fiscal 1993*. Washington, DC: World Bank.

———. 1992a. *Development and Environment*. New York: Oxford University Press.

———. 1992b. *The World Bank and the Environment—Fiscal 1992*. Washington, DC: World Bank.

———. 1992c. *World Development Report 1992: Development and the Environment*. New York: Oxford University Press.

———. 1991a. *Environmental Assessment Sourcebook*. Volumes 1, 2, and 3. World Bank Technical Papers 139, 140, and 154. Washington, DC: World Bank.

———. 1991b. *The World Bank and the Environment—Fiscal 1991*. Washington, DC: World Bank.

———. 1990. *The World Bank and the Environment—Fiscal 1990*. Washington, DC: World Bank.

———. 1988. "India: Country Strategy Paper." India Department, World Bank, Washington, DC.

World Bank and IMF (International Monetary Fund). 2008. *Global Monitoring Report—MDGs and the Environment: Agenda for Inclusive and Sustainable Development*. Washington, DC: World Bank.

World Bank, IFC, and MIGA. 2006. "Country Partnership Strategy for the People's Republic of China for the Period 2006–2010." China Country Management Unit, East Asia and Pacific Region, World Bank, Washington, DC.

World Bank Group with UNEP and UNIDO. 1999. *Pollution Prevention and Abatement Handbook 1998: Toward Cleaner Production*. Washington, DC: World Bank.